WERTHEIM PUBLICATIONS IN INDUSTRIAL RELATIONS

J. D. Houser, *What the Employer Thinks,* 1927
Wertheim Lectures on Industrial Relations, 1929
William Haber, *Industrial Relations in the Building Industry,* 1930
Johnson O'Connor, *Psychometrics,* 1934
Paul H. Norgren, *The Swedish Collective Bargaining System,* 1941
Leo C. Brown, S. J., *Union Policies in the Leather Industry,* 1947
Walter Galenson, *Labor in Norway,* 1949
Dorothea de Schweinitz, *Labor and Management in a Common Enterprise,* 1949
Ralph Altman, *Availability for Work: A Study in Unemployment Compensation,* 1950
John T. Dunlop and Arthur D. Hill, *The Wage Adjustment Board: Wartime Stabilization in the Building and Construction Industry,* 1950
Walter Galenson, *The Danish System of Labor Relations: A Study in Industrial Peace,* 1952
Lloyd H. Fisher, *The Harvest Labor Market in California,* 1953
Theodore V. Purcell, S. J., *The Worker Speaks His Mind on Company and Union,* 1953
Donald J. White, *The New England Fishing Industry,* 1954
Val R. Lorwin, *The French Labor Movement,* 1954
Philip Taft, *The Structure and Government of Labor Unions,* 1954
George B. Baldwin, *Beyond Nationalization: The Labor Problems of British Coal,* 1955
Kenneth F. Walker, *Industrial Relations in Australia,* 1956

Studies in Labor-Management History

Lloyd Ulman, *The Rise of the National Trade Union: the Development and Significance of its Structure, Governing Institutions, and Economic Policies,* 1955
Joseph P. Goldberg, *The Maritime Story; A Study in Labor-Management Relations,* 1958

THE MARITIME STORY

A STUDY IN LABOR-MANAGEMENT RELATIONS

JOSEPH P. GOLDBERG

HARVARD UNIVERSITY PRESS   CAMBRIDGE   1958

Library of Congress Catalog Card Number: 58–8077

Printed in the United States of America

to Selma
with love and gratitude

FOREWORD

The history of labor-management relations and the history of labor unions has been grossly neglected in the past generation. Events have been moving too fast, and university specialists often have been pre-occupied with practical responsibilities or current problems to the exclusion of the historical perspective. Since the 1920's there has been a major transformation in American labor-management relations. Union membership has grown four- or fivefold; the extent and scope of collective bargaining and the status of unions has been vastly extended at the work place and in the larger community. There have been significant changes in management policies and organization, and in the role of government.

It is timely to make a fresh and dispassionate review of the exciting events of the past generation and to place them in new perspective: the interlude of the open split between the AFL and CIO has come to an end with the merged federation; the relation since the thirties and forties between the labor movement and the administration in Washington has changed; new unions and new collective bargaining relationships have achieved a degree of stability, and older unions and relationships started before the 1930's have adapted themselves in a measure to the new conditions; there has been a prolonged period of relatively stable and high-level employment. By the mid-1950's an older era in the history of labor-management relations had come to a close and a new period had begun.

A series of volumes was projected, in coöperation with Professor Walter Galenson and Professor Lloyd Ulman, to tell the narrative of the major developments of the period, to point to new tendencies, to place events in the context of their long-run evolution — for it must be remembered that national unions and union-management relations in the American scene are more than a hundred years old — and to explain the old and the new features of the American labor movement and collective bargaining system. Some of these studies are to deal with the labor movement and collective bargaining as a whole, while others, devoted to particular unions, companies, or industries, are designed to illuminate major themes or to highlight sectors of intrinsic interest. The present volume on the offshore maritime industry is the first volume of these studies of the latter type to be published.

Dr. Joseph P. Goldberg has written a careful and detached narrative of labor-management developments in this industry since the turn of the century. The dramatic transformations in the past twenty years, and particularly since the end of the second World War, is seen in the perspective of more than a half-century. The bitter struggles for annihilation or dominance have given way to mutual accommodation; a casual and outcast labor force has become more regular and more comparable to industry generally; the foreign citizen has largely disappeared; the relations between master and men prescribed by ancient law have been gradually adapted to collective bargaining and the continuing needs of the work place at sea; the complex problems of control over hiring, and the distribution of available job opportunities with equity to the men and to the needs of efficient management no longer present unresolved issues of principle, despite the impractical provisions of the statute applied to hiring halls; the wages and conditions of employment in the industry have risen markedly relative to other industries, and vacations with pay, unemployment compensation, pensions, and other benefits previously unknown in the industry have been extended to maritime workers. The seagoing work force, their unions, and the managements of shipping companies have all been changed in the process. These major developments are in part the consequence of wider changes in the American community, reflected in this industry, and in part the result of specialized factors at work within the maritime sector.

A major theme of the maritime story is the continuing struggle against diversity and centrifugal forces; it is a quest for unity and for nationwide bargaining. The men at sea and their unions historically have been split and divided by craft (licensed officers, unlicensed seamen, deck, engine, and stewards' departments), by regions of the country (West Coast, Gulf and East Coast, and the Great Lakes); their alliances with shoreside unions have never been stable; they have been divided by race and nationality and by type of carrier.

The shipping companies also have had many divisive interests; some receive government subsidies, while others confront keen international competition without such assistance; there are specialized product lines such as oil, ore, or bananas, while other companies are engaged primarily in general cargo or passenger traffic; some operate old vessels and others new ones, and some vessels were acquired under favorable terms, while others were constructed for shipping companies at high costs; the economic position and competition faced by each route and each line varies to a degree, and the full range is very wide. The necessity for relatively uniform wages and conditions among lines and routes, which is a factor that binds carriers together, is continuously strained by these divergent economic and competitive positions.

These divisive factors on both sides help us to appreciate the very considerable developments and achievements of collective bargaining in the past twenty years. They also help us to understand why a national union, inclusive of both coasts and all factions of the offshore maritime industry, has so far not emerged, despite the continuing aspirations common to other sectors, and why nation-wide bargaining to prevent one coast being played off against the other is still to be achieved. This diversity likewise creates complex problems for the author, who has to weave together so many different strands to make the narrative complete.

A second major theme of the maritime story is the distinctive role of the federal government in the economics of the industry and in labor-management relations, even in peace time. In no industry outside of the railroads has so wide a range of governmental policies had a larger impact on the problems of collective bargaining. Subsidies to sustain a merchant marine vital to the national security affect the competitive position of companies and the wage scales that can be negotiated. The licensing of seagoing personnel and security clearances by government also involve interests fundamental to both sides. The inspection of vessels and the administration of safety and other standards bring federal agencies into intimate contact with the parties; the special features of maritime law shape the relations between the parties at many points. Collective bargaining between private shipping companies and the offshore maritime unions in an industry so permeated with public interest and regulation must deal with numerous problems.

A third major theme of the maritime story is the long-term substantial improvement in the status of the offshore work force. In a previous day, whose harsh imprint has not yet faded from the memory of the parties, the seaman frequently lived up to his reputation in fiction for the rough and tumble; he was often the victim of the crimp and lodging house keeper who served as labor recruiter; conditions at sea were primitive, and seamen were often immigrants unable to speak English. Dr. Goldberg chronicles the hard course by which not only wages and conditions have been sharply upgraded, but the status of the work force has been fundamentally changed in the American community. The seaman is now more like other workers; he has vacations, health and welfare benefits, pensions, and unemployment compensation and private supplements; he is more likely to be a family man. Despite the continuing unique effects of the work place at sea, he is less isolated and more integrated into the community.

A fourth major theme of this volume is the operation of the distinctive

maritime collective bargaining system. Every collective bargaining system is shaped and constrained by the technological and market environment of the parties. In the offshore maritime industry these factors are
unique: the isolated work place, the necessity to live and work at sea,
the casual nature of employment with trips of varying duration, the
hazards and working conditions aboard ship, the special interests of
the government, and the keen competition from foreign flag ships in
view of the relative levels of American and foreign wage levels. The
offshore maritime context thus poses distinctive problems for the parties,
affects the scope and topics included in an agreement, and highlights
the basic problem of control over hiring and the allocation of job opportunities.

Dr. Goldberg's study will attract the attention of a wide range of
readers: those actively engaged in the maritime industry who are concerned with perspective for current problems, collective bargaining prac-
titioners, students interested in new chapters in the history of labor-
management relations and the history of the American labor movement,
and those pondering public policy formation and administration in the
collective bargaining and maritime fields.

The financial support for the research and writing of this series of
volumes on labor-management history has come from a wide variety of
sources; this arrangement has been deliberately designed to underscore
the traditional academic standards of scholarship and integrity. The
sources have included charitable foundations, companies, and labor organizations. A full listing of such gifts and grants to Harvard University
for this purpose will be set forth in the foreword to the projected volumes which are to treat the history of labor-management relations and
the history of the labor movement in the period since the 1920's as a
whole. These grants and gifts constitute in the main a new type of support for research and scholarship and such pioneering is to be both
admired and appreciated.

August 12, 1957   John T. Dunlop

CONTENTS

TABLES

AUTHOR'S PREFACE

The extent of public concern over maritime labor matters is substantially greater than the importance of the industry, in terms of the nation's employment and income. This concern has arisen out of a combination of factors: the patriotic appeal of a merchant marine and its role as a naval auxiliary, the militancy of the organizations of both seamen and shipowners, and the colorful and forthright character of the leaders of both labor and industry.

The scope of this study is the evolution of the present collective bargaining relationships involving the offshore seamen's unions — a major outcome of this evolution has been the development of effective bargaining relationships in an atmosphere of mutual endeavor to maintain stability. This is in sharp contrast to the early relationships in the industry, but these too require treatment to sharpen the understanding of the current relationships. The keen antagonisms of the past have received numerous polemic treatments in union and employer periodicals, pamphlets, handbills, and even government reports. The major objective analyses, however, were published about thirty years ago; and these dealt merely with the histories of segments of seamen's organization and activities. The report of the Maritime Labor Board in 1940 was admirable in its scholarliness and scope, but it did not attempt a thorough analysis of the history of organization and of the development of collective bargaining. The role of the federal government in maritime labor relations has heretofore received no comprehensive, careful, and disinterested analysis. The more recent aspects of collective bargaining have received only sparse treatment.

My interest in this subject originated in an early assignment with an *ad hoc* panel of the National War Labor Board which dealt with maritime shipping cases. Later, I prepared a study of phases of this subject as a doctoral dissertation at Columbia University, under the sponsorship of Professors Allan Nevins and Leo Wolman. I was assisted in limited field work on both coasts in 1947–8 through a grant from the Yale Fund for Merchant Seamen Studies.

I am greatly indebted to Professor John T. Dunlop of Harvard University for both the opportunity to continue with my studies in this field

as a Research Associate in the Graduate School of Public Administration, as well as for the insights which resulted from his critical evaluation of my manuscript and from the numerous discussions I have had
with him. I am also greatly indebted to Professor Walter Galenson of
the University of California for recommending that I carry on the study,
and for his careful reading of the manuscript. Professor Lloyd Ulman of
the University of Minnesota has also provided many useful suggestions.
I wish to express my appreciation to Mr. Ewan Clague, Commissioner of
Labor Statistics, for authorizing my leave to conduct the field contacts
and research necessary to the completion of this study—even more, for
the support and encouragement Commissioner Clague has given to me
in the course of my work on the university project.

The study is based upon the periodicals, proceedings, and other publications of the various unions and shipowner's associations; congressional hearings and debates, reports of administrative agencies of the
Federal and State governments; documents of the United States Shipping Board, the Maritime Labor Board, and the NRA Shipping Code
Hearings in the Archives of the United States; the labor files of the
American Merchant Marine Institute; contemporaneous newspaper and
periodical accounts; letters of President Wilson and the C. E. Plummer
letters at the Library of Congress; papers of Walter Macarthur at the
Bancroft Library, University of California; papers of Andrew Furuseth
in the possession of Paul Scharrenberg and Silas Blake Axtell; and the
collective bargaining agreements in effect in the industry. Limited field
work was conducted on both coasts in 1947–1948; the financial assistance
provided by Harvard University permitted extensive field work in 1956–
1957. The field work furnished the opportunity for direct personal inter-
views of leading figures in labor-management relations in the maritime
industry.

I wish to express my appreciation for the advice provided by Professor
Paul F. Brissenden, Columbia University; Professor Elmo P. Hohman,
Northwestern University; Professor Leo Simmons, Yale University; Pro-
fessors Clark Kerr, Ira Cross, and Arthur Allen, University of California;
Professor John P. Troxell, Stanford University; J. Paul St. Sure and
James Robertson, Pacific Maritime Association; Ralph Casey, William
Mullins and Alvin Shapiro, American Merchant Marine Institute; Ralph
Dewey, Pacific American Steamship Association; Joseph Curran, John
MacDougal, Alex Stecyk, Herman Cooper, Solon de Leon and Bernard
Raskin of the National Maritime Union; Paul Hall, John Hawk, Matthew
Dushane and Herb Brand of the Seafarers' International Union; the late
Harry Lundeberg and Morris Weisberger of the Sailors' Union of the
Pacific; V. J. Malone, formerly of the Marine Firemen's Union; Ed Turner
of the Marine Cooks and Stewards; Lloyd Jenkins, the NMU Pension

and Welfare Fund; Captain M. K. O'Sullivan, Maritime Administration; James Marshall, Maritime Trades Department, AFL-CIO; Hoyt Haddock and Ben Man, AFL-CIO Maritime Committee; Paul Scharrenberg, formerly of the California Department of Industrial Relations; and the late Victor A. Olander, Illinois State Federation of Labor. I wish to express my appreciation for the effective assistance of Mrs. Ruth Whitman of the Harvard University Press, and to the librarians of the U. S. Department of Labor; the Industrial Relations Center and the Bancroft Library at the University of California; and the American Federation of Labor and the Congress of Industrial Organizations.

All of the views set forth in the study are my own, and any shortcomings must be attributed to me.

August 12, 1957   Joseph P. Goldberg

Errata

Page 46, line 42, *for* longshoremen *read* Longshoremen
Page 47, line 34, *for* International *read* international
Page 49, line 11, *for* make *read* made
Page 69, line 25, *for* Congressional Committees *read* congressional committees
Page 144, line 3, *for* union *read* unions
Page 149, line 28, *for* again, *read* again
Page 165, line 42, *for* difference *read* differences
Page 217, line 41, *for* finance *read* finances
Page 243, line 14, *for* assume *read* accept
Page 248, line 40, *for* Inland-boatmen's *read* Inlandboatmen's
Page 274, line 23, *for* operator's *read* operators'
Page 288, line 34, *for* government provided *read* government-provided
Page 300, line 14, *omit* on a national scale
Page 334, footnote 75, *for* 1952 *read* 1956

THE ECONOMIC SETTING

International shipping, although encrusted with the traditions of the sea, has made tremendous progress during the past half century in order to keep pace with the demands of twentieth-century economies. At the turn of the century the rapid replacement of small, wooden wind-propelled ships by larger steam-driven ships was both the product of, and the response to, the demands of expanding industrial technology. The traditions of the sea could have made this process of change a more difficult one, in contrast to the relatively tradition-free heritage of rail and air transport. But the service traditions of the seafaring nations, coupled with the historic urge of growing nations to assert their political and economic identities under their own flag ships in seeking external markets, resulted in a competitive drive that hastened the transition.

The disparity between rapid technological change and the lag in the social relationships which accompanied such change has been even more apparent in shipping than in shoreside industries. The hazardous nature of maritime travel in ancient, medieval, and even into relatively modern times; the tight and unpleasant life on board small ships; the rowdy character of the crews, originally resulted in the development of a legal tradition in which iron discipline on board ship was virtually sacrosanct. But the seamen were entitled to be cared for properly by the owner of the vessel even under this hard code, although in the legal expression of these rights they were treated as wards of the courts rather than as full-fledged citizens.

Laboring under a legal code that subjected them utterly to the direction of the master on board the vessel and to the potential charge of mutiny for any joint effort to improve their conditions, the seamen found that the obstacles to recognition and to collective bargaining loomed substantially larger than those of shoreside workers. With the nature of their casual employment, the unrestricted entry of foreigners into seafaring employment, and the extreme volatility of shipping in an industrial setting, the opportunity for the organization of seamen was particularly difficult, despite the increasing necessity for it.

In analyzing the past half century of labor-management relations in the offshore shipping industry in the United States, therefore, the focus

is on understanding the manner in which the very obstacles to organization, recognition, and collective bargaining have become motivating
forces for their achievement. The history of the development in shipping enterprise is not unique or peculiar — parallel developments can
be observed in any number of shoreside industries. The intensity in offshore maritime labor relations has been matched in such activities as
mining and longshoring. Postwar developments in all these fields,
however, suggest that labor-management relationships are now being
brought into line with the requirements of our new technology.

Labor-management relationships in offshore shipping during the past
decade have included the extension to the seafarers of many of the gains
in wages and working conditions which have been achieved by shoreside workers. These gains have integrated the American seaman into the
American industrial community. The forces behind his integration are
many and complex, arising out of such factors as the economics of the
American shipping industry and its role in the larger national and world
economy; the history of the labor-management relationship; the role of
the seamen's organizations and their leaders; the role of management
organizations; the major role of government in determining policies for
the merchant marine through defense policies, subsidies and seamen's
legislation. The revolution in the status of American seamen can only
be understood and fully appreciated through an analysis of the development and impact of these factors.

Before the opening of the Panama Canal, there was great diversity
between the West Coast and the East Coast. With the canal opening and
the establishment of both concurrent and competitive operations on both
coasts, and particularly with the resultant increase in contacts among
seamen, a substantial similarity of interest developed affecting the offshore, coastwise, intercoastal, and noncontiguous sectors of the American
merchant marine. The ship operators in all these fields have utilized the
same sources of labor with which to man their ships, and transferability
among these ship operations has been almost unlimited; the labor-
management relationships on the Great Lakes and the Rivers have differed substantially from those on the ocean waterways, by virtue of
different economic and physical circumstances. (The opening of the
Great Lakes to ocean vessels in the next few years, however, may have
a substantial impact on previously existing institutional arrangements.)

The limited space which can be given the economic organization of
the industry in this intensive study of the labor-management relationship and its history is not intended to detract from its importance. The
complexity of this industry's structure is obviously a basic factor in its
system of labor-management relations. Although the core of the labor-
management relationship is the formal organization of seafaring labor

as a common pool for offshore shipping companies, the structure of the industry is quite diversified. Perhaps the easiest basis for classification is in terms of the geographical sphere of operation — offshore or foreign-operating to foreign ports; coastwise — restricted to either the Atlantic or Pacific Coast; intercoastal — operating from one coast to the other by way of the Panama Canal; noncontiguous — operating from the mainland to the United States territories of Puerto Rico, Hawaii and Alaska. But this classification has only a surface simplicity — there are numerous routes in the deepsea trades on which the ships of American companies ply their trade. Over thirty foreign trade routes have been designated as "essential" as a basis for providing operating subsidies. The market structures of the respective routes vary substantially, although all are subsumed in the American Merchant Marine. Cargo opportunities are a function of the economics of the countries with whom trade is conducted, as well as of the nature of the shipping competition encountered. These vary substantially, for example, between the Central American, the Atlantic Europe and United Kingdom, and the East and South African routes.

The character of ownership and service further complicate the diversity in ocean shipping; these factors influence the relative importance of ship operation costs to the entire enterprise. To a company with ship operations as its focus, these costs are of paramount importance. Among these are liner operators who offer common carrier passenger and/or freighter services relatively regularly over a predetermined and fixed itinerary on a given ocean route. The ships of "irregular" companies are, as the designation implies, operated irregularly, both as to frequency and route, or may be chartered to other companies for operation in liner or industrial service; these include both dry cargo and tanker vessels. Where ships are operated as an integral part of a company's larger industrial or commercial enterprise, as in the case of bulk carriers transporting ores or petroleum, the costs of ship operation can be distributed over the entire enterprise and are of lesser consequence. Such operations, involving either ships owned directly, or chartered for the account of the integrated company, are designated as "industrial service"—but even here such ships may be operated as liner services on the outbound service, and as industrial carriers on the inbound.

The American merchant marine as an economic enterprise occupies a relatively minor role in the American economy. Gross receipts from shipping represent less than one-half of one percent of the national income. Shipping earnings play a prominent role in the total earnings in international trade of countries such as Norway (40 percent) and Denmark and Sweden (over 15 percent) and figure prominently in maintaining a favorable net balance in the accounts of the United Kingdom and the Netherlands. In the United States, shipping earnings in 1955 amounted to only 5 percent of total earnings, and contributed only about one-third of the favorable net balance.

It is significant that despite the relatively lesser prominence of the merchant marine in the American economy, our active merchant marine is the third largest in the world; the total merchant marine — including the inactive reserve — is the largest in the world. This growth in the prominence of American ship tonnage, largely the result of governmental construction to meet the needs of two World Wars, has also seen a reversal in the relative position of American flag shipping in the foreign trades. Following the Civil War, American flag shipping in foreign trade was largely restricted to a handful of companies engaged in the transpacific, Caribbean, and South American trades. American capital did seek to participate in the opportunities provided by shipping enterprise, but invested in the more profitable foreign flag companies, with their greater economies in ship construction and operation, and the advantages derived from large-scale operation, good will, and prior entry. It was in the protected coastwise trades that American flag shipping flourished for a time, enjoying the returns provided by the rapid industrialization of the nation. This was the period of bulk carriage in the great steam schooners, at a time when the European coastwise trade was already largely in steel ships. The substantial investments involved in steel ships in the coastwise trades resulted in the establishment of liner services carrying passengers and high grade cargoes.[1]

In 1900, the ratio of shipping in the domestic trades to foreign trade shipping was almost 3 to 1: 2 million gross registered tons to 800,000. Until the first World War, American flag tonnage in foreign trade remained almost stable, while coastwise shipping doubled. A measure of the state of American shipping just prior to the first World War is provided by comparison of ships under sail and steam — in 1911 over one third of the tonnage in both the domestic and foreign trades was under sail.

The provision of a great fleet as a result of the construction program of the first World War altered the situation in several respects. The American merchant fleet increased from about 6 million tons to 17 million tons between 1915 and 1921. Throughout the interwar period, much of the fleet was laid up. During the twenties, however, American flag ships participated to a fair degree in the foreign trade of the United States, carrying over 40 percent of the volume (one third of the value of the trade). With the depression, the active merchant marine declined, with the foreign trade segment declining more than the domestic trades. In 1939, approximately 80 percent of American ships were operated in the domestic trades.

In recent years, the domestic trades have been operating at a level of about 45 percent of the total fleet tonnage; this is due to the increase in tanker tonnage, for dry cargo domestic tonnage has decreased to about one third of the prewar level. American flag foreign tonnage is now about 45 percent of total tonnage, with both dry cargo and tanker tonnage having increased threefold since 1939. This shift has been the result of the decline in domestic waterborne dry cargo traffic, with the substitution of rail and truck transportation to facilitate the increased decentralization of industry into inland areas. The increase in tanker operation in the domestic trade has prevented an even greater decline in this trade. Efforts are currently under way to revive the domestic trade by providing shipping facilities — such as roll-on-roll-off ships which would permit of ready and economical integration of truck and ship operations. The contrasting growth in foreign service operations has been the result of the participation by American shipping in transporting aid cargoes, the provision of subsidies, the opportunity to obtain ships from the government fleet at low costs, the continued demand for coal, petroleum, grain and ore, and the increase in ship passenger traffic. A long-run growth has occurred, despite the decline from postwar peak levels as the merchant marines of the occupied and devastated countries of northern Europe have been reconstructed.

Ships of all flags pay the same longshoring costs in the same ports; the advances in ship design and technology are readily available in all the world's shipyards. The pressure of numerous international rate-setting conferences, in which most American berth lines participate along with their foreign flag competitors, results in the establishment of uniform rates and eliminates rate-cutting as a competitive factor. American companies are permitted to participate in these conferences under the provisions of the Shipping Act of 1916, subject to the approval of the Federal Maritime Board. A recent Senate study of the system of conferences concluded that rates were set high enough to allow American operators to meet their "out of pocket" costs of operations. The greater profits available to the foreign operator were balanced by the resultant stability of rates and the improved quality of service. Internal competition among conference members, the effort to obtain a larger share of the total traffic, and external competition — the ease with which new lines can enter a trade route — tend to restrict excessive rate levels.[2] "Irregular" ship operators are subject to the greater volatility in charter rates for their services which result from the marginal nature of the demand for their services.

Profitability in vessel operation, given the same rates and other identical conditions, is the function of national differences in construction and in operation cost, and in managerial enterprise in obtaining passengers

and cargoes. A separate study comparing the conduct of American shipping enterprises with those of the United Kingdom, the Scandinavian
countries, and other maritime nations to determine the success of our
competitors in carrying a dominant portion of our trade would be of
substantial value. For the purposes of this study, however, it is sufficient
to call attention to the differences between the costs of American and
foreign ship operation. And the differences, by virtue of the success of
American maritime unions in achieving and keeping pace with shoreside
trends in wages and working conditions, are substantial.

Higher ship construction costs in the United States, largely due to the
higher wage levels here, result in higher overhead costs in ship operation. The substantial differences in the direct cost of operating American
vessels arising out of higher wages and other factors is provided in
Table 1. In 1953, the excess of average wage costs on American freighters over those on comparable foreign flag ships ranged from 65 to 81
percent. Differences in subsistence costs ranged from a low of 12 percent to a high of 63 percent. In the case of ships' stores, the differences
were relatively negligible and in some cases in favor of the United
States. Maintenance and repair costs were also substantially greater in
the United States.

It is not sufficient, however, to view these unfavorable cost differentials without examining their relationship to total operating costs. The
items listed are the major items involved in direct operation of the
vessel. Total crew earnings probably range from 35 to 45 percent of the
direct vessel operating costs, depending on the nature of the ship and
trade, with subsistence costs amounting to an additional 5 percent. Consideration must also be given to crew costs against the total voyage
costs, including agency fees, stevedoring and other cargo handling costs.
A Maritime Commission study of intercoastal voyages in 1949 showed
vessel costs as about 45 percent of total voyage costs; stevedoring and
other shoreside cargo handling costs equaled at least the cost of vessel
operation — crew earnings were thus about 20 percent of the total voyage cost. Since vessel operating costs account for a greater proportion of
voyage costs in the deepsea trade, shipboard earnings on dry cargo
ships probably average about one-fourth of voyage costs. For tankers,
a recent government estimate showed crew earnings and subsistence as
amounting to 30 percent of voyage costs exclusive of overhead costs, and
to about 20 percent including overhead costs for depreciation and
interest.[3]

National policy to assist the merchant marine in overcoming the
handicap of higher labor costs in ship operation and higher ship construction costs arises out of more than mere economic considerations.
The government must maintain its national defense and prestige,

Table 1

Comparison of domestic and foreign operating expenses per ship (1953)

Countries	Wages			Subsistence			Stores		Maintenance and repair	
	Crew	Costs (monthly)	U.S. differential	Crew	Shipday Costs	U.S. differential	Costs (annual)	U.S. differential	Costs (annual)	U.S. differential
			Percent			*Percent*		*Percent*		*Percent*
United States	48	$29,426	...	48	$81.60	...	$71,294	...	$65,403	...
Denmark	43	7,990	72.8	43	71.81	12.0	69,795	2.1	30,403	53.3
France	47	10,274	65.1	47	60.50	13.6	71,533	-0.34	37,680	42.4
Italy	41	7,713	73.8	41	41.82	48.7	91,722	-28.7	32,753	49.9
Japan	56	6,273	78.7	56	30.24	62.9	78,202	-9.7	33,850	48.2
Netherlands	55	7,567	74.3	55	58.30	28.6	64,711	9.2	29,641	54.7
Norway	43	7,145	75.7	43	68.80	15.7	63,427	11.0	38,941	40.5
United Kingdom:										
White crew	54	6,444	78.1	54	63.72	21.9	63,111	11.5	27,440	58.0
Mixed crew	80	5,541	81.2	80	60.80	25.5	63,111	11.5	27,440	58.0

Source: House Committee on Merchant Marine and Fisheries, Hearings on Maritime Administration and Federal Maritime Board, 1955, p. 281.

through a naval auxiliary of ships and men, and continuous service on essential routes. It grants direct aid through construction and operating subsidies only to operators in the offshore foreign trade to enable them to meet foreign flag competition. Subsidies are based upon the principle of parity. Operating subsidies are restricted to ship operators who are deemed capable of rendering continuous service with appropriate vessels to the essential trade route. The conditions include provisions for the recapture of subsidies if profits exceed 10 percent of net worth, review of future payments, maintenance of economical and efficient operations, and additional stringent provisions. The amount of payment is based upon the difference involved in operation under the American flag on the route (measured by the fair and reasonable excess of the cost of insurance, repairs and maintenance, and wages and subsistence) as compared with the equivalent costs of operating the same vessel with a foreign crew by the foreign flag competitor.[4] The aids are not intended as guarantees of profitability; this is left to managerial enterprise. Operating subsidies are now granted to 16 companies operating approximately 280 ships. In 1954, these represented 27.5 percent of the total active American fleet, and 45 percent of American ships in the foreign trade.

The profits earned by subsidized as well as nonsubsidized operators have been determined by the traffic opportunities offered on their routes. Postwar freight-carrying opportunities for American ship operators have been more stable than in other years; berth operators particularly have carried a fairly steady amount of traffic, but much of it has consisted of aid cargoes. Nonliner, or tramp ship operations have fluctuated widely, particularly with the level of aid shipments, but their inbound operations have been fairly stable. Sharp foreign competition has also developed for American flag tankers.

Shipboard employment fluctuates with shipping opportunities. The secular trend in maritime shipping job opportunities, if post-Korean employment is indicative, suggests resumption of the employment level of the 1920's of a monthly average of 55,000 to 60,000 jobs on board American ships. The continuing casual nature of maritime employment results in employment of nine to ten months per year, when shipping opportunities are good. Under such circumstances, a reserve of 20 percent would be necessary to man the available jobs. The greatest fluctuations in maritime employment have resulted from the wartime programs of merchant marine expansion. Both during the first and second World Wars, and during the Korean crisis, the number of job opportunities increased substantially. They increased about threefold between the prewar years and the peak of 160,000 in 1945; then declined to 65,000 in 1950, and increased to 85,000 in 1952 during the Korean crisis. More recently, jobs have averaged about 57,000. These sharp fluctuations have produced periodic dislocations, characterized more frequently by unemployment than by labor shortages.

Job opportunities in the deepsea shipping industry are particularly vulnerable to cyclical factors. Employment in the domestic trades declined by only 5 percent between 1929 and 1933, while in the offshore trades it dropped 20 percent. The postwar predominance of deepsea shipping, over domestic trades, however, could intensify the impact of cyclical effects. There are also sharp fluctuations in shipping job opportunities due to short-run factors. International political crises, climatic conditions, and additional local conditions produce substantial and sudden fluctuations in shipping demand and in ship charter rates. Seasonal influences also are apparent in peacetime employment, particularly in passenger ship operations.

The foregoing brief review of the economics and tendencies of the maritime industry is our framework for the following history and analysis of the seaman's struggle to obtain institutional arrangements for his achievement of first-class status: collective bargaining between labor and management.

CHAPTER 1

THE SEAMEN IN 1900

WAGES AND WORKING CONDITIONS

It was recognized during the latter half of the nineteenth century that American seamen were disappearing from the ocean, as was American tonnage. Greater opportunities existed on land for both men and capital. Opportunities for American boys to rise from seamen to the commands of their own vessels were reduced with the introduction of steamships. Corporate organization replaced individual ownership, since the construction and operation of steam vessels required large amounts of capital. As the transition was made from sail to steamships, with their greater carrying capacity and smaller crews, there were relatively fewer opportunities for advancement open to capable and ambitious men. Besides, work on steamships was unattractive — it had to be done in the hold, in heated engine and boiler rooms, instead of on deck and in the rigging.

Wages were low, since they were set by world-wide competition after the eighties, for American shipping drew on a world-wide labor market. Legislation enacted in 1884 permitted American shipowners to sign on crew members in foreign ports, enabling them to take advantage of the lower rates prevailing there. "The rates of wages in American ports do not materially affect the cost of operating our transatlantic and transpacific steamships," was the opinion of the Commissioner of Navigation in 1894, for "they ship nearly their entire crews at their foreign ports of entry, paying virtually the same rates of wages for the same service as are paid on British vessels." [1]

Shipowners felt that since there were no skill requirements for men on board steam vessels, any man could be used who was physically able to perform the work. In the view of Andrew Furuseth, Secretary of the Sailors' Union of the Pacific, "The seamen must in the coastwise and in the foreign trade meet the world. The Japanese, the Chinese, the Malay, the European, all may come and need bring no previous training. . . .

These men from anywhere, with any or no kind of skill or experience, set a wage for which sailors and firemen must work or they must seek other employment. Our merchant marine is therefore manned by the residuum of the population, not only of our country and race, but of all countries and races." [2] During the nineties, only about 30 percent of the men signed on before shipping commissioners were American citizens. After 1900, the proportion increased to approximately 50 percent.[3]

American ships had the reputation for hard discipline in the nineties. The "Red Record" of American maritime industry drawn up by the Sailors' Union of the Pacific listed charges by over 100 ships' crews over a period of 11 years of 15 deaths from maltreatment; instances of loss of limbs, eyes, or teeth; other injuries of a permanent character, including insanity; and several suicides attributed to persecution. It was reported that only seven convictions were obtained against the officers involved, with punishments largely nominal. Although flogging had been prohibited by statute in 1850, corporal punishment was not prohibited, the effect being "merely to change its character from the specific to the general: it prohibited the cat; and by implication authorized the use of the belaying-pin and handspike. . . ." [4] Shanghaiing continued to be an important source of the labor supply. There was such ample evidence to the widespread existence of this evil that it was prohibited by Federal statute in 1906.[5]

The competition of unskilled labor, the resorting to foreign ports for hiring seamen, and the continued depression during the nineties all operated to prevent any substantial changes in wages. There was one important difference, however, between wage rates on the Atlantic and Pacific coasts. Wages in the coastwise West Coast trade were higher than those in deepsea operations off both coasts because of the continued shortages of labor and because of the greater degree of organization in Pacific coastwise shipping. On the Pacific, coastwise rates for able seamen were generally $25 to $30 per month; in the unorganized Atlantic and Pacific deepsea trades, rates were $15 to $20 per month. The rates varied by port of signing on, size of ship, and shipping routes involved.

Hours on duty were theoretically determined by industry custom; in fact, the captain's authority prevailed. It was considered established practice in the industry for the sailors, the members of the deck division, to work two watches each 12 hours per day (4 hours on and 4 hours off). In actual practice, with the hours of work controlled by the ship captain, the sailors frequently averaged over 14 hours of work per day.[6] Firemen were generally divided into three watches because of the grueling nature of the work, in close quarters under high temperatures (4 hours on and 8 hours off). The stewards worked from 15 to 18 hours per day. Work in all these departments was performed on the basis of seven days per week.

The crews bore additional burdens as a result of the policy of carrying as small a crew as possible to operate as economically as possible. This policy had become widespread among the merchant marines of the world. Although its origin may have been due to improvements as the result of using labor-saving devices, the Commissioner of Navigation acknowledged "the practice of taking light crews had been carried to an unsafe extreme on some American vessels." Thus, ships of 1200 tons should have been carrying a crew of 34; but British ships were carrying 26, while American ships were carrying 23.[7]

The crews' quarters were generally very poor — unprotected from the elements, cramped, and unsanitary. The forecastle was a "V-shaped room, tiered up to the top almost with bunks. In the center is a table where the men have to eat, and the balance of the space is taken up with benches. Very often . . . there are no mattresses on those bunks, and the men have to sleep on the hard boards unless the sailors aboard the ships have provided themselves with such accommodations." The moderate judgment of the Merchant Marine Commission in 1905 was that "as a rule this testimony is to the effect that general conditions of life in the American merchant marine — wages, food, quarters, etc. — are superior to those in foreign services, but the discipline is often more exacting, and the work more arduous." [8]

THE CRIMPING SYSTEM

The evidence herewith submitted clearly demonstrates the fact, already widely known, that the sailor, ashore, is looked upon as the legitimate prey of land sharks. From the day he arrives in port, until the day of his departure, he is never out of the hands of sharpers, who coax, wheedle, debauch and pander to his worst vices, until his last dollar is gone. Not even then is he a free agent. As the price of release from their clutches, he must submit to have his future earnings mortgaged. He must labor hard for many a day to repay the blood money and the "advances" given in his account by these Shylocks.[9]

Thus a government report describes the lot of the seamen as one of economic exploitation engendered by isolation and disorganization. As for remedying that hard lot, efforts were made by well-meaning individuals and groups to aid the seamen to improve themselves rather than to eliminate the causes for their unfortunate economic status, a view which was rationalized by the general popular theory that the seamen were a naturally improvident lot given to loose living and could not be expected to care for themselves. The seamen themselves, however, were becoming increasingly dissatisfied, and a leadership was developing on the West Coast which sought to attain improvement through organizing the seamen to act politically and economically to ameliorate their status.

The seamen had begun to realize that they were the victims of a system in which their labor had become a "will-less commodity in the hands of unscrupulous speculators, with which they [the speculators] could 'bear' and 'bull' the market." [10] An elaborate system had developed in every port whereby those could profit who trafficked in providing seamen to vessels which stopped in the port. Shipping of seamen was generally done through shipping masters, or crimps, who were paid for their services — always by the seamen, sometimes by the captain. These crimps or shipping masters were to be found among boardinghouse keepers, saloon keepers, and tailors.

Seamen had to patronize certain boardinghouses in order to obtain employment. The seamen on an incoming ship were subjected to all kinds of inducements by boardinghouse runners to desert, although frequently all that was needed was an opportunity "to exchange the dismal forecastle and the empty bread-barge for the fleeting pleasures of a bar-room." Those who deserted their ships forfeited their earnings. They were overcharged for transportation ashore, for food, for drink and lodging. Plied with drink from the time he left ship until such time as he was placed on board another ship by the boardinghouse keeper, the seaman was quickly separated from his money, if he had any. When his money gave out, or when the boardinghouse keeper or crimp decided it was time, the sailor was shipped. Under the law, the crimp would receive an advance on a seaman's wages before he was shipped. As a result, a substantial portion of the seaman's wages had been disposed of before he ever began to perform his work. If he refused to ship on the terms laid down by the boardinghouse keeper, his clothes could be retained for his debts, and he could obtain no "chance" or job.

Boardinghouse keepers and the ship captains made arrangements to ensure that seamen would be obtained only from certain boardinghouses. Also, captains frequently encouraged men to desert in order to avoid paying earnings accumulated over a period of months in the course of a foreign voyage. The captain might have to pay "blood money" to a crimp in order to obtain replacements, but he could still net a saving, especially since only part of the crew would be needed while the ship waited in port for a cargo — which might be a period of two months. During periods of labor shortages, shanghaiing was a frequent resort of those who made a livelihood from furnishing seamen. The situation was reversed when there was a surplus of men available for shipment: the crimp then would pay the captain for the opportunity to ship men in order to obtain advance payment of the debts allegedly due him.

It was not out of ignorance on the part of the public that this system was perpetuated, but the boardinghouse keepers were effectively organized to maintain their intermediary monopoly. As early as 1834, the *Boston Daily Advertiser* had condemned the advance system as a "traffic in the flesh of human beings, whom it first brutalizes in order to render them fit subjects for such traffic." There were voluntary efforts by merchants and mercantile organizations to eliminate the system, but these efforts came to nothing.[11] Even where state laws to license and control boardinghouse keepers existed, they proved ineffective because associations of boardinghouse keepers might frequently be allied with local political machines. Whenever any serious efforts were made to eliminate advance payments, these associations acted concertedly to delay sailings by failing to furnish men.

The combined strength of the crimps was effective even against Federal legislation enacted to eliminate the "advance" evil. In 1872, the shipping commissioners' offices were established by the government which theoretically were intended to assist the seamen to obtain berths free of charge. Out of the funds furnished them, the commissioners were expected to pay for rent, light, heat, and accommodations for seamen, as well as for their own salaries. Thirteen out of 21 commissioners each received a total amount of $1500 for all these purposes.[12] Naturally, the boardinghouse keepers continued in control in the face of such limited appropriations.

More stringent legislation was met by direct action. Advance payments were completely abolished by Federal statute in 1884, with the penalty of a fine and imprisonment of six months for violation. Immediately, the job merchants combined in refusing to furnish men for the ships; and, consequently, ships had difficulty in getting under way. The law was directly evaded by converting the seamen's wage into cash bonuses and wages of $10 per month. The bonus was paid to the crimp and differed little from the advance payment. Within two years, moreover, Congress was induced by shipowners and crimps to amend the act to permit an allotment for $10 for each month of the voyage to "an original creditor for any just debt for board or clothing." In effect, this was restoration of the advance system in another guise. An attempt by the Shipping Commissioner at New York to enforce the spirit of the act by inquiring into items included in amounts for which allotments were requested, was characterized by the Commissioner of Navigation as a "misinterpretation or perversion of the law in relation to allotments."[13]

SEAMEN UNDER THE LAW

American laws relating to seamen were based on English statutes; and, as is frequently the case, the imitation persisted after the original had been altered. After the Civil War, although slavery had been abolished, the Navigation Acts were made more severe. All American statutes relating to compulsory labor were stricken out in 1867, with the sole exception of those relating to seamen. And these provisions were made even more severe in 1872, when seamen were subjected to an additional penalty of three months' imprisonment if they deserted. Great Britain had abolished imprisonment as a penalty for desertion in home ports, but American law remained unchanged.

Why were seamen treated as a class apart? Because the concept of seamen as improvident individuals who could not look out for their own interests was an inherent part of the law. They were treated as wards of admiralty who, to cite an opinion by Justice Storey: "are protected and need counsel; because they are thoughtless and require indulgence; because they are credulous and complying and are easily over-reached . . . although not technically incapable of entering into a valid contract, they are treated in the same manner as courts of equity are accustomed to treat young heirs. . . ." [14] However, this was handling on a two-pronged fork, for as has been noted above, protection went hand in hand with restriction and the seamen were not permitted the freedom that shore workers possessed. Their clothing could be held for failure to pay their debts. If they deserted, they could receive none of their earned wages. Thus, it was held by the majority of the Supreme Court in the Arago Case in 1897 that "From oldest historical period the contract of the sailor has been treated as an exceptional one, and involving to a certain extent, the surrender of his liberty during the life of the contract. . . ."

There was a growing realization of the need for revision of these antiquated views, which had long anteceded the development of the modern means of transportation and the American Constitution. American seamen could derive some satisfaction from Justice Harlan's dissenting opinion in the *Arago* case, which stated that the ancient maritime laws "were enacted at a time when no account was taken of man as man, when human life and liberty were regarded as of little value, and when the powers of government were employed to gratify the ambition and pleasure of despotic rulers rather than promote the welfare of the people." His opinion stated further that the seamen's "supposed helpless condition is thus made the excuse for imposing upon them burdens that could not be imposed upon other classes without depriving them of rights that inhere in personal freedom. The Constitution furnishes no authority for any such distinction between classes of persons in this country." [15]

Thus, the seamen's hapless state was perpetuated by the law, and could not be changed without amending the law, that is, by political action.

A STEP TOWARD ORGANIZATION

Conditions thus made it inevitable that the seamen must organize to improve their status. The earliest continuing organizations were established on the West Coast, namely, the Marine Firemen, Oilers and Watertenders' Union of the Pacific in 1883, and the Sailors' Union of the Pacific in 1885.[16] The Marine Cooks and Stewards' Union of the Pacific was established in 1901. On the Atlantic, the Atlantic Coast Seamen's Union was established in 1888; the Marine Firemen, Oilers, and Watertenders' Union of the Atlantic in 1902; and the Marine Cooks and Stewards' Association of the Atlantic in 1901.

The impetus for organization and activity during the entire history of the seamen's unions up to 1921 derived from the compact organization and active leadership of the Sailors' Union of the Pacific. Organized in 1885 among the sailors on the coastwise sailing schooners, in 1891 this union amalgamated with a union of sailors on the steam schooners in the coastwise trade. A number of factors on the West Coast were favorable to organization among the seamen — the widespread and constant demand for labor on the West Coast which could not be satisfied because of the geographic inaccessibility of the coast; the protected nature of the coastwise lumber carrying trade through the exclusion of foreign flag ships; the unusually arduous work involved in this trade, requiring the sailors to discharge and load the lumber as well as man the ships; the existence of few ports — a fact which was conducive to ready organization and more facile administration by the union; a smaller volume of foreign trade than on the East Coast, consequently less direct competition from men with similar skills; and the relative homogeneity, in terms of their national origins, of the men sailing the ships. The discouraging effects of the hardships involved in loading and unloading the lumber schooners and the "astonishing number of Scandinavians" employed in the coasting trade were the subject of comment by one observer who attributed the small numbers of British seamen in the trade, despite the number of them who deserted at San Francisco, to the hard work.[17] The membership of the SUP in 1905, some 3500, included fully 75 percent of men from northern European countries.

The success of the SUP until the turn of the century must be measured primarily in the gaining and maintaining of an organization which served as a nucleus for the organization of all American seamen. Its aims included more than the attainment of economic benefits normally sought by labor unions. While it sought for "fair and just remuneration" and for "sufficient leisure," its constitution stated that its goals were also "healthy and sufficient food, and proper forecastles in which to rest," to be "treated in a decent and respectful manner by those in command" and "engagement without interference of crimps or other parties not directly interested."

Soon after its organization, the union directed its efforts at eliminating outside control of the seamen's labor market. Within a year of the organization of the union, an abortive attempt was made to set up a shipping office available to members of the union without charge. Again in 1891, a union shipping office was established which sought once more to provide members with equal opportunities for employment and to eliminate control by crimps or shipowner employment offices. A system of rotary hiring was established which, however, permitted seamen to remain in the employ of a ship, if mutually satisfactory to the captain and sailors. Separate lists were maintained for sailing schooners, steam schooners, and steamships. Any member who failed to get aboard on time after accepting a job, was subject to penalties under the constitution.

The establishment of a union shipping office was regarded by the union as striking a vital blow at the boarding masters and other parasites who had grown at the expense of the seamen. While the establishment of the union hiring hall was greeted with much enthusiasm and hope by the union, it was destined to be short-lived. The shipowners refused to accept the union's proposal for coöperation and charged that the masters were being deprived of their traditional right to select their own men.

The shipowners organized their own office and attempted to recruit nonunion labor through it. The combined attacks of the shipowners and the deepwater crimps, the onset of depression, and charges that the Sailors' Union of the Pacific was responsible for a series of acts of violence by unidentified persons resulted in a change of the union's shipping rules to permit free hiring by ship captains. While members were permitted to look for their own "chances," the union's shipping office would furnish crews upon request as heretofore. In effect, this was merely a recognition of the union's inability to maintain job control.

The continued influence of the crimps was evidenced in the agreement concluded in 1896 between the Shipowners' Association of the Pacific Coast with the Coasting Seamen's Shipping Association, an association of boardinghouse keepers. This provided that half of the seamen were to be furnished by members of the crimp association, and the other half from certain other boardinghouses and the Sailors' Home. The only sailors exempt from this agreement — that is, not required to live in the boardinghouses in order to obtain employment — were strike-breakers.[18]

During the nineties the Sailors' Union of the Pacific declared successive strikes against the Shipowners' Association of the Pacific Coast, an organization of operators of sailing schooners. But the continuing depression of those years, with the competition among unemployed and the laying up of the ships, prevented the union from meeting the combined economic strength of the shipowners. The failure of the union shipping office was symptomatic of the lack of collective bargaining. It is significant, however, that an effective organization was maintained during this period and that the Sailors' Union of the Pacific was able to provide the nucleus for a continuing though anemic national organization. This national organization, in turn, was to become the force behind the drive to alter the seamen's status on the legal front.

Only with the gradual improvement in economic conditions in 1899 were wages increased on the West Coast, and overtime payments made. The union scale was put in effect by virtually all companies. A number of companies also agreed to ship only union men. Within two years, collective bargaining was to be established on an active basis on the West Coast.

WEST COAST SEAMEN AND A UNITED FRONT

The leaders of the Sailors' Union of the Pacific — Andrew Furuseth, secretary, and Walter Macarthur, editor of the *Coast Seamen's Journal* — were constantly aware of the threat of lack of organization among seamen on other coasts to wages and working conditions on the Pacific Coast. It would be even more correct to state that they were aware at an early stage of the need for the world-wide organization of seamen to ensure that foreign conditions did not act as a drag on American wages and working conditions. As early as 1890, the Sailors' Union of the Pacific sent Andrew Furuseth and two other representatives to a convention of the British Seamen's Union at Glasgow, but the effort at an international federation failed. A more realistic view of the situation supplanted it; the West Coast seamen decided that what was needed first was an effective maritime federation of American seamen.

The first step toward such a federation would require organization of the seamen on the East Coast. But obstacles to organization were great. Competition of foreign seamen had been direct and almost insuperable for many years. Lack of skill requirements made it possible for shipowners to obtain men in any ports of the world and ship them at the lowest rates possible in offshore shipping. This limitation upon opportunities for employment in foreign trade, in turn, made for greater competition for employment in the coastwise trade. In addition, the fact that there were many ports on the East and Gulf coasts was a handicap to centralized, effective organization and ready administration for many years.

The desire to equalize conditions on all coasts at the highest levels and thus to protect West Coast standards led the Sailors' Union of the Pacific to urge formation of a national union of seamen. As a first step, in 1890, Furuseth sent Samuel Gompers $500 to be used to organize the seamen on the Atlantic Coast, and a committee was established which did some organizing work.[19] The SUP decided in 1891 to communicate with other seamen's unions with a view to holding a national convention to organize a national union. Such a convention was held at Chicago, and on May 11, 1892, the National Seamen's Union, later the International Seamen's Union, was established. It consisted of the sailors' unions on the Great Lakes, the Atlantic, Pacific, and the Gulf. The major result of the first convention was the decision to organize the Atlantic Coast and to eliminate the crimp element from the industry. Affiliation was open to all organizations consisting of seamen, and bonafide seamen's unions were to be grouped into districts having jurisdiction over their respective local affairs. Although the federation was originally based primarily upon sailors' organization, the hope was expressed that the firemen's organizations then in existence would become affiliated with the International Seamen's Union.

From the inception of the federation, the Sailor's Union of the Pacific opposed formation of one big organization consolidating all grades of seafarers as containing "more of the extremely liberal than the practicable quality." [20] This loose control was the basis upon which the International Seamen's Union was to operate until its demise in 1937 — a condition which was partly responsible for that demise.

The efforts to organize the East Coast during these early — and later — years were largely unsuccessful. Upon the organization of the National Seamen's Union, organizers were assigned to the Atlantic Coast. Efforts were made to enlist public support in getting rid of the crimping evil on the Atlantic Coast. Such organizations as the Central Labor Union and the Social Reform Club, as well as several newspapers, supported this drive; but Furuseth reported in 1900 that there continued to be a lack of organization on the Atlantic Coast, and that the crimps remained in full control. Therefore, in contrast to gains on the West Coast, wages on the Atlantic Coast remained generally unchanged.

The influence of the International Seamen's Union for many years stemmed from the influence of its leaders rather than from the numerical strength of its membership. In 1900, its membership was only 3400, with about 2100 in the Sailors' Union of the Pacific, 1100 in the Lakes Seamen's Union, and 300 in the Atlantic Coast Seamen's Union.[21] As a result of its affiliation with the American Federation of Labor in 1893, and the work of Andrew Furuseth, however, the International Seamen's Union was able to lay claim to some achievements in the matter of legislative improvements for seamen before 1900. Other than these, the sole benefit to its members was the recognition of their books of membership by the respective constituent unions. The impotence of this organization was due to its failure to fuse an effective organization, a failure which was to characterize its entire history.

THE SEAMEN'S LEGISLATIVE PROGRAM

Organization among the seamen did, however, bring with it the opportunity for careful analysis of the seamen's status by the seamen's own representatives. Their examination into the roots of the crimp system led to the conclusion that it did not involve only the crimp and the sailor, but permeated the entire business community. The inability to obtain recognition from their employers made seamen realize that while economic organization was essential to improve the seamen's lot, so was activity to change the statutes which were perpetuating the forces in which the crimping system was rooted — "the abolition of contract terms of servitude, the abolition of criminal process in that which is of right a civil case, and the total abolition of advance except to the seamen's mother, wife, or sister." [22] In Furuseth's view, the seamen should be permitted to enter into and break employment contracts like the land worker, and he should be free of the shackles that tie him to the crimp and to the ship.

The Sailors' Union of the Pacific drafted a legislative program in 1892 which it submitted as an "Appeal to Congress." This program was to become the program of the International Seamen's Union, and to be advanced through the latter's affiliation with the American Federation of Labor. Andrew Furuseth was appointed by the International Seamen's Union in 1893, and by the American Federation of Labor in 1895, to press for the achievement of the legislative program embodied in the "Appeal." Thus, Furuseth embarked on the activity of a lifetime that was to bring him the respect and admiration of many of the highest officials of the country. Numerous labor organizations expressed their support in petitions to Congress for the enactment of the seamen's program. The "Red Record" was widely distributed among Congressmen and the press.

The program adopted by the seamen (which was to form the basis for successive legislation from 1895 to 1915) sought to restrict employment on American ships, both in domestic and foreign ports, to men who had been engaged regularly as seamen and who were citizens or had declared their intentions of becoming citizens. The intention was to eliminate the drifter and Oriental labor from the industry. It sought to provide the seamen with a voice in the determining of a ship's seaworthiness — a matter which directly affected the lives of passengers

and crews — by permitting the right of the majority of the crew to request examination of a ship. Formerly this right had been restricted to
two officers, or an officer and a majority of the crew. It sought to protect seamen from unfair discharge in foreign ports without provision for
return to the home port. Imprisonment for desertion at home or abroad
was to be abolished. Seamen's wages were to be free from attachment.
A full scale of provisions was to be provided and expressly written into
the seamen's articles. Hours of work were to be protected by law — at
sea, sailors were to be divided into two watches, each of which was to
be kept on deck four hours alternately; and no unnecessary work was
to be required on Sundays or legal holidays at sea or in port. A printed
handbook was to be provided to eligible seamen, which would contain
the seamen's description with provision for entries which would be
limited to length of service, job description, and signature. Such books
were to be required for shipment on American vessels in domestic
ports.[23]

The seamen's program met with opposition from the shipowners and
related interests who conceded only that mandatory imprisonment for
desertion should be made discretionary with the court. This "might be
held *in terrorem* over the heads of these men" whom they characterized
as "the driftwood from their native countries where they cannot get
employment" and who are "deliberately invited to open mutiny and
rebellion by these sailors' unions." [24] Support for the view that continued
restraints were necessary to prevent seamen from deserting, particularly
where they failed to report after signing articles, came from government
representatives. "Where wages have not been earned," felt the Commissioner of Navigation, "it is a mere travesty on law to declare the forfeiture of wages a penalty for such desertion." Therefore, continuance
of imprisonment was recommended. In Congress, it was urged by some,
as by Senator Frye of Maine, that some restraints on the seamen were
necessary "so that they will not treat their contracts with utter levity and
leave without any decent excuse at all." Senator Frye also contended
that the seamen were well-organized and "had every advantage of the
ship and every advantage of the shipmaster." It was his view that the
"ships were entitled to some consideration." [25]

The activities of the seamen's leaders were soon successful in obtaining at least partial modification of the maritime laws. In 1895, the Ma-
guire Act was passed, which permitted seamen engaged in the protected
coastwise trades to refuse to join their ships and to desert at will, and
to receive one third of the wages due at any port of discharge, unless
their contracts specifically prohibited. It also prohibited the advance and
allotment in the coastwise trades, and prohibited anyone from withhold-
ing a seaman's clothes, under penalty of fine.[26]

It was soon apparent that this statute was not applicable to American seamen under foreign articles (i.e., in the deepsea trades) even while in American ports. In the *Arago* case, the Supreme Court, in 1897, sustained the enforced return of four seamen who deserted in an American port prior to leaving for foreign ports. Again the seamen appealed for public support to achieve their program. In San Francisco a mass meeting was held at which many local notables supported the seamen. An invitation tendered the Sailors' Union of the Pacific to participate in a Fourth of July celebration was declined with the statement that: "We, therefore, sir, being mindful of our status — that of involuntary servitude — which was in no way modified by that declaration of individual freedom, feel that it would be an imposition on our part to take advantage of your kindness and inflict our presence — the presence of bondsmen — upon the freemen who will on the Fourth of July celebrate their freedom. . . . Hoping that we also some day may honorably and as equals march in such parade. . . ."

Within a year, the White Act was passed which represented a compromise agreed upon by the seamen and the shipowners. While all imprisonment for desertion in domestic ports was ended, a maximum period of imprisonment of one month for desertion in foreign ports was retained at the urging of the shipowners who claimed that otherwise great difficulty would be encountered in foreign ports. This act also fixed a maximum allotment of one month's pay to original creditors.[27] It was not long, however, before efforts were being made to circumvent these allotment provisions.

By 1900, the seamen had established an organizational framework which, while largely unsuccessful in achieving collective bargaining, had made itself felt in the councils of the land. The American seamen were now free on American soil, at least. But the foreign seamen remained unfree, and their economic status affected that of the American seamen. Therefore, a new and more ambitious program was in the making.

CHAPTER 2

BEGINNINGS OF COLLECTIVE BARGAINING, 1900–1916

WEST COAST VERSUS EAST COAST

The differences in the status of organization and trend toward collective bargaining between seamen's organizations on the East and West coasts became more sharply defined during the period after 1900. Improvement in economic conditions brought with it improved wages and working conditions for the seamen on the West Coast. Strong and compact organization in the coastwise trades made it possible for these seamen to meet the associations of their employers on relatively equal terms. The growing strength of the unions in San Francisco reorientated the outlook of the employing groups. The seamen were among the first to enjoy the effects of this change, and from 1902 to 1921 enjoyed formal collective bargaining relations with the employers' associations. Throughout this period, however, the seamen's unions on the Pacific were unable to overcome the opposition of the major companies in the offshore trades.

The seamen on the East Coast presented an entirely different picture. Diverse ethnic groups within the various departments prevented effective organization. The leaders of the East Coast unions were unwilling to admit Spanish firemen and Negro sailors as members on equal terms. There was frequent disorganization and disaffection among the members because of policies of the officials. Strikes on the Atlantic and Gulf coasts were frequent during this period, but, with one exception, they were characterized by disunity; and the results were short-lived when any gains were made.

The leaders of the International Seamen's Union of America were aware of the weaknesses in the fabric of seamen's organization. Efforts to organize the seamen on the Atlantic failed, however, because of the loose structure of the international federation. The international was founded on a particularistic basis which it was unable to overcome. Crises in East Coast union affairs and the crushing of union organization on the Great Lakes by the Lake Carriers Association were met with indecision and inadequate action from the ISU. They did, however, achieve successes in warding off encroachments by the longshoremen and others in the seamen's work and in the legislative realm. But even success in the legislative realm was due essentially to the efforts of one man, Andrew Furuseth.

UNION ORGANIZATION AND TACTICS

By 1902, the International Seamen's Union had completed its organization of unions representing the respective departments of seamen on both coasts. Among the approximately 35,000 unlicensed seamen engaged in coastwise and offshore shipping on both coasts in 1903, a total of 8200 seamen were organized.

On the Pacific, the Sailors' Union of the Pacific and the Pacific Coast Marine Firemen were joined in 1901 by the Marine Cooks and Stewards' Association of the Pacific Coast. In 1907, the firemen's union was reorganized as the Marine Firemen, Oilers, and Watertenders' Union of the Pacific. These maintained their headquarters at San Francisco. Organization grew from approximately 3000 in 1900 to about 6700 in 1904, shortly after the first agreements were reached. Organization among seamen in the coastwise trades until the entry of the United States into the first World War was maintained at a level of 85 to 90 percent of the total personnel employed.

On the Atlantic, the Atlantic Coast Seamen's Union (reorganized in 1913 as the Eastern and Gulf Sailors' Association) was joined in 1902 by the Atlantic Coast Marine Firemen (reorganized in 1911 and again in 1913 as the Marine Firemen, Oilers, and Watertenders' Union of the Atlantic and Gulf) and by the Marine Cooks and Stewards' Association of the Atlantic in 1901. Headquarters were maintained at Boston for the sailors and firemen during most of the period, and at New York for the marine cooks and stewards. In 1900, some 1200 seamen were organized on the Atlantic Coast; a peak of organizational strength was reached in 1907 with a membership of 4800. Thereafter, the active membership fell off to 3900, which level was maintained until shortly before the entry of the United States into the war.

The organization of the seamen's unions on both coasts was either based upon, or similar to, that of the Sailors' Union of the Pacific. Branches were maintained by the unions at various ports along the respective coasts. The branches were under the jurisdiction of headquarters. Weekly meetings were held at headquarters and at branches.

Generally, a chairman *pro tem* was elected at each meeting. Permanent officers, usually a secretary as executive officer, a treasurer, branch agents, and patrolmen were elected either semi-annually or annually. (In the case of the Sailors' Union of the Pacific, the editor and business manager of the *Coast Seamen's Journal,* publication of that union and organ of the ISU, were also elected.) Strikes could generally be called only by vote of the membership at headquarters; they could not be called by individual branches without the sanction of such a general vote.

Membership was open to individuals who were members of the respective departments over which the union had jurisdiction and who either were American citizens or had declared their intention of becoming citizens. In virtually all cases, an applicant for entry into the union had to serve a six-month probationary period to determine whether he was capable of performing the tasks required and was suitable for membership in the union. The various constitutions generally permitted transfers from a like union in another geographical district without payment of an initiation fee. Initiation fees generally amounted to $5; the Pacific Marine Firemen, however, had a $50 fee which was reduced to $25 when the union was reorganized in 1907 to include firemen and oilers in its membership. Dues ranged from 50¢ to 75¢ per month. Benefits of membership included maximum shipwreck benefits ranging among the various unions from $25 to $50, depending upon the extent of a seamen's loss. This benefit was intended to provide seamen with necessary clothing and personal effects, and thus to keep them out of the crimps' clutches. All the unions provided death benefits ranging from $75 to $100 by 1914. Sick benefits, which ranged from 50¢ to $1 per week were small because they merely supplemented the medical care in public health hospitals to which seamen are entitled if they fall ill during the course of their employment.

Members who delayed ship sailings because of drunkenness or for any other insufficient reason were subject to punishment by fine or suspension for the first offense, and to expulsion for a second offense. Seamen who paid for chances on ships were subject to fines. Fines were also levied on members who brought the union into ill repute by bad conduct on board ship.

Recognition of the union generally gave its members the preference for available jobs, with the shipowner or master agreeing to obtain men through union representatives or the union hall when vacancies occurred. Men might be shipped through the union halls or off the dock. The system of rotary hiring or turn shipping was not in general use and was frowned upon by the leadership of the International Seamen's Union, who felt that it deprived the more skilled seamen of the advantages due them. On the East Coast, however, rotary hiring was put into effect for a short period during 1911 and 1912.

An additional feature of recognition was permission for union officers to visit docks and ships to make sure that union men were employed to fill vacancies and also to collect dues from members. It was the function of the union patrolman to visit as many ships on his beat as possible in order to carry out these duties.

Ship delegates, representatives of the union on board the ship and spokesmen for the crew, were chosen by the patrolmen or elected by the crew members of the respective departments. Unsettled grievances were reported by the delegates to the patrolmen, and were taken up with the company officials by the appropriate union representatives on shore. West Coast agreements provided for grievance machinery and arbitration of unsettled disputes.[1]

Where collective bargaining did not exist, efforts were made to persuade men on board the ships to organize. Launches would approach the ships and call on the men to leave the ship unless they obtained union conditions. On occasion, the "persuasive" tactics were extremely forceful, and recruiters on the launches might board the ships or be fired upon. Another tactic, intended to impede open-shop operations, was the use of what Furuseth called the "oracle." The men would sign on as nonunion men, and then, just before the ship was due to leave, would jump ashore with their clothing. Such tactics proved costly to shipowners who wished their ships to leave on schedule.[2]

The union organization and structure developed during this period were maintained with little change until the establishment of the National Maritime Union in 1937 and the Seafarers' International Union in 1938.

COLLECTIVE BARGAINING ON THE WEST COAST

Improved economic conditions during the last years of the century were accompanied by vigorous organizing activity in the San Francisco area among both skilled and unskilled workers. A strike of seamen in 1899 to restore the scale in effect in 1890 met with widespread success. Improved working rules were sought to fix hours of work in port and to provide for coffee periods. Some independent companies indicated their willingness to ship union men only and to permit union representatives on company docks to transact union business with members of the crews. Efforts of the Sailors' Union in 1900 to obtain a conference with the Shipowners' Association, however, were unsuccessful. In the spring of 1901, the Sailors' Union reached an agreement with the Pacific Coast Steamship Company, the principal line in the coastwise passenger service, which provided for exclusive employment of union members, so long as the union was able to furnish the necessary labor.

Growing strength was demonstrated by independence; an offer by the Shipowners' Association to carry only union seamen, if the Sailors' Union would refuse to furnish men to nonmembers of the Association, was rejected since the Shipowners' Association represented only a small proportion of the shipowners who were also considered the most rabidly anti-union. Matters stood thus when a major strike occurred in San Francisco which was to shape the destinies of union organization in that area for more than a decade.

The experience of the nineties, when the organized employers of San Francisco had effectively fought union organization, had demonstrated that the growing unions needed unified action in the city to forestall a similar drive. The activity of the Employers' Association of San Francisco (which consisted, as Father Peter Yorke put it, of "all the capital in the city of San Francisco engaged in the wholesale and manufacturing business, and, I am afraid, the banks also. . . .")[3] was viewed with open suspicion by the unions as a conspiracy to destroy their organization by coercing all employers into adhering to the open-shop principle by threatening to cut off their supplies. In February 1901, after several months of discussion, a number of waterfront unions, including the sailors', marine firemen's, longshoremen's, coal teamsters', pile drivers', joiners', clerks', packers' and hoisting engineers' organized the City Front Federation.

The City Front Federation participated in the strike of July 1901, in support of the teamsters who had been discharged for refusing to haul for a company employing nonunion teamsters. The sailors and firemen voted full support of the strike and provided financial aid to the longshoremen. The 16,000 waterfront employees sought a truce based on recognition of the right of employees to organize; the ending of discrimination against workers for membership in unions; and a return to the *status quo ante* the strike pending the settlement of differences by a conciliation committee consisting of representatives of both sides. The employers' position was characteristic of the open-shop sentiment of the times. They indicated a willingness "to live and let live," recognized the right of employees to organize to improve their conditions, and would not "trespass upon that right by refusing employment to any one solely because he does or does not belong to any labor organization." But the Employers' Association's declaration of principles also made clear that any provision for union security of any degree was, therefore, viewed as "being inimical to the liberties of the individual and in consequence productive only of harm to the community."[4]

The seamen were in the forefront of the strike activity. Andrew Furuseth was chairman of the executive committee of the City Front Federation and manager of the strike. Under his direction, every effort was made to ensure that the strike was carried out in a responsible manner without violence. Coal supplies for hospitals and for the lighting system were provided. Every effort was made to enlist the support of the public in the strikers' cause. Mass meetings were held. At one such meeting, Furuseth acknowledged that the seamen had broken their contracts, but felt that they had been justified in so doing. In his view, if it was all right for the United States to violate its treaty with Spain in order to help Cuba, "then it was right for the seamen and firemen here, in the interest of humanity to break their temporary arrangement. By whom should we, in point of ethics, be obliged to stand?" he asked. "Should we desert our fellow workmen, or should we stand by our class and suffer what consequences might come to us, all because we objected to the methods used by the Employers' Association. . . . ?"[5] He viewed the principle involved in the dispute as even more important than the sanctity of an agreement — a position which was opposed to his usual views.

The waterfront strike of 1901, called off after eleven weeks, demonstrated the strength of union organization, despite its failure to achieve success in the immediate struggle. The shipowners' associations had found themselves unable to cope with a combined organization of waterfront workers. The strength of organized labor generally was further demonstrated in the organization of the Union Labor Party and the successful culmination of its campaign for the mayoralty. The implications of the growth of a new force to be reckoned with were realized by the shipowners, who needed labor stability in order to operate their vessels during this prosperous period. The Shipowners' Association of the Pacific Coast, organized in 1891 by the operators of sailing schooners in the coastwise lumber trade primarily to fight the efforts of the Sailors' Union to obtain job control, was reorganized in November 1901 under the leadership of James Rolph, Jr. in order to enter into negotiations with the union.[6] After five months of negotiations, an agreement was reached for a trial period. At the end of the first six months, it was extended for a like period. Thereafter, on the basis of the union's demonstration of responsibility under the agreement, it was renewed for one year, with some modifications.

Under the agreement, all signing on and paying off in San Francisco would be done in a central office maintained by the Shipowners' Association. When men were needed, the owners and masters would either obtain crews from the Sailors' Union or from *bona fide* boardinghouses, in accordance with a pro rata to be agreed upon among the Sailors' Union, the boardinghouse keepers, and the Shipowners' Association.

While these provisions were a far cry from union job control, the union felt that shipping of crews through "'a shipping office' will remove that old sore, the 'scab shipping office'. . . . By investing the Union with authority to select a certain proportion of the crews from the houses of *bona fide* boarding masters, a guarantee is given that only those of that class who conduct their business in a legitimate way will be able to stay in business at all."

By 1904, the union became sufficiently strong to reach the point whereby the provision in the 1902 agreement relating to boardinghouse keepers could be eliminated; thereafter all men were to be obtained from the union. In ports other than San Francisco, agents of the Sailors' Union were to furnish crews when requested to do so by masters or owners. Provision was made for patrolmen to board vessels in order to oversee union affairs and also to see that all men were on board on time. The agreements from 1902 to 1904 spelled out the existing practice of employing crews in loading and discharging of vessels, either alone or together with longshoremen. The nine-hour day between the hours of 7 A.M. and 5 P.M., with one full hour for lunch, was recognized for work in all ports by 1904, with overtime payment for work outside these hours on weekdays, and for all work on Sundays and legal holidays. Coastwise rates were $40 per month for trips to inside ports, and $45 for trips to outside ports. Rates for offshore shipping ranged from $25 to $35 per month. The Sailors' Union put itself on record in these agreements as "not in favor of sympathetic strikes." A start toward grievance settlement was made in the provision for a joint standing committee to be appointed to adjust any grievances that might arise from time to time.

The operators of steam schooners, organized as the Steam Schooner Managers' Association, with Robert Dollar as president, were more reluctant to enter into collective bargaining relations with the unions. But the times were propitious for union organization, and the seamen's unions were gaining in influence among the seamen on the Pacific Coast. As a result, an agreement was reached between this association and the three West Coast seamen's unions in 1903 which permitted the unions the opportunity to see to it that crew members were members of the respective unions. Wage rates exceeded those on the sailing ships, and the port conditions were comparable.

A third agreement was reached with the Oceanic Steamship Company, which operated to Hawaii and Australasia under the direction of John D. Spreckels. It was the only deepsea company operating with white seamen because it was receiving a mail subsidy under the Act of 1891. This agreement, also reached in 1903, provided for preference to union members.

The wage demands during this period were described as intended "to establish a standard wage-rate capable of being maintained during a period of comparative depression as well as during periods of prosperity in the shipping industry, rather than to obtain the highest possible wage under the most prosperous circumstances."[7] Labor-management relations under these agreements were amicable for several years. The union stringently enforced penalties against failure to report to vessels on time. The Sailors' Union notified the City Front Federation that while it would be willing to aid striking unions financially, it was not prepared to permit any authority outside of the union to call its members out in a sympathetic strike. Recognition had brought with it the realization of responsibility, and the union leadership felt that the seamen would be placed in the position of having "to quit work for all time" if they were to participate in any agreement to refuse to handle nonunion cargo. In general, there appeared to be a willingness on all sides to maintain good relations.

The situation was altered in 1906, however, when the union voted against renewal of the agreement with the Steam Schooner Managers' Association in March because the latter refused to accede to the union's demands for a five-dollar wage increase, overtime increases, and messrooms for the crews where they were not already provided by companies according to the 1905 agreement on the grounds that they could not afford the adjustments.[8]

Discussions were still going on at the time of the San Francisco earthquake and the fire. It was apparent soon after the catastrophe that shipping prospects had, if anything, benefited from that event. The Sailors' Union decided to reopen negotiations. While the union acknowledged its obligation to do everything to aid in the rebuilding of San Francisco, it also pointed out that some 2000 of its 3000 members were working outside of the San Francisco area "under conditions which it had been determined should be improved" long before the earthquake. The steam schooner owners refused to accede and submitted the matter to the United Shipping and Transportation Association, which consisted of the unorganized offshore steamship companies (Pacific Mail, American-Hawaiian) in addition to the steam schooner operators. The United Shipping and Transportation Association supported the steam schooner operators and took over the active direction of the activities against the strike. The association decided to tie up all the steamships until the labor situation improved, and discharged 75 percent of the stevedores on the waterfront.[9] It was clear that an effort was being made to involve the City Front Federation in a showdown battle. The City Front Federation attempted unsuccessfully to obtain an end to the sympathetic lockout.

The seamen's unions indicated their willingness to arbitrate the controversy. However, arbitration was rejected by the shipowners on the grounds that they were paying the highest maritime wages in the world and that current conditions in San Francisco made entirely unjustifiable and inopportune any demands for wage increases.[10]

The actions of the owners' association in extending the lockout to longshoremen and seamen on freight and passenger vessels was viewed by Furuseth as an attempt "to give a death blow to union. . . . They have taken advantage of the situation, and misfortune of the city and the imperative demand for lumber, to take this opportunity to bring the matter to an issue once for all whether the sailors of the Pacific are to have any power." He denied that the wage demand had any real significance and cited the increased prices of lumber and freight.[11] The further charge was made that the United Shipping and Transportation Association was allied with the Citizens Alliance of San Francisco, and that both stood for the open shop, and would attempt to prevent individual ship operators from reaching agreement with the union.[12]

In order to forestall the possibility of arousing public animus against the seamen's unions for a strike which was threatening to involve the entire waterfront, the seamen's unions withdrew from the City Front Federation. This action was followed by the reëmployment of the locked-out longshoremen. The latter proceeded to load and unload ships manned by Japanese, Hawaiians, and other nonunion labor, imported as strikebreakers, and in some cases even to perform the work of seamen in moving the struck ships from dock to dock. The seamen's representatives, however, felt that the situation had been cleared and the pressure eased.

Although ships were being manned with strikebreakers, the strike was having its effect. The railroads were unable to handle all the lumber routed over them and an embargo was declared on further shipments. Some lumber was towed down the coast by way of a huge log raft consisting of 9,000,000 feet of lumber, despite the fact that such a practice was viewed with disfavor as a peril to navigation in the event that the raft broke up.

The strike also retarded the progress of building construction in the city. Increased pressure, therefore, was placed upon the parties by the mayor and the newspapers to submit the matter to arbitration. While the unions indicated their willingness to arbitrate, the shipowners announced that they stood for the open shop and that the strikers would have to work with the strikebreakers. The owners of the steam schooners attempted to enlist the support of the owners of sailing schooners who were members of the Shipowners' Association of the Pacific Coast, and who were the principal means of supplying San Francisco during the strike. On July 14, the Shipowners' Association joined the United Ship-ping and Transportation Association.[13] The members of the Shipowners' Association were divided, however, and on August 31, the group agreed to a wage increase. By this time, a number of steam schooner operators were feeling the effects of the strike and were attempting to obtain union men to replace the inefficient and costly labor employed during the strike.[14] Finally, on November 3, the unions were fully recognized and their requested increase in wages was granted.

After this trial of strength, an even tempo of peaceful collective bar-gaining relations between the seamen and the shipowners was main-tained until 1921. In 1907, the two associations of coastwise operators (sailing schooners and steam schooners) merged into the Shipowners' Association of the Pacific Coast. Organization of seamen and operators on a coastwide basis, hence agreements on a coastwide basis, was viewed by both sides as facilitating the settlement of disputes. Relations were apparently established so firmly that by 1908 the parties were operating on the basis of "tacit" agreements embodying the provisions of earlier formal written agreements.

The primary reason for attainment of such a position by the seamen's unions in coastwise shipping was succinctly accounted for in the *Pacific Marine Review,* a shipowner organ:

With the disappearance of sail before steam the difficulty of securing and/or training experienced seamen becomes intenser every day and has become a national problem of concern to every maritime nation. The fact that in the large steamers of the present day a majority of the crew must engage in the hard and unpleasant occupation of shovelling coals adds to the difficulty, while in our coastwise trade, the ability to secure more congenial occupations on land at far higher wages places the shipowners at a disadvantage.[15]

The seamen's unions had achieved a virtual monopoly of the skilled labor on the coast. They were especially valuable because they were skilled in loading and discharging lumber as well as in discharging the customary duties of seamen. Even with the depression after 1907, and the numerous unemployed on the beach, good relations were maintained in anticipation of the return of better times when skilled seamen would be needed.

There was only one big fly in the ointment so far as the unions were concerned. In intercoastal and offshore shipping, two important com-panies maintained their operations with nonunion labor. The American-Hawaiian Steamship Company was charged with carrying "incompetent landmen." The Pacific Mail Steamship Co., part of the empire of James J. Hill, was operating across the Pacific with Chinese sailors and firemen who were being paid $7 per month, out of which they purchased their own food. R. P. Schwerin, one of the moving forces in the United Shipping and Transportation Association during the 1906 strike and general manager of Pacific Mail, denied that his company was antagonistic to American labor, explaining the situation as follows: "We are in competition with other flags on the Pacific Ocean, taking the same class of cargo carried by these ships, and we are out to live and make dollars and cents . . . if we can obtain no better rates with a mixed crew than with a European crew, we can not pay the wages demanded by the European crew." [16] From these companies came numerous attacks on the seamen's unions, and the favorite charge leveled was that the unions were controlled by foreigners who restricted the entry of American boys into the merchant marine.[17]

To this charge that a substantial portion of the Sailors' Union consisted of foreigners, the *Coast Seamen's Journal* could only reply that "The Union simply organizes the material at hand without reference to the accident of birth, color, or creed. Come to think of it, there is a certain humor in the reference to the nationality of the seamen on the Pacific Coast, considering the fact that the reference is made by the most notorious employers of Chinese labor in the whole country. . . ." [18] The threat of the low standards prevailing for Oriental labor was to be met by the unions in the fashion which was characteristic of the times, by seeking legislative exclusion of oriental labor from American ships. Furuseth was instrumental in having such provisions attached to ship subsidy and Chinese exclusion bills in Congress. When these failed of enactment, an indirect approach was to be taken by the Seamen's Bill (see Chapter 3).

(see Chapter 3).

FAILURE ON THE EAST COAST

Conditions on the East Coast were the exact reverse of those on the West Coast during this entire period. While the seamen maintained unions, their membership fluctuated greatly, and occasionally dissolutions occurred. Only among the stewards was there a stable organization which grew steadily. The eastern unions were unable to cope with the constant influx of unorganized foreigners to employment on deck and in the engine rooms. Efforts to organize the foreigners and Negroes who were used in the coastwise trades, as well as in deepsea shipping, were spasmodic and largely ineffectual. East Coast leaders had none of the stature or ability of men like Furuseth and Patrick Flynn of the Pacific Coast marine firemen. Efforts to center job control in the unions were unavailing. Unions, religious and charitable agencies, and crimps all competed to obtain employment for seamen. Although the first two operated without interest in direct pecuniary gain, it was the last who exercised substantial control among the foreigners. Disorganization permitted East Coast shipowners to maintain virtually complete control of the labor situation, except for periods of short duration, until America's entry into the first World War.

The primary problem on the East Coast, that of organizing Negro sailors and Spanish firemen, was recognized by the leaders of the International Seamen's Union, but concrete action was slow and limited. At the eighth convention of the ISU, in 1903, resolutions were introduced by the only Negro delegate to organize Negro seamen into separate agencies "where they can maintain the good will of the seamen without violating the principles of trade-unionism, or arousing the race prejudice of the country." The matter was referred to the executive board for action, but it died there.

Progress was being made in organizing the English-speaking white seamen in the coastwise trades. "The main obstacles in our way are the colored and Latin elements," reported the general organizer at the twelfth convention of the ISU in 1907. It was his view that organizing the approximately 3000 Negro sailors, who were carried on 75 percent of the coastwise schooners and were receiving $5 less than the union scale, was essential in order to protect organized sailors on the Atlantic. However, the efforts of five Negro organizers in the field for a period of five months, and mass distribution of literature, appear to have been unsuccessful. The convention resolved to attempt to organize Negroes into separate branches.[19]

In 1908, the Marine Cooks and Stewards opened a branch office exclusively for Negroes, and it was stated that "in establishing this branch, every right and privilege which the colored men could justly claim has been fully considered, anticipated, and most generously provided for by their white comrades." They had their own hall, their own offices — "no arrangement could be more genuinely fraternal in conception, nor more generously liberal in execution." David Grange, described as "himself a most intelligent and energetic colored man, whose record in the Cooks and Stewards' Union is a credit to his race, and a guaranty of able, honest, and effective service as well," was placed in charge of the new branch.[20] This group was to maintain a continuous and effective organization.

When organization among Negro seamen did progress, and a number joined the Atlantic Coast Seamen's Union in 1911, that union, by referendum vote, denied Negro seamen the further right of membership. Negro seamen, thereafter, managed to maintain organization only by joining the Negro branch of the Marine Cooks and Stewards. That year the ISU convention voted to recommend that the Atlantic Coast Seamen's Union admit the Negro seamen under a system of separate locals "or other safeguards against discrimination between white and colored members";

an amendment to prohibit the right of transfer of such seamen to unions on other coasts was defeated,[21] although apparently nothing was done to implement this recommendation. Grange unsuccessfully introduced a resolution at the twentieth convention for the appointment of Negro organizers to organize Negro sailors on the Atlantic. The failure of the ISU to meet this nominally local problem which had nationwide ramifications for all the seamen was demonstrated by the weak substitute action which "urged" the district unions of the Atlantic and Gulf "to use every means in their power, educational and otherwise, to the end that all colored seamen be brought into the folds of the ISUA where they rightfully belong." [22]

The problem of organizing Spanish firemen and Spanish-speaking Latin Americans was of equal importance, for their numbers had increased. By 1915, they constituted over 50 percent of the firemen on the Atlantic.[23] They were the victims of the crimps, their victimization being intensified by the added isolation arising from their inability to speak English. These seamen were docked pay by the masters for all kinds of petty, trumped-up, and alleged charges, and the language difference made explanations difficult when they appeared before the U. S. shipping commissioners.

No real efforts were made to organize this group by the leaders of the Atlantic Coast Marine Firemen, although they denied discrimination. Open suspicion and hostility existed between the Latin firemen and the Anglo-Saxon leaders of the union. The latter were suspected of being in league with the crimps. Following charges that its secretary had been guilty of mismanagement, incompetency, and one-man rule in violation of the constitution, the Atlantic Coast Marine Firemen's Union was dissolved. The secretary was also engaged in the saloon business and "in the shipping of firemen . . . defrauding his victims on a larger scale than does the average crimp shipping master in New York." [24]

The union was reorganized in 1909 to include coal-passers, wipers, oilers, and watertenders, in addition to firemen. In accordance with the policy laid down by the ISU, the Spanish firemen were organized into a separate branch. Upon assurances by Furuseth that this branch would be virtually autonomous, there was a great impetus to organization under the guidance of their own leaders. One leader in particular, James Vidal, a former fireman, proved especially effective in building a strong organization. Furuseth said of these leaders that they were "men of an exceptional type" and that they had "sufficient scholarship in both Spanish and English to very readily translate from one language into the other, an appreciation of the international aspect of the seamen's movement, and of its ultimate aim and purposes. . . ." [25] They published their own weekly newspaper, which received financial support from the

ISU. Within a year, about 1000 of the 2100 Latin firemen in the Port of New York had been organized. This group was to play an important role in the major effort at union recognition on the East Coast during the 1912 strike.

The inability and actual unwillingness to organize important groups among the seamen was a byproduct of the general incompetency of leaders and the dictatorial organization which existed on the East Coast for most of this period. The conservative and limited view of the leadership of the sailors' union was symbolized by its unwillingness to have the headquarters moved from Boston to New York. New York had already become the center of shipping activity, with the replacement of schooners by steamships, and it required complete organizational concentration if any success was to be obtained at all. The circumstance of the reorganization of the Marine Firemen's Union by the ISU has been mentioned above. The new leadership of the firemen's union was hardly an improvement. Within a year of the reorganization, Oscar Carlson was found to have discriminated against the Latin element and to have been elected agent of the Philadelphia branch at a meeting attended by a small minority of the membership. He was permitted to retain office even though the election itself was found to have been in violation of the authority of the ISU. The ISU deemed it "unwise to remove Carlson," despite the fact that temporizing could not make for harmony.[26] Again in 1911, there was evidence of East Coast disunity when the New York branch of the Atlantic Coast Seamen's Union condemned the Boston leadership for refusing to permit the membership a referendum vote on the matter of sending more than one delegate to the ISU convention. It also condemned the leadership for ordering the New York branch to cease contributing to the support of the *Waterfront Journal* (an ILA-dominated publication advocating federation of marine transport workers). Upon appeal from the members of the New York branch, the ISU evaded the issue with a decision to the effect that the matter was one to be handled in accordance with the constitutional provisions of the Atlantic Coast Seamen's Union, although it did recommend that referenda might be used where they were not already specifically provided for by the constitution. This lack of action was to be regretted; for within a year, the ACSU secretary disappeared and his books showed a shortage of over $3000; within a year and a half, the unions of sailors and firemen were to be in a state of virtual disintegration following the failure of the 1912 strike (see below).

The disunity within the ranks of organized seamen, and within the ranks of seamen generally, made simple the employers' task of meeting efforts at organization on the East Coast. The lack of any skill requirements, the availability of a substantial supply of unskilled labor, and the constant turnover in East Coast shipping personnel were the main supports for continuance of the open-shop policy. The operators of coastwise companies acted in combination whenever union organization threatened to make inroads on shipowner control over employment. Their view of the unions was reflected in the accusation by a shipping trade journal of having "created dissension among a class of men that were before their coming, prosperous and happy. . . ." Furuseth was called a "foreign-born agitator" and the seamen's unions described as being 95 percent foreign.[27]

Growth of organization among the sailors on coastwise sailing vessels in 1902 had been countered by the organization of the owners of these vessels into the Atlantic Carriers' Association. With Field S. Pendleton at its head, the association had attempted to establish an independent union. In 1904, the Atlantic Coast Seamen's Union was locked out by the members of the association in a successful effort to reduce wage rates. In 1904 some success had been achieved by the firemen's union in organizing the Spanish firemen. These men were thereupon discharged, and German immigrants substituted. The union then opened a union boardinghouse in a successful effort to organize the German firemen.[28]

Coördinated strike action was generally lacking on the East Coast. Success came, and then only temporarily, when competent seamen were in short supply.[29] The most concerted action by the East Coast seamen's unions occurred during 1911 and 1912. A successful international strike of seamen in British, Dutch, and Belgian ports during June 1911, in which American seamen did not participate, provided the background for a strike against the Morgan Line by the three East Coast seamen's unions.[30] Five hundred strikers paraded through the streets of New York bearing placards demanding the abolition of the crimping system. It was reported that the strikers issued a statement in English, Spanish, and German, a paragraph of which stated: "We are not getting enough to eat, and on account of the padrone system upheld by this company, we are held in more abject slavery than the Negroes of the South before the Civil War." [31] Coming at a period of brisk shipping and at a time when the international strike of seamen might furnish American seamen with a strong basis of support, an agreement was concluded.

Agreements were also reached with the United Fruit Co., Southern Pacific Steamship Co., Old Dominion, Savannah, Clyde, and Mallory Lines (in the case of the last two, H. H. Raymond, vice-president, signed a "Memorandum of Understanding"). The agreements provided that union representatives would be able to visit the docks and ships, and that the crews would be obtained from the unions. Ships' officers could reject men furnished by the unions if they were unsatisfactory, and the unions would be required to furnish satisfactory substitutes. The agreements which were to be of one year's duration, did not contain a renewal provision or provisions relating to the handling of grievances.[32]

This, however, was to be but a brief interlude during a period of employer control. Shortly after their recognition in June 1911, the seamen's unions on the East Coast organized into the Waterfront Federation of New York and Vicinity for more effective action in the event of future strikes. The organ of this Federation was called the *Waterfront Journal*. Support for the Federation had been received from the International Longshoremen's Association, which was fostering a "national federation of all national and international unions engaged in transportation. . . ."[33] In line with this aim, the ILA encouraged the formation of local transport federations. A number of longshoremen's locals in the New York area, therefore, became affiliated with the Waterfront Federation, which then took a stand in favor of a transport workers' department in the American Federation of Labor — a position opposed by the leaders of the International Seamen's Union, who feared that such a department would be dominated by the longshoremen.

The view of James Vidal, leader of the Spanish firemen, diverged from those who were concerned solely with the limited goal of establishing a transport workers' department. He was a former fireman who had done an effective job of organizing his brother firemen to overcome the hold of the crimps and to improve their conditions on board ship. Dissatisfied with the conservatism of the leaders of the ISU, he took the firemen out of the union in early 1912. Apparently the major factor in this withdrawal was the denial to the Spanish firemen of the right of free transfer to firemen's unions on other coasts.

Apparently influenced by the widespread syndicalism in his native country, as well as by the current activities of the Industrial Workers of the World, the American version of syndicalism, Vidal sought to "propagate the idea of the general strike in the transport industry." The change in the name of the Waterfront Federation to the National Transport Workers Federation was viewed by Vidal as being consistent with "the desire of the authors of the movement to meet the demands of the mass of workers throughout the country, both organized and unorganized. . . ."[34] It is unlikely that the leaders of the longshoremen's locals and of the other seamen's union would have gone that far. The longshoremen, the Atlantic Coast Seamen's Union, and the Marine Cooks and Stewards, continued their affiliations with the ILA and the ISU, respectively.

A system of rotary hiring had been adopted by the firemen during the period of recognition by the employers to provide equal job opportunities to the members of the union. This system became a point of united attack by the employers organized in the American Steamship Association who apparently intended to weaken the unions' position by forcing them to strike against all major East Coast ship operators simultaneously. The rotary hiring system was described in these terms by the secretary of the association: "They have a book. That is the part of the philosophy of the union, that a man must be employed as he comes in. They send a man to you, and unless he is absolutely incompetent you must hire him. The consequence is that you never have a properly coördinated crew. . . ." [35]

With the termination of the contract in June 1912, the association announced that the agreement would not be renewed, on the grounds that recognition had had the effect of making the crews mutinous. The Association's refusal to negotiate resulted in the calling of a strike against all the coastwise shipping companies by the National Transport Workers Federation of America. The National Transport Workers Federation proved to be an abortive organization, with the Marine Cooks and Stewards and the ILA defecting.[36]

The shipowners were prepared for the strike. Negro strikebreakers were brought in from Wilmington, Philadelphia, and other points to replace the strikers. Mexicans were brought in by the Morgan Line. The employers claimed that not a single ship's sailing was being delayed, while Vidal claimed 20,000 were out. The union charged that the ships were being manned by "mere tailors and shoemakers' apprentices." The strikers attempted to involve the American Line operating to Europe so as to bring about competition between the transatlantic lines and the coastwise lines for strikebreakers. This tactic failed, however, for apparently there was no shortage of labor available for strikebreaking.[37]

The strikers were supported by the Socialist Party in New York, which was especially indignant at the action of the Federal government in using Navy bluejackets to man ships of the Government-owned Panama Railroad Line which had been struck by its civilian employees. A meeting was held under the joint auspices of the Socialist Party and the Federation at Union Square on July 18 (an anticipated attendance of 20,000 dwindled into an actual attendance estimated variously at from 1400 to 3500). In Galveston, the strikers received the support of the IWW.

On July 20, the leaders of the ILA reached an agreement with the Morgan Line whereby striking longshoremen would return to their jobs with that line, the scabs would be discharged, and the union men reemployed without any discrimination. The union men were to be permitted to wear their union buttons while at work, but they received no other concessions. On July 27, the Atlantic Coast Seamen's Union called off their strike, leaving the firemen to fight the losing battle alone.[38]

The loss of the strike resulted in complete demoralization of the sailors' and firemen's unions on the East Coast. Splinter groups formed the Sailors' and Firemen's Union of the Atlantic, which subsequently was issued a charter by the International Longshoremen's Association. The Executive Council of the American Federation of Labor later ordered the ILA to revoke this charter, whereupon the Sailors' and Firemen's Union went out of existence. Despite an initial unwillingness to take action, the ISU was forced to take a stand regarding the "loyal members" of the ACSU — those who had not bolted to the ILA; their organization was chartered by the ISU as the Eastern and Gulf Sailors' Association, with headquarters at Boston.[39] The Spanish firemen's group became affiliated with the IWW in April 1913 as the National Industrial Union of Marine Transport Workers; apparently a fair degree of organization was maintained, although the leadership changed.[40] In 1914, the ISU issued a charter to a group of "Anglo-Saxon firemen" led by Oscar Carlson, who wished to remain with the ISU.

With the loss of the strike, control of employment reverted almost completely to the crimps. Wages and working conditions deteriorated and remedy was further hampered by the outbreak of the first World War, which left many competing European seamen stranded on American shores. Only the Marine Cooks and Stewards were able to maintain an effective organization with good working conditions. Their skill in dealing with passengers was apparently of sufficient importance to the ship operators to warrant maintenance of a verbal understanding with their union and to permit union officials access to the docks and ships.

The Pacific Coast unions recognized the complete demoralization existing on the East Coast as a threat to their own status. They therefore furnished $5000 for the purpose of reorganizing East Coast sailors and firemen. Andrew Furuseth and Patrick Flynn, later the secretary of the Marine Firemen's Union of the Pacific Coast, undertook an organizing campaign early in 1915 on the East Coast. But efforts to obtain the shipowners' permission to allow union officials to visit docks and ships to explain the Seamen's Bill, in view of its imminent enactment, were unsuccessful. Furuseth and Flynn found that racial and national antagonisms were the main obstacles to organization on the East Coast. The advice furnished by the West Coast leaders was

to utterly disregard the question of nationality, and to disregard, at least for the present, any race question. It is not necessary to meet that question now, and if it necessarily must be met at a later period, it will be time enough to worry seriously about it when it has to be met . . . And further, that the men must get on board of the vessels, so as to work from the inside of the vessel by conversation with the rest of the crew and by distribution of literature.

Their advice, however, does not appear to have made any great impression.

THE EMPTY SHELL OF THE ISU

While the period from 1900 to 1915 saw a threefold increase in the membership of the unions affiliated with the International Seamen's Union, this growth merely reflected the limited extent of organization existing at the turn of the century. The total membership of 19,000 in 1915 included about 5000 fishermen and harbor workers whose organizations had affiliated with the ISU. About 7500 seamen were organized on the Pacific Coast, but only 4600 were organized on the Atlantic, although the tonnage there was at least three times that on the Pacific. On the Lakes, as a result of the crushing of the unions by the Lake Carriers Association after 1908, organization was at a low ebb, comprising about 2400 out of 13,000 to 15,000 seamen.[41]

The growth of the ISU in total membership during this period was not of any great significance; the organization remained a relatively small and not especially compact one. The ISU provided a means whereby a group of seamen's leaders, particularly those from the West Coast, were able to obtain the support of organized labor. The force of Andrew Furuseth's personality, together with his complete concentration on furthering the seamen's interests as he saw them, made it possible for the ISU to enjoy a position of influence in the American Federation of Labor which went way beyond its numerical strength. This position provided a means of protecting the seamen's jurisdiction and work from encroachment by unions of shore workers, particularly the longshoremen. The support furnished by organized labor, together with Furuseth's activities, made for success in the legislative field. Nevertheless, in its own right, the International Seamen's Union was never to achieve an effectively fused organization. Its annual conferences accomplished little more than the passing of well-meaning resolutions which were usually ineffective. Crises within constituent unions were met in a positive manner only when such a course could hardly be avoided.

Furuseth, elected president of the ISU in 1908, and its president until the organization's demise in 1937, viewed the ISU as being "not a Federation of three unions, but one union in three divisions arising from the three divisions of the labor which seamen perform" (the deck, engine, and stewards departments), with members "who are all seamen and under the same law." This may have been an ideal view, for it varied substantially from the true situation. The respective unions on the East and West coasts, and on the Lakes, acted independently of one another. On the West Coast, the three unions acted in general concord in matters of collective bargaining; on the East Coast such combined action was sporadic. The various district organizations acted generally at will, without the support or advice of the executive board of the ISU.

Efforts to achieve a mere nominal unity among the constituent unions were met with delay and lack of interest. Even the major immediate benefit made possible by the existence of the ISU, the opportunity for free transfer from a division in one district to a like division in another geographical district, was restricted. In 1907, at the insistence of the firemen on the Great Lakes and on the Pacific, the ISU constitution was amended to restrict free transfers between the various marine firemen's unions to transfers by mutual understanding. In practice, such an understanding was not reached, and the Spanish firemen on the East Coast charged discrimination. Motions to establish an "International Membership Book," symbolizing the rights of free transfer among all the seamen and simplifying the procedures for such transfer, although frequently discussed, could achieve but limited success where the rights themselves were restricted. The conventions of 1911 and 1912 considered establishing such a book, but interest lagged after the proposals of East Coast delegates for the actual right of free transfer were defeated. An international book for sailors alone was finally adopted, but the "International Membership Book" for all members of the constituent unions of the ISU never became a reality.[42]

ISU funds, whose source was largely the West Coast unions, were used to aid organization on the Atlantic and on the Great Lakes during the first years of the century. These organizing activities usually netted immediate gains. But these gains lasted only temporarily, being wiped out with the first attempt at obtaining recognition or at obtaining concessions in wages and working conditions from the employers. Efforts to combine aid to striking or locked-out affiliates with international control over strike action came to naught. Although SUP leaders supported such a proposal, the membership of the Sailors' Union of the Pacific, who were furnishing most of the financial support for the ISU, rejected it. Even when provisions to the effect were incorporated into the ISU constitution, they proved fruitless. Another provision of the constitution to the effect that "each affiliated organization shall have jurisdiction of its local affairs" carried greater weight.

Crises in the affairs of affiliated unions usually found the ISU in the position of not wishing to intervene in local matters until all the possible damage had already been accomplished. The ISU proved its ineffectuality when the organized seamen on the Lakes were locked out in 1908 following a five-year period of apparently successful collective bargaining relations with the Lake Carriers Association. An unsuccessful effort by the Lakes unions to carry on a strike, which began in 1909 and continued until 1912, was supported by voluntary donations in excess of $20,000 each by the Pacific Coast unions of sailors and firemen.

A proposal for an ISU strike assessment to support Lakes seamen was the occasion for a split between East and West Coast seamen, with the former opposing the proposal. As a result, no positive action was taken by the ISU and support continued on a voluntary basis by the individual unions. We have already observed the hesitant manner in which the ISU met internal difficulties in the East Coast unions of sailors and firemen. Where dual organizations developed, as in the case of the East Coast sailors' unions in 1912, the ISU at first adopted a policy of keeping out of the situation. Only after actual invasion of jurisdiction by other unions was threatened was the ISU moved to action. This fumbling did not enhance the prestige of the ISU so far as the sailors were concerned.

Furthermore, fundamental differences between the positions of the East and West Coast unions in 1911 became apparent in the convention held that year after the East Coast unions had acquired the confidence and voice that came with recognition by their employers. A serious split developed on virtually every major issue that came before the convention. Organization among West Coast seamen had anteceded that among longshoremen; West Coast seamen had to contend with the ILA in the invasion of their right to engage in longshoremen's work; West Coast seamen were well organized and apparently assured of recognition by their employers; therefore, West Coast seamen did not feel the need for the security that would come of federation with the allied waterfront trades. East Coast seamen, on the other hand, had but recently organized and obtained recognition and therefore felt the need of support from shore workers; the ILA actively supported the Waterfront Federation of New York and vicinity; and there was ideological support for industrial organization among the leaders of the Spanish firemen. Therefore the position of the West Coast leaders in opposing the proposal of the ILA for the establishment of a transportation department in the American Federation of Labor was contrary to that of the East Coast leaders. A variety of charges were made by the East Coast leaders against Furuseth, and a strong effort was made to replace him with an East Coast leader. The East Coast met with defeat in all these matters.[43] A split developed on the Seamen's Bill (see below, Chapter 3) also. East Coast representatives appeared before the House Committee on Merchant Marine Fisheries during the course of the 1911 convention, opposing either all or parts of the bill with the argument that the good features might possibly be struck out during the course of enactment while the bad features, such as the severe punishment provisions, might be retained. They also opposed the language provisions of the bill, which might operate against the interests of the Spanish firemen.[44] The threat to the West Coast leadership of the ISU was removed after the failure of the 1912 strike on the East Coast and the disorganization which accompanied it.

The ISU's inability to become a positive and independent factor in unifying American seamen during this period seems epitomized in the constant refusal by the delegates of its constituent unions to allow the establishment of a headquarters office independent of and physically separate from the offices of the East Coast sailors.[45]

GRAND ISOLATION FOR THE SEAMEN

"Never beg bread from friend, nor mercy from enemy, live by your own strength and die" — was the philosophy of action laid down by Andrew Furuseth in his "Second Message to Seamen" in 1919. This analysis of the relationship of seamen to shoreworkers and to shipowners primarily reflected the experience of West Coast seamen during the twenty years preceding its publication. In it, Furuseth stated that originally seamen had been highly skilled craftsmen, responsible for the maintenance and repairs of the ships and for the loading and discharging of cargo. Development of such skills had made for a maximum of efficiency with a minimum of cost in ship operations. But inherent in the development of such skilled personnel was the provision that they be employed "to do all possible work in port. This develops skill and the steadiness of employment keeps it with and in the business." However, as he saw it, shoreworkers were encroaching on the seaman's work, thus robbing him of his skill. They had joined with the shipowners in getting the seamen off the ship promptly on arrival in port. As he put it,

In fact while in port, they will only permit the seaman to sit on the rail smoking his pipe while they are doing the seamen's work, but the shipowner says to the seamen "Get out of the vessel, I don't need you." And the seaman goes ashore to eat up what he has earned. The owner loses the seaman's work, the seaman fails to develop that skill so essential in a real seaman and necessary in the world competition that is surely coming as things get back to a normal basis.[46]

After analyzing the past history of the seamen's unions' relationship with the longshoremen and with other shoreworkers, Furuseth concluded that the seamen had been accepted by shoreworkers only when their assistance was needed; but as soon as their assistance was no longer needed, the shoreworkers had dropped the seamen in order to take over their work. In the past, the seamen had asked for no assistance from shoreworkers in their economic struggles. Even the support of the American Federation of Labor had been "expected and received" only in the matter of legislation. The seamen "took their whipping without a whimper; but in their defeat they adopted the motto: 'Tomorrow is also a day,'" he went on grandiloquently, but ominously. Alliances with shore-workers could only be to the seamen's disadvantage; for any agreement on the part of the seamen to refuse to deliver cargo or to receive it from nonunion men would always end in the seamen's being deprived of the opportunity to work. Improvements in the longshoremen's status only injured the seamen; for "growing out of his system of bookkeeping and the human dispositions to follow the line of least resistance, he — the shipowner — came to believe what the economists long ago in their scientific jargon called the 'Wage Fund.'" Shipowners maintained the seaman in a position of serfdom, thereby keeping his wages down to compensate for the higher wages they had to pay the shoreworker, who was free to take his labor with him where he chose.

This philosophy of isolationism for the seamen was the result primarily of West Coast experience with the longshoremen. On the East Coast, the presence of a substantial and cheap labor supply, coupled with the great turnover among seamen, had resulted in the development of longshoremen's organizations with a clearcut title to longshore work. On the West Coast, it had been necessary to utilize the seamen in loading and discharging ships, particularly in out-of-the-way Pacific ports under adverse conditions where longshore workers were not available. The seaman's right to load and discharge ships in the coastwise trade was an important source of earnings. Such work could almost double the monthly wages he might receive for his regular activity in manning a ship. Furthermore, the skill and experience required for loading and discharging were additional factors protecting men regularly following the sea from the encroachments of unskilled labor. Not infrequently the leaders of the seamen took the position that the seamen were making a concession when they stood "merely upon the right to receive or discharge cargo 'over the rail'; for if they stood upon the letter of the law by which they were governed ultimately they would insist upon the right to work cargo 'on board, in boats, or on shore.'" [47] However, in the interest of maintaining harmony, the seamen were willing to demand only the right to work loading or discharging cargo within the rail of the ship.

Such practices and views were bound to come into conflict as longshoremen's organizations developed among the growing body of longshore workers on the West Coast. The clash was to be all the more intense and lasting because the seamen had aided the West Coast longshoremen in organizing. The seamen's unions had been members of the City Front Federation along with the longshoremen, and the seamen had withdrawn from the Federation in order to end the lockout of longshoremen during the course of the 1906 strike (see p. 31). In reciprocation, the longshoremen had gone aboard the schooners and performed work done customarily by seamen.

The clash with the longshoremen had developed out of invasion on two fronts: the province for organization and province for work. The ILA had extended its jurisdiction to marine firemen, engineers, and tugmen on the Lakes; and in 1902 had changed its name to the International Longshoremen, Marine and Transport Workers' Association of North and South America. This action was regarded by the ISU as intended "ultimately to assume authority over the whole works of commerce" and to eliminate the ISU. The suspicion was intensified by the constant difficulties experienced by the West Coast seamen and longshoremen in delineating their respective jurisdictions. In 1900, an agreement was reached whereby seamen were to do all work within the rail on their own ships; and longshoremen were to work on the docks and to have first chance to work on a vessel when additional men were needed. Both groups agreed that neither should receive cargo from, nor deliver cargo to, nonunion men. However, the longshoremen violated the spirit of the agreement by having the shipowners send nonunion crew members ashore while they were loading or discharging the vessel.[48] Apparently, the seamen violated the agreement as well by going aboard to work ships when additional men were necessary, since they were supposed "not to go aboard another vessel to work longshore except in case of necessity." After a two-year period of peaceful relations, controversy broke out again regarding the work to be done on deepsea ships. In June 1904, the Pacific Coast district of the ILA stated that its men would refuse to work with sailors doing longshore work on such ships. The Sailors' Union replied by reasserting the right of seamen to perform all kinds of labor, including cargo handling inside the ship's rail.

The constant guerilla warfare between the two international unions had finally come before the American Federation of Labor in 1902. However, the issue was evaded, after prolonged discussion, by a recommendation that each of the two unions select two representatives and that these four should select a fifth — to form a committee to settle the dispute.[49] No agreement was reached and the matter was again placed before the AFL. An impasse was also reached over the question of ordering the longshoremen to reduce the "longnomen" (as it was referred to by the seamen's leaders) to the previous name. The West Coast seamen met this failure to act by refusing to work with locals of longshoremen "which claim jurisdiction over 'marine and transport workers,'" thus encouraging the secession of West Coast longshore locals. A Pacific Coast Federation of longshoremen was established among the seceded locals. Furuseth charged that the ILA longshoremen and the boardinghouse keepers were working together and that they were harrying officials of the Sailors' Union of the Pacific.

It was apparent even to the reluctant members of the AFL executive council that some positive action was necessary. At the AFL convention in November 1905, the longshoremen were instructed to resume their earlier title; and both the ISU and the ILA were each instructed to appoint two members, who, in turn, would select a fifth member to constitute an arbitration board. If the four were unable to reach agreement on the fifth member, President Gompers was to select a fifth with approval of the AFL executive board.[50] The parties were unable to reach agreement and decided to submit the entire question to arbitration by Gompers, whose award was finally forthcoming in June 1907. Gompers directed the ILA to cease using the long name. He found that under modern conditions it was the custom and practice for longshoremen to perform loading and unloading; therefore, such work belonged to longshoremen, with the following exceptions:

(a) In the coastwise trade, when seamen bring a vessel into port, remain with the vessel for its onward course or for its return to the initial port, the work of loading and unloading the cargo to the extent of the ship's tackle may be performed by seamen. (b) Seamen may load or unload cargoes beyond the ship's tackle, but only with the consent of, or by agreement with, the longshoremen.

Under the first exception, the seamen had to be members of the ship's sailing crew. This decision coincided substantially with the seamen's position.

The ILA refused to accept the award, and the 1907 convention of the AFL again "instructed and directed" the longshoremen to use the shorter name, and two representatives were delegated to attend the next ILA convention to obtain an agreement on the award. Another secessionist movement was encouraged among the Pacific Coast longshoremen over the ILA's refusal to accept the Gompers' award. Agreement was finally reached between the two international unions during the course of the 1908 AFL convention. It was agreed that the ILA would assume the short title, and that representatives of the International unions would meet regarding any problems that might arise.[51]

Peace reigned for a period of three years, after which the ILA brought charges that the ISU was violating the terms of the Gompers' award. The entire matter was reopened before the AFL convention in 1913; the ISU was claiming the right to load and discharge offshore ships as well as coastwise vessels. An agreement was reached defining the following as offshore trade: on the west coast of South America, any port to the south of the Panama Canal, New Zealand, Australia, South Africa,

China, and Japan; and the loading and unloading of all ships engaged in such trade was restricted to longshoremen.[52]

Further differences developed in 1912 when President T. V. O'Connor of the ILA proposed the establishment of a Transportation Department in the AFL. When Furuseth opposed this, O'Connor replied that this position was not representative of the wishes of the rank and file. The role of the ILA in aiding the subsequent development of the Waterfront Federation of New York and Vicinity has already been described. The disintegration of the East Coast Sailors' and Firemen's Unions after the unsuccessful 1912 strike resulted in the chartering of the Sailor's and Firemen's Union of the Atlantic under the aegis of the ILA. The ISU reported the distribution of a circular to "Seamen, Harbormen, and Transport Workers" warning such men "not to join any union of Seafaring men unless such union is legally chartered and officially recognized by the International Longshoremen's Union." Whereupon the AFL executive council found that the charter had been issued in violation of the ILA's jurisdiction and ordered it revoked.

Relations between the ILA and the ISU were not improved by the action of the ILA convention in July 1914 in passing a motion to the effect that the ILA would "leave no stone unturned to see that the bill [Seamen's Bill] is defeated in its present form" unless "an amendment is added to the bill providing that sailors shall not do longshore work when ships are in port." President O'Connor felt that as a result of an increase in the number of seamen on the ships following the passage of the Seamen's Bill "it would go without saying that these men would be utilized which would mean that they would be performing our work." [53]

CHAPTER 3

ANDREW FURUSETH AND THE SEAMEN'S ACT

MAINTENANCE OF POLITICAL ACTIVITY

The uncertain or partial success in establishing collective bargaining on a firm basis up to 1916 contrasted sharply with the lasting qualities of law which had been so well demonstrated by the duration for centuries of the old navigation laws. Even more, these very laws were viewed as placing substantial handicaps on the seamen's rights as workers.

Their familiarity with the maritime laws of other nations, gained by employment on the ships of these nations, earned such seamen's representatives as Andrew Furuseth and Walter Macarthur the reputation of being experts in international maritime law. Comparative analysis of the various national maritime laws make them feel justified in demanding certain economic and social requirements in legislation to protect American seamen. To these requirements they added an ideological principle which had little currency among European seamen's leaders at that time — the abolition of penalties for desertion and establishment of complete freedom for the seamen.

The legislative campaign which culminated in the enactment of the Seamen's Act in 1915 had more immediate purposes than the achievement of a broad principle. It was devised to protect the conditions which had been achieved by West Coast seamen by recognizing, entrenching, and protecting the seamen's calling from the onslaughts of Asiatic and/or other unskilled foreign and native workers, as well as by establishing uniform hours and working conditions throughout the country. The achievement of these goals through legislation was not considered a substitute for economic activity; on the contrary, the seamen's leaders constantly stressed the need for organizing to meet their employers on equal terms.

This program was strengthened by being identified with the interests of the American merchant marine and with the protection of safety of life at sea, as well as with the general trend toward social democracy in the United States. The work of formulating the philosophical justification for the program and of forwarding it through direct pressure was greatly that of Andrew Furuseth.

ANDREW FURUSETH'S CALLING

Andrew Furuseth, for many years secretary of the Sailors' Union of the Pacific, the president of the International Seamen's Union from 1908 until the demise of that organization in 1937, more than any other individual was responsible for the legislation which freed the American seamen from a legal status comparable to that of an eighteenth-century wage servant. Furuseth was born in Norway in 1854, the fourth child among eight in a poor family. He had a brief elementary school education, and went to sea at the age of 19. He sailed on sailing ships under the flags of Norway, Sweden, Holland, England, and the United States; on steamships of Germany and of the United States. Within seven years of his coming to the United States in 1880, he became secretary of the Coast Seamen's Union (later called the Sailors' Union of the Pacific). In 1892, Furuseth came ashore permanently, and from that time until his death in 1938 almost continuously represented the interests of the seamen in Washington — as Samuel Gompers described him — "like a panther watching, like a lion attacking." As president of the International Seamen's Union he would accept only such compensation as would barely cover the minimum living requirements.

His entire life was devoted to the seamen's cause and matters related directly to it. In his own words . . . "I have tried to inform myself on the laws of the different countries, trying to find a reason for the decay of seamanship; trying to find some reason why the oriental takes the place of the white man on the seas; trying to find reasons why the white man refused to go to sea. . . ." His knowledge of the maritime laws of the world was a persuasive tool in support of the seamen's legislation. Furuseth's forthright and sincere manner, both personally and in his numerous pamphlets, impressed many. President Wilson confessed to the "deep impression (Furuseth always makes) on me." [1] Furuseth was constantly in attendance where his presence might aid the seamen's cause. Before Congressional committees, with individual Congressmen, and with Supreme Court justices, he constantly sought to advance his — the seamen's cause.

It has been said that in Furuseth, "The distinctive American labor philosophy found a complete and picturesque expression." [2] He associated the skill requirements in the sailors' calling with the strength of the maritime nations of the world. He practiced the principle of voluntarism in the relations of craft labor unions, in the affairs of the seamen's unions, and in the affairs of labor unions at large, with vehemence and directness. In the councils of the American Federation of Labor, he protested any forced amalgamation of crafts, insisting that amalgamation should be the product of voluntary action. His concern for freeing the seamen from serf status led him directly into the study of labor injunctions, and he attacked their use as a means of defeating peaceful collective action. He lashed into the labor injunction as undermining the basic traditions of the United States and accused it of making the Constitution "nothing but an indirect means of again establishing slavery in some form." [3]

A measure of Furuseth's position may be derived from the divergent sources of the attacks upon him and the conflicting views regarding his activities. To the shipowners he was a "foreign-born agitator" who had created "dissension and dissatisfaction among a class of men that were before his coming content, prosperous and happy. . . ." [4] To the leaders of some foreign seamen's unions, his proposals for freeing the seamen and for the international equalization of wages and working conditions, together with his opposition to social legislation as an end seemed a "Utopian dream." [5] To the Industrial Workers of the World, Furuseth's philosophy and activities were anathema, for they were the very antithesis of the basis for the IWW: the feeling was a mutual one — Furuseth's emphasis upon voluntary craft organization went directly counter to the "One Big Union" of the Wobblies; his insistence upon the necessity for skill and its retention was regarded as an anachronism by the IWW; and his stress on political activity was regarded by them as an unnecessary drain on the finances of the ISU in a worthless cause. [6]

Some who had been closely associated with the efforts to improve the seamen's status felt that Furuseth received substantially greater credit and adulation than were his due. Writing in later years, Walter Macarthur, author of the original Seamen's Bill and long associated with Furuseth, described Furuseth as a dogmatic individual who consistently "pursued the policy of browbeating and libeling every man who has shown a disposition to think for himself and speak his own mind. . . ." His influence was the product, according to Macarthur, of "his eccentricity of manner and speech. He inspired the confidence of the seamen by an assumption of superiority to ordinary human weakness and by an affectation of profundity. . . ." He charged Furuseth with being little concerned with the affairs of the SUP, having spent most of his time in Washington. [7] No one can discount, however, the persistence with which Furuseth sought the enactment of the Seamen's Bill.

RATIONALE FOR THE SEAMEN'S BILL

Andrew Furuseth's activities on behalf of the Seamen's Bill have been enthusiastically likened to the activities of the early classical economists. He was "self-trained, as the early classical economists were, and like them he is remarkably secure in his faith and cogent in his reasoning." [8] Furthermore, he applied the doctrines of the classical economists to the seamen's demands for legislation to improve their status. Furuseth argued that the proposed legislation fundamentally was not labor legislation in the narrow, ameliorative sense, but rather that it would assist labor only to the extent of removing the obstacles to effective operation of the factors of supply and demand in the seamen's labor market.

Furuseth contrasted the legislation which placed the onus upon the seamen with the legislation lightening the shipowners' burden. Any incentive for the shipowners to employ men skilled in the seamen's crafts had been eliminated in 1884 when legislation had been enacted limiting the liability of the shipowners in the event of shipwreck to the value of the vessel and freight surviving the wreck.[9] The same act had made it possible for shipowners to hire men in foreign ports for round trips to American ports in order to permit the hire of the cheapest possible labor. As Furuseth expressed it, "The shipowner cared no longer for skill, ability, nationality or race. . . ." [10] The Seamen's Bill sought to redress this lack of balance in the relative positions of shipowners and seamen.

Furuseth argued that only by eliminating imprisonment for desertion and by making seamen's lives more attractive through improving working conditions aboard ship would the American boy be induced to return to the sea to ward off further encroachment by the "Oriental." Only under improved conditions would the art of seamanship be restored and seamen become more than mere "hewers of wood and drawers of water." Only in this way could the United States ensure that a rejuvenated merchant marine could be maintained, for "seapower is in the seaman; vessels are the tools of seamen; tools ultimately belong to the races or nations who can use them." [11] Hence, in order to ensure this maritime superiority, it was necessary for the government to encourage the "American" to take to the sea. However, Furuseth objected to any limitation of employment on the basis of citizenship since this would have had the effect of outlawing the foreign seamen then comprising the bulk of the labor force of the American merchant marine.[12]

To those who attributed the greater cost of operating American ships primarily to differences in wage costs, Furuseth held out a panacea which became extremely popular among the proponents of the bill. Elimination of the forced aspect of the labor of seamen, and application of this principle to the seamen of foreign ships in American ports as well would strengthen the position of the American merchant marine. The effort to reduce American wages to foreign levels had failed, he reasoned, because seamen's wages were subject to the same influences as those governing the wages of any other class of workers. Wages are determined not by the flag of the ship which pays them, but by the port in which the seamen are engaged; and the wages paid in the port are determined by the standard of living in the country in which the port is situated. Permit seamen to desert at will in the ports of the United States, he argued, and the forces of the economic law of supply and demand will be released, enabling seamen on foreign as well as American ships to demand wages prevailing in American ports. Operating costs of American vessels will thus be equalized with those of foreign ships. He contended that the provisions of those treaties with foreign countries providing for the detention of deserting seamen should be abrogated, since they only act against the economic interests of the American merchant marine. Furuseth acknowledged, however, that this action in itself would not restore the American merchant marine; to accomplish that would require free ships as well as free men.

An integral part of the equalization process was to assure the seamen that they would have adequate finances to tide them over until they could get another ship; otherwise they would be subject to control by the crimp, and the purposes of the bill would be defeated. Therefore it was necessary for the seamen to have the right to request half of their earned wages in each port of lading or discharge.

Equalization of costs would also be provided by requiring foreign ships to meet American standards of safety while in American ports. In particular, Furuseth argued that the proposed language clause, requiring at least 75 percent of the crew members in each department to understand any orders given by the officers of the ship, would eliminate competition from British and other foreign ships which carried Oriental crews shipped at wage rates of $7, as contrasted with American rates of from $35 to $45 on the West Coast. Incidentally, of course, the effect of that provision would be to require the elimination of Oriental crews on board the American transpacific ships of the Pacific Mail Line, but this would assure greater safety at sea for American passengers and cargo.

The Seamen's Bill would also meet the essential requirements for safety at sea by establishing a standard of skill for the protection of passengers' lives. To the talk of unsinkable ships, Furuseth replied: "Vessels that can not sink and will not burn have not yet been built." Safety could only come through sound ships, sufficient lifeboats, and adequate and properly trained crews. For him, the A.B. seaman, the man who had at least three years of deck experience at sea, was the means for assuring safety at sea. At least 75 percent of the deck crew, he felt, should consist of men carrying A.B. certificates. These men should be responsible for the safety of passengers and crew since their varied training and experience provided them with the necessary experience. While some members of the engine and steward departments might be capable lifeboatmen, the possibility would be sheerly accidental; the duties of lifeboatmen belonged to the deck department, he maintained.

Furuseth acknowledged that the provisions of the bill might have the effect of raising wages somewhat on the Atlantic and Great Lakes since a better class of men would be required, but he doubted that Pacific Coast wages would rise. While it was not explicitly stated, conditions on the various coasts would be further equalized because the hours provisions proposed in the Seamen's Bill, particularly for work in port, were those prevailing under existing West Coast collective bargaining agreements. Furuseth acknowledged that the ISU had sought constantly to bring working conditions on all coasts to West Coast levels. The Seamen's Bill would tend to create the conditions which would make this possible.[13]

The three justifications for enactment of the Seamen's Bill: inducing the American boy to return to the sea, promoting safety of life at sea, and equalizing opportunities for the American merchant marine with those of foreign countries, were thus very skillfully interwoven by the sponsors of the bill with a program for partially improving the status of the American seamen.

ATTEMPTS TO GAIN SUPPORT

Furuseth sized up the seamen's lack of political strength in the following terms: "The seamen are poor; few of them are voters; fewer still can vote, being at sea; they have nothing with which to quicken sympathy and induce action except their plainly told tale. . . ."[14] Furuseth was ever available to Congressmen and others to tell that tale. He arranged for the introduction of the bill in virtually every session of Congress from 1900 on.

The organized seamen were furnished an opportunity to present their views during the intensive inquiry into the state of the American merchant marine by the Merchant Marine Commission in 1905. Representatives of the seamen's organization testified before the commission, pressing for support of the Seamen's Bill. The commission report cited the differences in wages and subsistence on American and foreign ships in support of mail subsidy legislation to aid the merchant marine. The seamen's proposals were disposed of by recommending them "to the friendly attention of proper committees."[15]

A subsequent development was a bill containing a provision that 25 percent of the crews of ships receiving subsidies would have to be members of the naval reserve. Seamen who were citizens or who had declared their intention of becoming citizens could join the naval reserve and receive $25 per year.[16] Furuseth did not raise any objection to the subsidy proposal as such, but he vehemently opposed involving the seamen in it. Furuseth's proposal that the Seamen's Bill take the place of this naval reserve provision was unsuccessful, as was the mail subsidy bill itself. In his view the seamen were being made a "pack mule" for subsidy legislation.

Although major ship catastrophes attracted some consideration for the Seamen's Bill, the proposals remained abortive. The *General Slocum* disaster in 1904 was followed by an enactment in 1908 which left the composition of steamship crews to be determined by the local steamboat inspectors as it had been in the past. The *Coast Seamen's Journal* viewed the revised act as a surrender to the shipowning interests, since the local inspectors "are dependent upon the favors of the shipowners for appointment to and retention of their positions." [17]

To counteract the attacks of the shipowners and related groups on the Seamen's Bill, the leaders of the ISU submitted numerous petitions to Congress and to the President. Analyses of the bill were prepared and delivered to all members of Congress. A pamphlet was circulated describing the skills of the "Able Seamen." Letters were mailed to correspondents in Washington and to newspapers throughout the country. The appeals for press support stated that the seamen would never succeed in compelling the shipowners to hire a sufficient number of skilled men without such support.

Failure to obtain action on the domestic front resulted in an effort to get the international seamen's movement to support the principles and provisions of the Seamen's Bill. In 1908, Furuseth was sent abroad by the ISU to ascertain the condition of seamen in the various European nations, and to attend the convention of the International Transport Workers' Federation, with which the ISU had been affiliated since 1907. Furuseth related of his mission that "I had in mind at all times the sailor. I never forgot for a minute that we alone are made felons for quitting work." However, he found that European seamen were not as aware, or perhaps not as concerned about the unfree status of the seamen.[18]

Furuseth attempted to introduce for discussion an "Appeal to the World" at the two-day convention of the International Transport Workers' Federation in Vienna. The "Appeal" was addressed to "those who govern nations, to those who make the laws, to humanitarians, democrats, Christians, and friends of freedom everywhere." It called attention to the continuing serfdom of the seamen. In the vivid language so typical of Furuseth's style, it stated: "We now raise manacled hands in humble supplication and pray that the nations issue a decree of emancipation and restore to us our right as brother men. . . ." In addition, he proposed that the federation demand enactment of changes in maritime law including the following: abolition of imprisonment for desertion and for refusing to obey commands in safe harbors; abolition of all continuous discharge certificates kept by the master, and replacement of these by certificates to be kept by the seamen: and provisions similar to those in the Seamen's Bill regarding advances and allotments, A.B. manning, and language provisions. Furuseth reported that his proposals never got beyond the committee stage.

This experience caused Furuseth to realize that the seamen of the world were as much in need of enlightenment as the general citizenry. In 1909, therefore, he addressed a letter "to the World's Seamen" pointing out the essential similarity of the seamen's status under all the maritime codes. He called for a meeting of representatives of seamen of all nations in order to arrive at a common legislative program to be submitted to all governments.

An effort was made to draw public attention to the forthcoming meeting of the International Transport Workers' Federation to be held during the summer of 1910. A parade was held, followed by a mass meeting of 2000 seamen at Cooper Union in New York City on December 6, 1909. Furuseth, Samuel Gompers, Victor Olander, and J. Havelock Wilson, leader of the British seamen, addressed the group. A banner in the hall expressed the sentiment of the meeting; "Lincoln freed the Negro slaves of the South; let the people free the White slaves of the sea." Resolutions called upon all seafaring men to join "in asserting their own ownership over their own bodies." [19]

The meeting of the International Transport Workers' Federation at Copenhagen during 1910 was primarily concerned with the question of an international strike to be held in 1911 if the shipowners of each country did not agree to recognize the seamen's organization and establish machinery for handling seamen's grievances. (This strike subsequently was carried out during June of 1911.) Here Furuseth again submitted his "Appeal to the World," but it met with numerous objections, particularly on the grounds that it constituted "begging." A compromise was finally reached whereby the legislative demands, which were separated from the appeal, were agreed to unanimously, subject to the significant proviso that each country might use "its own form or such form as it thought most suitable." [20] Furuseth's bid for international support had failed.

OPPOSITION TO THE BILL

Shipowner concern with the Seamen's Bill had been apparent from the very first submission of the bill to Congress in 1900. The proposal was viewed by them as the work of a group of foreigners and "ignorant mobocrats" aiming a blow "against the welfare of one of our most eminently important industries." This concern with the Seamen's Bill was apparent up to its passage and thereafter. It could hardly be stated that the provisions of the final act came as any surprise to the shipowning groups.

Ample opportunity was furnished both shipowners, related groups and the seamen to present their views at the numerous and protracted hearings held by Congressional committees between 1910 and 1915. The groups which appeared in opposition to the bill and which appealed to Congress for its defeat were representatives of the organized American shipping groups; foreign shipping interests; interests allied to shipping, such as local maritime exchanges and boards of trade; and local chambers of commerce. All the West Coast steamship interests, including coastwise and offshore operations, joined in opposition to the bill.[21] The American Steamship Association, representing Atlantic operators, indicated its strong opposition to the basic proposals of the bill.[22] The views of the Shipowners' Association of the Pacific Coast in opposition to the bill were clearly expressed in its official organ, the *Pacific Marine Review*. The opposition viewed the bill as "class legislation" designed to further the power already exercised by the already powerful International Seamen's Union. The strength of the seamen's organizations on the West Coast and the working conditions in effect there were cited as evidence that the seamen's status was not at all as bad as had been alleged. Further, it was constantly pointed out that the leadership and the great majority of the members of the seamen's unions who would be the sole beneficiaries of the legislation were foreigners. The bill was described as "a sham and a fraud perpetrated by the Seamen's Union to control the manning of ships on the Atlantic Coast and the Great Lakes as they do on the Pacific."[23]

The attacks against specific provisions were leveled against those which were regarded as most important by the seamen. While there was a general expression in favor of the abolition of all imprisonment for desertion, it represented an unwilling concession to the tenor of the times. The difficulties involved in changing some twenty or more treaties were pointed out; as was the inevitable increasing of freight costs, the effects of which would have to be borne by the American public, according to the opposition. However, the provision for half pay in every port was attacked vehemently. Captain Robert Dollar referred to it as a "disgraceful provision" because "90 percent of them [the seamen] . . . drink every cent they have outside of the bare necessities of life. . . . This law carried to its logical conclusion means having a veritable hell on earth in every port. . . ." [24]

The provision for the establishment of A.B. ratings, and the requirement that a certain proportion of the deck crew have these certificates, were attacked as providing the seamen's unions with a virtual monopoly over the men who could meet the requirements set forth by the bill. It was held that such a classification was the product of the sailing ship era and unsuited to the increasingly dominant steamship. The work of deckhands aboard a modern steamer "is of the most ordinary kind of unskilled labor . . . consisting for the most part of washing decks, scrubbing paint, and polishing brasswork . . ." was the employer view. It was argued further that the mere requisite of three years' experience was no test of ability, for the bill required no examination in order to obtain a certificate. The shipowners argued that it was unnecessary to have two A.B.'s for each lifeboat, and that such work could be done effectively by strong men in any department on board the ship. The result would be "with the bill enacted, that the only recourse of a shipowner for a crew would be to some seamen's union. . . ." [25]

R. P. Schwerin, appearing on behalf of the Pacific Mail Steamship Co. operating to the Orient with American officers and Oriental crews, warned that the effect of the language provision of the bill would be to drive the American flag out of the transpacific trade. He described the long and difficult battle of the Pacific Mail Line to overcome the obstacles of higher operating costs in the face of foreign competitors using Oriental labor. The action of the Pacific Mail Line in suspending its operation after the passage of the bill was to become a national issue.

The provisions regarding hours of work were most strenuously opposed by the representatives of the shipping interests on the Great Lakes. The president of the Pittsburgh Steamship Co. attacked the three-watch provision for firemen as being unwarranted on the Lakes with its high wages and good conditions. He indicated that a maximum of 12 hours in 24 would be an acceptable provision. East and West Coast spokesmen contended that the watch provisions for sailors and firemen were already in effect.

A spokesman for foreign shipping interests stated frankly that the foreign lines were not raising objections to the abolition of imprisonment for desertion simply "because they have been advised that it is a sine qua non, and there is no use talking about it." [26] He was not as reticent about the language clause, however, and argued that enactment would be to the detriment only of American shippers and the American public.

The hope was expressed by another representative of foreign shipping interests that "diplomatic intervention might succeed where the arguments of American owners have failed," especially since it was felt that this "most pernicious piece of legislation" would "affect foreign owners even more than American." [27] This fervent wish was granted. Great Britain presented three protests against the bill; Germany, two; the Netherlands, two, and Spain, one. While there were some objections raised to the arrest of seamen for desertion, they were not pressed. The principal objections were directed first at the jurisdiction granted American courts to apply our laws regarding seamen's wages to all seamen in our ports regardless of their nationality or of the nationality of the ship on which they served; and secondly, at the elimination of consular supervision of ships and seamen which existed under the treaties then in effect.[28]

ENACTMENT OF THE BILL

Not until Progressivism was able to make itself felt in politics was the Seamen's Bill to be given any serious consideration. The Congressional elections of 1910 resulted in gains for the Democratic Party with some 15 trade union members elected to Congress. William B. Wilson, former secretary-treasurer of the United Mine Workers of America, was appointed chairman of the House Labor Committee. The Seamen's Bill then received the sponsorship of Representative Wilson in the House and of Senator LaFollette in the Senate.

The election of Woodrow Wilson to the presidency in 1912 could readily be viewed as a victory for labor. The Seamen's Bill, with its catch phrase "emancipation of the seamen" would be assured thorough and favorable consideration. Other factors made the time auspicious — the *Titanic* disaster in April 1912 was stark testimony to the inadequate provisions existing to ensure safety at sea, and a rash of proposals was submitted to meet this need. The Seamen's Bill was a readymade solution, at least on the side of assuring adequate and experienced personnel; and with a few adjustments it could fill in much of the gap in safety legislation for the sea. Furthermore, the widespread antagonism to corporate interests was directed against the shipping interests as well. An investigation of shipping pools and combinations was conducted by the House Committee on Merchant Marine and Fisheries. The comparison between organized shipping interests and the unfree American seamen furnished a picture which was very favorable to the seamen.[29]

Despite all these favorable factors, the seamen had to wait until March 1915 for "freedom." During the years between 1910 and 1915, the bill received thorough analysis before Congressional committees and both houses of Congress. Both Republican and Democratic party

platforms in the election of 1912 promised enactment of legislation ending arrest for desertion and legislation assuring safety at sea. A bill
based on the Seamen's Act, and acceptable to the ISU leaders, passed
both houses within one day prior to the end of President Taft's term of
office. The bill failed to become law, however, for President Taft refused
to sign it on the grounds that he had been given insufficient time to
study such an important measure which "conflicts in its operation with
the treaty obligations of the United States and in its possible friction
with the commerce of foreign countries. . . ."

The members of the newly installed Wilson Administration almost im-
mediately set about carrying out the preëlection promises. William B.
Wilson, now Secretary of Labor, and William C. Redfield, Secretary of
Commerce, supported the Seamen's Bill as reintroduced by Senator
LaFollette. Senator LaFollette opposed any delay in the consideration
of the bill, charging that only when "property rights are involved, the
Senate is keen for prompt action";[30] and a measure coinciding substantially with the purposes of the original Seamen's Bill finally passed the
Senate on October 23, 1913. President Wilson intervened at this point
and, in a message to Congress sympathetic to the aims of the Seamen's
Bill, requested postponement of action on the bill until the results of
the International Conference in London (which the United States had
initiated) were made public.

Hearings were held by the House Committee on Merchant Marine
and Fisheries, and an amended bill was passed by the House in August.
The bill went to conference where compromise was reached on the
A.B. provision. The conference report was the subject of the final debates
on the measure during February 1915, with favorable action being taken
in both houses by February 27. The arguments pro and con the bill
during the final debates were identical with those in previous Congressional considerations of the bill. The outbreak of war in Europe, however, placed greater emphasis upon the possible international involve-
ments in terminating provisions of existing treaties. Opponents charged
that the bill would interfere with our commercial relations with every
foreign nation that had a merchant marine. To the reported intimation
that the part of the law applicable to foreign vessels in our ports "would
be enforced with a soft pedal," Senator Burton replied that it could not
be enforced at all under existing conditions.[31]

President Wilson, despite his desire to aid the seamen, gave the bill
serious and critical consideration even after its passage by both houses.
He advised Furuseth on March 2 that while his concern for the seamen
was as great as ever,

what is troubling me at this moment is that it demands of the Government
what seems a truly impossible thing, namely the denunciation of some twenty-

two commercial treaties. . . . To throw the commercial relations of the country into disorder and doubt just at this juncture might lead to the most serious consequences, and upon that ground I am debating very seriously whether it is possible for me to sign the bill or not.[32]

The President finally resolved his doubts in favor of the bill, signing it on March 4, despite pressures from Great Lakes shipping interests for a veto. As he justified his decision, "I debated the matter of signing the bill very earnestly indeed, weighing the arguments on both sides with a good deal of anxiety and finally determined to sign it because it seemed the only chance to get something like justice done to a class of workmen who have been too much neglected by our laws." [33]

Andrew Furuseth, overcome with emotion and gratitude at the passage of the Seamen's Bill, wrote to the President:

In signing the Seamen's Bill, you gave back to the seamen, so far as the United States can do it, the ownership of their own bodies, and thus wiped out the last bondage existing under the American flag. The soil of the United States will be holy ground henceforth to the world's seamen, if you should need them; you would only have to call on them. It is my prayer that you may not need them. I am saying, them, because I realize that I am a little too old.

Furuseth went on to say that the test of time would demonstrate that "your greatest and most courageous act will be deemed your signature to the Emancipation Proclamation of the Seamen." [34]

The bill as finally enacted contained the basic features of the long-pending Seamen's Bill. Only in the matter of manning had a radical change been made. In this respect, whereas the bill originally had called for a manning scale, the act left unchanged the existing authority for local steamboat inspectors to determine the number required for a crew. However, 75 percent of the crew in each department was now required to understand "any order given by the officers of such vessel." In addition, 65 percent of the unlicensed deck crew was to consist of able seamen.[35]

The act also called for the providing of life-saving appliances in accordance with the agreement reached by the International Conference on Safety at Sea in 1913. This provision of the act also required that lifeboats be manned by specified numbers of certificated lifeboatmen who might include "any member of the crew" holding a certificate of efficiency obtained by practical demonstration of competency. However, while the ISU had failed to get this function restricted to deck personnel, a compromise clause was included requiring that a licensed officer or an able seaman be in charge of each lifeboat or pontoon raft.

In virtually all other respects, the seamen's program appeared to have been achieved. Arrest and imprisonment for desertion of American seamen in foreign lands, and for the arrest and imprisonment of foreign seamen in the United States and its possessions, were abolished. Within ninety days of the signing of the act, notice was to be given to foreign governments who were partners to treaties containing provisions conflicting with the act that such provisions would be terminated upon expiration of the time limit required by such treaties for abrogation of provisions. The sole penalty for desertion was to be forfeiture of personal effects left on board ship and all earned wages. Further, seamen were to have the right to demand payment of half of their earned wages at every port at which the ship put in to load or discharge cargo. All advances and allotments (except allotments to close relatives) were prohibited; this prohibition was to "apply as well to foreign vessels while in the waters of the United States." Seamen's wages could not be attached.

The act called explicitly for a minimum of two watches for sailors and three watches for firemen, oilers, and watertenders — these men to be kept "on duty successively" in order to perform the regular duties of operating the ship. There was a further requirement that these men were not to be required to work in a department other than the one for which they had signed on. In safe harbors, a nine-hour day was to be the maximum, except for Sundays and specified holidays when no unnecessary work was to be required. The only recourse for seamen when these provisions were violated was the right to demand a discharge with full wages. A majority of the crew could request an inspection in a foreign port to determine the seaworthiness of a ship, the adequacy of her manning, or the adequacy of her stores and provisions. Provision was made for crew space equal to 120 cubic feet per crew member; separate berths limited to two tiers; proper light, drainage, washing places, and ventilation; and a hospital compartment on ships making voyages of over three days' duration. All forms of corporal punishment on board ship were prohibited, and the owners as well as the captain were made liable in damages for illegal punishment. The act provided that in any suit by seamen to recover damages for injuries sustained in the service of a ship, officers were not to be considered fellow servants.

The act was to take effect on all American vessels by November 1915; and on foreign vessels by March 1916, one year after its passage. In the case of matters covered by treaties with foreign nations, the period required by the treaty would determine the date of effectuation.

BIG GUNS LEVELED AT THE ACT

The great hue and cry which was heard through the land immediately upon the passage of the Seamen's Act was louder than the opposition which had preceded its passage. Any event which might be construed in the slightest degree as injuring the merchant marine was attributed to the "Furuseth-LaFollette Folly." The attack on the act was linked to the attack on the Administration's bill for the establishment of a shipping board to purchase, equip, maintain, and operate merchant vessels. The alleged ineptness of the administration's Seamen's Act was cited as evidence of the likely ineptness of a measure providing for government ownership and operation of merchant vessels. Resolutions attacking the act and the pending measure were submitted to Congress by the National Association of Manufacturers; the National Foreign Trade Council, consisting of merchants, manufacturers, railroad men, steamship owners, and bankers; the American Manufacturers' Export Association; and the Governors of India House, consisting of businessmen interested in foreign trade.[36] The San Francisco Chamber of Commerce was reported as having "organized practically every one of the commercial bodies on its side of the country into making a united effort against the new law"; and this was repeated in many major ports throughout the country.[37]

The very passage of the act (which was not to go into effect for eight months), in the words of the chairman of the Foreign Commerce Committee of the New York Chamber of Commerce, caused "a chill" to come over "our shipping merchants." He went on to ask rhetorically: "Could anything be more unwise or spell greater disaster to our flag?" And apparently referring to proposals to establish a shipping board, he himself replied: "But, as though the Seamen's Law were not enough, merchant ship-owners are menaced by government ownership and operation. . . ." [38] A substitute title suggested for the act was "An Act to discourage American shipping; to involve the Administration in irritating controversies with friendly powers; to ensnare the votes of organized labor."

Following the outbreak of the European war, the selling of the most ancient American ships to foreign buyers at inflated rates was attributed to the effects of the Seamen's Act. Captain Robert Dollar, who had removed his offshore ships from British registry with the outbreak of the World War in 1914, now announced that he would return them to British registry. He didn't; he sold his ships because "I found, however, that a sale would be more profitable. . . . Conditions enforced by the Seamen's Bill which will go into effect early next November make it impossible for us to operate profitably American ships in any but the coastwise trade." [39] At the same time, Captain Dollar expressed the hope that Great Britain would not accept the change in the treaty provisions under the Seamen's Act, with its "humiliating" requirements enacted by a nation "that has practically no ships in the foreign trade." [40]

The announcement by the Pacific Mail Steamship Co. that it was withdrawing its transpacific ships because the enactment of the bill would make it unprofitable to operate these ships with English-speaking personnel was to become the rallying point for opponents of the act. Shortly after the passage of the act, and without waiting for the promulgation of the administrative regulations enforcing the act upon its going into effect in November 1915, the company announced its withdrawal from the Pacific and the sale of its ships to Atlantic shipping interests. This was immediately hailed by the opposition as evidence of the destructive effects of the Seamen's Act — the elimination of the one line which had been struggling so gallantly against adverse conditions for many years in order to maintain the American flag in the transpacific-orient trade.[41] Secretary of Commerce Redfield's explanation was that the officers of the line had threatened to end its operations several years before the enactment of the Seamen's Bill because the Panama Canal Act had denied the use of the Canal to steamships operated by companies allied with railroad interests. Little circulation was given to other facts cited by those who denied that the Seamen's Act had caused Pacific Mail to end its operations. Such facts included the rise in the selling price of the company's stock from $18 to $30 after the passage of the Seamen's Act, and the handsome selling price commanded even by the company's antiquated steamers because of war conditions.[42] By way of epilogue, it may be noted that the Pacific Mail Line reëntered the Pacific trade in 1916 with a new fleet because the rise in freight rates had "operated as an offset to the greatly increased running expense entailed by the passage of this bill." [43]

Direct appeals were made to Congress and to the President for repeal of the act. The Maritime Association of the Port of New York even appealed to President Wilson to call a special session of Congress for this purpose.

The battle was fought for months in the newspapers of the country. Some newspapers carried editorials condemning the act almost every other day. The Pacific Mail Line incident virtually became a matter for national mourning.[45] Several months before the act was made effective, it was referred to as a "botch" because it deprived the seamen of jobs by driving the ships off the sea. It was constantly reiterated that safety at sea was imperiled by the act, and even a ship disaster — that of the *Eastland* at Chicago — was attributed to the Seamen's Act four months before the act went into effect.[46] It was frequently charged that the act had been "furtively passed by the Senate while its chief opponents were out of the Chamber." [47] Senator LaFollette and his constituents came in for snide criticism by reference to their national origins: "Multitudes of the people of Wisconsin — excellent citizens in every way — are of German and Scandinavian descent, and not familiar with American tradition." Ship delays were attributed to lack of manpower arising from the able seamen requirements of the act which, it was maintained, would only benefit foreigners brought in from Europe who could meet such requirements.[48]

So effective was the propaganda against the act that it could be said that "the mere mention of it has got to be as alarming as the mark of the beast in Revelation."[49] In the words of a disinterested observer, it was "many a year since this country has seen a propaganda as skillful, as extensive, and seemingly as irresistible as that which has been conducted against the LaFollette Seamen's Law. . . ."[50]

Those who had supported the act in Congress fought the attacks. Senator LaFollette charged that the press was conducting the campaign "at the instance of the shipowners," and had failed to study the history of the act or its provisions. Senator Fletcher of Florida pointed out that no opportunity had been given to the Department of Commerce to adopt administrative regulations to enforce the act before the attack had been launched. Senator Robert Owen pointed out that the act had been passed on each occasion without a record vote, and "yet this bill, upon which statesmen of neither party wished a record vote, is charged with being fatally destructive to the American Merchant Marine. But no man seems to be willing to specify with precision how this bill could kill the American merchant marine." Secretary of the Treasury McAdoo sought to present the complete story of the facts relating to the Pacific Mail incident; while Secretary of Labor Wilson charged that the press campaign was a "conspiracy."[51]

Disinterested comments, while generally favorable to the purposes of the act, were few and were given little circulation. They contrasted the privileged status of shipowners with the inadequate protection furnished passengers and crews under earlier statutes. The Seamen's Act was presented as redressing that lack of balance. The National Consumers' League had supported the passage of the bill in the interests of safety of life at sea, and continued to defend it after its enactment. Mrs. Florence Kelley, general secretary of the League, cited the "family resemblance" between the editorials written by "the Maritime experts in the Rocky Mountains, Oklahoma, Kansas, and Vermont" and those in the seaports. This "singular likeness" was especially remarkable in the opposition to the language requirement.[52]

There were disinterested individuals who took calmer views of the possible effects of the act. One held that while unionism would be advanced as the result of the establishment of standards of seamanship, it would hardly result in union domination. It was his judgment that freight and passenger rates would be increased by the act. He doubted whether the act could produce the complete equalization of wages its proponents had promised. He cited such obstacles as differences in language and race, Oriental exclusion, laws of foreign countries penalizing desertion, trade between ports outside the United States, and the general limitations on the mobility even of seafaring labor. However, it was his final judgment that the act would achieve its announced purpose to a considerable degree. While national legislation to achieve international effects was viewed as makeshift pending international agreements, this observer felt that the act was a "piece of international bad manners forced upon us because foreign nations are as yet unwilling to surrender the advantage which lower wages give to their shipowners." [53]

Attempts at objective analysis bore little fruit. The opponents of the act continued their attacks, even finding ammunition in the administrative regulations and actual enforcement of the act by the Department of Commerce which proved to be mild in restricting shipowning interests. In a number of respects, the administrative regulations promulgated by the department went directly counter to the express intent of the leaders of the seamen, and were the subject of strong protests. The language provision was interpreted to require only the understanding of customary orders given by the officers of the respective department under normal conditions, rather than the orders in emergency conditions also; and it was not restricted to the understanding of any particular language. Under this interpretation, ships could continue to carry English-speaking officers and Oriental crews, with orders being given in pidgin English. Foreign vessels in American ports were to be inspected to see whether they met the requirements of foreign laws which "approximated our laws subsequent to the passage of the Seamen's Act," rather than to see whether they met the requirements of the Seamen's Act.[54] "Approximate" conformance of foreign laws to our own was subject to liberal interpretation, and the extent to which local steamboat inspectors could determine by inspection whether actual conditions on the foreign ships met the provisions of foreign laws was open to the same degree of loose construction. The provision for watch and watch at sea was interpreted by the department as requiring only watches of equal length of time, rather than of equal numbers of personnel as well as equal length of time, which was the interpretation of the seamen.[55]

These interpretations only added to the intense feelings engendered by the act. Those opposed to the act from its inception could now attack it as being unenforceable and as permitting "a wholesale exercise of arbitrary power utilized to destroy the effect of the statute . . . [although] it must be admitted that the power has been exercised equitably. . . ." [56] Furuseth, with the support of the American Federation of Labor, attacked the construction given to some of the key provisions by the Secretary of Commerce. He pointed out that despite the passage of the act, American, English, Dutch, and Norwegian ships "are departing the ports of the United States manned by lascars and Chinese." [57] He charged that, in general, the Department of Commerce was acting in the interests of the shipowners, and against that of safety at sea.

Secretary Redfield defended the act's construction as having been based upon careful study of the Congressional debates and "for the single, sole, and impartial purpose of its proper enforcement and without the question of favors to anyone entering therein." Even President Wilson, while accepting the judgment of the law officers of the Department of Commerce, expressed the hope "that in the course of time a very satisfactory administration of the bill can and will be worked out." [58]

THE ACT DURING THE WAR AND AFTER

The attacks upon the act and the demands for repeal or partial revision subsided with the growing opportunities for shipping resulting from the high level of wartime freight rates. With our entry into the war, requisition of private shipping by the government ended the concern with the act for the time being.

The adoption of an extensive program of expansion for the merchant marine by the newly-created United States Shipping Board brought about the need for an expanded merchant marine personnel. Increases in the price level, plus the need of overcoming the attractions of better paying shore occupations, led to substantial increases in seamen's wage rates. These world-wide influences, added to the extraordinary demand for shipping and seamen, the prosperity of the merchant marines of all nations, and the degree of reliance on American production, created a situation in which ships under foreign flags had to meet American wage increases to ensure adequate personnel to man their ships. The alternatives were discontent or loss of men to American ship operators by quitting or desertion. The Seamen's Act might have made desertion more facile; but the primary conditions for equalization of wages were certainly not created by the act.

Investigations of trends in seamen's wages from 1916 to 1919 clearly demonstrated the tendency of the wages of the seamen of foreign countries to follow American adjustments, with virtual equalization of rates among the major maritime nations of the world. This was so pronounced that the British Shipping Control even considered the possibility of reaching some agreement with American representatives to prevent wage action in our country from forcing up the rates in their country.[59] These studies acknowledged the effect upon wages of the wartime economic conditions. However, they also gave credit to the Seamen's Act for some effect upon wages, particularly with reference to the direct manner in which increases in American wage levels were followed in foreign countries. Robert P. Bass, Director of the Marine and Dock Industrial Relations Division of the United States Shipping Board, after describing the effect of wartime economic conditions on wage increases, insisted that "considerable weight should be attached to the fact that since the Act's going into effect in 1915 and 1916, the greatest wage changes in the history of seamanship have taken place, and almost simultaneously with this upheaval, wages have found an international level." [60] However, he did not impute a direct causal relationship between the two events.

Andrew Furuseth was also circumspect in his early judgments regarding the effect of the act on international wage levels. He acknowledged that the widespread wage increases in 1916 were due to the war. However, with the passage of time, the Seamen's Act was assigned an ever more important role in these trends. By October 1916, the *Coast Seamen's Journal*, while taking cognizance of the effect of the war, was to refer to the Seamen's Act as "the most powerful" in achieving these gains. By 1918, the Seamen's Act in the eyes of its proponents was the determining factor in the war. Furuseth attributed all of the wartime gains to the workings of the act — "The law is equalizing wages" he announced to the world.[61]

This emphasis upon the role of the act was not restricted to the seamen alone. In 1920, Raymond B. Stevens, vice-chairman of the Shipping Board, stated that in his judgment "the evidence clearly indicates that the LaFollette Act has tended to increase wages paid by our foreign competitors." [62] So widespread had this view become that there were some who considered the equalization principle of the act as worthy of consideration as a scientific principle, along with the law of gravity, and referred to it as "Andrew Furuseth's law of the sea." [63]

The termination of the war immediately produced demands for the repeal of the objectionable features of the act. The American Steamship Owners' Association drafted a postwar program calling for return of the merchant marine to private ownership and for the elimination of those features of the Seamen's Act which added to the competitive burden of the American merchant marine.[64] Vehement attacks were forthcoming. The Pacific American Steamship Association called for the restoration of imprisonment for desertion "without cause" from American flag ships in foreign ports; the repeal of the half-pay provision which "gives the money which keeps them in a drunken condition while they are ashore . . ."; elimination of shipowner liability for corporal punishment by the officers; granting of subsidies to pay for the increased costs resulting from the language provision; and enactment of a statute to keep persons (that is, union officials) off ships at anchorage or at dock, unless the master first gives his consent.[65]

The Supervisor of the Training Service of the Shipping Board in attacking experience and manning requirements which had not been enforced during the war as resulting in manning by foreigners, went so far as to imply that the bill may have been one of the plans "by which Germany and those friendly to her hoped to render this country helpless if the time ever came when she needed to transport an overseas force." [66]

The Commissioner of Navigation also charged that an effect of the act was to increase the number of aliens sailing on American ships. However, the statistical data contained in the annual reports of his bureau showed that of all those seamen signing on before shipping commissioners, the percentage of American citizens had been: 43.5 in 1915; 43.2 in 1916; 42.9 in 1917; 41.9 in 1918 (the A.B. provisions were not enforced during the war years); 47.6 in 1919; 50.5 in 1920; 48.3 in 1921; 47.6 in 1922; and 50.2 in 1923.[67]

So effective were the renewed attacks on the act, that Chairman Lasker of the Shipping Board stated during the course of a Congressional hearing in 1922: "I want to take the occasion to say that the Seamen's Act has been one of the most misrepresented acts of which I have ever heard. I came down to Washington believing, as most people in my part of the Country do, if you repeal the Seamen's Act, you would have a merchant marine. That is pure bunk. . . ." [68]

Andrew Furuseth was now devoting much of his energies to the defense of the act on all fronts. He appeared on numerous occasions before Congressional Committees to contend that the act had equalized wages and had brought the American to the sea. He successfully opposed proposals to reduce the requirements for the A.B. certificate with the claim that the training ship could not provide the seamen with necessary training and experience which could only be acquired in actual operation of ships at sea.

Up to January 1920, the ISU had expended about $70,000 in defense of the act. Much of this had been used to prosecute cases in the courts in the hope of obtaining favorable decisions which would overcome the shortcomings of the administrative regulations laid down by the Secretary of Commerce. But only limited success was obtained in the courts. The outstanding victory was one achieved over foreign shipowners — a decision by the Supreme Court in 1920 that the provisions of the act were intended to apply to foreign seamen while in American ports, and that this application was entirely within the authority of Congress.[69]

Furuseth's efforts to have the act's prohibition of advances and allotments extended to American and foreign seamen while in foreign ports were unsuccessful. A Supreme Court decision failed to sustain his position, even following inclusion of a provision intended to achieve this in the Merchant Marine Act of 1920. Furuseth also fought the battle of the Seamen's Act on the international front. Almost immediately after the Armistice, he warned President Wilson that Great Britain would try to weaken the Seamen's Act at the Peace Conference. He warned dramatically that "they know that with this act standing unmutilated and fully enforced the United States will become a dangerous rival on the ocean. . . ." He conceded that he was not thinking only of the interests of the United States, but as well "of the seamen who may again be made unfree and deprived of all hope." [70] The president assured Furuseth that he would keep the danger in mind throughout the Peace Conference.[71] Furuseth went to Paris to protect the Seamen's Act, and to support Gompers in obtaining a provision in the labor charter of the Peace Treaty providing for freedom for the seamen. Gompers failed to obtain this provision, although a saving clause was included in the charter protecting existing conditions. As a result, Gompers and Furuseth fell out on the question of ratifying the labor clauses of the Peace Treaty. The ISU delegation alone voted against ratification at the AFL convention.[72] In the interest of obtaining the support of the foreign seamen, the ISU extended to Furuseth the standing authority to go to Europe whenever necessary. Furuseth attended meetings of the International Seafarers' Federation during June and August 1920. At the latter meeting, resolutions were unanimously adopted endorsing a request to the separate nations to adopt the principles of the Seamen's Act relating to arrest and imprisonment for desertion.[73]

The decline in trade after the spring of 1920, and the laying up of much of the world's shipping tonnage, left many seamen unemployed. The attempt by the ISU and the constituent unions to maintain collective bargaining relations and to obtain enforcement of the Seamen's Act were to be unsuccessful during the "strike" of 1921. The relative significance of the Seamen's Act in the face of adverse economic conditions was completely apparent. The rout of the unions following the 1921 strike subjected wage conditions completely to the unilateral will of the shipowners and the Shipping Board. Andrew Furuseth's "equalization law" could not withstand the combined assaults of economic depression, restrictive immigration laws, and disorganization among the seamen.

Following the collapse of union organization, the shipowners continued their attacks on the act, restricting these to the provisions which interfered with unlimited control over seamen on shipboard. In a joint statement, the American Steamship Owners' Association, the Pacific American Steamship Association, and the Shipowners' Association of the Pacific Coast in 1928 stated that only "minor changes" in the act were sought, not its repeal. These "minor changes" included revision of the half-pay provision, making payment subject to the master's discretion; and excluding sailors needed only for the ship's upkeep from its coverage, from the watch and watch provision.[74]

In effect, these provisions would have vitiated the last remnants of the act's provisions. What Furuseth had hoped to achieve through skill, language, and manning requirements had not materialized under the regulations promulgated for the administration of the act. The provisions setting restrictions on hours of work during a period of limited job opportunities were also meaningless, for the sole recourse of the seaman was to demand his discharge where the law's provisions were violated. The result of such action was blacklisting.

The most that could be said for the Seamen's Act was that it had provided seamen with the same freedom to work or quit which was available to shoreworkers. In its effort to protect and entrench the seafaring crafts, and to equalize wages and working conditions nationally, and even internationally, it failed. It only appeared to succeed when economic conditions made for optimum employment of ships and seamen, and only when a fair degree of control was exercised by the seamen's unions.

CHAPTER 4

THE FIRST WORLD WAR AND AFTER

FACADE OF UNANIMITY

The period of the first World War, both preceding and following our entry into it, brought great prosperity to the American merchant marine, and substantial improvements in the wages and working conditions of the personnel. The great reliance upon American shipping both by American and foreign governments created a need for stability in labor relations which would make it possible for private shipping companies to take advantage of wartime prosperity. The increases in both shore-side wages and the cost of living made adjustments necessary in order to attract and maintain an adequate labor supply for the merchant marine. These forces had already made themselves felt early in 1916, and adjustments had taken place on both Atlantic and Pacific coasts.

Our entry into the war brought a new and potent factor into the maritime labor relations picture. The United States Shipping Board, created in 1916 as an agency whose primary functions would be to regulate and promote the development of the American merchant marine, now took on an entirely altered aspect. Under the wartime powers of the president of the United States, the Shipping Board would take over and operate virtually the entire American merchant marine. The board would inevitably become more and more concerned with attaining stability in the labor-management relations of the maritime industry, to prevent disputes which might hamper the effective prosecution of the war.

Substantial improvements in wages and working conditions on both coasts resulted in virtual uniformity of wages and a fair degree of uniformity in working conditions on the respective coasts, and by 1919 on a nationwide basis. The unions gained tremendously in numbers and in funds. Apparently, a new era had begun for collective bargaining.

But even before the end of the war, there was evidence of shadows in this idyllic picture. Improvements had come about largely as the result of governmental decision, although both shipowners and unions had agreed voluntarily. But there continued to be an undercurrent of employer resentment against the unions. This was even reflected in the operations of the Shipping Board, where operating officials were drawn generally from shipowner ranks.

With the end of the war, the departure of the National War Labor Board from the scene, the failure of the president's labor-management conference in 1919, the widespread general industrial unrest in the United States and elsewhere resulting from substantial rises in living costs, together with prevalence of management's desire to "go to the mat with labor," all indicated the approach of chaos in labor relations generally. The prospect was intensified in the case of the war-maintained and government-dominated maritime labor relations, in view of the Shipping Board's imminent departure from its dominant position. The continued responsibility of the government for shipping operations and the increasing size of the fleet required that some provision be made to fill the threatening void in maritime labor-management relations.

Both shipowners and seamen's unions favored the board's withdrawal from its controlling position in labor relations. Withdrawal of government controls in the face of emergency conditions was obtainable only if private interests could demonstrate that they could carry on shipping activities at least as efficiently as the board, and could maintain at least the same degree of stability as had existed during the war years. This accounted, in part, for the unions' success in the strike of July 1919. A superficial harmony was achieved following this strike; but it did not require deep probing to discover the actual underlying instability in labor-management relations. Both the ship operators and the ISU reorganized. The inadequacies of the latter's efforts were soon apparent.

Harmony in labor relations continued so long as economic conditions were beneficial. But with the accelerating decline in freight rates and the laying up of many ships late in 1920, latent threats to the union came to the fore. Operating economies were demanded of the board by Congress, and changes in board officials were increasingly to affect administration of labor relations. While the board assumed a position of neutrality, its actions worked to the detriment of the seamen. Expiration of West Coast contracts, and the imminent expiration of East Coast agreements, were accompanied by increased indications of widespread intent by the shipowners to terminate relations with the unions and to establish open shop conditions.

The union leaders, in the face of adverse economic conditions, mistakenly hoped for support from the Shipping Board and from the administration. But this support was not forthcoming. Instead, the unions' position appeared to be an arbitrary and unwarranted refusal to accept economic adjustments in face of widespread wage reductions in other industries.

A strike in the face of declining shipping opportunities, and the joint interest of shipowners and Shipping Board in reducing costs was to serve as the *coup de grace* to the unions. The unions, particularly those of unlicensed personnel, were crushed completely; and the open shop came into full operation, with job opportunities under the complete control of the shipowners.

WARTIME IMPROVEMENTS

The outbreak of the war in 1914 and the withdrawal of foreign flag ships from the customary travel lanes found the United States with virtually no foreign-going merchant marine. The shortage of available tonnage, the risks of war, and the needs of the warring nations combined to provide excellent opportunities for substantial profit to those who had the ships. Freight rates rose to extraordinary heights; in some cases by as much as five hundred times. Ships which could be sold for only $80 a ton before the war, now brought as much as $300 per ton, since it was not unusual for a ship to earn its original cost in one voyage. American-owned ships under foreign flag which had been admitted to American registry could hardly meet increased shipping demands. The twofold increase of American shipping tonnage in the foreign trade by 1916 was largely at the expense of domestic shipping. By 1916, the gain in the number of American ships in the trade to Europe had virtually made up for the losses due to the withdrawal of foreign ships. Substantial advances had also been made in trade with South America and Asiatic Russia and Australia. The impetus to shipbuilding in American yards was amazing, and by July 1916 "the amount of work on hand was more than double the corresponding amount at any time in our history." [1]

The immediate effects of the war were disadvantageous to the seamen on the Atlantic Coast. The stranding of many foreign seamen in American ports as the result of the blockade of the Central Powers acted as a further depressant to low conditions due to the disorganization following the unsuccessful strike of 1912. Wages and working conditions had continued to deteriorate after 1912, and the crimps had been able to reimpose their control over the employment of seamen. To protect the East Coast unions, efforts were made to bring all the stranded foreign seamen into the union fold; but they were issued trip cards rather than entered into full membership status.

The efforts of Furuseth, Flynn, and other organizers appointed by the ISU bore fruit under the improving shipping conditions, and the mem-

bership of the East Coast unions increased from 2400 in 1913 to 9400
in 1916. By the spring of 1916, the static wages and poor working conditions on American ships, contrasted with the increasing cost of living
and increased shoreside wages and job opportunities, showed the need
for developing a strategy to obtain improvement in the conditions of
seamen on the unorganized East Coast. At a meeting of Furuseth and
the leaders of the East Coast unions in March 1916, it was deemed
propitious to demand a uniform scale on all ships, with wage increases
and overtime payment. They decided to demand an increase in war risk
compensation from the 10 percent being paid by most companies to 25
percent.[2]

Upon the companies' refusal to negotiate with the unions, it was
deemed necessary for crews to bargain on an individual basis. The Atlantic Division of the ISU, therefore, sent out a circular in English, German, Spanish, and Portuguese calling on the seamen to strike unless
they were signed on at the requested rates. The efforts of the seamen
to obtain the higher rates and the refusal of some of the ship companies
to accede resulted in a series of strikes, with consequent delays in sailing. The demands of the seamen were regarded by some of the shipowners as unreasonable, since the men involved had "never served on
sailing vessels and cannot expect to be treated as skilled labor." Another
argument used against granting increases was that the war prevented
American companies from using the "best" firemen and seamen, namely
Austrians and Germans, since they could not sail into Allied ports. However, the fact that the ISU demand had been circularized in various
foreign languages, which "ought to have included Asiatic language,"
was cited as evidence that the demand was not being made for American seamen.[3]

Most companies were willing to come to terms without risking ship
delays. Delays were much more costly than wage increases, in view of
the state of shipping, and seamen were becoming more and more scarce.
By May 1916, Furuseth reported that most of the major companies in
coastwise and foreign shipping had met with the union demands. Complete uniformity, however, did not yet prevail. Moreover, these conditions were apparently granted grudgingly.

Similar influences operating on the West Coast also resulted in improvements in wages and working conditions. Here, the shipowners had
been operating under tacit or verbal agreements which had remained
substantially unchanged during the decade since the 1906 strike. During
the spring of 1916, with the entry of coastwise companies into the boom-
ing foreign-going trades, the West Coast unions, acting jointly, negotiated an agreement obtaining the equalization of the rates for both
coastwise and foreign-going shipping at the highest rate then prevailing.

Preference to union men in hiring was continued, with hiring to be done through the unions' offices or on the docks. So tight had the labor market become by 1916, and so effective was union organization on the West Coast, that even companies employing nonunion men conformed to union conditions.[4]

With our entry into war, there were substantially greater improvements. Between 1916 and the end of the war, wage rates on the Atlantic increased from $27.50 and $30 to $75 for A.B.'s; firemen's rates, from $40 to $75. Overtime rates increased by 50 percent. Earnings were increased further by the 50 percent war risk bonus for sailing in the war zone. In addition, the working rules agreed to during the spring of 1917 provided for preference to be given union members in employment, and for improved working conditions, such as separate messrooms and shipowner-furnished bedding and blankets. Wages and working conditions in many respects were equalized on the East Coast with those on the West Coast in 1917, and this new equality was to be maintained until 1921.

Improvements in wages and working conditions went hand in hand with organization on both coasts. By 1916, the ISU could report that the membership of its constituent unions had increased to 30,000, almost twofold that in 1914. In addition, for the first time in the history of the organization, the Atlantic Coast unions now exceeded the Pacific Coast unions in total membership — 9400 as against 8400. This expansion in membership was exceeded by the advances made in 1917–18, as the maritime labor force expanded. By 1918, the total membership of the ISU had increased to 50,000 with 22,000 on the East Coast, 10,000 on the West Coast, and the remainder on the Lakes and in other than seagoing occupations. Even then, the major increase was yet to come with the culmination of the shipbuilding program undertaken by the Shipping Board's Emergency Fleet Corporation.

THE GOVERNMENT ENTERS THE SCENE

The outbreak of the European war had demonstrated the complete helplessness of American foreign trade in the face of the withdrawal of foreign ships. This had been the most effective force in bringing about consideration of a concrete program for building an American merchant marine. The Shipping Act of September 1916 was the first step in the program. It was intended to resolve the fears of the American shipowners that government ownership and operation would ensue. The board established under the act could arrange for the construction, purchase, or lease of vessels; these vessels, however, were to be sold, chartered, or leased to private operators. Only under the most restricted conditions could the board be permitted to operate ships directly. It also met the wishes of those who were opposed to subsidies and attacked the "shipping trust" by granting the board regulatory authority over combinations of shipping companies.[5]

American entry into the war in April 1917, shortly after the organization of the Shipping Board had been completed, radically changed the board's actual operations from the original legislative conception. Under his wartime powers, the president delegated to the board the authority to acquire vessels and to operate, manage, and dispose of such vessels. Under these wartime powers, the Shipping Board and its agent, the Emergency Fleet Corporation, embarked upon the task of constructing and operating a wartime merchant marine. The Shipping Board's control over shipping operations was immediately effective and was to continue to be a significant factor for several years after the war, particularly since the significant results of the construction program in increasing American tonnage were not to be realized until after the war's end.

While labor problems early became a direct concern of the board, the board did not approach them with any clearcut program or administrative organization. The program and administration were to develop only out of the experience in solving the particular problems which arose during the war. In January 1917, Vice-Chairman Raymond B. Stevens, former Congressman from New Hampshire, was assigned the task of dealing with any labor problems with which the board might be faced. During November 1917, Robert P. Bass, former governor of New Hampshire, was employed as a labor expert and assistant to Commissioner Stevens. Bass was placed in charge of labor matters in January 1918, and given a small staff of labor experts. It was not until September 1918, however, that the Marine and Dock Industrial Relations Division was formally established, with Bass as director. This division was assigned the general supervision of all labor questions involved in ship operations, subject to the direction of the board.[6]

The wartime rapport between the board and the unions developed primarily out of the efforts of Commissioner Stevens and Mr. Bass to administer as fair and impartial a labor relations program as possible, in spite of the fact that the Shipping Board was in a position to make arbitrary decisions. These officials attempted to make the labor leaders "feel that there was a place in the Shipping Board where they could come with their grievances and that they would at all times receive a considerate hearing and an impartial judgment or decision." Even if the labor leaders did not always get what they wanted, they were given the opportunity to express their views; and full and frank explanation was given for the actions of the board. Bass felt that this close relationship and the board's emphasis upon uniformity in wages and working conditions had enabled the Marine and Dock Industrial Relations Division to limit wage increases to "such amounts as seemed reasonable under all the circumstances . . . at a time when the unions had it in their power to enforce unreasonable increases had they been so minded." [7]

There were others on the board and among its staff who did not share this attitude toward the unions. They felt that the unions should not be given any privileged status, and that hiring should be done on the basis of the open shop, with no discrimination on account of union or nonunion membership. It was their view that the labor relations function of the board should be placed under the jurisdiction of the Operations Division, although that division was constantly being charged with discriminating against union men and its chief was viewed by union leaders as one of the leading proponents of the open shop.[8] The union leaders were aware of these sentiments and regarded them as evidence that a strong element in the Shipping Board was seeking to destroy the unions. The fear of destruction was heightened by the great influx of nonunion seamen through the Training Service and the Sea Service Bureau which threatened to engulf union organization. Another cause for fear was the increased number of merchant ships manned by Navy crews. Lack of labor representation on the Shipping Board, as contrasted with operator representation and direction of operations, crystallized these fears.

The vast manning requirements of wartime, and the uncertain role of the Shipping Board could overwhelm the unions. But the ISU sought to turn the situation to its advantage. The first problem raised by America's entry into the war was that of ensuring an adequate and stable labor supply with which to man American ships. Andrew Furuseth, immediately upon the declaration of war, approached the Shipping Board with a proposal for carrying boys on board ships, in addition to the regular crew, to train under the supervision of experienced seamen. The ISU offered the support of the organized seamen in training novices in return for allowing union representatives to conduct union business on the docks and ships. In addition, the union offered to subscribe jointly with the shipowners in an appeal to experienced men to return to the sea, and to novices to come to the sea. Furuseth also proposed that offshore ships, which had been largely unorganized prior to the war, carry only the best able seamen.[9] Acceptance of such a proposal would solve the employment problem for union members who had been put out of work by shifts in shipping tonnage from the coastwise to the offshore trades, and at the same time provide the unions with a means for protecting and expanding organization — since most experienced seamen were members of the unions.

A conference was called by the Shipping Board on May 8, 1917, which was attended by the shipowners on the Shipping Committee of the Council of National Defense and representatives of the International

Seamen's Union. The representatives of the shipowners and unlicensed seamen agreed that action was necessary to ensure an adequate labor supply for the expanded offshore shipping and the continuing coastwise trade.

A tentative agreement was reached whereby "substantially all the steamship lines will agree" to a 25 percent increase in the A.B. rate, to overtime pay for both cargo and ship work, to a war risk bonus of 50 percent for going to the war zone, $100 compensation for loss of effects due to war conditions, and to letting representatives of organized seamen have access to docks and ships. The provisions arising from the war were to be terminated with the war, and the wages were to remain in effect for one year "to the end that wages be stabilized and that the men now on shore may be induced to return to the sea." On their side, the unions agreed that boys should be carried in addition to the usual crew; that the number of able seamen would be diluted in proportion to the number of ordinary and apprentice seamen employed; that experienced seamen would coöperate with officers in training the novices; and that the unions would join with the shipowners in appealing to seamen employed on shore to return to the sea. This tentative agreement was approved by many East Coast shipowners and by the membership of the unions of unlicensed personnel.[10]

Continued anticipation of manning problems, the need to ensure general stability in labor relations, and the desire to extend these conditions to the Pacific Coast and Great Lakes resulted in the calling of a general conference by the secretaries of Commerce and Labor. The conference, which was held in Washington on August 1 and 2, 1917, was attended by representatives of the unions of licensed and unlicensed personnel, shipowners, stevedores, and government. A tripartite committee was established which unanimously recommended to the government agencies that similar agreements be entered into between unions and shipowners on the Pacific and Great Lakes.

"The Nation's Appeal for Men to Man its Merchant Ships," to be known generally as "The Call to the Sea," was also drafted by the committee. This Call advised those who had left the sea that, as the result of the Seamen's Act, "the importance of the seamen as a factor in the life of the nation is being recognized" with improved wages and working conditions. To the novice, the possibility of a real career was held out. Attention was called to the Atlantic Agreement, which was now countersigned by the chairman of the Shipping Board and the secretaries of Commerce and Labor. The major achievement of the August conference, thus, was the formal ratification of the Atlantic Agreement of May 1917.

The unions now felt that in the Atlantic Agreement they had realized a significant achievement because the East Coast shipowners had agreed to recognize them, a uniform wage scale had been adopted, and preference was to be given to union members in the hiring of able seamen.

The Shipping Board had played a relatively passive role in the negotiations leading to the Atlantic Agreement; it was shortly to play an increasingly greater role in maritime labor relations. The first occasion for direct intervention was a strike threatened by the Lakes unions to take effect on October 1, 1917. Following the lockout of the unions in 1908, the representatives of the organized seamen on the Lakes had persistently charged that the "Welfare Plan" which had been adopted by the association was serving as an effective blacklisting system. The savings, death, and accident benefits of the plan accompanied a system of employment control which was maintained by hiring seamen through the association halls, and by requiring every member of the welfare plan to carry a continuous discharge book furnished by the association. In this book officers entered their evaluation of the quality of a seaman's service.

The threatened Lakes strike was postponed after Vice-Chairman Stevens brought the parties together, obtained agreement on wages, and promised a Shipping Board investigation of the welfare plan and the discharge book system. The board's negotiations with the Lake Carriers Association continued until October 1918, directing and finally achieving elimination of the continuous discharge book and hiring through the association's hall.[11]

The action of the Shipping Board in the Lakes situation indicated the manner in which labor relations affecting seamen would be directed for the remainder of the war period. The board had gradually been forced to assume the role of sole arbiter in matters over which there were differences between shipping labor and management. This was also to be the role played in East Coast relations. This position regarding seamen was to differ from that which the board occupied with reference to shipbuilding labor, harbor employees in the Port of New York, and longshoremen, where tripartite adjustment commissions were established for the purpose of determining wages, hours, and working conditions, and for arbitrating any differences over interpretations of awards or agreements. (In the case of labor relations generally, disputes were dealt with by a tripartite body, the National War Labor Board.)

This assumption of a central role by the Shipping Board in shipboard labor-management relations on the Atlantic and Lakes was symptomatic of a fundamental lack of mutual understanding and trust necessary for successful negotiations over wages and working conditions. Although war conditions had brought about the Atlantic Agreement for the Atlantic and Gulf — albeit under government auspices — the lack of an established pattern of collective bargaining relations meant that further agreement could be reached only through governmental decision. The one undirected point of accord between shipowners and unions seemed to be the desire to have the merchant marine operated by a civilian agency rather than by the Navy.[12]

The unions were willing to accept the decisions of the Shipping Board because the men handling labor relations, Vice-Chairman Stevens and Mr. Bass, were regarded as being generally fair and "even friendly to the Seamen's Act." In addition, the actions of the board in encouraging the signing of the Atlantic Agreement and in the Lakes situation seemed indications that the seamen would get at least impartial treatment at the hands of the board.

The shipowners, too, were willing to substitute the Shipping Board's judgments for the burdens of direct labor-management relations. Wartime arrangements were regarded as being only temporary, as Franklin D. Mooney, president of the American Steamship Owners' Association, expressed it at the Marine Conference held in April and May of 1918:

we believe that nothing that is done at this particular time should continue after the termination or the cessation of hostilities . . . no legislation should be had and no rules adopted which would prevent the American merchant marine from competing with the world in the foreign business. We are perfectly willing to agree to any proposition that is considered fair and reasonable and consistent for the duration of the war.[13]

Changing conditions brought about by expansion of the board's operations, increases in the cost of living, charges of failures to obtain adequate numbers of recruits, and the hope of obtaining agreements applicable to all groups of personnel and to all coasts, led to the board's calling of another Marine Conference in April and May of 1918. Representatives of ship operators on all coasts and of both licensed and unlicensed personnel attended. A wide range of problems were thrashed out. The net result, however, was an agreement between the East Coast ship operators and the unions of licensed and unlicensed personnel to leave to the board the determination of wages and working conditions, and the adjustment of all disputes involving grievances or the interpretation of awards or rulings. In short, the Shipping Board was given in addition to its own rights and powers, a general commission by both employers and employees to settle all marine labor questions rising during the war on the Atlantic and Gulf coasts. It was only on the West Coast that the parties were able to reach agreements through collective bargaining, and the board accepted those terms.

The Shipping Board, under the authority granted to it at the Marine

Conference, issued a series of wage awards for the East Coast during May and June of 1918. Under one award, the wage and overtime rates were increased. The war risk bonus of 50 percent for sailing into the war zone was not changed, however, although licensed officers were awarded an additional 25 percent bonus for points in the western hemisphere. The wage scale was to remain in force until, in the judgment of the board, a change was warranted.[14] In reaching its decision, the board considered the cost of living, shoreside wages, and the need for seamen; it was also concerned with establishing a "standard" wage scale for all vessels sailing from Atlantic and Gulf ports. These criteria were consistent with the principles laid down by the National War Labor Board for disputes arising in industry generally.[15]

The lack of direct representation for the labor groups was subsequently to become increasingly irritating to the unions. One effort — a tripartite committee to give both unions and shipowners opportunity to discuss the general problems affecting the personnel of the merchant marine — achieved no tangible results. Union leaders felt that the shipowners were adequately represented both on the board and among the operating officials, whereas the unions were devoid of any direct influence. This irritation was aggravated because of the lack of any machinery for the handling of specific questions or grievances, many of which required intensive research or hearings. The situation had become sufficiently serious by November 1918 to warrant a warning by the director of the Marine and Dock Industrial Relations Division to the board, citing the lack of any established agency for handling marine labor disputes on which such labor was represented.[16]

The decisive role of the Shipping Board in East Coast labor relations contrasted sharply with its function in West Coast affairs. On the West Coast, the action of the Shipping Board was restricted to that of approving agreements reached by the seamen's unions with the members of the Shipowners' Association of the Pacific Coast. The provisions of these agreements were also adopted by the unorganized offshore companies. The agreement of 1916, which equalized rates for all trades, was followed by an agreement in 1917 and 1918 which provided for further increases. During July 1918, the Shipowners' Association voluntarily offered to reduce the workday in port from 9 to 8 hours, after the longshoremen were granted a similar change.

Here, too, there was agreement between shipowners and the Sailors' Union of the Pacific to dilute the supply of skilled sailors, patterned after the Atlantic Agreement. Through this agreement, the union voluntarily gave up part of the control it had exercised over the labor supply because at least 90 percent of the experienced sailors on the Pacific Coast were members of the union.

THE SHIPPING BOARD — A CHANGING WIND

With the conclusion of the war, the continued shipbuilding program begun during the war and the continued need for expanding shipping facilities placed the Shipping Board in an anomalous position. It was the owner of the majority of American ships, and it was responsible for supervising shipping operations essential for moving supplies to troops abroad and to war-devastated countries, as well as for returning troops home. Simultaneously, it was being subjected to pressures from shipowners to end its direct operation of shipping and to sell or charter government-owned ships soon. Accordingly, a ship sales policy was adopted by the board whereby nominally it was selling ships at world market prices, but actually it was turning them over to private operators for down payments averaging only 10 percent of the sales price. Thus, for a relatively small payment, private operators were able to profit from the boom conditions in shipping during 1919 and 1920. Ships which the board chartered to private operators were operated under terms by which the board assumed the burdens of all losses, while the private operators enjoyed a share of any profits.[17] With the collapse of trade opportunities after 1920, and the resultant decline in freight rates, many of these ships were to be returned to the board. The favorable opportunities thus afforded shipowners could be developed only through maintenance of harmonious labor relations.

The board's announced intention of leaving the field of labor-management relations to the unions and private operators was greeted with favor by both those parties. To the operators, this decision marked one phase of the replacement of direct governmental control over merchant marine operations with a policy of governmental assistance for restoring the American merchant marine to a plane of equality with foreign merchant marines. As Captain Robert Dollar, expressing the views of "all the big shipowners of the United States," conceived it, this restoration program would, in addition, require the sale of ships "at fair prices," the payment of subsidies where necessary to equalize differences between American and foreign ship operating costs due to higher American wage levels; the revision of the Seamen's Act, particularly by reducing the experience requirements for A.B.'s and by eliminating the language requirement; and reduction of engine room manning requirements. Other operators' proposals included support for the continuance of the Shipping Board's Recruiting Service and Sea Service Bureau "to assure shipowners an adequate supply of officers and seamen." [18] This program was obviously not calculated to bring about better relations with the unions.

The unions, on their part, felt that withdrawal of the Shipping Board from direct operations would be best in view of the express intent to restore shipping eventually to private operation in any case. An underlying factor undoubtedly was the realization that public opinion would not countenance strikes against the government. Since exclusive public ownership and control were not likely, immediate exclusive private ownership and control would be preferable to prolongation of the confused labor relations atmosphere growing out of the assertedly "neutral" position of the government. Part of the unions' uncertainty grew out of the continued existence of the war-created Shipping Board Recruiting Service and the Sea Service Bureau, which were increasingly considered as threats to union security and as possible strike-breaking resources.[19]

THE QUEST FOR UNION SECURITY

The entire history of wartime and postwar labor relations was bound up with the union quest for security through employer preference for its membership. To the seamen's leaders, the issue was a matter of life and death. The possibility that the vast expansion in the maritime labor force might be used to crush the unions when job opportunities decreased was ever in their minds.

It was realized early that the expansion of the maritime labor force through the shipboard training program envisioned under the Atlantic Agreement would be slow and small. Therefore, in June 1917, the Shipping Board had authorized the establishment of a Recruiting Service to recruit and train officers and crews. The training was restricted to American citizens. In July the board established the Sea Service Bureau to find positions for the officers and crews trained by the Recruiting Service and, also, to furnish experienced men where vacancies existed. While the training of officers was stressed during the first stages of the program's development, by the autumn of 1917 the ship construction program of the Emergency Fleet Corporation had reached a stage where rapid training of unlicensed personnel was mandatory. The men were given four- to six-week intensive periods on training ships, and were then added to the regular crews of the merchant marine on the basis of the ratio established by the Atlantic Agreement. Later, as the shortage of seamen became more acute, the ratio was altered to six A.B.'s and four boys. By the time of the armistice, over 30,000 applications for entry into this training program had been filed.[20]

Under the direction of Henry Howard, a chemical manufacturer with an interest in the sea, the Recruiting Service was successful in its efforts to obtain the support of the unions. Howard established advisory committees consisting of union and ship operator representatives. He pointed out the magnitude of the training job and gave the union representatives full information regarding the program. In addition, he assured them that the Recruiting Service, "as long as I have anything to do with it, shall not be used to crush out the unions; that I will, on the other hand, see that it is not used by the unions to force unionism where it does not already exist." Thus, he reiterated the policy laid down by the War Labor Policies Board, and applied by the National War Labor Board.[21]

The unions were generally the sources of skilled manpower for the manning of the ships during the war period. The Atlantic Agreement was widely regarded as requiring preference to be given to union members in filling the 60 percent-ablebodied-seamen requirement in the deck department, the condition upon which the unions had agreed to dilution of their craft.[22] Similarly where vacancies existed in other departments, the Sea Service Bureau first called upon the appropriate unions to make up the shortages before taking men trained by the Recruiting Service. Nevertheless, instances of discrimination against union men by the Shipping Board itself were brought to light.[23]

The entire question of union preference was reopened when, with the extension of the training program to the West Coast, the unions proposed that similar instructions be issued to the West Coast. Strenuous objections were raised by West Coast open-shop operators through the Division of Operations, and it appeared that some board members might wish to consider reopening the matter of permitting the open shop on the Atlantic as well as on the Pacific.[24] Furuseth appealed to President Wilson, who expressed his sympathy with Furuseth's position. Thereafter, no action was taken to change the situation.

With the termination of the war, the continued expansion of the merchant marine and the maritime labor force, and the maintenance of the Board's Recruiting Service and the Sea Service Bureau as entry avenues into the labor force, union security was a primary concern. In view of the operator's demands for reduced experience requirements, it was feared that the government agencies might be used to flood the industry with inadequately trained men who would displace union men when vacancies occurred.

It was argued in defense of the Recruiting Service and the Sea Service Bureau that assurances had been given that they would not be used to undermine the unions, and that every effort had been made to give the unions an advisory role in their operation. The continued existence of the Recruiting Service was justified on the grounds that substantial expansion of the merchant marine would entail expansion of its personnel. Thus it was estimated in 1920 that about twice as many A.B.'s alone would be needed as in 1918. In the case of the Sea Service Bureau, it was argued that its services were essential to all ships, private as well as Shipping Board, in order to undercut the power of the crimps in such ports as New York, Baltimore, and Newport News. Although assurances of impartiality were carried out to a substantial degree so long as the original directors of these agencies continued in office, the pronounced interest of the shipowners in continuing these services for the purpose of eliminating union control would make them anathema to the unions, whatever the good intentions of their administrators.[25]

The unions were not demanding complete job control through the closed shop, or hiring through the union, on a rotary basis or otherwise. On the contrary, the leaders of the ISU and its constituent unions generally opposed turning the unions into employment agencies. Rather they wanted job opportunities to be "free and open" so that masters could employ men on the piers or call upon the union to send qualified men, without the intervention of shipping agents of any kind.

The situation in June 1919 was not substantially altered from that of the war years. The formal and informal agreements of the Shipping Board upon the manning of Atlantic and Gulf shipping remained in effect, although the unions charged that they were not being carried out properly by the Sea Service Bureau. Except for a few of the large operators, employers were granting preference to union members in hiring; and even the large operators generally relied upon the Marine Cooks and Stewards' Union for experienced personnel. The unions' claim that 60 percent of the members of all departments were organized in the ISU was not denied by the companies. The nonunion companies, whose ships were manned by Spaniards, Portuguese, Italians, Central Americans, and West Indians, were employing the bulk of the membership of the Marine Branch of the IWW. On the West Coast, the situation was much the same, with at least 90 percent of the tonnage of privately-owned ships carrying union men. Here, too, however, it was charged that the Sea Service Bureau was being used as an instrument of discrimination against union men.[26]

The achievement of a transition to a more "normal" state of labor-management relations was hardly helped by the complete wartime reliance on the Shipping Board. Unlike the situation in longshore labor relations where the tripartite National Adjustment Commission continued to function after the war, in seafaring labor relations no machinery representing both labor and management had been established to take over when the Shipping Board relinquished control.

To meet the basic problem of providing a machinery for harmonious handling of peacetime labor-management relations in the industry, the Shipping Board, at the urging of Commissioner Stevens and Mr. Bass, called a Joint Industrial Conference in June 1919, inviting representatives of the unions, shipping companies, stevedores, and harbor vessel operators. The announced purpose of the conference was to obtain agreement upon an organization and machinery to handle labor questions. In sounding the keynote of the conference, Commissioner Stevens pointed out that in peacetime reliance on the Shipping Board for final arbitration was inappropriate. A resolution was submitted by Mr. Bass calling for a committee to consider the establishment of a Maritime Board with representation by labor and management to consider labor policies for the industry and to establish arbitration machinery.

The representatives of the shipowners indicated their willingness to consider the establishment of such a board. The representatives of the unions of licensed and unlicensed personnel, with Furuseth as their spokesman, however, contended that agreement on the question of union preference in hiring was basic to any agreement establishing a Maritime Board. Their feeling was that, although they had been invited to this conference as representatives of labor organizations, the intention was to hamstring the unions rather than to give them an equal and effective voice on the proposed board. Failure to provide immediately for any degree of union preference in hiring was taken by them as evidence "that instead of having the preference, we were to agree to fill up the gaps wherever those who had the preference, for one reason or another, failed to respond to the demands of those who employed them." [27]

The union demand for consideration of preferential hiring was rejected by the shipowners and the Shipping Board. This in effect was a reversal of the board's former policy. It justified this reversal on the grounds that "it would be manifestly improper for the Shipping Board as a governmental agency to adopt a policy to give the members of the Seamen's Union or affiliated organizations preferential treatment with regard to the manning of vessels operated by or under the control of the Board." [28] As a result of the disagreement on this basic issue, the conference failed completely in accomplishing its stated purpose. It was agreed, however, that representatives of the unions and the American Steamship Association would meet shortly in New York to negotiate on wages, working conditions, and grievance machinery. In view of the inconsistency between the board's announced position of neutrality and its actual position as the predominant operator, employing representatives of shipowning interests to administer operations, it was Mr. Bass' judgment that "the instinct of the labor leaders to settle only immediate issues at this time and to let the determination of a permanent policy await a clearing up of the Government's attitude toward them, is, all things considered, the right one." [29]

STORM WARNINGS

After the failure of the Joint Industrial Conference the representatives of the licensed and unlicensed seamen's unions met separately in conferences with the American Steamship Association and with the Shipping Board. The issue of union preferential hiring was now wrapped in the cloak of Americanism by both its proponents and antagonists. The private operators refused the unions' demand for preferential hiring, charging that it would result in discrimination against American seamen, since the membership of the unions of unlicensed seamen was predominantly foreign. The ISU leaders promptly offered a compromise, suggesting an agreement to grant preference to Americans, whether union or nonunion; and, if properly qualified American citizens were not available for employment, to grant union aliens such preference. The Shipping Board apparently found the revised union preference proposal satisfactory at first, but the members of the American Steamship Association balked at it, calling it a mere camouflage.[30]

The newly announced policy of the Shipping Board to leave labor matters to the private operators and the unions, and to follow the terms of private agreements, was now to be tried sorely by this basic disagreement between the board and the ship operators' association. The association refused to accede to the unions' demand in order to ward off recognition of the unions "because the percentage of Americans was so small that it was tantamount to recognizing the unions." [31] In effect, the association was prepared to hold the Shipping Board to its announced policy, and sought the determination of the issues in private negotiations.

Since the dam in labor relations continued and stemmed-up demands failed to be met, a break was inevitable, especially in view of the generally unstable labor atmosphere of the time with its numerous unauthorized strikes by union rank-and-file members.[32] On July 8, 1919, despite the announced intention of the seamen's union leaders to maintain existing conditions while attempting to obtain recognition through "calmness in our deliberations and discussions"; the members of the firemen's union of the Atlantic voted to strike, and walked off the privately owned coastwise ships.[33] Many sailors and cooks immediately joined in support of the strike, although their unions did not give official support until July 17. The unions were reluctant to strike the ships engaged in transatlantic shipping, for this would mean striking against government-owned ships as well as privately-owned ships. Decision regarding this matter was delayed pending the outcome of discussions with Vice-Chairman Stevens. The Shipping Board offered to grant a wage increase, an eight-hour day in port, and establishment of joint grievance committees in important ports. However, it denied the three-watch system for deck crews on the grounds that it would mean increasing crews at a time of personnel shortages; and it remained silent regarding the crucial union preferential hiring issue. A spokesman for the American Steamship Association announced that the shipowners would go along with the

Shipping Board's offer, but only under protest, for they considered it disturbing to the international equality in wages then existing. The unions, however, rejected the Shipping Board offer, and struck transatlantic ships on July 15. By the following day, paralysis of shipping on the Atlantic Coast was complete. Further support came from the Marine Engineers' Beneficial Association, which announced that although it was not on strike, its members would not sail with nonunion crews. Estimates of the number of ships tied up ranged from 500 to 800; but the success of the strike was not disputed in any case. This success brought many recruits into the unions' ranks.

H. H. Raymond, president of the American Steamship Association, charged the unions with taking an "un-American and bad" position in demanding what he alleged was a closed shop. His contention that the unions were demanding the displacement of faithful nonunion aliens was denied by union leaders who stressed that they wished vacancies only to be filled by union preference.[34]

Despite the unfavorable light in which the strike was put, its outcome was telling. A significant contributory element to its success — outside of the favorable economic conditions and the increasing union strength (at least in numbers) — was the role played by the Shipping Board during the strike. While instructions were issued at first to the Sea Service Bureau to man Shipping Board vessels, but not privately owned ships in the event of a strike, these were rescinded almost immediately and the bureau was directed not to furnish men to any struck ships.[35] During the course of the strike the Shipping Board announced that, while it could not agree to alter its position on the three-watch system, it was prepared to continue its former policy of obtaining personnel through the unions, and was willing to accept the modified union preference proposal.[36] Such a policy was unacceptable to the private shipowners, however, who (as reported by the Acting Director of the Marine and Dock Industrial Relations Division) requested the Shipping Board "to join with the private operators to take more drastic action to break the strike." To their proposal, Vice-Chairman Stevens replied "that the Government could not commit itself to a joint policy with the shipowners in matters of this kind because the responsibility would rest upon the Shipping Board as a government agency." Accordingly, the members of the American Steamship Association had the choice of taking whatever action they deemed advisable, while the board would act with regard to its own vessels.[37] This independent position of the board was to contrast sharply with the subsequent role played by the Shipping Board in the fateful strike of 1921.

Since the dominant operator, the Shipping Board, was willing to grant union preferential hiring, and the private operators were willing to grant economic concessions exceeding those offered by the board, provided the unions waived preference on privately owned ships, and since the unions felt that they were in effect assured of security through the substantial growth of membership due to the successful prosecution of the strike, the strike was terminated on July 26. Despite their former objections to the earlier and lesser Shipping Board offer, the private shipowners now agreed to wage increases; an eight-hour day at sea and in port; the three-watch system at sea for lookoutmen and wheelsmen, with the remainder of the deck crew working eight hours during the day. Since it was understood that there would be no increase in the size of the crew, despite the reduction in hours, overtime earnings would be increased substantially, even though the overtime rate remained unchanged. In lieu of union preference in hiring, authorized union representatives were to be permitted on the docks and ships at time of paying off, and at other times approved by the owners. The changes were to remain in effect until May 1, 1920.

The Shipping Board agreed to the more favorable economic conditions granted by the private shipowners, despite its earlier stand. It also carried out the agreement reached with the unions regarding preference by issuing instructions on August 8, 1919, to the effect that: "With the exception of giving the first preference to American citizens (union or non-union) properly qualified [to perform the work for which they are shipped], the Sea Service Bureau will continue to call upon the local offices of marine labor organizations for properly qualified men to the extent that union men are available and willing to ship." [38]

Increased shipping operations on the West Coast and the continued shortage of seamen in that area resulted in agreement between the coastwise operators and the West Coast seamen's union which provided for adjustments comparable to those on the East Coast. The agreement continued the long-established practice of preferential hiring. However, the new organization of major deep sea companies, the Pacific American Steamship Association, continued the policy of nonrecognition which had long been maintained by its major constituents.

MARSHALING OF THE FORCES

The period following negotiations of agreements after the 1919 strike was outwardly one of good feeling. The wisdom of maintaining good labor relations during a period of economic opportunity had been demonstrated. Amiability was to continue with the shipping boom until the spring of 1920, when the onset of the recession first manifested itself with a reduction of opportunities for profitable shipping. It was not until the precipitous decline in freight rates towards the end of 1920, however, that labor relations were to become strained to a breaking point.

But all through this period of outward respite, a behind-the-scenes realignment of forces and a changing strategy were in progress within the industry, both among the shipping operators (including the Shipping Board) and among the unions.

With the growth in shipping and with the greater opportunities in the offshore trade than in the coastwise trade during the war, the principal shipping interests reorganized to meet changes in operations and to assure a united front in dealing with unions and government agencies. The American Steamship Association, organized during the early years of the century to represent the combined interests of the coastwise steamship interests on the Atlantic, was reorganized during 1919 as the American Steamship Owners' Association. Among its sixty-odd member companies were included the major coastwise and deepsea operators on the Atlantic and Pacific. In addition to acting as spokesman for its member companies before Congressional committees and the Shipping Board, the association's Committee on Wages and Working Conditions provided a united front for negotiating with the East Coast unions.

On the West Coast, negotiations with the unions continued to be carried on by the Shipowners' Association of the Pacific Coast, representing the coastwise operators of the lumber schooners. In 1919, a new organization was formed, some of whose members were also members of the American Steamship Owners' Association. This Pacific American Steamship Association, which was to deal with problems peculiar to the Pacific, represented primarily the major Pacific offshore operators who were among the leaders of the open-shop drive which was renewed in San Francisco after 1919. One of its avowed purposes was working together with the American Steamship Owners' Association in matters of common interest. While individual members had informal agreements with the seamen's unions, the Pacific American Steamship Association as a whole did not recognize the unions.[39]

While these associations favored immediate withdrawal of the Shipping Board from ship operations, they were not opposed to government support on labor relations matters. The Associations' demands for continuance of the Recruiting Service and the Sea Service Bureau and for reduction of A.B. requirements in the Seamen's Act were presented as efforts to break a monopoly exercised by alien members of the unions.[40] By September 1920, when the effects of the decline in foreign trade were clearly apparent, the work of the Sea Service Bureau in placing some 160,000 officers and unlicensed personnel on American ships during the previous year, was viewed by the *Marine Journal* with satisfaction as demonstrating that "whatever may be the future problems of the new American merchant marine, there will assuredly be no difficulty in fully manning it. . . ."[41]

With continued opportunities for profitable shipping in 1920, the ship operators were ready and willing to maintain relations with the unions, and to take steps to avoid disputes arising over minor grievances. In contrast with 1919, the negotiations on the East Coast regarding wages and working rules to be effective after May 1920 resulted in an agreement to maintain wages and working rules substantially unaltered.

Despite the continued refusal of the operators to grant preference to union men, both sides stated that the agreement was evidence of the gradual maturing of labor relations. The willingness of the leaders of the unlicensed seamen's unions to refrain from making demands for improvements in existing conditions because of the slight decline of freight rates — despite the continued high cost of living — was lauded by a shipowners' organ, the *Marine Journal,* as "a patriotic desire to do their share toward keeping the American merchant flag on the ocean." The operators' position was described by the *Journal* as welcoming "every possible improvement in the conditions of seafaring life," and as recognizing that the "coöperation of their crews was essential to the successful prosecution of the industry in which they and their men had such a close community of interest." Hope was expressed that the negotiations marked "the beginning of a new and better era in the human relationships of our merchant marine." A more charitable view was expressed toward the "alien" seamen during this honeymoon period, cautioning against undue haste in Americanizing the personnel of the merchant marine. These expressions reflected a sentiment which was to be shortlived. By August, marine labor was to be accused of "sojering" on the job in order to obtain as much overtime pay as possible.[42]

The role of the Shipping Board, largest of all the operators, was to continue to be an uncertain factor in labor relations, and in shipping operations generally, during this period. The board's concern with shipping operations was to be reflected directly in its labor relations policy — or lack of policy. It had come under fire of Congressional investigations and drives for economy in operation with the Republican victory in the 1920 elections, and its discomfort was increased by Congressional consideration of a postwar merchant marine policy. In addition, private operators were pressing for return of shipping to private interests. Management of the board and determination of its policies for a year during this trying period were to be largely those of one man: Admiral William S. Benson, former chief of Naval Operations. Admiral Benson had been appointed chairman of the Board in March 1920 and was to continue in this position until June 1921. Despite the passage of the Merchant Marine Act in June 1920, which provided for seven commissioners, the board consisted of only two members, including the chairman, until November 1920, when recess appointments made by President Wilson failed to receive the confirmation of the Republican Senate. The terms of the recess appointees lapsed on March 4 with the new administration. Admiral Benson, however, was designated by President Harding to direct the activities of the board until appointment of new commissioners in June 1921.[43]

The unlicensed negotiations in 1920 indicated that the board was increasingly following the lead of private operators. The board's announced policy of granting second preference to qualified alien union members, after first preference had been granted to American seamen (whether union or nonunion) was continued, although its wisdom was constantly debated by the frequently changing members of the Shipping Board. The presence of Commissioner Stevens until June 1920 served as some assurance that the policies adopted in 1919 would continue. Thus, a proposal to grant preference in employment on Shipping Board vessels to graduates of the Recruiting Service program was voted down largely through the efforts of Stevens.

The rapidly changing scope of shipping opportunities during the latter half of 1920, the spreading recession with resultant decline in price levels, and the pressures for governmental economies complicated Admiral Benson's task of administering the board. While Admiral Benson pointed out the possibilities of economizing in repair and fuel costs, he also made early and continual recommendations for obtaining economies through more efficient use of personnel, particularly through reducing or eliminating overtime payments.

The two aims of the Shipping Board's labor policy after June 1920, therefore, became (1) withdrawing the board as a signatory party to agreements negotiated by private operators, but apparently continuing in practice to be bound by the provisions of such agreements; (2) reducing operating costs. These aims were very soon to prove conflicting. In the interests of obtaining economy, the board was to be drawn into exercising pressure on the outcome of private negotiations to the extent of sending "impartial" representatives to the negotiations, coming to understandings with the associations of private operators (who were also operators of Shipping Board vessels), and seeking press support for its policies.[44]

Admiral Benson questioned the advisability of the Shipping Board's participating in agreements between the private operators and the unions during the negotiations involving the unlicensed seamen's unions in the spring of 1920. He consented, however, to have the board join in renewing the agreements, since the negotiations had virtually been completed by the time he was appointed. The subsequent negotiations with the licensed officers were actually held up because Admiral Benson objected to continuance of overtime payment to licensed officers by the ship operators as "contrary to the traditions of [the] sea. . . ." [45] Although the practice was continued, he warned the associations of licensed officers that he expected them to coöperate in the next few months "in minimizing the abuse and amount of overtime which will greatly aid in the economical operation of American ships. . . ." [46]

As the level of freight rates dropped — descending more than two-thirds by the fall of 1921 — the attitude of both private shipowners and the Shipping Board was to stiffen in negotiations. Agreements negotiated earlier in the year with other marine personnel had been made effective for a year; but now the operators balked at entering into agreements with marine engineers and radio operators for the same length of time, agreeing to be bound only for a period of six months — until May 1, 1921. Here again, the Shipping Board was to intervene by placing pressure on the parties to accept existing wage scales.[47]

A circular letter "to All Seafarers in the American Merchant Marine" was issued by Admiral Benson in which he called attention to the drop in ocean freight, the growing foreign competition, and the resultant tying up of Shipping Board and private vessels. He called, therefore, upon the "public spirit" of the personnel of Shipping Board vessels to help reduce expenses, and to make the merchant marine self-sustaining, by increasing efficiency through performing necessary repairs during regular hours, and by keeping overtime to a minimum. His message warned that additional ships would be tied up with consequent additional unemployment unless there were improvements in efficiency.[48] The evidence was ample to union leaders by the end of 1920 that extremely precarious times were in order for the merchant marine, its personnel, and the maritime unions.

The auspicious conditions of 1919 and 1920 had encouraged increases in the membership of the unions of unlicensed personnel to reach new heights. The membership of the ISU reached a peak of 115,000 in 1920. The East Coast unions had mushroomed from a total membership of 4500 in 1915 to 81,000 in 1920, with almost a twofold increase between 1918 and 1919. The greater stability in West Coast operations during the war and afterwards was reflected by a less spectacular growth of membership, from 7300 in 1915 to 12,600 in 1920.[49] It was estimated that about 90 percent of the unlicensed seamen on both coasts were organized. The marked increase in the number of American citizens who joined the merchant marine during the war years and shortly thereafter was reflected in the increased proportion of American citizens in the membership of the various district unions of the ISU; the percentage of native American members increased from about 30 in 1917 to 50 in 1920, with much of the remaining percentage consisting of naturalized American citizens.[50]

The wartime gains in wages and working conditions, and the gains in union membership and funds did not delude the leaders of the seamen's unions into the easy belief that collective bargaining rested upon a firm foundation. The union leaders recognized early the threat of depression with consequent ship lay-ups and unemployment, and the constant hazard presented to organized labor, including seamen's unions, by the nationwide postwar open-shop drive. This realization was not followed, however, by any comprehensive effort to reëxamine ISU policies in order to reorient them to rapidly changing requirements of the shipping industry. The ISU continued to be an ineffectual instrument, its weakness arising from placing too much emphasis upon voluntarism among its constituent unions, its power limited by the fact that many of these constituent unions failed to carry out the resolutions it adopted. What actions the ISU leaders were to take may be described as being "too little and too late."

To meet these threats, the seamen's union came up with the following strategy. Shipowner charges of foreign domination in the seamen's unions were met with evidence of increased American membership, and with the unions' announced willingness to grant preference in hiring to qualified Americans, whether citizens or not. Attempts were made to organize all recruits to the merchant marine. A program of education and training of the new members was proposed by the ISU leaders which was intended to serve a manifold purpose: to make union members most efficient and reliable so that all shipowners would turn to the unions for the best workers; to meet the increasing Shipping Board demands for economy and thus to curry public favor; to eliminate any justification for continuing the Recruiting Service and the Sea Service Bureau; and to indoctrinate the many new members. The process of carrying out this program was to be a slow one, however. The Sailors' Union of the Pacific established its own seamanship school in December 1920, when the full impact of the slump was already clear and many were unemployed. But despite Furuseth's earlier emphasis on this matter, the ISU made no effort to adopt a formal plan for all its constituent unions to follow until the convention of January 1921. Then a proposal was made to provide a fund for a vocational training program. Even at that late date, however, a long debate was to ensue on this, the sole proposal which had been made to meet the threatening situation, and the proposal received approval only after the district unions had been assured that contributions would be completely voluntary.

The ISU leaders also made efforts to strengthen the seamen's unions by closer coöperation with the unions of licensed personnel. On the Pacific Coast, a Seafarers' Council was organized in 1920 which comprised the three unions of unlicensed personnel, as well as the Masters,

Mates, and Pilots of the Pacific Coast; and the Marine Engineers' Beneficial Association, Local 35. The establishment of a similar organization among the Atlantic coast unions in February 1921 was hailed by the shipowners as evidence of preparation for joint action when the agreements for unlicensed personnel and engineers would expire three months later, on May 1.[51]

Isolation from the unions of shoreside waterfront workers had become an absolute fetish on the part of the seamen, largely because of Furuseth's influence. His "Second Message to Seamen" in 1919 had argued that safety for the seamen lay in the sharpening of their skills, in the development of discipline and responsibility in carrying out agreements with the shipowners, and in maintaining an aloof position in the controversies of shoreside workers. This separatist policy had grown out of a long history of jurisdictional controversy on the West Coast and a long list of additional grievances against the longshoremen.[52]

Internal revolts also confronted the leadership of the ISU, entrenched since the days of the small, compact, and relatively uninfluential organization preceding the war. It was now faced with an expanded and substantially altered rank-and-file membership unfamiliar with the sailing ship tradition. Rank-and-file independence from the views of the union leadership were demonstrated in the policies adopted by the membership of particular branches. In Seattle and San Francisco, the new union members, "natives," as they were referred to by Furuseth, had voted against the union leadership and in favor of establishing a system of rotary hiring from a union list. Furuseth, in derogation of their action, attributed it to the fact that these men had been unable to get jobs "because they did not have the skill" and believed that they could equalize job opportunities in this fashion. Even in Furuseth's own domain, the Sailors' Union of the Pacific, significant shifts were occurring. In January 1921, Paul Scharrenberg, editor of the Seamen's Journal for many years, was defeated for reëlection by J. Vance Thompson. At the ISU convention which was then in session, Furuseth introduced a resolution to repeal a long-standing action of the ISU which had made the Journal its official organ. He stated that this action was not intended "as a criticism of the membership" of the Sailors' Union of the Pacific for choosing an editor "of whose discretion we have no definite knowledge," but "to protect the International. . . ."[53]

On the East Coast, some recognition had been given the changed conditions. In August 1920, the headquarters of the Eastern and Gulf Sailors' Association was finally moved from Boston to New York, which had clearly been the center of shipping operations for some time. As a result of complaints regarding the failure to organize Negro sailors, as well as Negro cooks and stewards, a Negro branch of the Eastern and

Gulf Sailors' Association was established to act in "close coöperation with the colored branch of the Marine Cooks and Stewards." [54]

The views of the changed rank and file were reflected in the ISU convention of January 1921. A resolution was introduced calling for the amalgamation of the respective seamen's unions on each of the coasts into single district unions. The proposal was defeated, however, after it was attacked on one hand as being a proposal for the "I.W.W. system of organization," and on the other, as lacking feasibility in view of past experience rather than as having any radical intent.[55] Proposals to establish national headquarters in Washington with both the president and the secretary-treasurer to be located there were rejected. No action whatsoever was taken on a proposal to set up the jobs of the ISU officers on a full-time paid basis. The net result of the 1921 convention in the face of apparent difficulties was continuation of failure to adopt any positive program which would be binding upon all the constituent unions. The sole positive action was the adoption of the abortive vocational training program described above, which could hardly be called a constructive and adequate plan for contending with the difficulties anticipated from reduced job opportunities, Shipping Board efforts at economy, and ship operator antagonism.

The seamen were not even given a little hope with which to face the impending disaster of a serious shipping slump and unemployment. Furuseth foresaw the possibilities in typically pessimistic terms: "I fear that it is going to be worse before it is better. Nearly all of us are without families, and we can, therefore, endure more of idleness than other men. If we must endure to convince our employers that we really mean what we say, then endure we must and will. In this we have no choice. The world has not consideration for those who whimper and then surrender. We must act otherwise." [56]

THE ROUT OF THE UNIONS

By June 1921, over one-half of the Shipping Board's fleet tonnage was laid up because of decreased cargo offerings. Depression had also resulted in a reduction of approximately 15 percent in the cost of living between June 1920 and May 1921. It was clear that readjustments in wage scales and working conditions were in the wind. Furuseth and other leaders of the ISU recognized their inevitability. The major concern was to minimize the extent of these readjustments.

The initiative in the matter of readjusting conditions was taken by a number of Pacific Coast companies which, early in January, gave the unions the thirty-days' notice required for terminating their agreements. It was understood that these companies were thereafter proposing to determine wages and working rules unilaterally. This view was reported

as having "aroused the keenest interest . . . among American shipowners and operators of the Atlantic and Gulf." [57]

Although Admiral Benson had decided on the termination of overtime
payments, he restrained the ship operators from taking arbitrary and
hasty action to terminate relations with the unions. A decision was
reached instead to support the American Steamship Operators' Association in proposing immediate reductions to the East Coast unions. The
operators, with the tacit support of the Shipping Board, then carried on
the negotiations.

The leaders of the unlicensed seamen's unions indicated their willingness to negotiate reductions, provided that certain other conditions —
namely, the matters of union recognition and union preference — were
satisfactorily settled and that agreements would be effective for the
period of a year. In return, the Association's Committee on Wages and
Working Conditions recommended early in February against entering
into any agreement which would extend beyond May 1. The decline in
the cost of living was cited as the basis for a proposal to reduce wage
rates by 25 percent, to eliminate overtime payments completely, and to
make other reductions in working conditions to reduce costs. No mention
was made of union preference. Further negotiations were postponed for
a period of almost two months, despite a union request for a conference.
Some of the members of the association, not bothering to wait for the
outcome of the negotiations to alter the agreement, had already taken
advantage of the widespread unemployment among seamen to reduce
wages and eliminate overtime.[58]

Continued pressure by West Coast operators and some East Coast
operators to end relations with the unions was thwarted by Admiral
Benson's continued unwillingness to terminate relations with the unions
by arbitrary action. His position was reinforced by uncertainty as to
what would be the policies of the new Shipping Board which was due
for appointment after March 4; and by a substantial group of shipowners
who, while supporting the open shop on the East Coast, were opposed
to arbitrary termination of relations with the unions.

President Harding's action in appointing Admiral Benson as his personal representative on the board during March made it possible for the
admiral, as sole member of the board, to act more decisively in the
matter of labor relations. The admiral's position in favor of continued
negotiations was strengthened when the American Steamship Owners'
Association advised the board it had reversed an earlier decision to
refuse to deal with the labor unions. But this willingness for orderly
negotiating procedures was accompanied by proposals for even larger
reductions than those proposed on the West Coast. Admiral Benson privately advised the Pacific American Steamship Association, which had

been urging him to act jointly with it to end all relations with unions, that he preferred the negotiation of new agreements. However, he also informed the association that "If the attitude of your association is unanimous and unyielding against negotiations, the Shipping Board will decline to negotiate." He asked for assurance that in the event of a tie-up the individual members of the association would agree to be bound by the joint decision of the association and the board.[59]

The prolonged lapse in any negotiations from early February to early April, and the conviction that the very existence of the unions was at stake, finally aroused the seamen's leaders. Furuseth appealed to Secretary of Commerce Hoover on April 6 to arrange a meeting with the American Steamship Owners' Association, and also to enforce the Seamen's Act in accordance with its original purposes. But his appeal achieved no action. In mid-April, however, the association met with the unions, proposing wage reductions of 20 to 30 percent, elimination of overtime pay, and the open shop. It was not seriously expected that these drastic terms, which were reported to have the approval of the Shipping Board and the West Coast operators, would result in agreement.[60]

Furuseth insisted that wage considerations were secondary, and asked for prior negotiations on the following points: abolition of the Sea Service Bureau; enforcement of the language, life-saving, and watch provisions of the Seamen's Act; preference to qualified union members "to develop efficiency"; and a union guarantee to limit membership to reasonably qualified men. In their meeting, the engineers opposed any wage reduction, but were willing to discuss revisions in the working rules. Negotiations were broken off when all these proposals were rejected by the operators, who announced that "The Shipping Board and the American Steamship Owners' Association confidently appeal their case to the judgment and patriotism of the American people."

Admiral Benson called a meeting attended by the unions as well as East and West Coast operators in a last minute conciliatory effort. As reported by one newspaper "Benson, as Chairman of the Shipping Board, and therefore one of the large ship operators was firm in his attitude." In a prepared statement, Benson cited the current depression and the reduced cost of living as justifying a 15 percent reduction in seamen's wages, elimination of overtime "which has been subject to such notorious abuses and which is so foreign to the spirit and customs of the sea," and such other modifications of the working rules "as will make for efficiency and economy of operation." He announced that in arriving at these changes, "I have weighed this matter carefully and long, and have taken advice freely, and have come to a mature and well considered conclusion." Bargaining "would not only be impossible when dealing with the

Government, but would also be repugnant to my sense of fairness," he stated, specifying those reductions which he regarded as irreducible minima. Regarding the ISU demands, his views virtually coincided with those already expressed by the ship operators.[61]

Furuseth continued in his efforts to avoid a break, but the Marine Engineers' Beneficial Association willing to negotiate on changes in working rules, but opposed to a wage reduction, had set May 1 as the strike date. Realizing that a successful strike was unlikely, and despite Benson's strong ultimatum, Furuseth called upon the unions to attend another meeting. Furuseth was not averse to granting preference to Americans, a policy already in effect; nor to eliminating overtime at sea; neither did he strongly oppose wage reductions.

The ship operators announced at the final meeting on April 29 that representatives of the American Steamship Owners' Association, the Pacific American Steamship Association, and the Shipowners' Association of the Pacific Coast had met in New York and "in deference to the views of the Chairman of the United States Shipping Board" agreed to his terms.[62] To Furuseth's request for a clear statement from Benson on issues other than wages, the admiral replied that discussion of such matters should come only after agreement upon the reduction. However, what his final decisions would be were apparent from his comments on questions put to him by Furuseth.[63]

Furuseth stated that the terms offered by the board and the private operators required the unions "to surrender everything to the pleasure of the employers and sign an agreement which does not guarantee employment for one single one of the members that were present." In desperation, the union leaders asked that the entire question be turned over to the president of the United States for the appointment of a board of arbitration. Admiral Benson, with the support of the private operators, rejected this proposal, claiming that the entire matter was his responsibility. He issued a public announcement that: "The efforts of the U. S. Shipping Board and the Steamship interests to avert a break with marine labor have come to naught. The refusal of the men to recognize the need for readjustment on a reasonable basis had ended prolonged negotiations. . . . I must record my regret at their misguided action which threatens such a blow to our new national shipping enterprise. . . ." By contrast, he praised the coöperation of the private operators in agreeing to his proposals. His announcement contained the portentous statement that the Shipping Board "is reluctantly compelled to meet with all the resources at its command the situation which confronts it." [64]

Benson's action, implemented through the board's ownership of more than half of the merchant marine, forced the unions to act at once, despite their declaration against striking if President Harding would act to accomplish arbitration of the issues. The unions announced that they had been locked out and that their members on both Atlantic and Pacific coasts would only sign on ships at terms which had existed prior to May 1. After this announcement, they succeeded in tying up many ships on both coasts.

The Shipping Board and the private operators met and decided upon the strategy to be followed during the "strike." In accordance with his threat that the full power of the government would be utilized to move government-owned ships, Benson called upon the Navy to man ships carrying United States mails. A "sign or get off" order was issued by the board, after conference with the private operators of Shipping Board vessels, under which all crew members were required to sign on under the new working rules or get off the ships. The private ship operators agreed to follow the Shipping Board in obtaining replacements for crew members who refused to sign on through the Sea Service Bureau. The board's instructions guaranteed preference in future employment to those men who accepted the new terms. Those who refused were threatened with listing upon the Shipping Board's deferred list (tantamount to blacklisting), regardless of their prior service. Benson also threatened to withdraw government ships from any operators who signed men on under former wages and working conditions; execution of the threat against one company which violated this order served to discourage any other company from doing the same thing. With some 35,000 unemployed seamen available after the unions were forced out, the Sea Service Bureau was able increasingly to keep the ships crewed and sailing on regular schedules. Concern with efficient operation and with manning by Americans apparently went by the board; ships were manned "through the employment of foreigners and less efficient men who, due to malfeasance or other misconduct, had been debarred from again sailing on Shipping Board vessels." According to a report issued by the Shipping Board during the strike, ample numbers of American citizens were available; however, a later report acknowledged that less than 5 percent of the seamen signing on during the strike had been American citizens.[65]

Mediation activities were conducted during the course of the strike by Secretary of Labor Davis and Secretary of Commerce Hoover. Efforts to obtain arbitration, however, were opposed by the private ship operators as being "contrary to business judgment, principle, and precedent"; and the operators refused to accede further to any modifications in wages or working conditions which were proposed by Davis and Hoover. When Secretary Davis was able to get the ship operators and the Shipping Board to participate, a "compromise" proposal was presented which was virtually the original Benson proposal. A split developed between the unions — the MEBA president, over internal opposition, accepted the terms offered; Furuseth refused to accept.[66]

Chairman Lasker and the other members of the new Shipping Board who had finally been appointed by the president in June were to sign for the board. Ship operators on both coasts protested against such action by the board, charging the unions with "a long record of defiant lawlessness and attempted destruction of human life and Government property," and warning that "under a signed agreement the loyal men who stood by their ships and their flag in this emergency would be sacrificed in violation of the solemn promise of the Board." This protest influenced the new board sufficiently to reduce the term of the agreement signed on June 13 with the engineers to six months; in addition, Lasker issued instructions for retention of competent engineers who had taken the place of the "strikers."

The new board offered the unions of unlicensed personnel an agreement for a period of six months which was substantially the same as Benson's proposal at the end of April. It eliminated any union preference, and denied union representatives the right to visit ships and docks. This proposal was rejected by the unlicensed unions; however, within a few days — on June 23 — the East Coast unions of the ISU voted to return to work, preferring to return without any agreement than to agree to the ignominious terms offered by the board.[67]

The East Coast seamen had been defeated for all practical purposes as soon as the Shipping Board had taken active steps to replace the "strikers" and had placed pressure on any ship operators reluctant to follow suit. The defeat was made possible by the presence of a substantial reservoir of unemployed seamen on the East Coast. The only difficulty experienced by the operators had been in getting engineers, and even there defections from union ranks had been on the increase. The agreement on the part of the MEBA was to break the back of the strike on the East Coast.

The situation was somewhat different on the West Coast. A stronger bond had been forged among the unions of licensed and unlicensed personnel in the Seafarers' Council. A stronger and more deeply-rooted union consciousness existed among the more compact membership, which had expanded to a much lesser degree than that on the East Coast. Men to replace the "strikers" had to be brought in from the Atlantic and Gulf coasts by the shipowners. The tie-up of West Coast shipping was effective, therefore, for a longer period than on the Atlantic. The steam schooners in the coastwise lumber trade were almost completely tied up. The San Francisco local of the MEBA refused to be bound by the action of the president of the union in signing an agreement with the board. It protested first, because the agreement failed to protect the right of the "strikers" to return to their jobs, and secondly, because the unlicensed seamen had been left in the lurch. The "strike" continued on the West Coast for more than a month after it was terminated on the Atlantic, with the Pacific American Shipowners' Association refusing to have any dealings with the unions as the Sea Service Bureau increasingly met their needs for men. The members of the Shipowners' Association of the Pacific Coast, however, made a last offer based on the 15 percent wage reduction and an open shop, which was rejected by the unlicensed unions. Shortly thereafter, the engineers decided to return to work.[68] Both associations now announced that they would operate with nonunion crews, and would establish a joint employment office to enforce this policy. Upon Furuseth's advice, the unlicensed unions called off the strike on July 30.[69]

A minority of public opinion saw the "strike" in the same light as Senator LaFollette did: "It is not a question of wages at all. It is a question of destroying the men's organizations and of subjecting them to working conditions which they will not stand, and ultimately a question of driving American seamen and the American merchant marine from the sea, enabling the shipowners to employ cheaper foreign labor and make still larger profits." [70]

The seamen had fought a lost cause — their rout could be followed only by a Carthaginian peace. In Furuseth's words, "the old reactionaries of the Robert Dollar type, who have bitterly fought the Seamen's Bill and have never become reconciled to the new status of the American seamen, hand down the new marine policy." [71]

CHAPTER 5

THE COLLAPSE OF UNIONISM, 1921–1933

THE SHIPOWNERS TAKE OVER

With the loss of the "strike" of 1921, job control was effectively vested in the shipowners and was to remain completely in their hands until 1934. Dissension within the ranks of the ISU had accompanied the fatal attack from without, and it became more articulate during the course of the losing battle. To the West Coast rank and file, increasingly affected by growing "Wobbly" views, it appeared that the particularism of craft union organization was responsible for the disunity that lost them the strike. Efforts to strengthen the International Executive Board were meaningless gestures, since union membership decreased by more than half by 1922 and was to decline still further during the decade.

As a result, "labor" no longer troubled the operators as a major problem of operating efficiency. It had resolved itself into a mere matter of providing an adequate labor supply which could be controlled with a minimum of friction. The success of this control was assured by the establishment of a shipowners' Marine Service Bureau on the West Coast; the continued operation of the Shipping Board's Sea Service Bureau for both government-owned and privately owned ships; the almost universal use of operator-issued continuous discharge books with blacklisting propensities; and the lax administration of the Seamen's Act, particularly with regard to fulfillment of experience requirements and watch provisions. Wages and working conditions could now be unilaterally determined; maintenance of satisfactory working conditions was of little concern, wages were adjusted upward and downward according to the relative attractiveness of shoreside job opportunities. And if dissatisfaction among the seamen made them prone to some inroads by the IWW Marine Transport Workers' Industrial Union and the Communist Marine Workers' Industrial Union, the matter was considered of little concern — a minor problem of temporary and isolated character.

A major concern to the many shipowners, however, was the decline of earning opportunities in the foreign trade during this period. Possibilities for profitable returns in that trade were small for American interests during the twenties. High tariff barriers and a restrictive American immigration policy reduced further the earning opportunities that were limited initially by the competition of more efficient foreign flag operators. As a result, in 1925 about 80 percent of American tonnage in overseas operations was controlled by the government; privately owned ships had been returned to the more lucrative coastwise trade. Governmental shipping policy during the twenties and early thirties, sponsored by shipowning and allied interests, was to be directed toward building up participation of private ownership in foreign trade through financial or other assistance by the government. A ship sales policy was adopted by the Shipping Board to this end in 1921, under the provisions of the Merchant Marine Act of 1920, setting $30 per dead-weight ton as a fair price for ships in contrast with the rates of $210 to $225 set in 1919; but sales lagged. (Subsequently, the ships were sold for rates as low as $6.10 to $18 per dead-weight ton.)[1]

The associations of shipowners joined in announcing in 1925 that the ship operations of the government during the preceding five years had conclusively demonstrated "that the government cannot efficiently conduct a shipping business and that, with the exception of a few services, no marked progress has been made toward the goal of a permanent merchant marine in the foreign trade, notwithstanding the expenditure of millions of dollars from the public treasury." The greater efficiency resulting from private operation, they asserted, was necessary; but so was government assistance to overcome the handicaps intrinsic to American shipping.[2] This appeal for assistance was finally granted under the Jones-White Act of 1928, with its mail subsidy provisions. The sale of government-owned ships was accelerated after the passage of this act. This was due in measure to the fact that the Shipping Board had adopted a concurrent policy of guaranteeing to those purchasers who would subsequently be granted mail subsidies by the postmaster general that they would not be subjected to competition from Goverment-aided sources along the same routes. Purchases were made by operators with complete assurance that they would be granted mail subsidies as a consequence, although the act required advertising for competitive bids.[3]

The postmaster general's investigation in 1935 was to reveal that this emphasis upon aid to private ownership resulted in perversion of the intent of the law. Whereas Government officials were required by the Act of 1928 to award mail subsidy contracts by open competitive bidding, they negotiated private contracts with favored bidders and went through the "mere formality" of advertising the contracts. Numerous abuses developed in this period out of the diversion of grants under the Jones-White Act "to other than sound shipping operations." Direct government aid in mail pay, discounts in sales of Shipping Board vessels, and granting of low rates of interest on Shipping Board loans to private operators for construction of new ships and reconditioning of old ones accounted for an expenditure of over 162 million dollars by the government; this contrasted with a direct cash investment of about 85 millions by private mail contractors. Despite the expenditure of such substantial sums by the government it could be said "that comparatively little of the enormous grants . . . [had] gone into the building of a permanent merchant marine on a sound basis." [4]

Since scrambling to get on the "gravy train" proved of greater immediate concern than long-range planning for a permanent merchant marine, little could be expected by way of development of a well-trained and adequate merchant marine personnel during this period. Interest in the status of seamen was virtually nonexistent and was not even stirred by the problems of unemployment among seamen which followed the onset of depression in 1929.

MECHANICS OF EMPLOYER JOB CONTROL

The extent of union domination in job control extravagantly alleged by shipowners during the heyday of the seamen's organizations was nothing compared to the degree of actual employer domination during the period from 1921 to 1934. The West Coast shipowners coöperated in the administration of a shipping office, supplementing this control through the issuance of continuous discharge books. On the East Coast, continuous discharge books were issued and the formation of "coöperative" unions was encouraged among licensed and unlicensed personnel. The Shipping Board, through the placement activities of its Sea Service Bureau, was able to exercise control over its personnel.

Plans for the establishment of a shipowner employment agency were formulated by the Pacific American Steamship Association and the Shipowners' Association of the Pacific Coast in joint conference with the Waterfront Employers' Union of San Francisco. The Waterfront Employers' Union had previously demonstrated the success of its tactics in breaking the former Riggers' and Stevedores' Union in 1919, and in assisting to establish the "blue-book" Longshoremen's Association of San Francisco which had furnished no support to the seamen during the 1921 strike. The two shipowner associations decided in September 1921 to set up a jointly-operated Marine Service Bureau in San Francisco through which all member companies would have to obtain their crews. As a condition for employment, officers and unlicensed seamen were required to resign their union membership.

In a circular announcing its establishment, the shipowners stated that the bureau was intended to take charge of the "employment feature" which "has been the great lever that has enabled the representatives of the trade unions to cause difficulties between the men and employers." The fundamental role of the service was to be "a square deal for the employee," and its operation was to be "in the nature of a clearing house for all marine disputes." The seamen were welcomed by the bureau to present their grievances to a "labor committee, composed of the members of the two associations acting jointly, who will consider these complaints to determine the justice and, when warranted, to take the matter up with the individual owner for adjudication of such reported grievances." This procedure for handling the grievances of the men was intended to demonstrate to them that the shipowners would give more prompt and fair consideration "to any claims justly made than could delegates of any unions, and this without cost. . . ."[5]

The shipowners viewed the bureau as permitting the operation of the ships on a "business" basis. Continued high wages, the maintenance of stable labor relations, and reduction in turnover were all cited as advantages accruing from the bureau's operations.[6] The mechanical details of the operation of the Marine Service Bureau were simple. The men registered at the bureau when they wanted employment. They were assigned to jobs on a rotary basis, the man with the lowest number (that is, the one longest on the beach) got the job. The men who were shipped through the bureau were required to carry continuous discharge books which were issued by the bureau. These contained a complete description of the holder's sea service, including a rating of his service and of his personal character by each master under whom he served. The seaman turned the book over to the master whenever reporting on board ship, and it was kept by the master throughout the voyage.[7]

The continuous discharge books, of which 44,000 had been issued on the West Coast between 1922 and 1926, were reported by the operators to be satisfactory to the men. The manager of the Marine Service Bureau ascribed, among the manifold utilities of the book, the fact that it

provided a meal when the men were broke, and a bed when they had no place to sleep. It has been a certificate of good character when they have been picked up by police officers on suspicion. . . . It gives him a character and conduct rating that he is entitled to, as every human being is entitled to, when he is seeking employment; and our seamen show a commendable pride in holding a period of efficiency and honesty aboard ship.[8]

The American Steamship Owners' Association, once again primarily representing East Coast shipowning interests, did not seek to control the direct hiring process of its member companies. These members hired men through company employment offices, on the piers, or through shipping masters (crimps). However, efforts were made by the association to control the labor force through the use of continuous discharge books. The success of the book on the West Coast resulted in its adoption on the East Coast in November 1922, along with the advice of the Pacific American Steamship Association regarding the details of its operation. Within two years, over 35,000 books had been issued on the East Coast. Arrangements were also worked out whereby the shipowners' associations on both coasts would mutually recognize each other's books, thus providing for controls on a nationwide basis.[9]

East Coast ship operators were actively concerned with the establishment of "coöperating unions." According to Winthrop L. Marvin, vice-president of the American Steamship Owners' Association, a leader in the movement to "Americanize" the personnel of the American merchant marine, young American-born seamen had left what they called the "squarehead and dago" union to establish a union of their own — the American Seamen's Association. This association (whose chief founder was Nellie Bly), he reported, consisted of officers and unlicensed seamen as well as top supervisory personnel, such as marine superintendents and port captains, all of whom had "no anticipation of devoting their energies to agitate over wages and working conditions." Instead, the association was supposed to be "purely fraternal and patriotic" and its purpose was to ensure that foreigners would man coal burners and "juggle soup plates," while Americans received preference in working under the more pleasant conditions of oil-burning vessels.[10] Eventually, the shipowners' association recommended that its members give preference in employment to the members of this seamen's association. Similar preference was given to an association composed of the white leaders and membership who broke away from the Marine Cooks and Stewards' Union of the Atlantic Coast after the 1921 strike and established an independent organization whose purpose "was to coöperate with the shipping companies and were . . . absolutely averse to strikes and other arbitrary union methods."

The new Shipping Board, with Albert D. Lasker as chairman, announced its intention of adhering to the proposals made earlier by Admiral Benson which included the open-shop policy. The board's willingness to discuss wages and working conditions with the unions and to enter into formal agreements with them did not constitute any change in this position. The members of the board were divided on the unions' demand for passes to board Shipping Board vessels, and Chairman Lasker announced that he would confer on the matter with the "New York shipowners in an endeavor to secure mutual coöperation" on the matter. The upshot was that the board finally decided to deny passes to the unions.[11]

To carry out the "nondiscrimination" policy, Lasker issued instructions in August 1921 to all managers and operators of Shipping Board vessels providing that preference always be given to American citizens when crews were being engaged and that crews should be obtained through the Sea Service Bureau. The instructions also ordered that "no discrimination shall be practiced against any man because of his union or nonunion affiliations" under the penalty of withdrawal of Shipping Board vessels.[12]

Under the chairmanship of T. V. O'Connor (former president of the International Longshoremen's Association), Shipping Board chairman until 1933, the board continued its policy of entering into formal agreements with the licensed personnel and the longshoremen on the Atlantic and Gulf. The board made no effort to enter into formal agreements with the unions of unlicensed seamen after the ISU leaders had refused to accept open-shop conditions. On occasion, however, the board did meet with Furuseth and other ISU officials at their request. The board's actions were usually taken after "conference and frank discussion" with the private shipowners. The board granted passes to representatives of the ISU in November 1923 without prior consultation with the shipowners because it viewed the matter as being of "minor importance." However, the representatives of the American Steamship Owners' Association censured this action. Such concessions upon the part of the board were very rare, however, and unilateral actions of this nature did not recur.

The private shipowners actively supported the continuance of the Shipping Board's Sea Service Bureau as an employment agency for furnishing personnel on government-owned ships. Shipowners joined the board in lauding the bureau as a means of achieving the Americanization of the personnel of the merchant marine. A further effort to cooperate occurred when the board and the shipowners' associations joined unsuccessfully in supporting legislation to compel the universal use of the continuous discharge books.

The union view of these methods to achieve a more "business-like" mode of operating American ships was radically different from that of the Shipping Board and the private operators. An impartial observer reported that the seamen felt an intense antipathy toward the Marine Service Bureau, particularly because of its potentialities as a strikebreaking weapon. The bureau was charged with maintaining a current list of potential strikebreakers. The discharge book, or "fink book" as it was called by the seamen, received its share of dislike. The discharge book and the records of the bureau lent themselves to blacklisting; and the blacklisting was usually for "personal or political" reasons rather than because of an individual's capacities. It was charged that despite the rotary hiring system, there were loopholes for assigning men to jobs on the basis of favoritism. The staff of the bureau, reported as being composed of "uncompromising union-haters," were deputy sheriffs and were constantly armed.[13]

Action taken by the ISU against the Marine Service Bureau through the courts forced some adjustments in the bureau's activities, but the broader outlines of employer control remained unchanged. An initial action which charged the bureau with being a blacklisting device interfering unlawfully with the rights of free contract and a free labor market was lost when a circuit court decision found the bureau to be neither unfair nor discriminatory. A second action, in the case of *Anderson vs. Shipowners' Association,* was more successful: The Supreme Court, reversing lower courts, found that the activities of the association violated the antitrust laws in that it posted the wages to be paid by the members and that "when a seaman's turn comes, he must take the employment then offered or none, whether it is suited to his qualifications or whether he wishes to engage on the particular vessel or for the particular voyage and the officers of the vessels are deprived of the right to select their own men or those deemed most suitable." The association ceased posting wage scales and discontinued the requirement that all seamen had to be registered in the bureau and hired there. These adjustments in the bureau's operation made it possible for member companies to hire seamen outside the bureau.[14]

Furuseth's efforts through Congressional action to free the seamen from employer domination were equally unsuccessful. He charged the Sea Service Bureau with maintaining a deferred list, or blacklist, which served the purposes of the private shipowners. However, despite his demonstration that the bureau had no legal sanction and was completely a creature of the Shipping Board, it was not until 1934 that the bureau was abolished. He was equally unsuccessful in getting the shipowner-issued continuous discharge book, with its character rating, displaced by a government-issued book which would bear no reference to a seaman's character or efficiency in service. While the shipowners favored a government-issued book, they opposed exclusion of a rating of the seamen's service. Furuseth's proposal was enacted — but not until 1936 when a changed condition in union organization made it a measure obnoxious to the unions and palatable to the shipowners (see Chapter 7).

ECONOMICS OF EMPLOYER CONTROL

The seamen enjoyed little of the prosperity of the twenties, but felt the full impact of the depression of the thirties. Economic conditions deteriorated to the lowest levels; wages were reduced by about one-half since 1921. Except on the West Coast lumber schooners, overtime pay was eliminated; the two-watch system on deck had been restored, and in many instances hours worked exceeded those permitted under the Seamen's Act — the two watches to be worked by deck personnel and the three watches to be worked by engine-room personnel — for the law had no teeth.

Complete employer domination in hiring resulting from the rout of the unions was accompanied by changes in wages and working conditions designed to restore prewar levels. The initial downward adjustments, made effective on May 1, 1921, had been justified on the basis of reductions in the cost of living, widespread wage reductions in industry generally, and the depressed condition of the shipping industry. Wage rates were reduced by approximately 15 percent to rates of $72.50 per month for able seamen and firemen on Shipping Board as well as privately owned vessels on both the Atlantic and Pacific. Overtime pay was virtually eliminated, and equivalent time off was substituted. Firemen who did not stand regular watches (8 hours per day at sea) could be required to work 10 hours out of 24. Working hours in port were no longer fixed at 8 within a fixed period during the daytime, but were set at any 8 during the course of 24 hours. The provisions relating to the living conditions of the men, such as provision of bedding, were completely eliminated. Only the Shipowners' Association of the Pacific Coast, whose lumber schooner operating members relied on seamen experienced in and capable of loading and discharging, maintained overtime payment provisions and paid a higher rate of $77.50 to able seamen and firemen.[15]

Even these conditions, however, proved to be but temporary steps toward achieving a more complete "reversion to the status of the years preceding 1919." [16] Individual members of the steamship owners' associations were soon paying rates below the scales published by their parent associations and the Shipping Board. By September 1921, although there had been little further appreciable decrease in the cost of living, the American Steamship Owners' Association was already considering a further wage reduction because of the aggravation of the shipping depression. Shipping Board representatives joined the association in discussions regarding further reductions, with a view to adopting a uniform policy after the new year. The Shipping Board counseled further that wage reductions should be based on conservative policies, despite the opportunities for obtaining personnel at virtually any wage rates.[17]

The American Steamship Owners' Association announced a wage scale in January 1922 which reduced the rates for able seamen and firemen from $72.50 to $47.50 and $50 respectively, and decreased the rates for other unlicensed seamen by comparable amounts. While decreases to unlicensed personnel ranged from 20 to 35 percent, those for licensed officers were generally only about 15 percent.[18] In addition, the three-watch system was eliminated and the two-watch system on deck (twelve-hour workday at sea) was restored. The Pacific American Steamship Association, while following the lead of the American Steamship Owners' Association, regarded the wage reductions as being excessive and reduced rates by an average of about 12 percent — to a rate of $55 for able seamen and firemen. On the lumber schooners where rates were decreased by smaller amounts, a $65 rate was established for the key job classifications.[19]

The Shipping Board, in line with its policy of "collective bargaining" called union representatives to attend conferences with the Shipping Board to discuss wage reductions, following the actions of the private employers. The representatives of the unlicensed unions continued to refuse to participate contending that drastic wage cuts had been prede-cided. In the meetings with the licensed officers' union representatives, the union men expressed their opposition to the wage reductions in strong terms. It was reported by the board's Marine and Dock Division, however, that "they were finally induced to accept the reductions in the [friendly] spirit in which they were insisted upon." It was felt that their resentment was assuaged by entering into formal agreements for a definite period of six months. The Shipping Board established a wage scale which generally equaled or exceeded the scale of the Pacific American Steamship Association. The American Steamship Owners' Association commended the board for the manner in which it "approached and concluded a very knotty problem," arriving at a solution which was very close to "sound business lines"; however, it expressed the reservation that "we all realize wages, generally speaking, are still too high." [20]

Increases in the basic hours of work in all departments were accompanied by reductions in the manning scales on both privately owned and government-owned vessels, thus increasing still further the workload per man. The Shipping Board, to compensate for its higher wage scales, led the private operators in this approach to reduced operating costs. Manning scales on Shipping Board vessels were reduced in December 1921 to such an extent that a staff member of the board testified that Shipping Board vessels were "carrying a smaller complement than which prudent owners might carry . . . the board's complement is often far below that of both the private owners and the British vessels." [21]

Savings effected through these changes in wages and working conditions on Shipping Board vessels in operation in 1922 were estimated at five million dollars a year.[22] The continued deterioration of the American merchant marine during the twenties and early thirties, however, suggested that the ineffectuality of such palliatives as drastically reduced wages and working conditions indicated that additional and perhaps more basic weaknesses had to be overcome to cope with foreign competition. The scales established by the shipowners' associations were meaningless during the period of postwar depression when member companies could reduce wages at will; in some cases able seamen were being paid as little as $30 per month. With the upturn in the general level of shoreside wages in 1923, the shipowners were forced to raise the seamen's wages to avoid a possible shortage of men. The American Steamship Owners' Association increased its scale to that of the Shipping Board (for example, the rate of $55 for able seamen); but when the Shipping Board in turn increased its scale in May 1923 to $62.50 for able seamen, and put back into effect the three-watch system on deck, the association as a whole did not follow suit. In actual practice, however, most of the individual companies were finding it necessary to pay higher rates in order to retain their personnel. The Shipowners' Association of the Pacific Coast added a $5 increase in rates in 1923, apparently hoping to induce seamen experienced in lumber schooner operations to return to their former vocations.[23]

The Shipping Board was more responsive to external pressures for improvements in wages and working conditions during this period of the "return to normalcy" than were the private operators. A threatened strike by the ISU and an actual strike by the IWW Marine Transport Workers' Industrial Union early in May 1923 provided the immediate impetus for reëxamination of the status of seamen on Shipping Board vessels. Secretary of Labor Davis called President Harding's attention to the shortage of labor on land, and the consequent desertion of the seamen to land-based jobs to escape from the poor conditions which had been foisted upon them since 1921. He pointed out that the private operators were maintaining the pretense of paying a $55 rate by paying an additional bonus, "but urging the Shipping Board to fight the battle against an increase in the $55 rate." He suggested an increase of from $10 to $15 a month. He also suggested that the officials of the ISU be given passes to board Shipping Board vessels, an act which "would accomplish more than anything else in overcoming the activities of the IWW." [24]

Under these combined pressures, commissioners O'Connor and Benson met with the representatives of the ISU. After an investigation by a committee appointed by the board, the board announced a scale which increased wages by $7.50 generally (to $62.50 for able seamen; $65 for firemen on oil-burning ships, and $67.50 for firemen on coal-burners); granted the three-watch system on deck; an eight-hour day in port; and an increased manning scale. These adjustments were in line with those which had been made by many private operators.[25]

The wage levels attained in 1923 were generally maintained by the board and the private operators until the full impact of the depression was felt in 1929. However, the division of the men on deck into three watches instead of two proved to be a temporary concession on Shipping Board and privately owned East Coast ships; it was withdrawn when less difficulty was encountered in obtaining personnel. Many operators on the West Coast, however, were forced to grant the three-watch system in 1927 to get necessary personnel. But Furuseth's efforts to have the three-watch system restored on Shipping Board vessels in 1927 were successfully protested by the American Steamship Owners' Association.[26]

The sharp reduction in wages and working conditions immediately following the 1921 "strike," together with the shoreside depression attendant on postwar readjustment, had left a large force of unemployed seamen who were fertile field for organization by the "Wobblies." However, operator concern with the "radical" element among the personnel of the merchant marine had declined after 1923. The "weeding out" process permitted by the use of the continuous discharge books had eliminated the "undesirables." Low wages and poor working conditions had driven many experienced seamen from the sea; they had been supplanted by young men who went to sea for short periods and were not concerned with the permanent improvements in wages and working conditions which might be achieved through organization. Furuseth charged in 1928 that despite the fact there were some 156,000 men with able seamen's certificates to fill less than 30,000 jobs, there was a shortage of truly qualified men. Statutory requirements for able seamen were being met by employing men who had been issued certificates by local steamboat inspectors without any supporting evidence of claimed experience. This malpractice in obtaining certificates was not ended even after the Director of Steamboat Inspection called attention to the fact that such "procedure is not in accordance with the intent of the law." [27]

Despite the emphasis they placed on the need for Americanizing the merchant marine, private shipowners carried substantial numbers of alien personnel because Americans preferred the more attractive employment conditions on shore. Even the proportion of Americans which was placed by the Sea Service Bureau fell from 92 percent to 78 percent between 1922 and 1924; but by 1929, the proportion had again risen to 89 percent. Evidence regarding the number of aliens in the merchant marine was also furnished by the Commissioner of Navigation, who reported that the proportion of American citizens signing on before the Shipping Commissioners ranged from 50 percent in 1923 to 60 percent in 1929.[28]

Senator Hugo N. Black criticized the contradiction in the position taken by employers regarding the Americanizing of the merchant marine when he reported in 1936 that: "Our investigation showed that in spite of activities of certain interests to obtain subsidies, always based on the ground that it was for American labor, it developed that certain shipping interests were at the same time trying to have as high an exception as could be obtained so that as many foreigners as possible could be employed." This was borne out by the shipowners' opposition to measures supported by the ISU which would have had the effect of prohibiting the employment of Oriental and Filipino seamen on American ships. Strongest opposition to these measures came from the West Coast operators who argued that "There isn't a member of the association on the Pacific Coast that would not rather employ American citizens on his vessels, but in that Oriental trade, with our competition employing Orientals we, if we are going to compete with them, have got to be allowed some privileges and rights in that regard." The provision in the Jones-White Act requiring 50 percent of the crew on ships receiving mail subsidies to be American citizens was largely the result of the efforts of the shipowners, who opposed a larger percentage on the grounds that Americans were unwilling and unsuited to serve in the stewards' department.[29]

Furuseth's attacks upon the quality and efficiency of the personnel of the merchant marine during this period were met with indignant rebuffs by the Shipping Board and the private shipowners. The annual Merchant Marine Conferences conducted by the board from 1928 to 1934 would have been love feasts for the Shipping Board and private shipowners, but for the discordant notes of Furuseth's charges. These charges were given little credence; typical of answers to them were the following:

Our Americans . . . make the more efficient sailors. There may be something in it that they do not belong to a certain organization, and because of that possibility they are not so efficient in the minds of some people. [Laughter] But I am convinced that as a whole American seamen are just as efficient as those of any other nation. . . . There are American steamship owners and masters aboard ship quite as capable of discussing these matters as he [Furuseth], and why should we permit it to be said in this country that American seamen are disloyal, inefficient and cowardly? [30]

World-wide depression after 1929 and restrictive national economic policies were doubly effective in reducing the opportunities for profitable engagement in foreign shipping. The volume of cargo carried by American ships fell by 55 percent between 1929 and 1933. With the loss of business in the North Atlantic, many American passenger ships were diverted to use as part-time cruise ships to the West Indies. Many ships in both the foreign and coastwise trades were laid up. Some of these had skeleton crews aboard to keep them in readiness for going into operation on twenty-four-hour notice. Others were laid up completely, with only watchmen aboard.[31]

Ship lay-ups and reduced trade were accompanied by widespread unemployment among seamen. Employment opportunities for seamen were reduced by about 20 percent between 1929 and 1932.[32] Competition for employment among seamen, on the other hand, was increased by a substantially greater amount because many former seamen returned to the sea; fewer departed, continuity of service was greater; many young men who had never been to sea before now entered the industry.

A study by the U. S. Shipping Board indicated that shipping wages were reduced by approximately 15 percent between 1930 and 1932; subsistence costs were lowered by 35 percent; total payrolls, by 20 percent.

Recruits could be obtained to sign on as workaways at one cent a month in order to have a berth and food. Placements by the Sea Service Bureau dropped sharply from 65,000 in 1929 to 31,000 in 1931, while applicants increased in large numbers. Over 95 percent of those placed were now American citizens.[33]

To obtain employment, men were accepting jobs below their qualifications; men with officers' licenses were sailing as able seamen or oilers; and A.B.'s and oilers in whatever jobs they could obtain. Hiring practices in the industry were chaotic. On the East Coast, hiring was done by personnel managers for some companies, but in most cases by mates and boatswains on the piers. On the West Coast, while many men were hired through the shipowners' Marine Service Bureau, a substantial proportion were also hired on the piers. With the exception of the bureau, these hiring practices required the services of some central agent; and shipping masters furnished the various companies with men at 50¢ to $1 a head. Shipping masters, licensed under the laws of the State of New York, and presumably permitted legally to receive only a fixed fee from companies for furnishing men, were now reportedly receiving kickbacks from the men in violation of the law. Counterfeit A.B. certificates were being sold widely to many men who reportedly had no knowledge of the sea. The crimping evil was widespread again, particularly on the East Coast.[34]

Private charitable institutions aided the seamen in obtaining shoreside employment. The Federal Government furnished funds for relief beginning in November 1933. It was estimated in September 1934 that some 2300 seamen were being cared for by nine charitable institutions in New York alone, with at least 3000 additional idle seamen there.

Statistics alone cannot measure the problems facing the unemployed seamen. C. W. Sanders, Director of the Sea Service Bureau, described the results of a personal survey in October 1932 as follows:

I visited a number of steamship pier offices and found a noticeably large number of seamen outside of all piers. Even though there are no positions open on the ships docked, the men report daily in large numbers expecting that there may be a possible chance to be employed. In my conversation with marine superintendents, I find the majority of the seamen are keeping their jobs and are more contented than they have been for a number of years. The seamen who are not fortunate enough to be employed have in many cases listened to the organizers of "The Marine Workers Industrial Union" which is an IWW [sic] outfit that is causing all the discontent among the unemployed seamen and longshoremen. . . . The daily attendance of seamen at our New York branch is estimated at about 2500 men. We have the only waiting room in the port where seamen can come inside out of the weather and await a call for a position. . . .

He reported that some shipowners were permitting crews to remain aboard laid-up ships in order that they might have a place to sleep and to cook their own food.[35]

Living conditions on the ships, most of which had been jerry-built back under the Shipping Board program between 1919 and 1921, deteriorated along with economic conditions. The food was often poor. The crews' quarters contrasted sharply in their lack of adequacy and livability with the passengers' quarters, even on the newer ships. The *Marine Engineering and Shipping Review* described them authoritatively as follows in June 1936:

When the progress of ship design is considered, the matter of crews' quarters has hardly emerged from the sailing ship era. . . . The housing of large numbers of men in open forecastles, the crowding of entire crews in spaces never designed for that purpose, the lack of proper washrooms with decent sanitary equipment, the disinterestedness of many commanding officers in providing for regular cleaning of crews' quarters on the ship's time and the lack of adequate insulation on steel decks, bulkheads and doors, surrounding such quarters, are but a few matters which should claim the attention of the enlightened ship operators.[36]

This view was supported by a survey undertaken for the American Steamship Owners' Association in 1936 and 1937 which found that there were frequently as many as fifteen to twenty-five and sometimes up to forty members of the crew berthed in a single room on passenger ships; that with but one exception, recreational facilities for the crew were lacking and that on many ships "not even the primitive requirement of a chair or bench to sit on had been provided"; that with regard to sanitary facilities, there was "complete lack of privacy on many ships"; and that men had to wash from pails frequently, and where there were washbasins, only cold water was furnished and seamen wanting hot water had to resort "to a pail heated on the steam pipes." [37]

The fruits of these conditions were summarized in a Maritime Commission report in 1937, as follows:

the shipping industry is now paying for the shortsightedness in repressing labor for so many years. Some of the operators who paid low wages during the depression were at the same time receiving substantial subsidies from the Government for the preservation of an American standard of living. By denying their employees the right to organize, shipowners created a condition favorable to un-American doctrine. . . .

COMATOSE CONDITION OF THE ISU

The entire labor movement had suffered a setback from the postwar open-shop drive which had been aided by the conditions produced by the depression of 1921; but the seamen's unions had been laid low as if by a tidal wave. By 1923, the ISU membership had returned to prewar levels; even this is no complete measure of the extent of deterioration in the seamen's unions.

The impotency of the unions confronted by complete catastrophe was bound to bring to the fore the disaffection which had been smoldering against the inflexibility of the policies of the union officials in facing changing conditions. Rank-and-file rebellions against union leadership, aided by IWW members and sympathizers, had developed on both coasts. Within Furuseth's bailiwick, the Sailors' Union of the Pacific, the movement had obtained almost complete control under the leadership of J. Vance Thompson, who had been elected editor of the *Seamen's Journal* in January 1921. Upon Furuseth's insistence, the ISU had taken action to discontinue the *Journal* as its official organ. During the course of the "strike" on the West Coast, the *Journal* had become increasingly vocal in demanding that "Transport Workers Awake," and actively support the formation in every port of marine transport worker federations of seamen and longshoremen. This idea was hardly new in view of the earlier City Front and Waterfront Federations of San Francisco.

Furuseth's opponents had been strong enough to obtain an overwhelming support from the SUP membership to override ratification of the agreement offered by the Shipowners' Association of the Pacific during the 1921 strike. This agreement had provided for open-shop conditions. Thereupon, Furuseth had rushed back to San Francisco to persuade the seamen to return to work, proclaiming the failure of the strike and advising those who could to leave the sea for the time being. He denounced as IWW members those who had supported a federation of marine unions. Upon his recommendations, the membership had then voted to terminate the strike.[38]

Furuseth and other leaders of the ISU now turned their guns on the radical elements within the Sailors' Union of the Pacific. A new publication, *The Seaman*, was started by the ISU in October 1921 to fight the *Journal*. During the four issues it lasted, the columns of *The Seaman* were replete with attacks upon the disruptionist and conspiratorial tactics of the "Wobblies." In person, Furuseth sought to recapture control of the Sailors' Union by appealing directly to the membership to support the old policies and to expel the radicals whom he accused of conspiring with the IWW. His forceful personality was largely responsible for his success in regaining control. Thompson and about thirty additional members were expelled on charges of being radicals and members or supporters of the IWW in violation of the SUP's constitutional ban on membership in any dual organization which opposed the principles of the Sailors' Union of the Pacific.[39]

To guard the union against any such "insidious" attacks in the future, the constitution was amended to make the chairman, who had formerly been elected at each meeting, a permanent official, and to facilitate trial and expulsion for membership in dual organizations. In addition, the *Seamen's Journal* was turned over to the ISU.

On the East Coast, immediately after the strike, there was also a threat to the established leadership of the Eastern and Gulf Sailors' Association from a group within the union which was charged with consisting of IWW members or supporters. This threat was met by returning the union headquarters from New York, the center of insurgent activities, to Boston.

The leadership of the unions affiliated with the ISU were to weather the storm; but their victory was to prove meaningless. They were to be leaders without any following during the next decade. Following his successful effort "to wash the Sailors' Union clean," Furuseth permitted himself one of his few optimistic statements in forecasting "it is possible to save all the organizations and it is almost certain, nay, I may say certain that the Sailors will come back with lessons learned from the past." [40] However, it was to take more than a decade of bitter experience with complete employer domination before his forecast was to be realized.

Lacking the strength furnished by strong and widespread union organization, widespread strikes to obtain recognition or economic improvements were doomed to failure. Furthermore, the ISU leaders were unwilling to resort to strikes, apparently in the hope that, by contrast, their position would place them in a more favorable light than the Wobblies. When the IWW struck on both coasts in May 1923, Furuseth warned against participation in the strike. His warning went unheeded on the West Coast, however; the shipowners retaliated by extending the Marine Service Bureau's activities to San Pedro. The fact that the ISU officials opposed the strike was cited by Secretary of Labor Davis in suggesting to President Harding that the ISU officials be given passes to board Shipping Board vessels.[41]

Under the existing conditions of employer domination, the only actions possible to obtain redress of grievances were on an isolated and individual basis. Under penalty of mutiny charges if they struck at sea, the seamen were denied use of the landworkers' tactic of striking on the job. Their action was necessarily limited to strikes when the ships were in port. "Wobbly" philosophy and tactics were sympathetic toward "job actions" by a few men against individual ships. Since no recognition was granted the ISU for the purpose of meeting with the employers regarding wages and working conditions, even that conservative union was forced to recommend use of its own version of job action — the "oracle." This ISU tactic called for the men to leave a boat just before it sailed; the IWW tactic called for the men, once aboard, to refuse to operate a ship so that it was prevented from leaving the harbor or proceeding on its voyage. The "oracle" had to be used with caution because the shipowners identified it with IWW tactics. Furthermore, the "oracle" could be used with greatest effect only on the lumber schooners where the special experience requirements of the trade gave seamen assurance that it would be difficult for shipowners to replace them. Although the tactic was used, ISU officials apparently sanctioned its use only rarely. Both the ISU and the "Wobbly" tactics could only achieve temporary and limited gains. Ringleaders could be displaced and prevented from obtaining further employment in the industry through the employer-issued continuous discharge book.

The Seamen's Act provided recourse to find additional impediments to place in the way of ship operation (for as Furuseth put it, "the Seamen's Act is not a roasted goose, it is a gun with which to shoot the goose."). Seamen demanded their discharge with full pay where shipowners were violating the provision for two watches for men on deck and three watches for men in the engine room. Where no violations of the act existed, the seamen exercised the right the act granted to demand discharge with half pay in any port where the ship might load or discharge cargo.[42]

These tactics reveal the precarious existence which the ISU and its constituent unions were able to maintain during this period. Where experienced men continued to be at a premium as on the lumber schooners, and where wages and working conditions were maintained at high levels, some semblance of organization continued on the West Coast. On the East Coast, organization was maintained among the cooks and stewards. The ISU continued to hold annual conventions for several years, but with dwindling funds and customary inactivity; only three conventions were held between 1927 and 1936. The membership of the ISU affiliated unions, which had dropped from 115,000 to 50,000 within a few months after the 1921 debacle, decreased further to 15,000 by 1926; and 5,000 during the depression years.[43]

Prompted apparently by fear of the inroads of the Wobblies and Wobbly sympathizers who might seek to change the basic organization of the ISU, the ISU leadership made an abortive effort in 1922 to strengthen the central authority of the executive board through constitutional revisions radically altering the seat of authority in the international union and its constituent unions. (The following statement was added to the preamble: "The absent members, who cannot be present, must have their interests guarded from what might be the results of excitement and passions aroused by persons or conditions . . ."; and the revisions sought to prevent such changes.) Authority formerly vested in the individual unions was now given to the executive board of the ISU. The board was given the final authority to issue and revoke charters of constituent unions, and to supervise use and distribution of strike funds. Direct control of membership of the constituent unions was provided for the first time through a provision which excluded from membership any individual who was a member of a dual organization or an organization hostile to the ISU; and the provisions of the ISU constitution were made binding on the individual members of the constituent unions as well as upon the unions themselves. Formerly hope had frequently been expressed that the unions on the respective coasts would work together. But now, the constitution clearly spelled out the organization of the constituent unions into districts (Atlantic and Gulf, Pacific, and Great Lakes) and into separate district unions (deck, engine, stewards); it provided for joint district union meetings for educational purposes and for the development of coöperation; and it delineated the functions of the respective district committees.

Furuseth characterized the constitutional revisions as involving a change from "a government by discretion into a government by law . . . with penalties attached to the violation of the law." However, these changes proved to have little significance either in strengthening the ISU during this period, or in warding off the IWW inroads. The ISU continued to have the same lack of influence in the affairs of its constituent unions which characterized its entire history; its organizational activities were almost nonexistent, and the constituent unions had few relations with other unions in their respective districts.[44]

The major activities of the ISU during the twenties and thirties centered around the efforts of Andrew Furuseth: first, to obtain some degree of recognition for "legitimate trade unions" of the seamen (as Secretary of Labor Davis distinguished them), in order to counter the effects of the Wobblies; and secondly to undermine employer domination through enforcement of the Seamen's Act, and reinforcement of any shortcomings of that act through court action and legislation. While Furuseth was able to enlist the support of several Congressmen, he was unable to overcome the basic unwillingness of the Republican administration of the "normal" twenties to intervene in behalf of labor.

In 1920, Furuseth had cautioned against restrictive labor legislation arising out of the antiradical hysteria. Furuseth had always been an opponent of the IWW tenets, however, which were at odds with everything for which he stood and fought since they opposed industrial unionism to craft unionism; saw skill play an increasingly smaller role under modern industrial conditions of mass production; emphasized direct action, opposing collective bargaining and time agreements; and were against engaging in any political activity. In Furuseth's eyes, the IWW and the shipowners were basically in agreement for "as the employer is utterly and absolutely opposed to any qualification of skill that he is bound to respect, so the IWW stands in exactly the same position. . . ."

Following the strike of 1921, Furuseth's philosophical antipathy to the Wobblies blossomed into open hatred. His experience with their infiltration into the Sailors' Union of the Pacific and his fear that their strength was growing at the expense of the ISU unions after 1921 made him join the ranks of those who were not opposed to the use of repressive methods against the Wobblies. He expressed his view of the IWW and its activities in no uncertain terms: "Like a blighting pest coming through the air, IWWism has descended upon place after place to leave nothing but wreckage, misery and despair behind." [45]

Furuseth sought to use action against the Wobblies as an opening wedge for restoring the ISU and its constituent unions to their previous role of recognized spokesmen for the seamen. The reason for the IWW and Communist influence in the ISU unions, he charged, could be attributed to the shipowners' failure to grant preference in hiring to his organization during the postwar expansion of the merchant marine. Now, he proposed to private shipowners and to the Shipping Board, ". . . in order to get the wobblies out of the vessels the owners ought to give us passes for the docks and ships . . ." in order . . . "that we . . . point them out."

The Shipping Board granted the ISU representatives some passes to board its vessels, but the private shipowners rebuffed all advances of the ISU on the grounds that its members, too, were "practically" under the control of the IWW and had "lost the privilege of collective bargaining and the control of shipping arrangements, and stand today on a platform based almost solely on class hatred — sinister, intense hatred for the American shipowner, whether private, corporate, or federal." [46]

Furuseth's unsuccessful attempts to obtain a renewal of relations with the shipowners were accompanied by renewed activity in Washington. He enlisted the support of numerous Congressmen for his legislative efforts, including both the elder and younger Senators LaFollette, Senator Shipstead of Minnesota, and Senator King of Utah. In virtually every session of Congress Furuseth-sponsored proposals were introduced whose purpose was to strengthen the Seamen's Act where it had failed. One frequently recurring proposal included a provision prohibiting American flag ships and foreign flag ships which entered American ports from carrying among their crews any seamen who could not enter the United States as immigrants, unless such seamen were citizens of the country under whose flag they were sailing. This proposal — justified by Furuseth in terms of the number of Orientals deserting in American ports, who he declared, sailed solely for the purpose of entering the United States illegally — would have had the effect of keeping Oriental and lascar seamen off American and foreign ships, except those flying the Japanese flag. A companion feature of this proposal was the requirement that all ships depart with the same number in the crew as they had upon arrival. This measure was successfully opposed by American shipowners, supported by foreign shipowners, on the grounds that it was a device to give the jobs to American seamen and would be to the competitive disadvantage of American shipping enterprise.[47]

Reference has already been made to the efforts of the ISU by court action and by statute to overcome the suffocating effects of employer job control through employer-controlled employment agencies and employer-issued continuous discharge books. In view of the weakness of the unions, the ISU hoped elimination of employer control might be accomplished by placing the employment of the seamen under the jurisdiction of the U. S. shipping commissioners. It contemplated continuous discharge books issued by the government and containing no references to character or efficiency. East and West Coast operators joined in opposing these proposals on the grounds that only the "lawless" element among the seamen would desire the elimination of character ratings.[48]

All of these efforts, which occupied most of Furuseth's energies and involved the expenditure of much of the ISU funds, accomplished only minor and transitory victories. The Shipping Board granted passes to the ISU, but maintained its open-shop policy. Politically, the sole achievement was inclusion of a provision in the Jones-White Act of 1928 whereby 50 percent of the crew on ships receiving mail subsidies had to be American citizens; the percentage was to be stepped up to two-thirds after four years. The specific exclusion of Filipinos from citizenship under this act was viewed with additional approval by ISU officials.

DIRECT ACTION BY THE WOBBLIES

The intense hatred of the IWW for the craft organization of the AFL, the stress placed by the IWW on direct action, and its antagonism toward political activity could only result in an impenetrable wall of hostility between the ISU and its leaders and the Marine Transport Workers' Industrial Union of the IWW. This organization had its origins among the Spanish firemen on the Atlantic in 1912 who had resented their treatment at the hands of the "Anglo-Saxon" leadership of the Atlantic Coast firemen's union. The IWW union had been able to maintain a precarious organization among these seamen during the period immediately following. Its main source of strength for several years, however, was the predominantly Negro local of longshoremen in Philadelphia which had been organized in 1913. The successes of the ISU during and immediately following the war restricted the growth of the IWW union among seamen. Growing unrest within the rank and file of labor, and an influx of many Wobblies and Wobbly sympathizers into the ISU unions from 1919 to 1921 weakened the control exercised by the ISU leadership. The virtual collapse of the ISU with the 1921 "strike" resulted in vigorous acceleration of IWW organizational activity among marine transport workers.

The Marine Transport Workers regarded the ISU as an abhorrent symbol of a departed era. It saw the ISU as the product of "the days of wooden ships and iron-headed men"; and classed it and the International Longshoremen's Association as "outworn institutions . . . [ready] for the junk pile . . . [that] don't fit in with the 'Electric Drive,' the 'Radio-compass' and the 'manless ship'. . . ." Craft organization, according to the MTWIU, promoted "organized scabbing" by one craft upon another. The ISU efforts to obtain recognition were interpreted as proof that the leaders of "capitalistic" trade unions were seeking to assure "the bosses that they have the unions under good control." [49]

Furuseth, for his activities to obtain the passage of the Seamen's Act, had been criticized as being a "faker" who had "drained the treasury" of the ISU. His continued efforts to obtain the enforcement of the act after 1921 were regarded as waste expenditure of valuable funds which "should have been spent for organization purposes" instead of being "handed over to a bunch of grafting lawyers," while "all radical and active seamen on the Pacific Coast were driven from the ships" by means of the Marine Service Bureau and the continuous discharge books. The Wobbly journal, the *Marine Worker,* announced on behalf of the seamen that they "are getting tired of being continually saved by Andy and at the same time seeing the conditions of forty years ago being forced upon them." The Wobblies derisively termed the Seamen's Act a "fraud" and "delusion."

The efforts of Furuseth and other ISU leaders to curry favor with the Shipping Board and the shipowners only added to the hatred of craft unionism. The granting of passes to ISU delegates to board Shipping Board vessels was cited as evidence that the ISU leaders were "professional stools" and "leeches in human form." Furuseth's charges that the Wobblies were being protected by the shipowners were answered with a request for an investigation and the countercharge that Furuseth was aiding and abetting the trial and imprisonment of seamen under the California criminal syndicalist law. The Wobblies attacked Furuseth's motives by calling him everything from a "reactionary" and "personification of narrow American bigotry" to a being unfit "to be called a Judas; a slimy, crawling snake, weaving his way through the labor movement." [50]

The Marine Transport Workers' Industrial Union followed the IWW pattern of aims closely. It sought to organize all workers engaged in marine transportation, at sea or on shore, without "distinction of race or creed" and to embrace "all the workers of the whole world" in "One Big Union of all Marine Workers of the World. . . ." Its ultimate goal was to achieve sufficient power "to enforce our World Wide Marine Strike and Demand (not beg) Universal Wages and Working Conditions." The international organization would seek a universal wage scale, equalized at the highest level. Its immediate economic goals were the three-watch system; double-time pay for overtime and holiday work; good food; decent living conditions; and a universal wage scale, with rates equivalent to those paid skilled mechanics for similar work ashore.

Greatest emphasis in structural organization was placed upon the ship delegates system. By assuring a maximum of democratic representation, it was felt, this system would assure a strong foundation. This MTWIU democracy was pointed out as being the basic distinction between the MTWIU and the ISU.

The MTW sought to achieve its aims through purely economic methods, as did the IWW unions generally. The emphasis was upon widespread strike activity and job actions on individual ships; with increased emphasis upon the latter as the former encountered constant reverses. Maritime strikes were called frequently during 1922 and 1923. The major effort during this period was a general strike in April 1923, affecting marine, lumber, oil, and construction workers on the West Coast. The first demand in all phases of this strike was for "release of class-war prisoners"; second the economic demands for the particular industry.[51]

In the case of the MTW these economic demands were for a $20 increase in the Shipping Board scale, with private owners to pay an equivalent scale; payment of the American scale by all foreign vessels signing men on in American ports; an eight-hour day and forty-four-hour week in port; and payment for overtime work. On the West Coast, the strike was effective for a short period in paralyzing the intercoastal trade. No negotiations were attempted by the union however; and, as one observer reported, "It was a joyous demonstration of power. It lasted a month and was called off willingly enough after the Los Angeles police department made wholesale arrests." According to the ISU, the strike resulted in the extension of the operations of the Marine Service Bureau to San Pedro. On the East Coast, the IWW threat to strike coincided with an independent announcement by the American Steamship Owners' Association increasing its scale to equal that of the Shipping Board. The ISU leaders had also been asking for wage increases, but they had made it clear that no strike was intended. However, the Marine Cooks and Stewards had announced that they would ship no men during the strike. Although early in the strike, the MTW leaders predicted mass support in New York, they were later forced to admit that only about 900 of the 30,000 seamen employed in that port had gone out.[52] The strike failed on the East Coast and it was dubious whether any gains could be attributed to it.

Other sporadic strikes were called. A five-day strike was called on the West Coast to protest the conviction of twenty-seven seamen and long-shoremen for violating the criminal syndicalist law. A strike was called on the East Coast in support of the longshoremen in October 1923, despite the fact that the longshoremen had not supported the MTW during the "general strike" in April. It was reported that the smaller ship operators had been willing to come to terms with the MTW during this October strike, but that the union had refused on the grounds that it would gain its demands from all or none. As a result, it gained nothing. All these strike activities achieved little or nothing. Even had there been any immediate success, the MTW would not have been prepared to capitalize on such gains by formal agreements. During the two years following the unsuccessful 1923 strikes, therefore, increased reliance was placed upon "job action."[53]

In March 1925, an effort was made to inject new life into the organization by calling the First International Conference of the Maritime Workers of the Western Hemisphere, including delegates from the transport workers of several South American countries. The conference went on record in support of an international strike in 1925 "to rectify the abominable conditions prevalent in the Marine Industry." An unsuccessful fifteen-day strike was called during September 1925 in "sympathy with the striking seamen of Great Britain, Australia, South Africa, Denmark and China" and in protest against bad conditions and wage cuts on American ships.

A second international conference, held at Montevideo in March 1926, was attended by representatives of South American marine transport workers and of the Red International of Labor Unions. This meeting was followed by a strike on the part of the claimed membership of 25,000 "throughout the world," but appears to have had virtually no effect on shipping operations.[54]

Continued failure in strike activities resulted in a renewed emphasis on job action. The numerically few Wobblies could exercise proportionately greater influence by using the job action tactic than through meaningless strikes. Job action was described as involving the crew of a single ship, "when enough get aboard a ship, they should agitate and get the crew together, and when the captain says 'let go,' hold on and then present your demands by means of a committee and 99 times out of a hundred you will be victorious."

The MTW failed to achieve any significant gains: its claim to internationalism was hardly well-founded, its foreign branches consisted merely of sea-going American Wobblies; employer control was too well entrenched to be overcome by its loose organization. Its members were discriminated against in obtaining lodging where officials of charitable lodging houses for seamen heeded the call of shipowners "to take a positive stand against agitators of the IWW" and refuse use of their buildings "to this lawless organization"; they were subject to prosecution under the criminal syndicalism laws in some states.

The failure of the MTW to achieve widespread support was acknowledged after 1926 in the adoption of a "sobering-up" tendency to place greater emphasis upon obtaining immediate economic gains rather than upon pursuing "the Ideal with its dazzling shafts from the Sun of one Utopia." However, this failed to accomplish the expected revival of the organization. The major significance of the MTW in the growth of seamen's organization was its tradition of militancy, its emphasis upon job action, and its persisting influence among seamen. Despite doctrinal differences, it contributed directly to the Communist-dominated Marine Workers' Industrial Union in the matter of tactics and economic demands.

DEPRESSION AND THE COMMUNISTS

Depression provided impetus to the entry of a new rival union into the maritime labor situation, the organization of the Marine Workers' Industrial Union as an affiliate of the Communist Trade Union Unity League. The Communists' active entry into the maritime field was foreshadowed in 1926 when the International Seamen's Club was organized with recreational facilities for members of both ISU and IWW unions who were "urged to organize and to struggle against the constantly worsening conditions." In 1928, the Marine Workers' Progressive League was organized to engage directly in agitation for improvements in the status of the seamen. It was not until the next stage of development, the reorganization of the Marine Workers' Progressive League into the Marine Workers' League in 1929, that the Communist program began to be "conducted in a more systematic manner and the organization began to emerge from a propaganda stage and became a class struggle organization conducted as a Union and the leader in the struggles of the Marine Workers." The metamorphosis in the Communist position was complete, at least temporarily, when the Marine Workers' Industrial Union was organized in 1930.

The Communist Marine Workers' Industrial Union attacked both the ISU and the IWW. Furuseth was attacked on the grounds of having diverted "the discontent of the seamen into ineffective legal channels and sabotaged and discouraged strike action; [he] has divided the ranks of the workers over the issue of race and nationality; has supported and proposed reactionary bills before Congress . . . aimed especially at the foreign born. . . ." The IWW leaders were attacked with equal vehemence as disrupters of the "united front of the workers" who, "while speaking of 'mass action' and general strike," failed to lead any action of the unemployed and opposed unemployment insurance. The "nonpolitical" IWW was accused of playing "the boss' politics by telling the workers they have 'no interest in politics.'"

The Marine Workers' Industrial Union announced its purpose was to unite all workers in the marine industry, including licensed and unlicensed seamen, longshoremen, and harborworkers; and to "lead them in their struggle against the employers for better working and living conditions and for ultimate freedom from wage slavery." The union declared it would not "handle ammunition for, or take part in, any imperialist wars . . . will defend the Soviet Union, the only workers' government in the world; . . . will not man or load ships to transfer marines to be used against the workers of any other country." The MWIU was prepared to organize all marine workers into one union regardless of "race, color or rank." [55]

The deterioration in wages and working conditions as the depression reached its lowest levels after 1932, and the increase in unemployment among seamen, provided the MWIU with effective weapons for increasing its influence. The MWIU demanded immediate unemployment compensation and the passage of an unemployment insurance bill; liberalized care at marine hospitals; three watches; elimination of the practice of workaways, or employment of seamen at nominal wages; abolition of all blacklists; the establishment of Central Shipping Bureaus under the seamen's control; and immediate recognition of Soviet Russia. A delegation of seamen was sent by the MWIU to demand federal relief for seamen.

The MWIU used the job action tactic frequently after 1932, adopting the strategy of concentrating upon the ships of one line. Having a limited following, the MWIU had no choice but to leave strike action to the individual crews. It was reported that about fifty job actions were called on the ships of the Munson Line during the period of a year, with winning of minor concessions. However, these victories proved to be of a limited and temporary nature, the MWIU journal, the *Marine Workers Voice*, explained, because: "we did not convince the Munson crews to stay on the ships after victories and make it possible to develop company scale action." The MWIU claimed greater success in the establishment of a seamen-controlled Central Shipping Bureau in Baltimore which was reported to have been in control of 85 percent of all shipping, and to have overcome the influence of the crimps in that port.

The MWIU, like the MTWIU, emphasized the central role of the ship's delegate in the organizational process. But this union and its other Communist counterparts had learned from the failure of the IWW that success in achieving permanent organization called for emphasizing and using the immediate grievances of the seamen. The tactics were described thus: "Such committee might be just temporary, elected to demand better food, overtime pay or remedy some other immediate grievance. But the Marine Workers' Industrial Union fights to make these committees permanent, to establish on every ship and dock a United Front Committee, that will be the daily leader in the struggle against the bosses and for better conditions and wages." Weak numerically, the MWIU hoped to enhance its effectiveness by getting control of the leadership of all organized and unorganized groups of seamen by this means. Ship's delegates were advised to counter the "Red Scare" by pointing out that while "there are Communists in the MWIU . . . it is not a 'Communist organization.' " [56]

The MWIU claimed a membership of 12,000 longshoremen and seamen in 1934. However, the same accusation could be leveled against it that it had leveled against the IWW — it failed to get any mass support. While it concentrated on immediate gains, it was unable to gain the confidence of the mass of the seamen. With the resurgence of labor organization under the National Recovery Act, it was to the ISU that the seamen flocked. The Communists, like the IWW, however, contributed a page of militancy in the history of seamen's organization and provided lessons in organization and tactics which were to be used with more lasting effect in the future.

CHAPTER 6

RESURGENCE AND DISORGANIZATION, 1933–1937

BACKDROP OF TURMOIL

The National Industrial Recovery Act, enacted in 1933 to cope with the depression through government-encouraged industry organization to control competition and through efforts to raise mass purchasing power, was also to infuse new life into the labor movement. The apparent protection promised to collective bargaining by section 7A of the NIRA, with its provision that employers should not interfere with their employees' right to "organize and bargain collectively through representatives of their own choosing," offered an immediate impetus to organization, especially among the largely unorganized workers in the new mass production industries. The lack of an adequate administrative machinery to enforce actual collective bargaining between employers and organizations representing their employees left a void, however, which could be filled only by economic strife; first, because of the rapid development of labor organization encouraged even by the limited scope of the act; second, because of the long-festering grievances of workers; and third, because of the continued refusal of employers in such industries as steel, automobiles, and shipping to deal with the unions.

With the widespread resurgence of the labor movement after 1933, stirrings were inevitable among the seamen; they had been laboring under conditions which were especially degrading and irritating. The revulsion against employer control stimulated the rise of militant rank-and-file groups. These groups gained strength from the failure of the NRA shipping code negotiations, the unwillingness of the shipowners to grant recognition and engage in collective bargaining even with the conservative ISU unions, and from the apparent readiness of the conservative ISU leaders to accept the restricted concessions offered by the employers. The conflicts of the period, therefore, were expressions of the demand for recognition and acceptance of what were, *de facto*, new organizations and their young militant leaders both within the established trade union community and by the shipowners. The new leadership had little truck with the policies of the old-line leadership as it sought to fill the organizational void. The new policies and alliances were intermixed with both ideological and pragmatic elements. But these rested on shifting sands which were readily dispersed by the impact of the AFL-CIO split, and the altered status resulting from employer recognition.

As had been true several decades earlier, the foundation for the organizational drive among seamen was again to come from the West. Now, however, it was the longshoremen in San Francisco who were to set the stage for a showdown battle between waterfront employers and workers which developed in 1934. They were joined by the seamen in their famous prolonged strike, and out of this effort to avoid isolation in the face of a common powerful adversary developed the Maritime Federation of the Pacific. Common fear of isolation from the labor movement at large, when the IWW and Communist influences were pressing for a single maritime union, produced this loose federation of unions of marine transport and related workers, organized to provide a common program and common strategy. Despite the fundamental differences regarding program and tactics which developed early between the new militant leaders, Harry Lundeberg and Harry Bridges, the federation was able to continue as an active counterforce to the employers at crucial moments until 1937 when the basic cleavage in the labor movement made this limited expedient impossible. The federation served also as an additional shield against efforts by the employers to bypass the new leaders and to deal with the ISU officials.

The development of widespread militant organization on the West Coast had a direct bearing upon the status of East Coast shipping labor relations. West Coast operators sought to enlist the support of the East Coast ship operators for a joint drive against the unions. While no more favorable to collective bargaining than their leading colleagues on the West Coast, East Coast shipowners could rely on less aggressive tactics to achieve similar ends. The conservative ISU leaders, recognized by the East Coast operators, were able to maintain their hold on the East Coast unions for a time. They could be relied upon to keep the militant rank and file, who were seeking conditions comparable to those on the West Coast, from obtaining control. The efforts to perpetuate themselves in office became rallying cries for the rank-and-file insurgents, whose efforts were heightened by a Communist clique which had entered those unions after recognition had been achieved. Demands for West Coast levels in wages and working conditions were coupled with efforts to throw out the entrenched officials who had been satisfied to accept the lesser levels.

Job actions were carried out by the eastern insurgents on intercoastal ships in West Coast ports where support of the West Coast unions was assured.

Union recognition was granted by the shipowners on both coasts only under duress; there were no accompanying changes in outlook and policies to ensure that collective bargaining would actually be achieved. Continued anti-union activity by West Coast employer organizations, in which shipowners were prominent, created mutual distrust and hostility and made the unions feel that they too had to organize and unite to strengthen "their position against the expected counterattack of organized antiunionism." "As a result . . . the course of labor relations in California . . . when organization gains were made, has been vexed by sympathetic strikes, sweeping organizing drives, and the use of the secondary boycott, so-called 'hot cargo' tactics."

The issues on both coasts were met jointly in the fall of 1936. The West Coast shipowners had demanded that the entire pattern of labor-management relationships be made the subject of renewed arbitration. Their demand to resubmit to arbitration the question of control of hiring through union hiring halls was viewed by the unions as another effort to undermine union status. The issue was met by a strike lasting ninety-nine days, with the ultimate victory going to the unions. Defying the ISU officials, East Coast insurgents joined in support of the West Coast strike to demonstrate their strength and to call attention to their grievances. Although the insurgents were initially successful in causing widespread tie-ups in East Coast shipping operations, the activities of the ISU leaders in furnishing replacements inspired so many defections in the insurgent ranks that their strike had to be called off before the West Coast strike ended. The strike served to demonstrate the weakness of the ISU leadership and the potential strength of the insurgents; thus, it was a direct factor contributing to the formation, shortly, of a new East Coast union representing all the unlicensed departments — the National Maritime Union.

THE NIRA

Governmental recognition in the National Industrial Recovery Act of the right of workers to organize without employer interference brought new life to the maritime unions as well as to the labor movement generally. Soon after the enactment of NIRA, West Coast longshoremen signed authorizations expressing their desire to be represented by the ILA, and repudiating the employer-dominated "blue book" union. The long dormant ISU took on new life, and the venerable Andrew Furuseth returned to San Francisco in July 1933 to stimulate and direct the work of the organization. The limitations of NIRA assistance in face of intransigent employer opposition to union recognition and collective bargaining was soon apparent. Only trial by economic battle could prove that the strength of worker organization was capable of achieving its intended purpose of collective bargaining and improved wages and working conditions.

The unions affiliated with the ISU hopefully prepared drafts of respective shipping code labor provisions for the Atlantic and Gulf, Pacific, and Great Lakes. On the Atlantic, proposals were drawn up jointly by the unions; the three Pacific Coast unions formulated their demands separately. Subsequently, the ISU coördinated the union demands to meet the employer proposals. The ISU proposed a National Maritime Board, made up of shipowners' and seamen's representatives to adjust differences, determine wages and working conditions, and operate joint employment offices. This was modeled after the British system.

The Communist-organized Marine Workers' Industrial Union, claiming to represent 12,000 seamen and longshoremen, included all the ISU demands in its program; in addition, it proposed a guaranteed annual wage. Both the ISU and the MWIU attacked the shipowner refusal to grant union recognition.[1]

The union proposals were submitted to the shipowners together with requests for conferences. The shipowners adopted a policy of opposition to union recognition which they maintained throughout the Shipping Code proceedings. They opposed the proposal for the formation of a Maritime Board. Furthermore, in all meetings, the shipowners announced that they were recognizing the labor representatives as the personal representatives of William H. Davis, Deputy Administrator for the Shipping Code, and not as representatives of any labor organizations as such.[2] The code proposals initially presented by the shipowners accepted the requirements of the National Industrial Recovery Act only for the protected domestic trade; in the foreign trade, it was proposed to request exemptions from the minimum conditions of the act because it was not possible to make these equally binding on foreign competitors.[3]

A final draft of the General Shipping Code was drawn up in May 1934 whose labor provisions represented shipowner concessions on some economic provisions, but none on union recognition. The code provisions reiterated the substance of section 7A of the NIRA; fixed minimum rates at $50 for able seamen and firemen, and $40 for messmen; three watches for members of deck and engine departments, and an eight-hour day in port; prohibition of the practice of carrying workaways to the exclusion of regular crew members; provision for a labor-management committee to study maximum hours for stewards; and a National Shipping Labor Board with functions stemming from those of the National Labor Board.

The matter of overtime payment was left for determination in connection with the divisional codes established for particular trades. No mention was made of union recognition; and no provision was made for permitting union representatives to visit ships.[4]

Even these limited concessions were never to be accomplished. President Roosevelt refused to approve the Code on the grounds that it might interfere with the treaty rights of foreign nations and might also increase the costs of transporting farm products in foreign export.[5] The long, drawn-out negotiations had done nothing to improve the relations between the shipowners and the seamen's organizations. The grievances remained, and there appeared to be no possibility of improvement.

ECONOMIC CONFLICT

The labor organization which had been stimulated by the NIRA would not be bound by the limitations of that legislation. Given an impetus, it soon looked toward achievement of recognition and elimination of long-standing grievances against employer domination with its concomitant deterioration of wages and working conditions and the discrimination against union members. Organization by employers thwarted actively the demands of the newly-organized workers. Industrial warfare was inevitable, with devastating effect upon the community. The West Coast, with its tradition of strong union organization, was to be the mis-en-scène for one such clashing of the forces. In San Francisco, the first significant organizational development was the formation of an ILA local to throw off the yoke of the "blue book" union.

The grievances of the longshoremen had paralleled those of the seamen. Following the defeat of the longshoremen in the 1919 strike, an employer-dominated "blue book" union had been established in San Francisco with which employers maintained closed shop relations.

After its formation, the ILA local warned that any attempt to force its members back into the blue-book union would result in a strike. The Waterfront Employers' Union, representing steamship and stevedoring companies employing longshoremen in San Francisco, recognized the rapidly growing strength of the longshoremen's local by entering into negotiations, beginning in December 1933, concerning the union's demands for wage increases, a six-hour day, a closed shop contract, and union control of the hiring hall.

The basic conflict between the longshoremen and their employers was crystallized in their difference over the union demand for control of the hiring hall. The longshoremen's antipathy to the shape-up system which had been in effect in San Francisco after 1919 was forcefully expressed by Harry Bridges, the new militant longshoremen leader:

We have been hired off the streets like a bunch of sheep standing there from six o'clock in the morning, in all kinds of weather; at the moment of eight o'clock, herded along the street by the police to allow the commuters to go across the street from the Ferry Building, more or less like a slave market in some of the Old World countries of Europe.[6]

The uncertainty of employment under the shape-up system, with its propensities for discrimination and favoritism, was aggravated by the fact that there were at least two longshoremen available for every job. When the employers proposed a joint hiring hall, Bridges argued, "it is not a joint hiring hall at all, but a shipowners' hiring hall with an impotent ILA observer. . . ." The union-controlled hiring hall, he maintained, is basic to achievement of the longshoremen's right to organize, for "it is the only guarantee against discrimination, blacklist, and therefore, against the destruction of unionism by the shipowners." [7] A union-controlled hall would insure regularization of employment and, also, equal distribution of work.

The negotiations came to a stalemate over the hiring hall issue. A strike vote was taken in February, but an appeal by President Roosevelt, accompanied by appointment of a mediation board, resulted in further delay during March. Since no satisfactory conclusion resulted from the activities of this board nor from the prolonged hearings conducted by the Shipping Code authority, a strike was finally called on May 9. The strike quickly spread to all the Pacific ports, with 12,000 longshoremen leaving their jobs. Soon seamen were leaving their ships to join in a sympathy strike with the longshoremen. The Marine Workers' Industrial Union reported that its members had left their ships.[8] Although ISU officials made a point of replying that their West Coast unions had taken no action, within a few days many ISU seamen were also leaving their ships. By May 15, over 4000 members of the sailors' and firemen's unions had walked out, and they were soon joined by 700 marine cooks and stewards. These actions by the rank and file forced the ISU leadership officially to call a strike on May 16, "partly in sympathy with the longshoremen, but principally to resume actively its long-clouded leadership of the men of its crafts." [9] The unions of licensed officers, whose grievances were comparable to those of the seamen and longshoremen, joined the strike; by May 21, some 15,000 seafaring men on the West Coast were out.

The ISU leaders called upon the West Coast shipowners for immediate ISU recognition or — if the shipowners insisted — for recognition after a ballot of the seamen before their return to the ships to determine the appropriate bargaining agent. They also demanded that the Marine Service Bureau be discontinued as an employment agency, and that the men be reëmployed without discrimination for union or strike activity. All issues unresolved within thirty days of the start of negotiations would be submitted to arbitration.

While the Waterfront Employers' Union, including shipowners and stevedoring contractors, had recognized the longshoremen, the shipowners were unwilling to recognize the seamen's unions, much less negotiate with them.[10] As the strike dragged on and the unity between the seamen and the longshoremen increasingly appeared indissoluble, the shipowners receded somewhat from their position of ignoring the seamen's proposals. Spokesmen for the Waterfront Employers' Union argued that their association could not deal with the seamen because their representation was not confined to ship operations.[11] Furthermore, the companies refused to accede to the union proposal to arbitrate all differences which were not settled through collective bargaining within a reasonable period of time.

From all sides came reports of the unprecedented character of the strike, particularly with regard to the determination, the unity, and the discipline of the strikers. The *Seamen's Journal,* voice of the conservative ISU leadership, commented on the unprecedented "creation of a new solid front. . . . All are standing firm and fighting together for a common victory — the seamen and longshoremen having pledged themselves not to return to work unless and until the demands of both are conceded." This unity remained a basic feature of the entire strike, and the efforts by the employers to break this unity were unsuccessful.

The acumen and tact with which the strike was conducted were cited in newspaper reports. Bridges was described as having "maintained perfect discipline, organizing his pickets like a field general, and even keeping strikers away from saloons. . . ."[12] An East Coast ship operator, while recommending a meeting of East Coast operators to consider collective bargaining with conservative unions, summarized the characteristics of the West Coast strike as follows:

From authentic sources, we are informed that the present strike on the Pacific Coast is entirely different than any strike that has occurred on the Pacific Coast in the last 25 years. The sincerity and determination displayed by the men is quite remarkable. The foreign element is in the minority and most of the men are cleancut Americans. It was absolutely astonishing the way both union and nonunion men walked off the ships. . . .[13]

The efforts of the first mediation board appointed by President Roosevelt could not change the grimly determined stands of both employers and the rank and file of waterfront workers. A "compromise" agreement reached between the Waterfront Employers' Union and Joseph Ryan, President of the ILA, was rejected by the membership of the San Francisco local on June 16. This rejection was based, first, on the exclusion of the seafaring unions from any settlement, and, secondly, on the provision for a jointly-controlled hiring hall. Simultaneously, the effectiveness of the strike was increased still further when the teamsters voted to refuse to handle goods affected by the waterfront strike. Newspaper reports on July 1 indicated that the Industrial Association of San Francisco (consisting of San Francisco businessmen) was prepared to counter the strike with imported strikebreakers and armed guards, and nonunion trucks, and was prepared to call upon the state government for aid through the National Guard. The association and the American Legion charged that the strike was inspired and led by Communists.[14]

The effect of the widespread and prolonged strike was business stagnation in almost all Pacific ports except Los Angeles.[15] Furthermore, its threatening possibilities were so apparent that President Roosevelt used the authority recently delegated to him by joint Congressional resolution further implementing the NIRA to appoint a National Longshoremen's Board on June 26.

While the function of the National Longshoremen's Board was primarily fact-finding under its grant of authority, it could also order and conduct elections to determine the representatives desired by the employees "when it shall appear in the public interest." The board could act as an arbitration tribunal, but only if the parties agreed to such action. The members of the board were the Most Reverend Edward J. Hanna, Archbishop of the Diocese of San Francisco; O. K. Cushing, a San Francisco attorney; and Edward F. McGrady, assistant secretary of labor.[16]

The President's action forestalled for the time being the use of force threatened by the Industrial Association to open the port of San Francisco.[17] But even as the preliminary conferences with the contending parties got under way, the Industrial Association was proceeding with its plans to break the blockade of pickets which was preventing the movement of cargo to and from the waterfront. On July 3, the Industrial Association made its first effort to "break [the] dock strike with guns and gas," and opened the way for hauling cargo from the waterfront to the warehouses, at which point the pickets blocked it. The hospitals were filled with injured and wounded men in this first test of power.[18] On July 5, trucks of the Industrial Association moved beyond the warehouses under police protection. The police drove the strikers and sightseers up Rincon Hill, using nauseating gas as well as clubs and firearms; two men were killed and 115 persons injured.[19] Governor Merriam intervened in the strike by calling out the National Guard to protect the shipment of goods on the state-owned Belt Line Railroad. In the view of two disinterested observers, these developments gave the strike the appearance of being directed against the police and the public. However, "a less obvious effect was to suggest to the strikers that the government itself was not impartial, but against them. Communists were not slow to point this out to the men, ignoring, of course, government feeding of needy strikers' families and other helpful services." [20] Bridges called upon the San Francisco Labor Council to authorize a general strike against the Industrial Association, charging it with attacking organized labor. This request was turned down.[21]

Mediation proceedings were conducted by the National Longshoremen's Board in this tense atmosphere. At first, both the longshoremen and their employers refused to agree to submit the question of the hiring hall to arbitration. With the entry of the teamsters into the strike, however, the Waterfront Employers' Union offered unconditionally to submit all matters in dispute with the longshoremen to arbitration. The situation was complicated by the refusal of the ship operators, who were now willing to bargain with representatives who might be chosen by the seamen and to agree in advance to arbitrate any differences which might remain unresolved during these negotiations. The longshoremen, therefore, refused to submit the offer of the Waterfront Employers' Union to a referendum until, first, the hiring hall question was settled; and, second, until a satisfactory arrangement was made for the seafaring unions. The unity of the maritime unions was regarded by the strike leaders as basic to final success for, as expressed by Harry Bridges, "The reason why the maritime workers have been so successful this time thus far in the strike is because of the fact that they have stuck together. Our experience has shown us that for any one maritime group to agree to go back to work without the others would be tantamount to strikebreaking. . . ." [22]

On July 16, 1934, the conservative leadership of San Francisco labor, forced to reverse its earlier position by an "avalanche" of rank-and-file pressure, called a general strike of San Francisco workers in support of the waterfront workers which was to last until July 19. This action resulted in the unleashing of a "torrential attack upon 'reds' and 'subversive influences' among the strikers" by the press and public officials.[23] "Vigilantes" raiding Communist headquarters and meeting places were followed by police who arrested over 300 persons as Communists.[24]

With public disfavor mounting under the pressure of inconvenience and unfavorable publicity, the conservative leaders were able to resume direction of the ranks of San Francisco labor. The general strike was called off with a pledge of "every resource, moral and financial, for the continued prosecution of maritime workers' and longshoremen's strike."

Mounting public dissatisfaction with the prolongation of the waterfront strike and economic costs finally forced the contenders to alter their positions. After an all-day conference attended by representatives of the Waterfront Employers' union, the San Francisco Industrial Association, the steamship companies, and six San Francisco newspapers, a public announcement was issued on July 21 expressing the shipowners' willingness to "arbitrate hours, wages and working conditions" with the appropriate seamen's unions, if the longshoremen agreed to submit all issues including that of the hiring hall to arbitration by the National Longshoremen's Board. Since the ILA representatives were unwilling to agree, the board decided that direct intervention was necessary, and conducted a referendum on the employer offer among the ILA membership under its own jurisdiction. The results, made known by July 26, were overwhelmingly in favor of arbitration of all the longshoremen demands. On July 29, the longshoremen voted to return on July 31.

Difficulties arose between the shipowners and the seamen's unions over the reëmployment of strikers. The steamship companies indicated their willingness to discharge only those men hired after May 16 (the date the ISU unions formally declared the strike) who had not regularly followed the sea prior to that date. Seamen who had struck were to be reëmployed without any discrimination, but only as vacancies occurred. Any question of unfairness or discrimination was to be referred to the board for determination. The seamen's unions, however, were not satisfied with the offer, demanding instead the immediate reinstatement of all of the strikers. To obtain the unions' agreement, the board assured them that it would use its influence to have all strikers reinstated in their former jobs.[25] On July 29, the Shipowners' Association of the Pacific Coast announced that the steam schooner operators would recognize the ISU unions without requiring an election, and that the men would be reëmployed without having to go through the hiring halls. The seamen celebrated this victory by burning their continuous discharge books, symbols of the old regime of employer domination. The strike was finally terminated on July 31, when the seamen voted to submit their demands to arbitration.

The National Longshoremen's Board conducted elections among the seamen beginning at the end of July and continuing through October. The bulk of the votes was not counted because, with one exception, the members of the Pacific American Steamship Association (offshore and intercoastal operators) in December 1934 followed the precedent of the steam schooner operators by recognizing the ISU unions without waiting for the votes to be counted.[26] Negotiations between the shipowners and the seamen's unions over the terms of the agreements were largely unsuccessful. In each instance they agreed only to grant union preference, to establish joint labor relations committees to handle grievances (with the labor members to be appointed by the ISU executive board), and to ban strikes, work stoppages, and lockouts for the life of the agreements which were to remain in effect until September 30, 1935. All other issues were to be decided by two tripartite arbitration boards: one for the coastwise steam schooner operations, and the other for the offshore and intercoastal operations. The award for the former was handed down in January 1935; that for the latter, in April 1935.

The basic question of employment controls was decided in both awards by prohibiting any requirement that seamen register at a private hiring hall to obtain employment. The shipowners were given the option of employing the men from the union hiring hall or directly from the dock, and the rotary system was prohibited. Thus, the awards coincided with the views of the old-line ISU leaders who opposed sole control through union hiring halls, and went counter to the wishes of the militant rank and file. Both awards provided for three equal watches for deck and engine departments; an eight-hour day in port; bedding and linens to be furnished by the companies; and mess rooms for the crew. The offshore and intercoastal award set rates of $62.50 for able seamen and firemen; rates ranging from 50¢ per hour for overtime for some classifications in the stewards' department to 60¢ for all other members of the crew, overtime to be paid for work in port over eight hours on weekdays, as well as for work on Saturday afternoon, Sundays, and holidays. On intercoastal and offshore ships, work at sea over eight hours per day could, at the employer's option, be paid for at the overtime rate or by compensatory time off in port.[27]

While final settlement of the seamen's demands was being deliberated by the arbitration boards, events had been taking place which were to make the terms of the subsequent awards anachronistic. Following the termination of the strike, most of the steamship companies had rebuffed the efforts of the National Longshoremen's Board to obtain reinstatement for all the seamen who had been out on strike. The unlicensed seamen, aided by the longshoremen, thereupon resorted to job action to reduce to impotency the job control exercised by the employers. The Seattle branch of the Sailors' Union of the Pacific, in which Harry Lundeberg was prominent, set the tone for these events by adopting a resolution which established the policy of requiring all men to ship through the union hiring hall. The rotary system was put into effect; any man caught shipping off the dock thereafter, according to Harry Lundeberg, "would be classed as a fink and treated as such." Job actions were used in reprisal against companies who refused to use the union hiring hall. Crews would quit and companies could not obtain replacements until they agreed to call upon the union hall for men. These tactics were also used to force the offshore and intercoastal companies to recognize the ISU unions and to obtain improvements in living conditions on board the ships.

The members of the National Longshoremen's Board surveying maritime labor relations in February 1935 came to the conclusion that "such relations have been established between the longshoremen and their employers and the seamen and their employers, that, with reasonable coöperation between the employers and the men, in other words 'united action of labor and management,' as expressed in the National Industrial Recovery Act, there would be no further labor disturbances in seafaring activities on the Pacific Coast." [28] The board's view was unduly optimistic. The terms of the arbitration awards were unsatisfactory to the militant groups among the seamen whose views, voiced by Harry Lundeberg, were that "there was no granting of the hiring hall; and what was worse, for the first time in many years, instead of a direct agreement with the SUP, the agreement was in the name of the ISU for all three unlicensed unions. . . ." [29] The first feature challenged the job control already achieved by the seamen; the second threatened the autonomy of unions whose members already resented the entrenched and conservative ISU leadership. Furthermore, the "reasonable coöperation between the employers and the men" so necessary to all collective bargaining was not to be forthcoming in West Coast maritime labor relations for several years. Basic breaches between the parties could only be healed temporarily by application of terms prescribed by outside agencies; the radical surgery of another economic conflict was necessary before an organic working relationship could be grafted between employers and seamen.

THE RESPONSE OF EASTERN OPERATORS

The waterfront strike on the West Coast caused East Coast shipowners to reexamine their labor policies. Some operators foresaw the possibility of Communist or Wobbly gains in the event of an East Coast strike and recommended forestalling such a possibility by granting recognition to the conservative unions.[30] However, the majority of the shipowners did not see any serious or immediate danger of a strike and therefore no action was taken for several months.

In February 1934, a Seafarers' Council for the Port of New York had been established consisting of the three East Coast ISU unions, the United Licensed Officers, and the Associated Marine Workers (harbor workers). The council, claiming 19,000 members, approached the American Steamship Owners' Association during June 1934 with a proposal for a conference to negotiate wages and working conditions and to avoid industrial strife in the industry. The council warned the association that the situation on the West Coast was "a dangerous one, and we are fearful of its contagious effect upon the seafarers within our jurisdiction," and gave assurance that it was representing "the conservative labor organizations in this port." [31] The council's proposal was rejected by the association during July on the grounds that no serious threat faced the shipping industry in New York; that going wage rates exceeded those approved by the labor representatives for the ill-fated shipping code; and that there was no evidence that the members of the council actually represented their employees. Until such evidence was available, the association maintained, "any act of the employers which might limit the choice of representatives by their employees would be most unfair. . . ." [32]

The failure of the ISU unions to take any decisive action to obtain improvements for the seamen on the Atlantic and Gulf enabled the Communist-controlled Marine Workers' Industrial Union to increase its prestige and influence through announcing a militant program and promoting individual job actions.[33] To meet growing MWIU influence the ISU leadership was finally forced to take a strike vote and to schedule a strike for October 8. Whereupon the MWIU announced that it would also strike at that time.[34] Demands to the shipowners reiterated the demands made a year before at the start of the hearings on the shipping code.

These developments altered the attitude of the East Coast operators. Lloyd K. Garrison, chairman of the National Labor Relations Board, personally intervened in the situation and succeeded in arranging a meeting between the representatives of the shipowners and the ISU. By October 1, some 28 companies operating 450 ships had agreed to recognize the ISU unions for purposes of collective bargaining, and the ISU called off the strike.[35]

The MWIU, outmaneuvered by these developments, was forced to proceed with the scheduled strike to justify its demands for recognition. The MWIU claimed that its strike succeeded in tying up twenty-eight ships and that crimping had been eliminated; but the strike proved to be a fiasco because of the weak hold of the MWIU among seamen and longshoremen, and the ability of the shipowners to get replacements for striking seamen from the ISU unions and the ILA. The strike was called off on October 14. Recognizing its own weakness, the MWIU now appealed unsuccessfully to the members of the ISU unions to join in formulating a program of united action. When collective bargaining negotiations between the ISU unions and East Coast operators resulted in an agreement, the MWIU offered to merge with the ISU. When this offer was rejected, the MWIU adopted another strategy, that of boring from within. By a "business meeting" held in February 1935, rather than by the democratic procedure of a referendum vote of its claimed membership on the ships, it was voted to approve the "unity proposals of the National Committee of the MWIU." These proposals called for the dissolution of the MWIU, with all the members joining the ISU unions as individuals; a campaign to make the ISU a "mass union" and to obtain "100 percent job organization and job control." This program was not viewed as "an act of desperation" but "as a necessary next step to organize a greater struggle against the shipowners, for the enforcement of what the seamen have already won, and for greater victories." [36] The grievances of the rank and file of the seamen against the conservative and undemocratic policies of the entrenched ISU leadership were to furnish Communist leadership with fertile ground. The success of the MWIU strategy was to be demonstrated subsequently when the Communists were able to obtain a strong hold within the ISU, and later within the National Maritime Union.

The negotiations between the committee of Atlantic and Gulf shipowners and the ISU, acting on behalf of its Atlantic and Gulf district unions, culminated in an agreement in December 1934. Fear by the conservative union leaders that their position was weak because of widespread unemployment among seamen led them to accept terms which fell far short of those originally demanded. The $57.50 rate ($62.50 on tankers) for able seamen and firemen increased average rates by only $3 to $4 per month. In many instances, higher wages were actually being paid.[37] These rates were $5 below those subsequently awarded in April 1935 to the West Coast seamen on offshore and intercoastal ships. While three watches were made effective on deck, with an eight-hour day at sea and in port for all members of the deck and engine departments, there was no provision made for overtime pay on the East Coast. This also was to contrast adversely with the optional overtime pay provisions later awarded West Coast seamen on offshore and intercoastal ships. The East Coast employers agreed to union preference in the filling of vacancies and to the granting of passes to union representatives to board ships. An elaborate grievance machinery was also written out; and strikes, lockouts, and work stoppages were banned for the life of the agreement, which was to terminate on January 1, 1936.[38]

The *Seamen's Journal* could crow with delight: "Three cheers for the International Seamen's Union — the only union in America authorized to speak for the sailor, the fireman and the cook — the true spokesman for all the unlicensed personnel." [39] By August 1935, the membership of the ISU unions had increased to 30,000. Events were shortly to demonstrate, however, that every action of the ISU was but another step toward its doom, and that despite the West Coast arbitration awards and East

Coast agreement, in reality the ISU had established no organic basis for sound collective bargaining relations.

The weakness of the maritime union was manifest shortly after the 1934 strike, when an unsuccessful strike was conducted against tankers operated by West Coast petroleum companies. It was out of this failure that the Maritime Federation of the Pacific developed. But joint action was only one facet of the tactics utilized by the seamen's unions to solidify their positions. Following the 1934 strike, the West Coast maritime unions tried to consolidate their positions by using job actions to force all employment through the union hiring halls; they also used job actions to obtain improvements on the ships. Both proved to be limited and transient tactics.

Following the certification of the ISU unions as bargaining representatives on all West Coast tankers, except those of Standard Oil of California, there were prolonged negotiations without any agreement. The basic issue involved was the demand of the unions for union preference in employment as had been granted by all other West Coast shipowners. The unions, charging that the oil companies under the leadership of Standard Oil were undermining them by displacing union members with nonunion men, called a strike in March 1935. Sympathy strikes by the radio operators and the marine engineers followed, and strikers and sympathizers boycotted the products of Standard Oil of California.

Plans for the formation of a federation of Pacific coast maritime transport unions were hastened by the success of the companies in operating their ships within a few weeks after the start of the strike. In April a conference was held in Seattle, and the Maritime Federation of the Pacific was organized to become a stormy petrel for West Coast maritime labor relations. Against the wishes of the old-line leaders, the rank and file of the West Coast ISU unions voted to have the newly organized federation handle the tanker strike. While threatening to take a general strike vote, the federation merely called upon the Secretary of Labor for arbitration. An arbitration board was appointed which was promptly ignored by the oil companies, who announced that they had "nothing to arbitrate." [40] As the companies continued to man the tankers with nonunion men without difficulty, the strike was called off in June by Harry Lundeberg, president of the Maritime Federation. The *Voice of the Federation*, official journal of the federation, found some basis for satisfaction that calling off the strike had not wrecked the federation.

The Maritime Federation of the Pacific had been organized by the longshoremen and by representatives of the rank and file of the seamen's unions. At its height, the federation included unions representing about 40,000 members, including longshoremen, licensed and unlicensed ship personnel, radio operators, and members of related crafts and trades. The original constitution of the federation restricted membership to "*bona fide* labor unions who work in conjunction with and who are in conformity with the principles of the American Federation of Labor." Officers, elected at the annual conventions, included a full-time president and secretary. The executive committee included the officers and one representative from each of the affiliated unions. Headquarters was located at San Francisco, with district councils in various ports consisting of representatives of the locals and branches of the member unions. Funds were raised by a per capita tax, and assessments could be levied upon agreement by component organizations.

The primary purpose of the federation was united action among all labor organizations associated with the maritime industry. This end was sought through simultaneous termination and renewal of agreements "with the realization that the strength of a combined federation of maritime workers demands fair dealing in all settlements for all affiliated organizations." The battle cry of the federation was "An injury to one is an injury to all." [41] Thus, while autonomy of the constituent unions was explicitly recognized, unity in action in trade disputes was to be obtained through the federation. The constitution of the federation, with more optimism than realism, called upon constituent organizations, before taking any action, to give the federation and the affiliated groups "ample time to prepare themselves and [to take] all other means for handling disputes as provided elsewhere in this constitution." Member unions were encouraged to call upon the district councils, in local disputes, or the executive committee, in coastwise disputes, for aid in adjusting minor disputes affecting a single organization. Where negotiations failed in such cases, the question of strike action might be referred through the executive committee of the federation to the component unions for a membership vote. In the case of major disputes which might force members of other unions off the job, however, a member union was required to conform to this procedure in order to receive federation support. Federation action on major issues was to be determined by referendum vote of the rank-and-file membership.[42]

The Maritime Federation of the Pacific was dominated by the personalities and policies of the two leaders most representative of the divergent militant influences in the West Coast labor movement: Harry Lundeberg and Harry Bridges. Harry Lundeberg, first president of the Maritime Federation of the Pacific, had become a rank-and-file leader in the Sailors' Union of the Pacific when the seamen rose almost spontaneously to support the longshoremen during the 1934 strike. Born in Norway in 1901, he had gone to sea at the age of fourteen, sailed under several flags for eight years, landed in Seattle in 1923, and sailed out of that port for a dozen years. His trade union philosophy was imprinted with the Wobbly emphasis upon direct action, the "one big union," and antipoliticalism. For Lundeberg, job action was an essential tactic to improve the seamen's economic status, especially in the matter of the union hiring hall and overtime payments. He opposed any restraint of the free use of this weapon by the seamen.[43]

Lundeberg's efforts to achieve leadership within the Sailors' Union of the Pacific had been thwarted by Paul Scharrenberg, editor of the *Seamen's Journal*, trusted lieutenant of Andrew Furuseth for over thirty years, and secretary of the California State Federation of Labor. In 1935, therefore, Scharrenberg was expelled by the rank and file of the Sailors' Union. Efforts by the ISU to obtain Scharrenberg's reinstatement, and to intervene directly in the affairs of the West Coast seamen's unions only furnished Lundeberg with additional ammunition for his attacks upon the ISU leadership whom he charged with being part of the "shipowners' controlled machine" when it finally revoked the SUP charter in January 1936.[44] Lundeberg early adopted a position in support of the "industrial form of unionism" as allegedly represented by the Maritime Federation of the Pacific. He also supported the Committee of Industrial Organization upon its organization in 1935 by several unions affiliated with the AFL.[45]

Harry Bridges, Australian-born leader of the San Francisco longshoremen, had come to the fore with the revolt against the blue-book union. A left-wing militant, influenced by the tactics and philosophy of the Communist Party, he viewed political activity in support of economic aims as an integral part of trade union activity.[46] His tactics were more flexible and opportunistic than those of Lundeberg. From the security of the presidency of the almost completely autonomous Pacific Coast District of the ILA, Bridges, unlike Lundeberg, could afford to urge that the SUP reaffiliate with the ISU. Reaffiliation, he apparently felt, would void charges that the Maritime Federation ran counter to the AFL in philosophy and organization. Although he had originally supported the use of job action to enforce control of hiring through the longshoremen's union hiring hall, Bridges was to alter his attitude toward the tactic after job control was achieved. With attainment of the union hiring hall, and the economic provisions of the 1934 arbitration award, the longshoremen had won their basic demands. Thereafter, Bridges was to concentrate the strength of the Maritime Federation on protecting the West Coast longshoremen's gains by aiding the development of organization inland and among waterfront workers on other coasts.

Bridges hoped by altered tactics to reduce the vulnerability of the Maritime Federation against attacks both from the AFL leadership and from the employers, especially since the attacks of the employers were directed particularly at the longshoremen.[47] The "hot cargo" tactic (boycotting of cargo produced or handled by nonunion labor) used spectacularly to further those ends might not be viewed as unorthodox, for it was not dissimilar to the secondary boycott tactic used by the most conservative unions. Bridges preferred this tactic with its use of concerted action; he opposed the use of job action, for he held that its undirected use by small groups to achieve limited economic gains might work to the detriment of the Maritime Federation members as a whole. Therefore, he advocated that the use of job action be controlled by Maritime Federation machinery — a position which Lundeberg considered as killing the tactic itself in killing its intrinsic element, namely, spontaneity.

The continuance of the Maritime Federation of the Pacific, despite frequent clashes arising out of these basic differences in interests (and, as a result, in tactics) between the two maritime leaders, bears testimony to the state of uncertainty and fear under which the maritime unions were laboring between 1934 and 1937. But its mere continuance was no evidence of the validity of its activities. The federation was impotent in the face of frequent jurisdictional disputes between its members because it could only deal with the disputes which were voluntarily referred to it. Individual unions disregarded the interests of other member unions, and made agreements or took actions which favored their own interests. Actions taken at federation conventions were disregarded by the member unions. The *Voice of the Federation* became the clearinghouse for the expression of the differences among the union leadership. All efforts to keep controversial matter out of the newspaper were unsuccessful. One federation president described the *Voice* as follows: "On the front page would be an article describing the solidarity and militancy of the Federation, and then the inside pages would belie those articles through the bickering and hatred described therein." [48] Unity was displayed only under the pressure of direct attack from the waterfront employers, and even then rifts existed among the leaders.

The first months following the formation of the Maritime Federation of the Pacific in April 1935 saw a fair degree of unity within the federation. Sympathy strikes were called by the seamen in support of striking radio operators and by the longshoremen in support of striking warehousemen. These strikes were met by employer threats to void the agreements resulting from the arbitration awards unless they were called off.[49] A united front was presented by seamen and longshoremen in supporting striking longshoremen at Vancouver, British Columbia, for several months by refusing to release ships carrying "hot cargo" loaded by striking longshoremen at Vancouver. Lundeberg, together with representatives of the West Coast marine firemen and marine cooks and stewards' unions, was called to Washington in August by Assistant Secretary of Labor McGrady to meet jointly with representatives of the Waterfront Employers' Union and the Pacific American Steamship Association, as well as with Andrew Furuseth and Victor Olander, who were representing the ISU. There Lundeberg insisted that the question of releasing the tied-up ships be decided by a referendum vote of the Maritime Federation membership rather than merely by the vote of the West Coast ISU unions — a position which had been taken by Furuseth who was aligned with the shipowners on the matter of living up to the agreements. Lundeberg prevailed on this point, and the subsequent vote of the Maritime Federation membership was to go overwhelmingly in favor of continuing the boycott.[50]

At the same time, a major break in the unity of the maritime unions occurred over the question of renewing the agreements originating from the arbitration awards which were due to expire on September 30. During August, a "Rank-and-File ISU Convention" had been held by the West Coast seamen's unions, which called upon the longshoremen to refrain from signing any agreement until the seafaring unions were also ready to do so. On August 26, a full-page advertisement inserted by the Pacific American Steamship Association and the Waterfront Employers' Association appeared in the principal San Francisco newspapers announcing that the shipowners were opposed to any change in the arbitration awards since they "were arrived at only after months of painstaking investigation and deliberation by Government arbitration boards and were intended to be, and can be, a basis of permanent settlement . . . abrogation is merely to renew last year's strike." Bridges' ILA, in subsequently voting overwhelmingly to renew the award, undercut the position of the seamen's unions who, in turn, were forced to renew their award.[51]

The members of the SUP, dissatisfied with this state of affairs, and contending that the shipowners had denied them the right of collective bargaining, voted to resort to job action wherever longshoremen's conditions were not met by steam schooner operators. An emergency convention of the Maritime Federation was called in November to deal with a number of pressing matters, the leading ones being the issue of job action and support of a strike of longshoremen at Gulf ports. An SUP proposal for Maritime Federation support in the event that drastic action would be necessary to win the demands on the steam schooners failed to receive support. Instead, a resolution was passed which obviously limited the application of job action. Job action could only be applied "to a job such as a ship, dock, shop or warehouse unless otherwise agreed by all maritime groups affected," according to the resolution; and joint consideration by all the unions involved was required wherever a job action "may jeopardize the Maritime Federation as a whole." The SUP retaliated by refusing to join in a boycott of "hot cargo" from Gulf ports affected by a longshoremen's strike. It did concede, however, that a strike vote of the membership of the various unions should be taken in the event that any member union might be threatened by lockout for refusing to handle such cargo.

Early in January 1936, the sailors resorted to job actions on the steam schooners, refusing to work longer than six hours in port. The steam schooner operators replied by laying up the ships. Over 60 ships and 1500 officers and men were affected. As suggested by the results of the November convention, support from the longshoremen was not forthcoming. After five weeks, the sailors offered to return to the steam schooners under the terms of the arbitration award, and the schooner operators accepted.[52]

Relations between Lundeberg and Bridges became even more strained over Bridges' urging acceptance of terms offered by the ISU following revocation of the SUP charter by the ISU in January 1936. The differences were further reflected in their respective stands on the immediate issue of industrial unionism. At the second convention of the Maritime Federation during the spring of 1936, Lundeberg sought to implement his advocacy of industrial unionism by obtaining the Federation's approval of a proposal to merge the unions of sailors, marine cooks, and marine firemen. The federation failed to act on this proposal. Consistently with his advocacy of industrial unionism, Lundeberg supported the application of the unaffiliated Industrial Union of Marine and Shipbuilding Workers for membership in the Maritime Federation on a coastwise basis. Bridges, again, opposing any action which might antagonize the AFL, prevailed, and the application was not accepted. Instead, the convention announced its desire to organize a National Maritime Federation "in accordance with the principles of the AFL."[53]

These basic antagonisms between the maritime leaders were overcome, and then only temporarily, when the shipowners' actions seriously threatened all the unions. The Maritime Federation supported ship tie-ups by East Coast insurgent seamen in West Coast ports during the spring of 1936, and later supported the "outlaw" strike of East Coast seamen. On one occasion, when the S.S. *Santa Rosa* docked at San Francisco, and the longshoremen refused to pass picket lines on the dock, the Waterfront Employers' Association announced suspension of all relations with the ILA. Under this direct attack, all the maritime unions supported the longshoremen. Although for a period of a week the majority of ships in the harbor of San Francisco were not worked, the longshoremen were finally forced to end the work stoppage and to agree to handle "hot cargoes." [54] Again, when the arbitration awards were about to expire during the fall of 1936, and the waterfront employers were demanding that all disputed issues of the contract, including the hiring hall, go to arbitration, all the unions were to engage unitedly with the three West Coast employers' associations in what was generally acknowledged to be another test of strength.

EAST COAST SEAMEN AND DEMOCRACY

The successes of the West Coast militant groups in eliminating conservative leaders, in achieving job control through the union hiring halls, and in obtaining better wages and working conditions served to inspire a rank-and-file insurgent movement with similar objectives on the East Coast. Simultaneously with the MWIU's going underground in February 1935, an "ISU Rank-and-File Committee" had been established which immediately started publishing the ISU Pilot. The stated aim of the new group was "to build one powerful ISU and organize every seaman in the industry." This was to be achieved through organizing "all bona fide seamen"; ensuring adherence by all companies to the agreement; obtaining job control through the union hiring hall; and democratizing the leadership and operation of the East Coast unions.[55]

The efforts of the "ISU Rank-and-File Committee" were directed henceforth at obtaining mass support for their program. The Pilot served as an effective means for crystallizing the grievances of the seamen against the union administration. The leadership was charged with consciously failing to perform its duty of organizing all seamen, including those who were unemployed, and failing to extend and protect union organization. Although the ISU claimed 30,000 members, only 14,000 of these came from the Atlantic, Gulf, and Lakes districts — three-fourths of the seamen in those districts remained unorganized, it was charged. Conservative leaders were also charged with having failed to act in the best interests of their constituents — in failing to obtain West Coast conditions or to eliminate the crimping evils through establishing job control via the union hiring hall. Evidence was cited of misappropriation of union funds by the officials, and of actual collaboration with company officials.

The old-line leadership, long in control of their sprawling jurisdiction, with its numerous ports and dispersed membership, assumed absolute power to meet this onslaught and charged the opposition with being Communist-inspired.[56] To center authority completely in the hands of the officers of the constituent unions, and to eliminate provisions for recall of union officials, packed meetings were used to hold elections and to revise the constitutions of the East Coast unions. Opposition to such tactics resulted in the expulsion of the protesters.[57]

Unable to unseat the union leaders, and apparently achieving limited success in getting rank-and-file support, the ISU Rank-and-File Committee resorted to court actions and to appeals to impartial citizens for aid in their fight against the union officials.[58] These indirect activities were overshadowed by the outburst of direct actions by the rank-and-file membership following the announcement by the ISU leaders that they were going to accept the companies' terms upon the expiration of the contract in January 1936.

The agreement then in effect, covering most Atlantic and Gulf ship operations, provided for a wage scale $5 below West Coast rates, contained no provision for cash overtime payment, and provided for elaborate grievance machinery which had never been operative. Furthermore, while it granted union preference, employment had continued on the same uncertain and disorganized basis which had existed prior to recognition — hiring was still done through company employment offices, through shipping masters (crimps), on the docks, and through the union. All these stimulated grievances among the rank and file, particularly those engaged in the intercoastal trade who came into direct contact with the members of the well-organized, militantly-led West Coast maritime unions with their better conditions and their union hiring halls. The ISU Rank-and-File Group, in behalf of all *"bona fide* seamen" had called upon the union officials to obtain West Coast conditions and union job control through union halls in negotiating the new agreement. As the *Pilot* advised the West Coast unions, these demands were part and parcel of the fight for a "rank-and-file union with unity of East, West, Gulf Coasts and Great Lakes, for one National Union with one Uniform National Agreement." [59]

In the face of this sentiment, the union officials had indicated they were prepared to accept the shipowners' proposals for renewal of the agreement without any change. This was an effective although inadvertent stimulus to overt expression of rank-and-file discontent. Three hundred members of the crew of the Panama-Pacific liner, *Pennsylvania*, walked off the ship in San Francisco on January 4, 1936, to protest the "sell-out" by the union leaders in signing an agreement without referring it to the membership. Meetings of the sailors' and firemen's unions up and down the coast successfully demanded the submission of the question of renewing the contract to a thirty-day referendum. The result of the referendum showed approximately 6000 opposed to renewal, with about 2000 supporting renewal. Whereupon the union leaders were forced to return to the shipowners and request a $5 increase and a 2-year contract "as a means of stabilizing the situation." [60] While this request was being considered by the shipowners, the accumulated grievances of the East Coast seamen were receiving further airing on the West Coast.

On March 2, 1936, while the intercoastal liner *California* was in San Pedro harbor, a group of sailors led by Joseph Curran refused to cast off the lines until they received West Coast wage rates. The remainder of the crew, which had been signed on in New York, supported this group by remaining aboard, but limiting its activities to feeding the passengers and keeping up enough steam to heat the ship. The tie-up was ended after two days when Secretary of Labor Perkins intervened, pledging herself to place the strikers' point of view before the committee negotiating the terms of the new agreement and to use her "best offices to see that there would be no discrimination against them as to future employment." Secretary of Commerce Roper took a different view of the situation, however, and requested the Department of Justice to take action against the leaders for mutiny. He was joined by John M. Franklin, president of the International Mercantile Marine Company, who charged that Curran's leadership of the strike constituted mutiny and attacked the Department of Justice for failing to act. The ISU leaders repudiated the strike as a violation of the agreement and did not dispute the validity of the mutiny charge. When the ship returned to New York, sixty members of the crew were logged two to six days' pay, and discharged; some received discharge certificates with D. R. notations (meaning "decline to report" — the equivalent of an unfavorable character rating).[61]

While the *California* incident was taking place, the ISU leaders negotiated an agreement, limited to only fourteen East Coast companies, which was signed on March 10. This agreement, which provided for a five-dollar increase, was to expire December 31, 1937. It had been signed without a referendum vote by the membership. The ISU leadership thus provided the rank-and-file movement with two bases for dissatisfaction: first, it had publicly repudiated the strikers on the *California* with a virtual charge of mutiny; and, secondly, without any apparent regard for the wishes of the membership, it had negotiated an agreement with only a small segment of the industry on the East Coast, which contained no provision for overtime, and expired during the worst season of the year from a tactical point of view. The ISU justified the contract on the grounds that: "we cannot hope for Utopia overnight. The past fourteen years have given us a great deal to overcome and we must not go too fast. . . ."[62]

The "rank-and-file group" sought widespread strike support to eliminate these conditions. Crew members of the *California*, smarting under the treatment accorded Curran's group on their return to New York and the nonsupport of the union leadership, prevented the next sailing of the ship on March 20 by refusing to sign on and by picketing the ship. Curran tried to get other East Coast crews, especially those on inter-coastal ships, to join his group in a strike. By concentrating on inter-coastal operations, the strike committee hoped, with West Coast support, to tie up ships sailing to the West Coast which might be manned by strikebreakers. Within two days, Curran, as chairman of the strike com-mittee, was able to report that 900 men were out. The strikers stated that they were seeking to force all companies — not merely fourteen — to sign an agreement which would provide for West Coast wages and overtime pay; an eight-hour day for stewards; union control of hiring; expiration of the contract on September 30, simultaneously with West Coast agreements; and reinstatement of the *California* crew.

The strikers were denounced as "outlaws" by the ISU leadership and were threatened with expulsion unless they returned to their jobs. The ISU leaders assured the companies that all crew needs would be met. Curran, denounced as a "tool of the Communist Party," was expelled from the Eastern and Gulf Sailors' Association along with eighteen others. The leadership claimed that the "outlaw" strike involved only some 1100 seamen, and that no ships were being delayed.

The strikers, however, claimed the support of 4500 East Coast sea-men. They were also receiving support from the West Coast unions until the latter were locked out during April following the tying-up of the *Santa Rosa*. They succeeded in presenting to public officials in Wash-ington their grievances regarding poor quarters, unsafe conditions, long hours, and their charge that inexperienced men were replacing the rank-and-file strikers. Charges of police brutality against the strikers, together with the publicity regarding the conditions on board ships and in the unions, elicited investigation and support by disinterested citizen groups.

In turn, the strikers were charged with receiving support from Com-munists. One supporting group, attacked by the National Civic Federa-tion as being "dominated by Moscow influence and . . . forwarding the Communist plan to encourage industrial unrest in this country," coun-tered that its funds were furnished only by its nonpartisan membership. Curran, while acknowledging "a few contributions from Communists and Communist Party groups," stated that "most of them come in small amounts from seamen on ships, from seamen's local unions, many on the West Coast, from other labor organizations and from many indus-trial sympathizers, including college professors and ministers." He stated emphatically that: "The Communist Party has never run this thing and it never will. We accept help from the Communists because we need all the help we can get." Curran denied charges that Harry Bridges was the instigator of the East Coast rank-and-file strike, although he acknowledged their interests coincided with those of the West Coast maritime groups, that is, in "the formation of a Maritime Federation that will help us in collective bargaining."

The strike was finally called off after nine weeks, when some 1200 seamen voted to accept the terms of the ISU executive committee. These promised ISU assistance in preventing discrimination against the strikers; implementation of the grievance procedure in the contract to ensure that seamen's grievances would receive proper attention; and intercession by the national leaders to ensure that strikers would receive equitable treatment from the district unions from which they had been expelled.

The strike had apparently been a failure. However, the strikers had received the promise that their grievances would be considered by the union leaders. As expressed by Curran: "we have made our case clear. We have had the attention of Congressional and civic leaders directed to the conditions against which we protested, and investigations which otherwise would not have been started. We also obtained valuable experience in group action. Now we are ready to go back to work. But that does not mean we are through. We are only starting. . . ." Efforts would now be directed at organizing the men on the ships in preparation for September 30, when Pacific Coast agreements would come up for renewal, he announced, ". . . and if the shipping lines then hold out against our demands the Atlantic Coast will be pulled with the Pacific in a general shipping strike that will mean something." [63]

The spring strike had also served to bring to the fore a new young and militant leadership. Joseph Curran had shown that flair which is particularly necessary to achieve leadership among seamen. He had been outspoken and aggressive in the *California* sitdown strike, and had shown organizational and leadership qualities in the wider strike. Thirty-years-old at the time of the strike, he had gone to sea since 1922. Popular with his shipmates, and often their spokesman, he typified, as well as led the rank-and-file seamen in their efforts to throw off the old-line ISU leadership.

Immediately following the termination of the strike, efforts were continued to eliminate the East Coast union leaders through court action. David Grange, President of the Marine Cooks and Stewards, was charged with misappropriation of union funds. A dispute over the results of an election in the Marine Firemen, Oilers and Watertenders' Union in August furnished the rank-and-file group with an opportunity to oust Oscar Carlson, long-time head of that union. [64] In reply to a request for passes to board ships by the leaders who replaced the Carlson faction, the American Steamship Owners' Association stated that such permission would be granted only to representatives designated by the ISU officials. The ISU confirmed Carlson and his colleagues as the only duly elected officials. Passes were, therefore, denied the representatives of the rank-and-file group. A strike was called on the liner *President Roosevelt* at the end of September, as a result of which an agreement was obtained allowing representatives of both factions to board ships of the International Mercantile Marine Co. Job actions continued to be called for the purpose of rectifying "poor and downright rotten conditions of work, of pay and of living," in lieu of more concerted action.[65]

THE UNITED FRONT

The impending expiration of the 1934–5 longshoremen's and seamen's arbitration awards at the end of September 1936 was the heralding of an endurance contest between West Coast shipowners and maritime unions. Leading West Coast lines, Dollar, Matson, and American-Hawaiian were reported by the press as having "believed for some time that there could never be peace on terms satisfactory to them as long as Bridges and Lundeberg, or men of their philosophy and tactics, continued in control of the unions, and in furtherance of this belief they have been making their extensive preparation for a shutdown for many months." [66]

The employers notified the unions in July that they wished to open the awards. The maritime unions established a joint negotiating committee, but agreed to permit the SUP to negotiate agreements independently in return for its coöperation. During negotiations, "a solid front of shipowners and waterfront employers" demanded that all matters in dispute be arbitrated.[67] A deadlock developed over the role of the hiring hall when suitable union men were not available.[68]

Contributing to the dispute were the seamen's demands for cash overtime payment for all overtime work at sea instead of the options of cash payment or compensatory time off in port — a cause of constant friction, since the option was exercised by the shipowners.[69] Although other demands of the licensed and unlicensed personnel remained unsettled, basically it was the issue of hiring controls that provided the source of insuperable disagreement.

Clear indications of conflict on the West Coast after September 30 influenced important developments in other areas. Later in September, East Coast shipowners, apparently seeking to forestall a sympathy strike on their ships, voluntarily opened their agreement with the ISU, although it still had more than a year to run, and agreed to optional overtime payments for the first time since 1921. The option of paying overtime at 60¢ per hour or of granting compensatory time off was established for all work by deck and engine crew members in excess of 8 hours per day at sea and in ports other than the home port, as well as for Saturday afternoon and Sunday work in the home port. These optional overtime provisions, however, remained less favorable than those which were a source of grievance on the West Coast.

The fear of a recapitulation of the 1934 San Francisco maritime and general strikes haunted labor and shipping agencies of the federal government. Assistant Secretary of Labor E. F. McGrady was active once again seeking to mediate the West Coast maritime labor disputes. Temporary appointments were made to the newly-established Maritime Commission to meet the emergency. The commission, with its statutory authority over subsidy payments and over minimum wages and manning scales on subsidized vessels, but with no authority over disputes, interjected itself actively into the situation in an effort to end the impasse. On the eve of the strike, telegrams were sent to the parties, calling upon them to postpone the strike.

The employers were "ready and anxious" to tie up the ships but were reluctant to alienate public opinion which, unconvinced that the basic issue was union irresponsibility, believed that "they [the employers] were out to do up the unions as such." Since a considerable degree of public sympathy supported the unions' stand on arbitration, the employers agreed to a maximum fifteen-day extension of the agreement, but refused any further extension unless the unions agreed to arbitrate. The unions agreed only to the extension. As the extension period drew to a close with no change in the situation, the Maritime Commission urged the parties to grant a further extension. It declared that "in the public interest" it proposed to use "to the fullest extent its power and authority both legal and moral to prevent a tie-up." [70]

The waterfront employers now accepted the Maritime Commission's proposal unconditionally. But widely publicized differences developed between Lundeberg and Bridges regarding the tactical stand to take on the Maritime Commission's intervention and its demand for an extension, in order to ensure continuance of favorable public reaction. The differences were resolved temporarily when the joint union committee agreed to an extension until October 26, and decided to conduct a referendum among the membership of the unions for authorization to order a strike on October 28 if necessary. The committee accompanied its decision with a blast at the sudden emergence of the Maritime Commission into the picture "with a vast range of authority over the seafaring and shore worker in his conduct of negotiations with the employer and his conditions of work." The current barrage of legislative proposals and enactments, which included the passage of federal legislation pertaining to the Maritime Commission and requiring seamen to carry continuous discharge books was ascribed to "a powerful machinery" which had been "created with the power and authority to reëstablish just those conditions which the shipowners were once capable of maintaining by themselves. . . ." The commission was charged with attempting to extend its authority with the encouragement of shipowners "far beyond that ever intended even by Congress."

The Maritime Commission announced that it could not "accept any limit of time as to the period of its investigation," going on to say that "It must insist upon compliance with its demands for continuance of operations under the present agreement" until the investigations were completed. The unions, now united, charged that Admiral Harry Hamlet, representing the Maritime Commission, had advised them that his function was to investigate the entire national maritime labor picture as well as the immediate situation and that this investigation would take from six months to one year to complete. Accordingly, the unions decided to conduct a strike vote.[71]

When the strike-approving results of the referendum were made known, the employers conceded to virtually all the demands of the longshoremen with the "apparent intention to divide and conquer." The steamschooner operators had also reached tentative agreements with the seamen's unions. The Pacific American Steamship Association, however, refused to grant the hiring hall to the unlicensed personnel and sought to split these unions by negotiating agreements separately. Its efforts failed and a strike was called, effective at midnight October 30. A last effort by Admiral Hamlet on November 2 also failed when the union representatives walked out from his hearing after a shipowner spokesman began to present testimony regarding alleged union violations of the 1934 awards.[72]

The strike on the West Coast now settled down to a test of endurance. The shipowners, particularly Matson, Dollar, and American-Hawaiian, had been prepared for the showdown, and they were prepared to use tactics quite different from those used during the 1934 strike. Ships were to be laid up, and strikebreakers were not to be employed immediately.[73] The shipowners denied any intention of destroying the unions and indicated that they were seeking through arbitration "to achieve a just and lasting solution of maritime labor troubles that have kept Pacific Coast shipping in chaos for the last two years." They contrasted their willingness to arbitrate and to submit the dispute to the Maritime Commission with the unions' refusal to arbitrate certain issues, including union preference and the hiring hall. The employers charged the union hiring hall and rotary shipment had been established in violation of the 1934–5 awards, and had deprived the employers of their prerogative to select their own employees and had interfered with the stable composition of crews.

The unions, also prepared for an inevitable showdown, were in a better position than in 1934. The militant organizations which had been developed during the two years had the support of the bulk of West Coast maritime workers. Strike funds had been built up. While uncertain and fluctuating, some basis for unified action had been developed among the seven unions of licensed and unlicensed seamen and longshoremen through the Maritime Federation of the Pacific.

The usual precarious unity of the maritime unions was maintained for the duration of the strike, with individual unions delaying action on their respective settlements until settlements were reached with all. In December, a tentative agreement was reached with the Sailors' Union which virtually met all of that union's demands. The announcement of this development caused an open rift between Lundeberg and Bridges, with Bridges charging that a false impression was being created that the strike was ended. He also charged Lundeberg with failing to furnish the ILA with information regarding the developments in negotiations. The split was healed for the time being, however, when Lundeberg announced that the SUP had no intention of making a separate peace.[74]

The unions, like the shipowners, sought public support. Through public meetings and radio broadcasts, often in joint debate with employer representatives, the unions charged that the major shipping companies had fomented the strike in an effort to break the unions. Every effort was directed to ensure that picket lines were orderly.[75]

As the strike dragged on through November, December, and January, the virtual cessation of all shipping activity on the West Coast had widespread repercussions. With 40,000 maritime workers idle, lumber cargoes piled up on docks, and logging camps and sawmills shut down or operated on a curtailed basis.

The outbreak of the strike on the West Coast was accompanied by important developments for maritime labor relations on the Atlantic and Gulf coasts. The recent adjustments providing for optional overtime payments failed to meet the grievances of the rank-and-file seamen. As Curran had forewarned at the end of the "outlaw" strike during the spring of the year, preparations were made for participation in the West Coast strike. On October 28, a meeting of some 1000 Atlantic Coast seamen empowered the Seamen's Defense Committee, with Joseph Curran as chairman, to call a strike if West Coast seamen walked out. On October 30, this rank-and-file group voted a sitdown strike on all ships to leave New York within twenty-four hours in order to place pressure on the ISU leadership which had scheduled a meeting for October 31 to consider participation in the strike.[76]

At the ISU meeting, from which Curran and the other members of the Seamen's Defense Committee were barred, the district and international officers of the ISU, forced to yield to some extent, called upon the seamen to restrict the strike to intercoastal shipping. The leaders read wires purportedly from Bridges and other West Coast leaders which warned against extending the strike to offshore shipping. The audience howled down the telegrams as "fakes." At the scheduled closing time, the ISU leaders left the stormy meeting, whereupon Curran and the other leaders of the rank and file Seamen's Defense Committee were invited into the meeting and a vote was taken in support of a sympathy strike. Faced with the opposition of the ISU leaders and the uncertainty of receiving united support from other East Coast seamen and longshoremen, the "rank and file" voted to remain at their accustomed places of work in a "sitdown" to prevent the use of strikebreakers. The Seamen's Defense Committee was now reconstituted as a strike strategy committee with power to negotiate a new agreement meeting all West Coast conditions, including the union hiring hall. It called a strike on all East Coast ships on November 6. The strikers received important reinforcement from the action of the East Coast locals of the Masters, Mates, and Pilots' Association and the Marine Engineers' Beneficial Association in calling "independent" strikes on November 23, upon expiration of their agreements. The American Radio Telegraphists' Association also walked out on December 1.

If the West Coast strike was a test of endurance, the East Coast strike was a knockdown dragout battle. East Coast shipping interests had been counting upon the ISU leaders to hold the seamen to observance of the agreements which had been negotiated with ISU leaders. Upon the calling of the strike, the East Coast shipowners charged it with being an "outlaw" action in violation of the agreement. The president of the American Steamship Owners' Association charged that "the better class of American seamen" were not in sympathy with the strike and were acting only "as a result of the duress and threats of physical violence made to them by a small group within the union intent on turmoil and confusion." Protection "against intimidation and violence" was promised to employees who would remain at work. Shipowners expected that with the closing of the Great Lakes navigation season, plenty of able seamen would be available with which to "smother" the insurgent strike and "smother it right." [77]

The ISU leaders actively supported the shipowners against the strikers. David Grange, head of the Marine Cooks and Stewards' Association, described the strike as forwarding "Communism against Americanism and we are on the side of America. . . ." ISU leaders would maintain all the agreements with the companies, he announced, promising to furnish replacements for the strikers, with protection for the replacements "to the extent of arming our men," if necessary. The ISU leaders were fortified by the action of Joseph Ryan, international president of the ILA, in refusing to permit East Coast longshoremen to support the strikers on either coast, despite Bridges' efforts to enlist his support. Ryan announced early during the strike that he would not furnish labor to any shipping company which was recognizing the insurgent seamen on the East Coast. Bridges was ousted by Ryan as international organizer of the ILA when he came East later seeking the support of the East Coast longshoremen for the strike.

New York was the center of the most vigorous East Coast strike activity. Constant claims and counterclaims were made regarding the strikers' success in tying up ships in the port. Early strike efforts were widely supported. Two companies even indicated their willingness to recognize the strikers in order to obtain crews, but they were induced to stand by the American Steamship Owners' Association.[78]

The most significant action during the course of the strike with respect to the future of union organization on the East Coast was taken at a coastwise conference on December 14 where rank-and-file delegates from the branches of the Eastern and Gulf Sailors' Association and the Marine Cooks and Stewards' Association voted to expel the old-line leaders. Trustees were elected to administer the funds, property, and affairs of the unions until replaced by officials elected at the next general election. These trustees, together with the officials previously elected by the rank and file in the firemen's union, were now to act as the District Committee of the ISU. For the first time, the rank-and-file leaders had succeeded in establishing a coastwise organization and were competing with the ISU leaders for recognition as duly constituted bargaining agents. The committee tried to have the 1936 East Coast agreement set aside through court action on the grounds that it was the fruit of a conspiracy between the ISU leaders and the shipowners; when this failed, it appealed to the National Labor Relations Board for such a decision. The American Federation of Labor sought to counter any further developments by announcing that plans were under way for a national maritime federation under the leadership of Ryan and the ISU.[79]

Meanwhile the strike, with divergent motives and circumstances on the part of its participants, continued. An anomalous situation had arisen due to the fact that East Coast strikers and West Coast shipowners were favoring arbitration of disputes; but West Coast strikers and East Coast shipowners were in opposition to it. The East Coast strikers, weakened because of the lack of unanimous support, and because of the opposition from ILA and the ISU leaders, were anxious for arbitration which might achieve early consideration for their grievances without further continuation of the strike. Conversely, East Coast shipowners opposed arbitration to prevent recognition of the rank-and-file leaders; West Coast shipowners, however, were supporting arbitration in the hope of winning public support. Bridges recommended that the West Coast strikers support the East Coast seamen, at least with regard to East Coast ships in the intercoastal trade. Such support, however, was not to extend to the point where the interests of the West Coast unions might be harmed. As Bridges reasoned, "the eastern seamen would not permit a complete sacrifice of the Maritime Federation of the Pacific." [80] Subsequently, it was reported that the longshoremen had delayed the final settlement of their demands until the East Coast seamen called off their strike. There was mutual support between East and West Coast seamen during the strike against the effectuation of the recently enacted law requiring seamen to carry government-issued continuous discharge books. However, a disagreement was to arise between Lundeberg and the East Coast rank-and-file leaders after the strike in regard to the tactics to be followed in connection with the book, a controversy which was to prove the basis for the first serious split between East and West Coast militant seamen.

The NLRB's scheduling of a hearing, meanwhile, to consider its jurisdiction over the strikers' demands was regarded as something of a victory. Nevertheless, the East Coast rank-and-file strikers were forced to call off their strike after 86 days. The secretary of the Strike Strategy Committee was later to report: "out of 30,000 members that registered in the beginning of the strike, we wound up on January 24th with less than 3,000 men left up and down the entire Coast. Presumably, the rest of the guys finked out." [81] A contributory factor to the weakened position of the unlicensed seamen on the East Coast was the action of the national leadership of the licensed officers' unions in calling off their strike.[82] On January 24, 1937, after authorization by vote of the striking seamen, Curran declared the strike formally ended, and listed the following among the achievements of the strike: "The East Coast ship owners have been kept so busy they have not tried to break up the West Coast strike. We have driven the fakers out of the union and we have managed to show the government that seamen will not stand for 'fink' books. . . ." [83] However, the Curran group had failed to obtain recognition; the employers were to carry on their negotiations at the close of the strike with the old-line ISU leaders.

The strike on the West Coast was finally ended early in February, after 99 strikebound days. The unions were victorious since the employers formally agreed to call upon the unions for men; however, the employers could reject men furnished by the union if written reasons were furnished. Thus job control through the longshoremen's and seamen's hiring halls was preserved and strengthened. The parties agreed to prohibit strikes and lockouts for the life of the agreement until September 30, 1937. The seamen benefited from wage increases of $10 per month, which brought rates for able seamen to $72.50 in deepsea operations, and to $80 in coastwise operations. Overtime work was now to be paid for by cash only, and these rates were increased by 10¢ per hour. Working hours for deck and engine crews remained unchanged; but maximum hours in the stewards' department were reduced to nine hours in a spread of thirteen on deepsea passenger ships, and to eight hours in a spread of twelve on deepsea freighters and in the coastwise trades.

CHAPTER 7

REORGANIZATION AND UNCERTAIN STABILITY, 1937–1941

THE NEW ORDER

Unity among the maritime unions had been a basic factor in their victory in the 1936–7 strike. The weakening split among them which occurred shortly thereafter, and the widespread unemployment among seamen during the years immediately preceding the outbreak of war in Europe, made it an inauspicious time for demanding improvements in wages and working conditions. The primary concern of the seamen during this period was to hold on to what they had. The unions were to forget their differences only when they felt the employer associations were threatening their hard-won gains.

The appearance of the National Maritime Union upon the scene acted immediately as a powerful catalytic agent in the realignment of affinities among the maritime unions. Until now, despite conflicting interests, the West Coast unions had been forced to coöperate to ensure survival. The appearance of a potentially strong East Coast seamen's union, whose membership already exceeded the combined membership of the West Coast seamen's unions a few months after formation, was viewed by the West Coast seamen's unions as a threat to their autonomy and to their recent achievements. The possibility that affiliation with the CIO might mean subordination to the jurisdiction of the NMU was to swing Lundeberg and the SUP from favoring the CIO to reaffiliating with the AFL. On the other hand, to Bridges the appearance of a strong potential ally on the East Coast, whose jurisdiction would not conflict with his, brought closer the goal of a national maritime federation. Affiliation with the CIO offered him leadership of the International Longshoremen's and Warehousemen's Union; authority to lead an organizing drive among Pacific Coast workers on behalf of the CIO; and, possibly, ultimate leadership of a national union of marine transport workers.

The reordering of union relationships was accompanied by a trend in maritime industry labor relations toward increasing stability, more so than in American industry generally. Idle man-days resulting from strikes of ship personnel dropped by over 90 percent between January 1936 and June 1939.[1] Sitdown strikes on board ship, following the trend in industry generally, increased more than twentyfold in 1937; but in 1938 they had declined in importance, and by 1939 had been virtually eliminated.

Divergent factors contributed to increasing this stability. By 1939, union recognition had been achieved on both coasts; the exercise of substantial job control through union hiring halls had been accomplished in the industry, except on oil tankers and on the Great Lakes; and sizable gains had been made in wages and working conditions. With the validation of the National Labor Relations Act by the Supreme Court, the ship operators had resigned themselves to collective bargaining with the unions. But their attacks upon the unions were to continue, particularly their charges of "irresponsibility" and "radicalism" for the purpose of obtaining federal legislation to restrict the activities of the unions. The activities and policies of the Maritime Commission and the frequent attacks in Congress upon the unions were regarded by the unions as evidence that the government was supporting the shipowners. The uncertainty engendered among the unions by these conditions was heightened by their disunity, occasional instances of internal dissension, and continued widespread unemployment. They laid stress, therefore, upon the need for responsibility and stability to protect the gains already achieved, to strengthen internal organization, ward off attacks, and to demonstrate the benefits of collective bargaining to the shipowners, the government, and the public.

The ability of the shipowners and the unions to overcome their differences and extend their agreements between 1937 and 1939 testified to the efficiency of this strategy. While it could hardly be claimed that collective bargaining was blooming hardily, there were some indications that the seeds of mutual understanding had been planted. The fact that the dominant groups in the Roosevelt Administration chose to proceed with caution in the matter of maritime labor legislation may have favored these developments. Even as the seamen's organizations appeared to be under attack on the legislative front, the prominence given to improvement in the seamen's status as a major underpinning for the new program of operating and construction subsidies served to strengthen the unions.

THE NEW ORDER ON THE EAST COAST

The 1936–7 strike sounded the death knell of the ISU, for it had demonstrated that the old-line leaders were as incapable of keeping the rank and file in check on the East Coast as they had been on the West Coast. Once again, however, the shipowners were prepared to resume relations with the conservative leaders to prevent the militant rank and file from exercising official control. Their very aiding and abetting the old-line leaders served only to hammer the last nail into the coffin of the ISU.

Immediately following the strike, members of the American Steamship Owners' Association sought to prevent the employment of "known agitators" by referring applicants for work to regular ISU union halls "to give the union an opportunity to determine whether an applicant is a bona fide member of the union in good standing." In conferences between the American Steamship Owners' Association and the old-line leaders of the ISU, agreement was reached to amend the existing contract to bring wage and overtime rates up to the West Coast levels, and to reduce working hours in the stewards' department.

Protests of the rank and file over negotiations with the old-line faction were ignored by the shipowners. Upon appeal from the rank and file to end these negotiations, the AFL executive council recognized the rank-and-file demands by authorizing William Green, president of the AFL to arrange for an election in the Eastern and Gulf Sailors' Association and to recognize the results of the earlier election in the Marine Firemen's Union.[2]

The split between the AFL and the CIO, however, left the AFL ill-equipped to follow-up on the maritime labor situation. Within a few months, the orientation of the East Coast rank and file was altered from reconstructing the ISU within the AFL toward establishing a new union within the CIO. The rank-and-file group appealed to the National Labor Relations Board, charging the shipowners with having attempted to superimpose a repudiated leadership on the union membership. As a result, some companies ended the practice of requiring clearance cards signed by ISU leaders. But since recognition of the rank-and-file officials did not follow, it was decided to adopt more drastic tactics. A sitdown strike on the *President Roosevelt* took place during April 1937 to protest refusal by the International Mercantile Marine Company to recognize the rank-and-file leaders of the marine firemen's union. The strike was called off when, through the efforts of Elinore M. Herrick, regional director of the NLRB, an agreement was reached to issue passes to both rank and file and ISU representatives for boarding the company's ships and to hold an election under NLRB supervision.

At this point, the AFL again indicated it was going to act to straighten out the situation, but again action failed to follow. Therefore, Mrs. Herrick sought to reconcile the difference between the contending groups within the ISU. These efforts, however, were frustrated by the delaying tactics of the old-line faction. In the meantime, the rank and file had succeeded in obtaining recognition from a number of companies through job action. Emboldened by these successes, chafing under the continued delays by the ISU and the AFL leaders, and anticipating only further delays, the rank-and-file leaders took the final and decisive step and announced the establishment of the National Maritime Union early in May. The ISU was now clearly doomed; by the time the first NMU convention was held in July 1937, the new union could already lay claim to a membership of 35,000. This convention unanimously supported affiliation with the CIO, and announced that the question would be settled by a vote of the entire membership, which subsequently gave its ratification.[3]

The founding of the National Maritime Union early in May 1937, in the midst of widespread sitdown strikes on board East Coast ships, provided the militant East Coast rank and file with the first opportunity for self-government. The spirit of democracy which permeated the proceedings of the twelve-day session of the first convention in July reflected the dissatisfaction with the former domination of the ISU leaders. Representatives chosen from the membership on shipboard predominated over those on shore. A draft constitution submitted for the delegates' consideration was subjected to close scrutiny. Every possible assurance had to be provided that final authority would rest in the membership rather than in the elected officials. The spontaneous expression of opinion was so broad and forceful that, according to one critical observer, "it completely swamped the so-called political clique that we have regarded with some distrust out here on the Pacific Coast. . . ."[4]

The preamble of the constitution, as finally drafted, announced that the NMU "shall not be committed to any particular religious creed or political belief; neither shall affiliation herewith interfere with the religious or political freedoms of its members. . . ." The goals of the NMU included: unification of all workers in the industry "regardless of creed, color, nationality, or political affiliation"; improvements in wages, hours, working conditions, and living quarters by legislation and/or economic action; the enactment of social security legislation, including old age pensions, unemployment insurance and accident insurance; legislation setting forth manning scales; and the national unification of all maritime workers.

The characteristic feature of the original NMU organization was its degree of segmentation and decentralization, clearly the heritage of the ISU. The basic units of organization at each branch were the divisions representing the deck, engine, and stewards' departments, respectively. At the next organizational level were the three districts — the Atlantic,

Gulf, and Great Lakes — with separately elected district officers and complete autonomy regarding district matters, including supervision of the affairs of the divisions and formulation of rotary shipping rules. The National Council, consisting of the three national officers and the district officers, was to act on all union matters of national import. On shipboard, the members of each department were to elect representatives to a ship's committee. The basic authority within the union was inherent in "the biennial convention of delegates elected from ship and shore by general vote."

At the initial convention, Curran and other leaders, while acknowledging the improvements in overtime pay and crews' quarters obtained through job action, stressed the need for restricting the use of such tactics, "otherwise we will become a thousand different unions on different ships and we will have no organization." These recommendations were reinforced by constitutional provisions which required that strikes involving individual ships could only be called by a branch agent upon a vote of approval by the branch membership. The calling of a general strike, between conventions, was made subject to a recommendation by two-thirds vote of the National Council and approval by referendum vote of the membership.[5]

Membership benefits included shipping through the union hall on a rotary basis; funeral allowances up to $125; shipwreck benefits up to $100; hospital benefits of $1 a week; and prison benefits of $5 a week if serving a sentence arose out of union activity.

During the first two years of its existence, the NMU was beset with a constant stream of difficulties from within and without. From its inception, it had been attacked as Communist-inspired. To charges of this nature, Curran replied that the NMU "is not a political organization, is not committed to the support of any political program and is controlled by the rank and file."[6] Before the first constitutional election in 1938, a "rank-and-file" movement developed charging Curran and the "political clique" with being Communist-dominated. The immediate occasion for attacks in the *Rank and File N.M.U. Pilot,* issued by this group, was the recently negotiated tanker agreement in which the union had failed to obtain job control through the union hiring hall. The "insurgents" succeeded in electing Jerome King as secretary-treasurer, and in gaining control of the National Council and the regular *Pilot;* Curran and Ferdinand Smith were elected president and vice-president, respectively. The insurgents unsuccessfully challenged Smith's qualifications as an officer by alleging he had been a strikebreaker during the spring strike of 1936.[7]

The differences within the union were brought to a head when the tanker agreement expired in 1939. Despite Curran's warning against making excessive demands of the tanker operators, a rank-and-file committee insisted upon pressing for hiring through the union hall. When the major tanker operators refused to accede, a strike was called whose failure was a major setback to the union. King and the other members of the rank-and-file group were charged with having been in the employ of a ship operators' group and with conspiring to disrupt the union. King was found guilty of the charges and was suspended for ninety-nine years. These events, occurring just prior to the second national convention, were accompanied by a secessionist movement by the leaders of the Gulf District, who charged the national administration of the union with being Communist-dominated. The leaders of this movement were expelled from the union.[8]

These were the difficulties facing the NMU when it convened for its second national convention during July 1939. The unsuccessful tanker strike and the problems of internal administration had reduced the union's finances to a point where it had to borrow $25,000 in order to conduct the convention. But there were bases for hope, despite the difficulties facing the union. The membership had grown from 30,000 to 51,000 during the two years since the union's formation. The union had been successful in negotiating an agreement which covered the bulk of the dry cargo operators on the East Coast; and, despite the loss of the major tanker operators, it had agreements with a number of the smaller companies. With approximately 13,000 members unemployed and numerous signs of weakness, it was felt that reorganization was necessary in order to strengthen the union so that a united front could be presented to the dry-cargo operators when their agreement expired in the fall.

The second convention, therefore, differed in spirit from that of the convention two years earlier. The emphasis now was upon critical self-examination to determine what direction to take. Emphasis was placed upon such reorganization and redistribution of authority as would permit greater resiliency and economy in operation, a less involved superstructure, and greater centralization.[9]

The union was reorganized by clearing away the geographical divisions and the craft divisions. The organization was now to consist solely of branches at important ports; the National Council, made up of the national officers and the port agents; and the National Office, consisting of the national officers. The distinctive character of the Port of New York, with its tremendous volume of shipping, was recognized by providing three agents to represent the deck, engine, and steward departments, respectively. Additional authority was given to the National Council, and the National Office was authorized to execute the resolutions of the council. The calling of strikes affecting more than one ship in one or more branches, which did not come under the category of a "general strike," were now subject to the vote of the council, with approval by a majority of the branches and crews of the ships involved. The council could determine the number of patrolmen to be employed in any given branch; it could also decide when the needs of the organization required additional suboffices. It was also directed to "establish an Educational Bureau to provide general trade union education to the members of the union." Further evidence of the increased centralization was furnished by the drafting of uniform basic rules for shipping through the hiring hall, subject to additional provisions to meet local conditions. This trend toward increasing the power of the National Council continued and additional powers were granted it in 1941.

The American Federation of Labor remained incapable of meeting the maritime situation in the face of the larger AFL-CIO split. Although the ISU charter had not been revoked, and the old-line ISU leaders still laid claim to their appropriate jurisdiction on the East Coast, the AFL had tacitly disowned them. Following the formation of the NMU, Ryan, president of the ILA, had started to press actively for a marine labor council of seamen, longshoremen, and harbor workers. In furthering this plan, the ILA had been issuing charters to seamen's unions. Meanwhile, the AFL hesitated to deal the *coup de grace* to the ISU and thus formally acknowledge its exit from the seagoing jurisdiction, particularly since Ryan was having little success among the rank and file of seamen. To save face, a board including Ryan and Green, was put in charge of administering the ISU. This proved to be but a temporary expedient. As a result of the lack of success in meeting the CIO drive, Ryan was to withdraw from the seamen's field in October; and the AFL was to revoke the ISU charter and, instead, charter the AFL Seamen's Union directly under the federation's administration. This federal union, which was chartered in December 1937, consisted of some 2000 seamen on the Atlantic and Gulf who were opposed to the political complexion of the NMU, as well as to the old-line leaders.[10]

This group subsequently had their misgivings at the AFL's granting Lundeberg the international charter in 1938. They feared retaliation because, as ISU members, they had accepted government-issued continuous discharge books, and because they had refused to join in the 1936-7 "outlaw" strike. Lundeberg overcame the fears of the East Coast seamen of being "eliminated and persecuted" by assuring them that the SUP would remain a distinct Pacific district and that the East Coast districts would have complete autonomy. Furthermore, there was to be no interference with the job rights of East Coast men on East Coast ships. However, it was understood that when East Coast men were permitted to ship on West Coast ships because of a shortage in West Coast personnel, preference would be given to East Coast men who had clear strike records (that is, no strikebreaking record in the 1934 or 1936–7 strikes), and who carried certificates of identification rather than continuous discharge books.

An aggressive organizing campaign was immediately begun upon the establishment of the SIU. The East Coast district of the SIU was organized along industrial lines comparable to the NMU organization. The secretary-treasurer was established as executive officer of the district union; other leading officials were the assistant secretary-treasurer and patrolmen representing the respective departments.[11]

The East Coast seamen affiliated with the SIU followed the same general philosophy and tactics as Lundeberg and the SUP, placing much emphasis on job actions, and manifesting lesser concern with appeals to obtain support of public opinion. Social welfare, political activity, and trade union education programs — so characteristic of the NMU — were of little or no concern to the AFL seamen. They were opposed equally to the "phonies" of the ISU and what they regarded as the "Communist partisan politics" of the NMU; they were militant "business" unionists.

THE SPLINTERING OF THE UNIONS

The split between the American Federation of Labor and the CIO in 1936 was to provide competing magnetic poles which split asunder the maritime unions as they split the labor movement generally. But the maritime unions were not beset by any conflict over the issue of craft versus industrial organization, for Lundeberg, Bridges, and Curran all supported closer integration. Rather the basic causes of conflict among the maritime unions arose out of the clashing ambitions of the union leaders, as well as over differences in trade union ideologies and tactics.

On the West Coast, the seamen's unions had been reconsidering the question of their affiliations in view of the moribund condition of the ISU. Under Lundeberg's inspiration, the now unaffiliated Sailors' Union had decided in April to conduct a referendum on the question of AFL versus CIO affiliation. Lundeberg's inclination was clearly indicated by the language of the ballot: "Do we want to accept the old ISU crew and the AFL representatives? Or do we want to follow under the banner of the CIO and the ideals of progressive industrial unions?" Bridges' policy at that time was described as involving the support of "the CIO organizational campaign, to fight efforts of the AFL fakers to wreck the CIO, and to remain within the AFL." [12]

The entry of the National Maritime Union into the circle of maritime unions, however, was to alter the orientations of the West Coast unions. The NMU, having gained a membership of 35,000 as early as July 1937, and demonstrating even greater growth potentialities, threatened to overshadow the three West Coast seafaring unions, whose combined strength was about 20,000. Antagonism between the East Coast insurgents and the SUP had developed almost immediately after the end of the 1936–7 strike. The action of the East Coast rank-and-file leaders in reversing an earlier position and voting to permit the acceptance of the continuous discharge, or the Copeland "fink" books, was viewed by the West Coast seamen as a traitorous act. The months following the termination of the strike were marked by SUP efforts to "dump" members of the NMU on intercoastal ships on the grounds that they carried the "fink" books, and by NMU charges that the SUP was seeking to invade NMU jurisdiction over intercoastal ships operating from the East Coast. The likelihood that a CIO charter would be granted to the NMU, giving it nationwide jurisdiction over unlicensed personnel, produced a more circumspect attitude toward the CIO on Lundeberg's part. At the convention of the Maritime Federation of the Pacific in June 1937, he was to introduce a resolution to have the constituent unions vote on the question of CIO affiliation, but with the express reservation that the identity and autonomy of the unions would be maintained. A truce in the jurisdictional disputes between East and West Coast seamen's unions was also arranged pending the outcome of discussions with John L. Lewis. Meanwhile, announcement of the results of the May SUP referendum was withheld.[13]

Leaders of the various maritime unions, including Harry Bridges, Robert Stowell (SUP), Vincent J. Malone (Pacific Marine Firemen), Eugene F. Burke (Pacific Marine Cooks and Stewards), Joseph Curran, Jerome King, and Ferdinand C. Smith (trustees of the deck, engine, and stewards' departments of the NMU, M. Rathborne of the Telegraphists, and representatives of licensed officers, shipbuilding workers, and of the West Coast inlandboatmen met with Lewis early in July. Out of their discussions, a five-point program was derived and a maritime organizing committee was formed consisting of John Brophy and Rathborne, representing the CIO, Curran, Bridges, Pinchin of the Masters, Mates, and Pilots, Malone, and John Green of the Industrial Union of Marine and Shipbuilding Workers. Bridges was also named Pacific Coast director of all CIO unions. The program called for the formation of a national industrial maritime union consisting of all unlicensed seamen to be organized at a national unity conference to be held in Chicago during August. This union and the autonomous national unions of the licensed officers, longshoremen, and any other related groups were to be joined in a national maritime federation.[14]

While the plan was accepted by the Maritime Council of the Port of New York (consisting of the NMU, Industrial Union of Marine and Shipbuilding Workers, and the New York locals of the Marine Engineers' Beneficial Association and the Masters, Mates and Pilots' Association), it met with opposition when the conferees reported it to the convention of the Maritime Federation of the Pacific. Despite Bridges' assurances that the West Coast seamen's unions would have a representation equal to that of the much larger NMU, the sailors' and marine firemen's unions rejected the proposal. Claiming that the CIO program had nothing to offer them, they charged that a charter was being contemplated which would give the NMU jurisdiction over all offshore and intercoastal shipping, with the jurisdiction of the West Coast unions restricted to the steam schooners. Lundeberg, who had been ignored when Lewis had made appointments to the maritime organizing committee, was primarily responsible for the convention's rejection of the CIO program in July. While a meeting was held in Chicago during August to lay the groundwork for a national industrial union of seamen, it was foredoomed by Lundeberg's refusal to have the SUP participate. Another meeting scheduled for January 1938 was to meet with a like fate.[15]

Lundeberg now chose to follow a policy of aloofness, bargaining with both the AFL and the CIO for affiliation upon the best possible terms. During October of 1937, he sent letters to both John L. Lewis and William Green proposing almost identical terms, namely, that the SUP be given a national charter covering unlicensed personnel and guaranteeing complete autonomy. Lewis replied that these were questions which would have to be decided by the seamen themselves at the January 1938 meeting. In his letter to the AFL, Lundeberg also proposed that the ISU charter be canceled. Lundeberg's interest in possible reaffiliation furnished the AFL with the hope of reëstablishing a national organization of seamen and in his reply, Green indicated that the AFL was willing to reorganize the ISU and to recharter it under terms acceptable to Lundeberg "and to the rank and file of seamen." [16]

Lundeberg's immediate decision, however, was to remain independent of both the AFL and the CIO and to seek to combine the West Coast seamen's unions in a seafarers' federation affiliated with the Maritime Federation of the Pacific.[17] The fallacy of such a hope was soon to be demonstrated. To what extent he could count on fellow members of the Maritime Federation was to become evident during a prolonged jurisdictional dispute over the ships of the Shepard Line in which Bridges supported the NMU against the SUP.[18] The significance of this development was clear; despite their membership in the Maritime Federation of the Pacific, the West Coast unions affiliated with the CIO, particularly Bridges' International Longshoremen's and Warehousemen's Union, would place the interests of their East Coast CIO affiliate above those of the West Coast seafaring unions.

Lundeberg therefore announced in June 1938 that he was in favor of affiliating with the AFL. In support of this position, he advised the SUP membership that "any union struggling for existence must reinforce itself with available allies; not those that correspond to the Ideal, but those ready to hand." A referendum of the SUP membership supported Lundeberg. The last vestige of maritime unity was ended when the SUP withdrew from the Maritime Federation of the Pacific on the grounds that it was dominated by shoreside organizations who were seeking to use the federation "as a weapon to club workers into the CIO."

In August 1938, the AFL issued an international charter for the Seafarers' International Union of North America, with jurisdiction over unlicensed seamen and fishermen, and entrusted its administration to the SUP, which in turn was to issue district charters to the AFL seamen on the Atlantic and Gulf and the Lakes. The earlier AFL Seamen's Union was absorbed by the eastern district of the SIU. An aggressive organizing campaign was immediately undertaken in these areas. By October 1939, the national SIU organization was to claim a paid membership of 15,000.[19]

Faced with the organizing drives of the rival AFL Seamen's Union on the East Coast and the hostility of Joseph Ryan's ILA, the National Maritime Union had continued to press for the formation of a CIO national industrial union of seamen. However, this goal became impossible when Lundeberg agreed to affiliate with the AFL. Failing in their effort to achieve an inclusive and integrated maritime organization, the CIO maritime unions were to content themselves with establishing a medium for more limited coöperation in 1938 — the CIO Maritime Committee. To this committee, consisting of the executive officers of the CIO maritime unions was to be assigned the function of coördinating the organizational and legislative activities of the maritime unions.[20] During the period prior to the war, however, the CIO Maritime Committee was to serve primarily as the legislative representative of the maritime unions. Its initial effort to coördinate the contract negotiations of the East and West Coast CIO maritime unions in the autumn of 1939 were to be largely unsuccessful. Divergent interests and situations facing East and West Coast unions were to prevent any agreement on unified action.

Thus, by mid-year 1938, the divisive processes had been completed. On the East Coast, the longshoremen and the Atlantic and Gulf districts of the SIU were aligned against the NMU. On the West Coast, the longshoremen and their satellite Marine Cooks and Stewards' Union aligned against the Sailors' Union of the Pacific, while the Marine Firemen's Union maintained its independence of both the AFL and the CIO. The Maritime Federation of the Pacific, now clearly under the domination of Bridges' ILWU, was being kept alive as a means of maintaining some bonds of unity with such non-CIO groups as the Marine Firemen's Union, Independent, and a local of the International Association of

Machinists; and with such a nonmaritime group as the cannery workers.

Interunion relations following the formalization of the differences among the maritime groups consisted largely of recriminations, jurisdictional disputes, rival organizing drives, and efforts to obtain greater concessions than rival unions had obtained. Lundeberg attacked the NMU leaders as following weak-kneed political policies which injured the seamen. Instances which he cited were the NMU's supporting of government training ships which would be used "for the training of scabs to break seamen's strikes"; accepting of government-issued "fink" books; and permitting seamen to ship through government hiring halls. Jurisdictional disputes between Bridges' longshoremen and Lundeberg's sailors, particularly over the sailors' work in loading and discharging cargo on the steam schooners, while not unusual before the formal split, now became increasingly frequent.[21] To meet an organizing drive of the NMU during 1941 among the West Coast tanker companies, Lundeberg was to reorganize the SUP on an industrial basis; in this situation, the competition was to prove beneficial for the SUP, for as a result it was to succeed in organizing virtually all West Coast tankers within three years.[22]

The basic precept of the Maritime Federation of the Pacific, simultaneous termination and renewal of agreements, was virtually discarded as the member unions conducted separate negotiations, extended agreements for varying lengths of time, and called uncoördinated strikes. Only in 1938, when it appeared that organized employers were preparing to end all relations with the longshoremen's union, were all the maritime unions including the SUP to join in a concerted effort — the support of the longshoremen. Unity served to ward off the attack and a new agreement was reached.[23] But the unity lasted only as long as the immediate threat. The Maritime Federation, having long since ceased to perform any real function, was finally put to death in 1941, without the benefit of a referendum of the membership of its constituent unions. At its funeral, Bridges was to warn the West Coast firemen and cooks to amalgamate with the NMU, and announce that "if it was necessary, and it might become necessary, for the best protection of the West Coast longshoremen, I would sponsor a move (I don't know how far we would get) to amalgamate the ILWU and the NMU. . . ."[24]

REORGANIZATION OF EAST COAST SHIPOWNERS

The emergence of the NMU as a new and potentially powerful organization among East Coast seamen necessitated a reëxamination of the nature and policies of the organization among shipowners for labor-management relations. It early became apparent that failure to deal jointly with the union would result in an imbalance of power between the large union and the individual companies — the early realization for the necessity for joint action served to keep instability at a low level, aided by the efforts of the NMU leadership to demonstrate their responsibility.[25]

Increasing the union's staying power and demonstrating its responsibility would build toward equality in dealings with the ship operators. But the first relations between employers and the NMU had been inauspicious. The NMU had originated in the midst of a rash of sitdown strikes to force the shipowners to grant recognition and to improve working conditions. Immediately upon the establishment of the union, however, NMU leaders had announced that sitdown strikes should be used only with caution for "by so doing we will still further impress the public with the fact that we do not take indiscriminate action, but that we work together smoothly as any sound organization is expected to function." [26] This was wishful thinking, for a smoothly working organization remained to be achieved; and so long as poor living quarters on board ship continued and the new organization was threatened by rival organizing activities, sitdowns were to continue. In a number of instances, the crews involved in sitdowns were brought to trial before the Bureau of Marine Inspection and Navigation; the certificates of about 100 men were suspended between March 1937 and July 1938. This use of the "ship disaster" statutes was condemned by the CIO as "usurping the NLRB's exclusive jurisdiction in the matter of adjusting the labor disputes." [27]

The NMU had filed petitions for certification as collective bargaining agent with East Coast companies during May and June 1937, almost immediately after its formation. With the virtual elimination of the ISU, Ryan and the ILA had sought to fill the void for the AFL. The result was sporadic violence and intensification of work stoppages on each side to prevent the other from obtaining recognition by the ship operators. A truce was arranged by the NLRB between the rival unions to prevent interference in the elections. Sitdowns continued when passes were issued to ILA representatives to board ships of certain companies. The NLRB restricted its activities in these disputes to assuring that when passes were issued, they were issued equally to both sides. Meanwhile, elections were being conducted on a company basis, with NMU successes in a number of cases. During September, the NLRB held hearings on an application for elections on 71 lines. The AFL obtained a stay of election in what proved to be an abortive attempt to act on the reorganization of the ISU; the NLRB subsequently proceeded with the elections. By March 1938, the NMU had been designated for 39 lines, and the ISU for 4; by July 1939, the results were 68 and 12, respectively.[28]

The position of the ship operators regarding the NLRB elections, as

expressed by the executive committee of the American Steamship Owners' Association in June 1937, was that they "were in favor of and desired
to coöperate with the NLRB in the holding of elections for the designation of representatives of their unlicensed seagoing personnel for the
purpose of collective bargaining. . . ." According to the NLRB, 90
percent of the shipowners had coöperated during the elections. As the
results of the first three elections became known, and the NMU started
negotiations with these companies, representatives of the association
conferred with the three companies in order to "work out a formula
for all collective agreements . . . with a view to having the members
of the Association agree to stand solidly behind such formula. . . ." [29]
The association sought to implement this policy of a standard or uniform
agreement, and to prevent defections by individual companies which
might grant too favorable terms, by calling a conference of shipowner
and union representatives during November 1937. As the negotiations
proceeded, it appeared that there would be a deadlock over the association's refusal to grant union preference via the union hiring hall and
to recognize the ship's committee for the purpose of dealing with grievances aboard ship.

Since the deadlock with the dry cargo operators continued, the NMU
called for negotiations with the individual companies. With the possibility of piecemeal negotiations now staring them in the face, the ship
operators acted to reorganize the American Steamship Owners' Association. A new president, Frank J. Taylor, was elected, and a resolution
was adopted calling "for sound and common sense coöperation between
government, steamship owners, labor, and the public."

The metamorphosis of the American Steamship Owners' Association
was completed with the organization of the American Merchant Marine
Institute. The new organization announced that as one of its purposes
"it will strive to foster, promote, improve, and maintain the best relationships among those engaged in operation of the American merchant
marine and all personnel employed thereon." [30] A committee of the
newly constituted institute finally reached an agreement with the NMU
at the end of July which was signed on October 31, 1938, following
ratification by the union membership.

The initial agreement reached with the NMU after almost a year of
negotiations was heralded by Taylor as forming "a sound and constructive basis for orderly labor relations and for assuring stability in the
industry in the future." The union leaders viewed the agreement as a
means of consolidating "our position firmly, then, with less danger to
what we have already won, we can proceed to fighting for gains we now
have to give up temporarily." Agreements were signed by the union with
the individual companies incorporating the terms of the standard agree-

ment negotiated by a committee of the institute. Except for vacancies in key (that is, more responsible) ratings, jobs would be filled exclusively by union members, provided they were satisfactory to the company. In effect, this provided for obtaining personnel through the union hiring hall. The agreement specifically permitted unlicensed personnel to remain continuously in the companies' employ where it was mutually agreeable. Work stoppages and lockouts were prohibited. Wages and hours provisions were comparable to those in effect on the West Coast. Detailed provisions regarding crews' quarters, working rules, and grievance machinery were set forth. The union agreed to special concessions regarding overtime for ships in the coastwise trade in recognition of "the critical economic situation which confronts the coastwise trade," namely, the competition from land transportation. The agreement was to remain in effect until September 30, 1939.[31]

The year 1939 did not augur well for the NMU. The role of the "rank-and-file" group in demanding that the tanker companies be made to agree to the use of the union hiring hall has already been mentioned. The tanker agreement negotiated in 1938, even before the dry cargo agreement, provided for only a limited degree of union preference, permitting the companies to retain employees who did not choose to join the union, to reship former employees, and to transfer employees from one ship or port to another ship or port. Passes were to be issued to union representatives, and the ships' committees were to be recognized. A number of the smaller companies agreed to the demand; but the major operators, Standard Oil of New Jersey and Socony Vacuum, together with Tidewater Oil and C. D. Mallory, refused the demand. A strike was called against these companies in April. Regarding NMU charges that unqualified men were being used as strikebreakers, the acting director of the Bureau of Marine Inspection and Navigation reported: "we found that there appeared to be justification for complaints. We found that one ship sailed with a crew of which not one member was properly qualified." The strike was finally called off in June since the tanker companies were encountering little manning difficulty.[32]

This major setback to the union was accompanied by internal difficulties, and the union's affairs appeared to be at a low ebb. These difficulties were augmented when the dry cargo operators, through the American Merchant Marine Institute, demanded modification of the expiring agreement to permit the company to hire nonunion men who would be required to join the union promptly. The institute, in commenting on the experience under the initial agreement, stated that "while the general record of observance of agreements is probably improving, there are still many instances of failure to observe agreements by unlicensed personnel." The difficulties in the main were attributed to the rotary system which, it was charged, caused discontent among employees, violations of the agreement, and "does not give the employer choice in the selection of his employees in keeping with his responsibility for safety at sea and the standard of service which it is desired to extend to the public." [33] The institute took a strong position on the hiring provision. Negotiations continued for four months, when a two-year agreement was reached which, in effect, continued the previous terms.

The outbreak of the war in Europe with the resultant opening of opportunities for the ships of neutral nations had made it imperative that an agreement be reached; otherwise, perhaps the companies might not have yielded the issue so readily. Curran, recognizing that in the future it might not be possible to come off as well, warned the membership to end job actions to avoid giving the employers any grounds for attacking the union on the charge of irresponsibility. As Curran expressed it, "We ought to impress upon the membership that they've got a good union; they've got a strong union, but they haven't got a union that can't be broken." [34]

The active organizing campaign by the Atlantic and Gulf district of the Lundeberg-led SIU was also successful in obtaining recognition. By mid-year 1939, separate agreements had been obtained with twelve companies which operated primarily in the coastwise trades. While the provisions for union preference varied, job control through the union hiring hall was an accomplished fact, as it was for dry cargo vessels generally on both coasts. Other provisions of the agreements were comparable to those of the standard NMU pact.

UNIFIED EMPLOYERS AND DIVIDED UNIONS ON THE WEST COAST

Disunity among the West Coast unions was to prevent the formation of an integrated organization comprising the members of all of the ship's departments. The clash between Lundeberg and Bridges prevented the vertical amalgamation of the West Coast maritime unions for which both had striven. Unlike the East Coast unions, therefore, the West Coast unions continued divided on a departmental basis, with virtually the same organizational structure that had existed since their founding: a system of branches, with the San Francisco branch as headquarters, and with union policy determined by weekly membership meetings at headquarters and the branches.

The Marine Cooks and Stewards' Union and the Marine Firemen, Oilers, Watertenders and Wipers' Union were subjected to internal dissension over the issue of supporting Lundeberg or Bridges, or of remaining independent. In the case of the Marine Cooks and Stewards, the "disruptive forces" who supported Lundeberg were to be ousted; and in 1938, the union was to be swung more fully into the Bridges' orbit by his supporters within the union. The Marine Cooks and Stewards' Union, with a membership of about 8200, was then affiliated with the CIO as well as with the Maritime Federation of the Pacific. However, the strength of particularism even in this Bridges' satellite was evident when the membership rejected a Bridges-supported plan to have the Marine Cooks and Stewards join the NMU as an autonomous union in 1941.[35] Within the Marine Firemen's Union, the supporters of independence, led by Vincent J. Malone, were to be victorious in 1938; and although the union's affiliation with the Maritime Federation was to be maintained, the relationship was to be extremely cool. Efforts by Bridges in 1941 to get the 4000 members of the union to affiliate with the NMU, and by Lundeberg to get them to affiliate with the SIU were to be defeated by overwhelming majority votes of the membership. Malone's sentiments on affiliation were: "In such a bargain, we believe the Marine Firemen's Union would be condemned to the role of nothing more than a despised and doglike auxiliary. We prefer to continue on our own course, thereby being dictated to by neither Harry Lundeberg or Harry Bridges. . . ."[36]

The unity among the ship operators contrasted sharply with the disunity among the seafaring unions. Immediately after the 1936–7 strike, which had won the unions much public support, as well as a substantial victory, the operators acted to recoup their position. In 1937, the two principal associations representing marine labor — the Pacific American Shipowners' Association negotiating with the seamen, and the Waterfront Employers' Association negotiating with the longshoremen — were brought together under one executive so that they could "act either jointly or independently, as the circumstances indicated." Almon E. Roth, former comptroller of Stanford University, was made president and executive manager of the two associations. The shipping groups, acknowledging that their recent experience had "taught them the value of new opinion from unbiased sources bearing on their own problems in connection with organized labor," announced that Roth's appointment was based upon "his ability to solve public relations problems and to reconcile diverse points of view." As a primary duty, the new executive was "to harmonize the shipping industry with the maritime labor unions on the Pacific Coast."[37]

The shipowners' point of view regarding relations with the unions was to be given a new translation under Roth. He called attention to the achievements of collective bargaining relationships as well as to the failures. He cited the good faith of the employers in reaching agreements and expressed the hope "that labor leaders will find it to their interest to observe contracts." "I do not predict continued peace upon the waterfront," commented Roth, "but I do unhesitatingly say that

there is no sound or common sense reason for serious trouble. . . ." [38]
He extolled the increasing ability to reach agreements on troublesome
items, and even attempted the self-critical approach: namely, the validity
of a number of Maritime Commission findings regarding conditions in
the merchant marine, particularly the need for improving crews' quarters. Union shortcomings continued to receive critical attention. Work
stoppages by the unions were attributed primarily to jurisdictional disputes. There were accusations that "a certain number of [labor] leaders
are elected upon platforms which call for trouble with the shipowners."
Although Roth acknowledged that few employees were Communists, he
maintained "there is no question, however, that the program and the
technique which has been adopted by some of the leaders on the waterfront is the program and technique of the Communist Party." On the
basis of these charges, he requested revision of the National Labor
Relations Act, particularly to provide some penalty for contract violations and to permit employers as well as the unions to ask for elections.[39]

Idle mandays due to strikes by West Coast seamen were to decrease
in comparison with work stoppages during 1937 (which saw the end of
the 1936–7 strike) by over 95 percent during 1938, and by over 97 percent during 1939. What strike losses did remain were primarily the
result of sporadic work stoppages. The Pacific American Shipowners'
Association reported that 144 of a total of 192 disputes between Pacific
Coast licensed and unlicensed seamen and the association during the
twenty-eight-month period following February 1937 resulted in work
stoppages in violation of the agreements. Approximately 40 percent of
these lasted more than twenty-four hours. As analyzed by the shipowners, approximately 50 percent of the disputes arose over issues in
the general category of wages, hours, and working conditions. Specifically, the major issues included disputes over crew quarters and
safety facilities, overtime payments, and manning scales. Furthermore,
approximately 20 percent of the disputes arose over the hiring issue, the
most frequent cause being the seamen's refusal to ship with men they
considered antiunion or objectionable in their manner toward subordi-
nates or coworkers and the employers' refusal to hire certain individuals.
About 5 percent were jurisdictional disputes; and about 13 percent of
the disputes involved sympathetic actions (usually refusal to cross picket
lines) in support of such groups as longshoremen, teamsters, and lum-
bermen. Although work stoppages had been initiated by the seamen, the
Maritime Labor Board was to observe "there is probably some merit,
although how much is difficult to determine . . . in the contentions of
the unions that the men are provoked to job action by 'chiseling' and
other irritating tactics on the part of employers, and by the adamant
attitude of employers with regard to grievances which are peaceably

presented." Since both employers and employees distrusted arbitration of grievances, and the ability to solve disputes through negotiation was slow in developing, there was a persistent, although reduced, tendency for seamen to seek improvement through direct action.[40]

Despite the Pacific American Shipowners' Association's charges that these stoppages were in violation of the contract, collective bargaining relations with the seamen were continued. The agreements were renewed between 1937 and 1939 without change, largely because the split among the maritime unions and widespread unemployment were effective deterrents to requests for changes. The only serious threat to this peace was to occur in September 1938, after the SUP had already negotiated its agreement. Almon Roth, as president of the Waterfront Employers' Association, had threatened to refuse to renew the ILWU contract unless guarantees would be included against work stoppages in violation of the contract. This action, which followed upon employer refusals to renew contracts with San Francisco warehousemen and retail clerks, was viewed by the unions as heralding another open shop drive. Factional disputes were temporarily laid aside, and rival unions united to meet this common menace. Lundeberg threatened a sympathy strike if the longshoremen were locked out. The SUP was willing, he said, to "back up the bona fide longshoremen. That doesn't mean we'll back up Harry Bridges and the bunch of Communist stooges who run his outfit. . . ." Faced with this united front of labor, the waterfront employers reached an agreement with the longshoremen.[41]

Following the example of the longshoremen, the seafaring unions agreed to an indefinite extension of their agreements with the Pacific American Shipowners' Association in 1939. In anticipation of the effects of the second World War on shipping prospects, the contracts were made subject to reopening on sixty days' notice.[42]

The start made toward maintaining the semblance of collective bargaining relationships between shipowners and seamen's unions benefited both parties. Increased stability made it possible to obtain increased efficiency and continuity in shipping operations. Recognition of the unions by the employers and increased demonstration of willingness to deal with them made it possible for the unions to exercise increasing control over their members, and assured the development of responsible organizations. The unions, through the demonstration of responsibility, were able to ward off the efforts at enactment of restrictive labor legislation for the maritime industry. The representatives of the new organizations of the militant rank and file were increasingly able to hold their own on the constantly threatening legislative front, as they had held it on economic matters.

THE FEDERAL GOVERNMENT AND THE SEAMEN

The Board desires to point out, to a degree which has never been adequately appreciated, the confusion in labor relations in the maritime industry is a reflection and a consequence of the confusion in the laws affecting these relations and of the confusion in the administrative policies of the governmental agencies entrusted with the administration of these laws. (*Maritime Labor Board, Report to the President and to the Congress* (1940), p. xiii.)

The activities of the administrative agencies of the Federal government during this period reflected the non-parallel policies of the administration. On the one hand, the agencies primarily concerned with labor relations, such as the NLRB, the Department of Labor, and the Maritime Labor Board, sought to advance the cause of collective bargaining to provide a firm foundation for stability in labor relations in the merchant marine. On the other hand, the agencies primarily concerned with the technical aspects of shipping operations, such as the Maritime Commission and the Department of Commerce, frequently showed impatience at the pangs attending the birth of collective bargaining. Although these agencies recognized the need for true collective bargaining, their impatience was generally directed at the unions and the seamen. And although the activities of the maritime agencies were generally restricted to the periphery of maritime labor relations, they frequently stimulated serious reactions on the part of the unions.

Amelioration of the condition of American seamen was a major argument in supporting the administration's advocacy of direct operating and construction subsidies for the purpose of improving the condition of the American merchant marine. The *Morro Castle* (1934) and *Mohawk* (1935) ship disasters heightened the public's awareness of the basic shortcomings in the conditions facing the seamen on shipboard, as well as the limitations in physical equipment on board ship which seriously threatened the safety of life at sea. The resurgence of maritime labor organization, with the growth of labor organization generally under the protective cloak of the administration's labor policies, also assured the seamen's representatives of a more favorable reception in Congressional circles than they had had for over a decade.

The unstable conditions in the merchant marine in 1936 and 1937, marked by the victories of the rank-and-file groups in their battles to control their own unions and to win recognition and economic improvements from their employers, brought employer demands for restrictive legislation. This campaign for restrictive legislation mustered sufficient force to obtain serious Congressional consideration. The maritime unions fought these proposals as attacks upon collective bargaining in the industry. Calmer counsels prevailed, however, in the compromise provisions which established the Maritime Labor Board in 1938, giving it mediatory functions differing little from those of the Conciliation Service of the Department of Labor.

With the possibility of direct government intervention removed, the responsibility for maintaining stable labor relations rested squarely on the willingness of shipowners and seamen's unions to establish sound collective bargaining relations. The increasing stability in labor relations during 1938 and 1939 was proof that a start had been made.

Legislative proposals relating to maritime labor relations and conditions were constantly before Congress following 1934. Early proposals, intended to buttress the public support for subsidy legislation, also contained provisions whose primary purpose was to ameliorate seamen's conditions. There were also provisions, however, which could be used to restrain the spread of militancy among the rank and file of seamen. Following the organization of militant unions, legislative proposals sought to circumscribe the use of the strike in labor disputes. The prevailing sympathy in administration circles toward the development of organization among American workers generally extended to maritime workers as well; seamen's legislation, therefore, was to have little restraining effect upon the growing strength of the unions.

The ISU leaders who had failed to obtain government sanction for their program through the NIRA were to be given a more favorable reception subsequently in connection with the administration's maritime subsidy program. Concurrently with President Roosevelt's proposal that forthright operating and construction subsidies "to make up the differential between American and foreign shipping costs," replace the thinly disguised and ineffective subsidies in the form of ocean-mail contracts, consideration was given to improving the caliber and condition of the men who manned the ships.[43] The *Morro Castle* disaster had heightened public interest in the need for safety at sea.

The proposals for a long-range maritime subsidy program were considered in prolonged Congressional hearings and subsequently became the objects of close scrutiny and sharp attack in Congressional debates. The proposals for seamen's legislation were less controversial, since the need for improvements was universally conceded. But there were basic differences between the ISU leaders and the shipowners regarding the manner in which these improvements could be achieved.

Andrew Furuseth, making a last valiant effort in behalf of his oft-repeated plea, advised the House Committee on Merchant Marine and Fisheries in 1935 that with proper enforcement of the Seamen's Act, operating subsidies would be unnecessary; however, he conceded the necessity for a construction subsidy. Regarding the proposals for seamen's legislation, he called for a provision which would restrict the hiring process to direct hiring by the master, of men shipped through the offices of the U. S. Shipping Commissioners.[44]

Once again, he supported government-issued continuous discharge books as insurance against the future reimposition of employer-issued books and as a means of restricting the seamen's calling to *bona fide* seamen. The proposal for character ratings, he rejected, however, as being shipowner-inspired.

Employer-issued continuous discharge books having been eliminated by the growth of strong union organizations, the shipowners reversed their earlier position on government-issued discharge books. They now supported these books and demanded, further, that they include provision for character and ability ratings as a means of exercising disciplinary control over seamen. Their strongest opposition was directed at the ISU's view regarding citizenship requirements for the stewards' department. Ira Campbell, general counsel of the American Steamship Owners' Association, arguing that Americans "don't make waiters and bedroom stewards," asked for exemption of the stewards' department.[45]

The elements which had caused the spectacular battle over the earlier Seamen's Act were now missing, however. The employers were now reluctant to fight, since some seamen's legislation appeared to be a *sine qua non* for the enactment of subsidy legislation. Furthermore, the ISU demands were hardly objectionable since they merely sought protection of the hours provisions already in effect under existing collective bargaining agreements. The government-issued continuous discharge book, even without the character rating, and other proposals relating to the issuance, suspension, and revocation of seamen's certificates of service could be effective in maintaining discipline among seamen.

The direction of the debates in Congress reflected the altered situation. The basic issue was that of subsidy payments, and the proposals for seamen's legislation were hardly debated. Both proponents and opponents of subsidies, however, resorted to arguments regarding the effects of subsidies upon seamen's conditions to support their respective positions. The sponsors of the subsidy legislation argued that this was the only avenue for improving the seamen's status.[46] The opponents of subsidy legislation viewed these arguments skeptically, pointing out that the interests seeking subsidies "always based on the ground that it was for American labor . . . were at the same time trying to have as high an exception as could be obtained so that as many foreigners as possible could be employed." [47] As finally enacted, the legislation relating to seamen was to be divided between the Merchant Marine Act and the Seamen's Act, which were passed almost concurrently during June 1936.[48]

The Merchant Marine Act of 1936 included a section (Title III) relating to "American Seamen," which was intended to set up a standard to be applied in the payment of the operating-differential subsidies provided for elsewhere in the act.[49] The act authorized the Maritime Commission to "investigate the employment and wage conditions in oceangoing shipping." After such investigation and "appropriate hearings," the commission was to establish "minimum-manning scales and minimum-wage scales and reasonable working conditions for all officers and crews employed on all types of vessels receiving an operating-differential subsidy." The act permitted increases over the minima to be added to the operating differential subsidies authorized for the vessels, thus protecting the operation of collective bargaining. The act also required all licensed and unlicensed personnel on subsidized cargo ships, and all licensed personnel and 80 percent of the unlicensed personnel (to be increased to 90 percent within 2 years) on subsidized passenger ships to be American citizens.

The companion Seamen's Act was intended to protect safety at sea by improving the caliber of American seamen through strengthening the provisions of the precursor Seamen's Act of 1915, and by maintaining discipline on shipboard. Whereas previously the law had required certificates only for able seamen, now all seamen were required to carry certificates of service, which were to be issued by local boards of inspectors.[50]

The individual discharge certificates formerly issued after each voyage were to be replaced by government-issued continuous discharge books which made no reference to character or ability. The book, to be retained by the seamen at all times, was to be issued within six months to all seamen on foreign and intercoastal vessels; and within one year to all other seamen, except those on ships operating on the rivers. The book was to include such personal information as the seaman's description, photograph, age, address, nationality, and signature. Upon a seaman's discharge, the shipping commissioners were to enter in his book such notations as the name and type of vessel he had just sailed on, the nature and length of voyage, and the kind of job he had filled.

The act extended the statutory three-watch system to sailors; and it limited hours of work at sea and in port to eight, except for the stewards' department. These conditions had, in fact, largely been achieved through collective bargaining. Crew quarters were to be inspected by local inspectors at least once a month, and penalties were prescribed where ships were found to be improperly ventilated, unclean, or unequipped with the plumbing and mechanical appliances required by law. Within six months after passage of the Seamen's Act, at least 75 percent of the unlicensed personnel and all of the licensed officers on an unsubsidized ship were to be American citizens.

Decided reactions to this legislation were to be manifested several months after its enactment. Confronted with the Maritime Commission's pressure to prevent the West Coast maritime unions from striking during the autumn of 1936, the unions characterized the legislation as seeking to undermine their growing strength by a "powerful machinery . . . with the power and authority to reëstablish just those conditions which the shipowners were once capable of maintaining themselves. . . ." [51] The provision for the government-issued discharge book, or "Copeland Fink Book" as it was referred to in maritime labor circles, was cited in support of this view.

The continuous discharge books were regarded by the rank-and-file seamen's groups as an attempt to restore the old employer "fink" book under governmental protection, thus ending one of the major gains which the 1934 strike had achieved. The opposition to the continuous-discharge book feature of the Seamen's Act, although slow in starting, gained momentum as the time approached for effectuation of the provision. Efforts to obtain postponement of the issuance of the books which had been scheduled for December 1936 were unsuccessful. During the course of the 1936-7 maritime strike, prevention of the issuance of continuous discharge books became a major objective of the striking seamen on both coasts. The basic differences between Lundeberg and Bridges were reflected in the tactics each used against the book. Lundeberg supported outright refusal to accept the book, while Bridges opposed such action as "striking against an Act of Congress," and favored political action to obtain revision. The East Coast seamen obtained an "informal" hearing before Senator Copeland in January 1937 after lobbying and demonstrating in Washington during the course of the "outlaw strike." Curran and other leaders of the East Coast rank and file charged that the book could serve as an effective blacklisting device against militant members of the ISU since it would show gaps in service during strike periods. [52]

The continuous discharge book continued to be an unstabilizing influence even after the termination of the 1936-7 strike. [53] This disturbing element in maritime labor relations was finally ironed out in March 1937, after a Congressional hearing at which Lundeberg, Curran, and other seamen's representatives appeared in opposition to the book. ISU and shipowner representatives supported continuance of the book. Under Representative Bland's direction, action was taken with notable promptitude after joint discussions between representatives of government agencies and the seamen had resulted in compromise terms. By March 24, 1937, a new act was passed by Congress and approved by the President which gave the seaman his choice as to whether he would carry a continuous discharge book or a certificate of identification, both of which were to contain the same information regarding his identity. With the latter, the seaman would be issued individual certificates of discharge by shipping commissioners which would provide him with evidence of his sea service.[54]

Hardly had this problem been met when labor relations in the maritime industry were again subjected to close study by the members of Congress. Immediately following the 1936–7 strike, bills were introduced by Senator Guffey and Representative Bland whose object was to stabilize maritime labor relations by making the industry subject to provisions similar to those established in the Railway Labor Act of 1926.[55] Support for even more stringent measures was forthcoming from the shipowners. The union opposition was sustained by the Maritime Commission at this stage, as well as by the Department of Labor and the NLRB. It was deemed inadvisable to apply to the maritime industry, in which collective bargaining had hardly taken root, a machinery which had been mutually agreed upon by the parties for the highly-organized railroad industry. The Maritime Commission reversed its position within a few months.[56]

During the months following these hearings, which saw the organization of the NMU and the split among the maritime unions, widespread publicity was given to the instability in maritime labor relations, charging the leaders with irresponsibility and radicalism and the seamen with insubordination and inefficiency. Largely ignored were the mélange of factors producing the unstable conditions. Not the least of these factors was the general state of instability in the labor relations of American industry in general. Almost unmentioned was the existence of a void in relations between East Coast shipowners and unions which went unfilled for over a year while NLRB elections were being conducted and negotiations with the shipowners were being carried on. This explained the absence of any contractual machinery with which to handle the grievances arising over food, quarters, and hours of work. The spasmodic sitdown strikes of individual crews to obtain concessions from their employers may be attributed to the lack of grievance machinery, the widespread suspicion of employer motives, and the inability of the newly organized unions to control their membership. Rarely, however, was the problem of labor relations in the American merchant marine considered in such context.

A report by Senator Royal S. Copeland, during August 1937, regarding conditions in the merchant marine attributed the difficulties facing the industry to "a group bent on getting control of the personnel on all ships of the American merchant marine" in matters regarded as properly under the control of the master to ensure proper discipline.[57]

A series of incidents receiving great play in the press during the months following the Copeland report were to be held up as object lessons by those who believed in the salutary effect of tightened discipline on American ships. The refusal of the crew of the government-owned, privately-operated ship, the S.S. *Algic,* to handle cargo being discharged by strikebreaking longshoremen in the port of Montevideo, Uruguay, in September 1937 was to set off a new drive against the maritime unions. The crew voted to advise the captain of their refusal to work on deck on the grounds of the danger in working with inexperienced "scabs" who were "throwing cargo around like hash," as well as on the basis of their sympathy with the striking longshoremen. Acting in a self-styled "prompt and decisive" manner, the Maritime Commission ordered the captain of the ship to place the men in irons if they persisted in their refusal to obey orders. The commission characterized the action of the *Algic* crew as "unlawful" and as constituting "a strike against the government." When informed of the commission's order, the crew agreed to return to work. The *Algic* incident was followed almost immediately by the commission's submission of proposals for maritime labor legislation, in reversal of its earlier stand.[58] The Maritime Commission's activities precipitated widespread newspaper and Congressional discussion of maritime labor matters. The *New York Times* viewed the commission's action in the *Algic* incident as "provoked directly by the chaotic conditions afloat" which were clearly "to a great extent the responsibility of the unions. . . ." It also predicted that the conviction of fourteen members of the *Algic* crew under the mutiny provisions of the Act of 1790 would have a "salutary effect upon the reign of lawlessness afloat that has marked our recent history." [59] Charges of Communist influence among the maritime unions were again given much coverage by the press. In articles during November 1937 receiving widespread attention, *The Washington Post* listed several leaders of the NMU among the graduates of a marine school conducted by the Communist Party, whose goal was to establish "a Communist unit on every ship." [60]

Hearings were held over a four-month period on the Maritime Commission's proposals for maritime labor legislation which were based upon modified provisions of the Railway Labor Act of 1934 and were intended to be applied to both seamen and longshoremen. The hearings on this proposal turned primarily into a clearing house for the charges which were currently circulating against the maritime unions. To Chairman Kennedy's testimony in behalf of the legislation was added the support of the shipowners' representatives. The Pacific American Shipowners' Association called for a separate Marine Labor Act which would "require the obedience of all parties to the same and . . . provide adequate penalties for noncompliance." Only in this way, stated its spokesman, could an end be put to strikes in violation of contracts and federal statutes.[61] The unions were again supported in their opposition to the proposals by the federal labor agencies. Secretary Perkins characterized the measure as "premature" and "unworkable administratively." [62]

Promise of fair examination of the merits of the maritime labor problem was held out during the course of the hearings on the commission's proposals. Senator Elbert D. Thomas indicated that the allegations regarding the lack of discipline on American ships would be examined with an eye to remedying the causes, rather than the symptoms. "A lack of discipline will never be remedied in this day and age unless it is remedied in the light of actual justice . . ." was his evaluation of the charges against the seamen; "when our labor becomes self-disciplined, we shall find that the labor leaders will assume their responsibility with all the consideration for the benefit of the men and their conditions, and a harmonious relationship between the men, their ship, and the owners. . . ." [63]

It was, therefore, no surprise when the labor provisions of the act amending the Merchant Marine Act of 1936, as formulated by the Committee on Education and Labor, differed substantially from the original proposals. The legislation finally enacted provided for a Maritime Labor Board with mediatory functions, but bore no other resemblance to the original proposals. The changes were explained by Senator Thomas as arising out of the failure of the parties to agree upon the original proposals.[64]

It had taken over a year to obtain the passage of this relatively insignificant piece of legislation. During this breathing spell there had been substantial progress toward increased stability. Agreement between the NMU and the American Merchant Marine Institute in July 1938 was to close the major gap then existing in maritime collective bargaining. Increased stability was sufficiently apparent so that a special Senate investigation in 1938 into "the alleged subversive activities in the merchant marine" was discontinued.[65]

Increased stability in maritime labor relations, however, was no complete insurance against renewal of campaigns for restrictive legislation to which the political activities of the left-wing unions added fuel. With the outbreak of the war in Europe in September 1939, the maritime unions were to be caught up again in an intensified drive upon "un-American activities." The left-wing-dominated maritime unions affiliated with the CIO Maritime Committee — the National Maritime Union, the International Longshoremen's and Warehousemen's Union, and the American Communications Association — opened themselves to attack by opposing American aid to the Allies following the pact between Nazi Germany and Soviet Russia. "The Yanks are Not Coming," a slogan popular with the left-wing maritime unions, found equal favor with the

Communist Party and the native Fascist groups who were espousing the cause of isolationism.

The National Maritime Union was the focal point for attacks on the maritime unions. The testimony of the ousted "rank-and-file" group of the NMU before the Dies Committee in 1939 and 1940 charging virtually complete Communist-domination of the union's policies provided a basis for a new exposé which received widespread publicity.[66] A web of implication was spun around the NMU in articles such as "Sea Going Soviet," "Stalin's American Merchant Marine," and "Hitler's Plan to Seize the American Merchant Marine." In addition to rehashing the charges made before the Dies Committee, these articles created an aura of suspicion, implying subversive intrigue and disloyal intent through statements of half-truths calculated to create ill-will toward the unions.[67]

The legislative proposals current during this renewed attack on the maritime unions would have deprived the vehemently anti-Communist unions as well as the left-wing unions of their major gains. The language of a report of the Chamber of Commerce's Committee on American Shipping Needs in March 1940 was in keeping with the agitated times:

To enable the American merchant marine to serve the public successfully it is essential that it be relieved of irresponsible leadership in the maritime labor field. The last six years have been marked by the infiltration of un-American activities into important branches of organized maritime labor. The motives in these activities have not been confined to normal labor objectives. Shipping is peculiarly vulnerable to such inroads because of world contacts, and it has been deliberately used by these subversive interests as a national avenue into shore industries. . . .

The unions' exercise of job control came in for indirect attack on the grounds that it had been the cause of numerous work stoppages and had made it "increasingly difficult" "for ambitious young Americans to enter our merchant marine service." The report renewed the appeals made in 1937–8 for amending the National Labor Relations Act so as to give employers and employees "equitable" rights, and for legislation penalizing maritime work stoppages in violation of contracts.[68]

That restrictive legislation failed of enactment was not only the result of the generally favorable climate for labor in Congress, it was also the product of, first, divergent shipowner views on specific legislative enactments, and soon after, of the growing desire to permit stability to develop through collective bargaining, if possible. Thus, despite the support given it by East Coast shipowners and the Maritime Commission, a bill requiring all members of the crews to be American citizens failed of enactment since the West Coast owners and Lundeberg objected to the 100 percent requirement, although they approved the intent of the measure to keep undesirables off American ships. Further, a remarkable transformation was to occur among the shipowning groups, when a bill was introduced in January 1941 to restrict the sphere of union prerogative, particularly by replacing union hiring halls by government halls.[69] Fearful of any action which would unstabilize labor relations and affect their participation in the war-induced expansion in shipping opportunities, shipowner representatives unanimously opposed the establishment of government hiring halls "as inopportune at this time." Stress was laid upon the possibility of jeopardizing "the peaceful relations now existing, if such legislation is now enacted." Under these combined objections, the measure was not reported out of committee.

This period also saw efforts to extend to the seamen the benefits of such social legislation as workmen's compensation and unemployment insurance. The proposals for workmen's compensation failed of enactment because of differences between shipowners and seamen — shipowners supporting application of the Longshoremen's and Harbor Workers' Compensation Act to merchant seamen; the unions opposing this action on the grounds that seamen already had more liberal benefits under the provisions of the Jones Act of 1920.[70] With enactment of the Neutrality Act of 1939 and the possibility of widespread unemployment among seamen, the administration itself was to seek the development of an unemployment insurance plan for seamen. Prolonged hearings and expert advice failed to produce agreement on basic issues, and the attempt at legislation failed. Although they were not opposed to the principle of unemployment insurance, the shipowners announced, they were opposed, first, to the proposals to administer the plans through the union hiring halls; and, secondly, to payments "to men who voluntarily leave their work." [71] However, old age benefits of the Social Security Act were extended to the seamen in 1939.

Responsibility for applying to the maritime industry the administration's policy of ensuring recognition of certified unions and of advancing collective bargaining rested primarily with the National Labor Relations Board and the Maritime Labor Board during this period. These agencies, together with the Department of Labor, saw in the contemporary instability in maritime labor relations a transitory situation which would disappear as collective bargaining relationships matured. The activities of these agencies in maritime labor relations were, therefore, directed toward promoting those conditions inherent in the industry under which collective bargaining could best develop. Proposals for the application to the maritime industry of techniques which had been developed for the railroad industry were viewed by the labor agencies as retarding such development.

The principles developed by the NLRB in its more general administration of the National Labor Relations Act were made applicable to the maritime industry with the modifications necessary to meet the conditions peculiar to this industry. The major activity of the NLRB in this industry, as in industry generally during this period, lay in the determination of appropriate bargaining agents. This was a major factor in the development of stability in East Coast relations. In connection with its other main function, the consideration of cases involving charges of unfair labor practices, the NLRB was presented with issues which involved tests of the degree to which the navigation laws affecting seamen jibed with the labor laws. Other cases involved problems arising out of the peculiarities of employment on shipboard.

In determining the appropriate bargaining units in representation cases involving West Coast tanker operators, the board was to recognize the traditional West Coast distinctions between the deck, engine, and stewards departments.[72] Where a company had refused to issue passes to union representatives to board its ships to consult with the unlicensed personnel, the board found that such action constituted interference by the company. In view of the seamen's short stay in port, their desire for normal recreational pursuits during that period, and the relative inaccessibility of union halls, the board decided against the company's argument that ship committees could refer unsettled grievances to the union at the union hall.[73]

Several cases involving charges of unfair labor practices required some resolution of the apparent clash between the provisions of the navigation laws relating to the seamen and the National Labor Relations Act. The companies involved had replaced crews affiliated with one union with members of a rival union, and had justified their actions by citing the statute which required the men to sign on the shipping articles before each voyage and to sign off the articles after each voyage. They argued that a seaman's employment terminated when he signed off the articles at the end of a voyage. The board found that the signing of articles was but one incident in the employment relationship, and that it was customary in the industry for a crew to ship and reship on the same vessel for several successive voyages. The board held that the employment relationship could only be terminated by a positive act, such as the employer's refusal to reëmploy a seaman or the seaman's refusal to accept further employment. Hence, discharge of employees following signing off the articles was found to be discriminatory, in the absence of other circumstances, where such action was intended to penalize the crews for union activity.[74]

In 1941, the Supreme Court reversed an NLRB decision (Southern Steamship Co. case) involving the issue of the right of seamen under articles to engage in a sitdown strike on board a ship moored to a dock in a safe American harbor. The Supreme Court's decision left little doubt that seamen under articles would be subject to penalties under the mutiny statutes if they struck and refused to obey the captain's orders on board a ship moored to a dock in a safe domestic harbor, no matter what the provocation.[75]

Provision for supplementing the activities of the NLRB in the maritime industry was made by the 1938 statute establishing the Maritime Labor Board for a period of three years. The three-member board was to encourage the shipowners and their employees to bargain collectively and to settle all disputes amicably; it was also to prepare a report suggesting a permanent policy for the stabilization of maritime labor relations.[76] Thus, once the appropriate collective bargaining agent had been determined through elections conducted by the NLRB, the Maritime Labor Board could assist the parties in reaching agreements and in maintaining amicable relations.

In 1942, the board reported having dealt with 195 separate disputes during the three years from July 1938 to June 1941. At least 80 percent of the strikes involved only one or a few ships' crews; and the seriousness of the "other disputes" was open to question.[77] the vast majority of American seamen were unaffected by the existence of the Maritime Labor Board, primarily because of the increasingly stable labor relations which characterized the period of the board's existence.

Whatever influence the board might have had was further circumscribed by the administrative confusion created by the multiplicity of federal agencies concerned with maritime labor matters. The legislative grant of authority to the board failed to extend exclusive jurisdiction to the board over the adjustment of disputes in the industry. Hence, a competition developed between the board and the Conciliation Service of the Department of Labor which had long included the maritime industry among its broader responsibilities. This situation of clashing jurisdictions left the government open to the charge, on at least one occasion, that a labor dispute "was being aggravated by a jurisdictional dispute between two governmental agencies." [78]

The problem was further complicated by the varying preferences of the maritime employers and unions as to what governmental agency would be called upon for assistance. Thus, the Sailors' Union of the Pacific refused to have any dealings with the Maritime Labor Board, preferring the Conciliation Service. West Coast maritime employers charged the board with prejudice. The board found a measure of popularity only among the CIO maritime unions.[79]

Although in its mediation function the Maritime Labor Board found the field complicated by competition, in its planning function, it found the field clear — or, rather, barren. Its efforts to obtain agreement between shipowners and unions on a permanent federal policy for maritime labor relations was to fail after many conferences. The board, therefore, decided unwillingly to issue its own report in March 1940, without the approval of labor or management. Perhaps the most lasting aspect of the board's report was that it raised questions regarding revision of the navigation laws pertaining to seamen, and particularly to the hoary practice of requiring the signing of articles, and the uncertain line between legal strikes and mutinies. The board's life was extended for only a year in 1941, and it passed out of existence in March 1942.[80]

The interest and activities of the maritime agencies in maritime labor matters further complicated the administrative maze in this realm. These agencies drew support for their activities in such matters from both specific statutory authority and from the administration's general policy of support for an adequate and efficient American merchant marine. The Maritime Commission and Bureau of Marine Inspection and Navigation tended to use discipline and expedition as their frame of reference for achieving stability in maritime labor relations, placing substantially less emphasis upon the administration's policy of fostering collective bargaining. However, the pronouncements of the Maritime Commission constantly referred to the principle of collective bargaining. The frequent clash between practice and theory often had an effect opposite from that intended and resulted in accomplishing greater, rather than lesser, instability in the industry.

The Bureau of Marine Inspection and Navigation, established as the result of a reorganization in 1932,[81] was assigned increased responsibilities for merchant marine personnel by the legislation enacted in 1936 which required all seamen to hold certificates of service and to pass examinations to gain higher ratings. The bureau was given authority to investigate acts of misconduct or incompetency on the part of holders of certificates of service, whether or not such acts were connected with any marine casualty. A finding of guilt in such cases, known as "C" Board cases, was to result in suspension or revocation of the certificate of service, without which seamen could not obtain further employment. The bureau's exercise of its authority in "C" Board cases became the subject of bitter union attacks, particularly during the unsettled period of 1937 and 1938. Under this authority, seamen who participated in shipboard sitdown strikes were tried for misconduct for refusing to obey the masters' orders.

The Maritime Commission's role in maritime labor relations was more direct and influential than that of the Maritime Labor Board. Its statutory authority was limited to the determination of minimum wage, minimum manning scales and reasonable working conditions on subsidized ships. However, its broad responsibilities for the development of an adequate and well balanced merchant marine, together with the possible impact of its own determinations, made it inevitable that it would play a part in filling the unstabilizing void in labor-management relations.

The abortive effort of the hastily appointed temporary members of the Maritime Commission to forestall the 1936–7 strike had made for an inauspicious start. The new permanent commissioners, with Joseph P. Kennedy as chairman, who took office in April 1937 in the midst of the Guffey-Bland proposals for maritime legislation, were to adopt a more cautious attitude. Initially opposing new legislation, the commission turned its attention to an investigation of conditions in the merchant marine. It was also confronted with the problem of arriving at "minimum" wages and manning scales and "reasonable" working conditions without disturbing conditions established under existing collective bargaining agreements or influencing the outcome of further collective bargaining.

The commission's determinations were not to be announced until October of 1937, and its study of conditions in the industry was not to be released until November 1937. In the meantime, however, the action it had taken in the *Algic* incident was followed by recommendations for maritime labor legislation, on the finding that "chaotic labor conditions, signalized by demands of the crews, 'sitdown' and 'quickie' strikes, and slipshod performance of duties are characteristic of the industry." [82]

Almost simultaneously, the commission issued its determination regarding minimum wage and manning scales and working conditions to be applicable to the approximately 10,000 seamen on board the more than 150 ships covered by the operating differential subsidies. Minimum wage rates were fixed at the levels previously agreed to by West Coast operators and by a substantial number of East Coast operators. Important innovations in the industry developed by the commission's determination included vacation pay for continuous service, and return to port of discharge designated in articles with full pay if ship was withdrawn.[83] A major development was the establishment of a committee on crew quarters to recommend the remodeling of quarters on subsidized vessels.[84] Minimum manning scales and working conditions would be resolved subsequently on a ship-by-ship basis. The commission stressed that its determination of minima did not preclude reimbursement through operating subsidies of higher wages agreed to by the contractor through collective bargaining or other cause.

The ameliorative actions did not alter the union view that the policies of the commission were hostile to their interests. When Chairman Kennedy departed to assume his new position as Ambassador to Great Britain, he was followed by Admiral Emory S. Land, whose policies were considered by the unions to be essentially the same.

The commission's policies for the operation of some forty government-owned ships through private operators became the focus of continuing controversy. The commission refused collective bargaining rights to employees on these government-owned ships, on the grounds that they were receiving "their wages out of funds appropriated by Congress for this purpose." The commission's hiring policy ignored the union hiring halls, with responsibility resting with the masters of the ships, and with nondiscrimination for union or nonunion membership.[85]

The commission's determination regarding this labor question was, at the minimum, a debatable one. The NLRB had already held that companies acting as managing operators of Maritime Commission ships were employers under the National Labor Relations Act, since the exemption of the Federal government from the act's provisions was "not intended to apply to a commercial venture of this sort." The Maritime Labor Board cited the precedent of the Shipping Board's practice between 1917 and 1921 in entering into agreements with the unions as being "diametrically opposed" to the commission's policy.[86]

The unions charged the Commission with seeking to undermine the union hiring hall and opposed the use of the Maritime Commission's "fink halls." Although the unions were unanimous in their opposition to the commission's policy, they differed sharply — as in so many other instances during this period — over tactics to follow. In 1938, the NMU originally directed its members to use only the union hall, and to picket the offices of the shipping commissioners; these tactics were altered to "pack" the halls of the Sea Service Bureau to ensure that only NMU members were employed, when it appeared that the AFL Seamen's Union and nonunion seamen were accepting jobs.[87]

On the West Coast, in 1939, when it appeared that the commission would apply its nonrecognition, nondiscrimination policy to a trans-Pacific operation from Seattle, the SUP, supported by the Maritime Federation of the Pacific, immobilized the four ships by picketing. The commission canceled the contract, charging the union's insistence on the union hiring hall as the cause. Lundeberg's reply to the commission's attack minced no words: "We sail the ships — and we, nobody else, will tell us how and where we will sell our labor. As an organization, the Sailors' Union of the Pacific will fight every attempt from any quarter whatsoever to push us back into slavery again." [88]

Shortly thereafter, under pressure from West Coast business interests, the Maritime Commission resumed negotiations with the unions. Agreement was finally reached for crews to be shipped through the union hall without having to register with the shipping commissioners, and the operations of the Pacific Northwest Oriental Line got under way early in September. On the East Coast, too, the commission altered its policy, rehiring the former NMU crews when it took over several privately operated ships for its "Good Neighbor Fleet." [89]

The establishment of the United States Maritime Service in 1938 under the jurisdiction of the Maritime Commission was regarded by the unions as a further reason for suspecting the purposes of the commission. The Service was established to train men to serve as licensed and unlicensed personnel on American merchant vessels. During the first years following the establishment of the Service, the Maritime Commission restricted the enrollment to experienced seamen, seeking to assuage the unions' fears that the program would be used to flood an industry where unemployment was already prevalent. Applicants were to be chosen, regardless of "race or creed, or because of membership or nonmembership in any organization. . . ." [90]

Because the West Coast unions opposed the training program from the very start, the enrollment in the Government Island station was frequently as low as one-fifth its capacity for unlicensed seamen. The SUP viewed the Service as setting the stage "for the first act towards regimentation of seamen" and saw as its end that "a brand new personnel, unaffiliated with Union Ideas, will be trained to supplant the present men in the industry. . . ." When the commission extended enrollments to include 500 inexperienced young men annually, the SUP renewed its attacks on the training program as a source of potential strikebreakers. "The whole system is an attempt to mold a man's opinion" was the way the *West Coast Sailors* put it, "and what plan is more perfect to accomplish that than the training ship routine with the uniform and everything else that goes with it." [91] The NMU had endorsed the training program at first, primarily because it had been restricted to experienced men. However, it was to become estranged from the program upon the commission's failure to carry out alleged promises to give the union a voice in such matters as the curriculum and the selection of applicants. [92]

With the outbreak of war in Europe, and subsequently with our own entry into the war, the role of the Maritime Commission, and of its agencies for carrying on wartime shipping activities became the center of labor-management relations. It is significant that despite this peacetime background of apparent clash with union interests, a wartime policy was evolved with which both unions and management were largely in agreement.

CHAPTER 8

AMERICAN SEAMEN IN THE SECOND WORLD WAR

THE SPECTRE OF GOVERNMENT DOMINATION

The American merchant marine increasingly became an implement of American foreign policy following the outbreak of war in Europe in September 1939, an intimate association which continued into the postwar period. American ship operators made high profits, despite the flat proviso of the Neutrality Act of 1939 that American flag ships could neither deal with belligerent nations nor traverse combat zones. They were able nevertheless to take advantage of the increased freight rates in the areas from which competitive foreign ships were now withdrawn. Furthermore, the administration, whose foreign policy was oriented toward supporting the Allies, looked with favor upon the transfer of American ships to foreign flags for operation by foreign seamen in trading with the belligerents. Therefore, as an alternative, and indeed, an attractive one, ships could be chartered or sold outright to foreign nations at rates which brought substantial returns. Average operating profits per deadweight ton rose threefold between 1939 and 1941; in the case of some twenty-eight major freighter companies, earnings after taxes rose over five times its previous amount during this period.[1]

Prosperity in the industry brought mixed blessings to American seamen. The effect of the Neutrality Act, with the resultant ship transfers and sales, was immediate and widespread unemployment. Administration promises to aid unemployed seamen were only partially achieved. The war-bred demand for shipping, on the other hand, furnished the unions the opportunity to demand, with fair assurance of success, improvements in the economic terms of their agreements. Thus, between May 1940 and the end of 1941, the rate for the A.B. seamen on dry cargo vessels was to increase from $72.50 to $100 per month, an advance which outstripped the wage trend in the economy generally, as well as the 10 percent rise in the cost of living index. During the entire period of the war, this rate was to remain unchanged. The most substantial increases in seamen's earnings were to develop out of the bonuses negotiated between operators and the unions to compensate the men for the risks run in sailing ships through warship and submarine-infested waters and into ports subject to air bombardment. These war risk bonuses, as they came to be known, together with the provisions for insurance against injury or loss of life resulting from war conditions, were to become a major cause for contention before Pearl Harbor.

The divergent affiliations and ambitions of the maritime unions, together with the rapidly changing character and locale of war operations, created a tense and amorphous situation in the American Merchant Marine. War risk and insurance provisions were subject to constant renegotiations as new areas became dangerous and as the perils in other areas were intensified. The NMU and SIU-SUP strove over the laurels for obtaining major advances, and operators charged that they were being whipsawed in the process. In view of substantial shipping profits, the unions had little sympathy for the operators.

The "Yanks Are Not Coming" stand of the Maritime Federation of the Pacific, echoed by the national leadership of the NMU, in the days preceding the Nazi attack on Soviet Russia had left the maritime unions, including those which were rabidly anti-Communist, open to attack. Political motives could be, and were, ascribed to maritime strikes and work stoppages. Union sensitivity to governmental intervention under such conditions can readily be understood. Governmental efforts through the Maritime Commission to establish uniform and stable bonuses only tended to aggravate matters. Fear of governmental controls which would restrict their activities was constant on the part of the unions until Pearl Harbor.

Immediately before Pearl Harbor, the government's primary concern with seafaring personnel extended first to stabilizing war risk bonuses, and second, to expanding manpower to meet the contemplated expansion of the merchant marine. Contrary to the commission's intentions, the bonus activities of the Maritime Commission were to heighten dissatisfaction and bring on a strike by one segment of the unlicensed personnel. Its manpower activities were to achieve only partial agreement.

The necessity for stability in labor relations following American entry into the war in December 1941 was particularly apparent in an industry so directly involved in the war effort. Agreements were obtained promptly to ensure stability in labor-management relations. These arrangements would have been meaningless, of course, unless underwritten and implemented by the Federal government, which was soon to become owner of a fleet several times the size of the prewar seagoing merchant marine, as well as operator of the entire merchant marine.

Fear that the merchant marine would be operated as a naval auxiliary was assuaged by administration assurances that the merchant marine would be operated privately. Implementing these assurances, the War Shipping Administration turned back requisitioned vessels, allowing their private owners to operate them as general agents of the WSA. Similarly, as government-constructed vessels came off the ways during the war, they were chartered to established private operators. Suspicious of WSA intentions, the maritime unions exercised a constant vigil over their rights. The combined strength of the unions was sufficient to obtain WSA "Statements of Policy" in which the administration agreed not to disturb the existing procedures whereby ship operators appointed as general agents of the administration obtained and dealt with seafaring personnel.

Strict adherence to these agreements during the war years was to protect the unions from being overwhelmed by the vast influx of new personnel as job opportunities increased fourfold on deepsea vessels. Union security under these circumstances could be guaranteed only by the certainty that the new entries would obtain employment through the union hiring halls on ships covered by collective bargaining agreements. The WSA's strict observance of its assurances on this matter was a major factor contributing to the almost perfect record of labor stability in maritime labor relations during the war.

There were rifts, however, between the WSA and the unions. These were the product of such factors as the continuous rivalry between the SIU-SUP and the NMU, the recurrence of SIU opposition to governmental intervention, and the limited opportunities for the free exercise of collective bargaining in a country at war. While the rifts were overcome, the opposition to government controls remained.

Wages and working conditions were altered but little for unlicensed seamen during the war years. The war risk bonuses were the major contributive factor to their increased earnings. As bonuses were adjusted by the Maritime War Emergency Board to meet altered war risks, union resentment mounted against that agency's control. This resentment was to reach its height at the war's end, when the board proposed to end the bonuses.

INTERUNION COMPETITION FOR IMPROVEMENTS, 1939–1941

The dislocation in American shipping operations accompanying ship sales and transfers to foreign flags immediately produced widespread unemployment among American seamen. Job opportunities for ocean-going American seamen decreased by about 12 percent. Thus, between October 1939 and November 1940, the number of jobs in the deepsea merchant marine fell from about 55,000 to about 48,000.[2] The efforts of the maritime unions to halt this trend by opposing the unrestricted sale and transfer of American ships were doomed to failure in the face of the administration's concern with the larger aspects of foreign policy. The effectiveness of the appeals of the maritime unions was undoubtedly reduced by the suspicion the Bridges'-dominated Maritime Federation of the Pacific and the National Maritime Union, which had adopted a strong neutrality stand following the Nazi-Soviet Pact, were motivated by political interests.[3]

Confronted with the plight of the unemployed seamen, President Roosevelt suggested the broad outlines of a relief program to include an expanded program of training, employment via the WPA, and social security legislation.[4] But the agencies called upon to implement this program achieved only partial success. The Coast Guard restricted enrollments in the training program to seamen beached by the Neutrality Act; the WPA formulated a plan to employ 5000 seamen on waterfront improvement projects.[5] Other phases of the program were less fruitful. While seamen were brought under the old-age provisions of the Social Security Act, they were not to be covered by unemployment insurance until 1946. The director of the Bureau of Marine Inspection and Navigation refused to exercise administrative discretion to restrict the issuance of certificates for new men to serve in unlicensed ratings on the grounds that "the law does not authorize us to throttle down the inflow of such men and on the contrary requires us . . . to issue without examination and without any previous sea service, certificates in certain ratings to all applicants, even including aliens. . . ."[6]

Always present in some form during this period, governmental influence in maritime labor affairs assumed its real significance only after our entry into the war. Job opportunities in the American merchant marine were not to expand appreciably until after the United States entered the war and the effects of the war-induced shipbuilding program were felt. In the meantime, however, as readjustments were effected in American shipping, and shipping profits attained tremendous levels, the maritime unions were increasingly able to demand and obtain some improvements for their membership. The growing shortage of skilled seamen due to the attraction of higher shoreside wages, particularly in shipyards where seamen's skills could best be utilized, provided an effective lever at a time when the emphasis was upon quick turnaround and delivery to obtain maximum earnings. The world-wide scope of the conflict, the changing character and locale of war operations, and the competing demands of the respective maritime unions made the ship operators more tractable.

Strong union organization protected the gains already achieved, despite the reduced job opportunities; it assured that further gains would be made by the seamen as shipping conditions improved. In anticipation of readjustments in American shipping, negotiations during the fall of 1939 had left the wage question open — on the West Coast, subject to sixty-days' notice; and on the East Coast, subject to a six-months' wage review. As these readjustments were made and shipping earnings rose still further, the unions were soon demanding a further share in profits. Intense rivalry among the unions of unlicensed seamen ensured that a high degree of uniformity in wages and working conditions would be maintained. Competition for the lead in economic gains was the concomitant of rival organizational drives, and wartime shipping prosperity opened the field to such play. The SUP claimed it had set a standard for the East Coast when the $10 "war emergency" increase granted to the West Coast unions in May 1940 was followed immediately by a similar adjustment for the NMU, although the six-month wage reopening clause in the latter's agreements still had some time to run.[7]

The success of the NMU in obtaining a $5 increase on vessels operating in the Atlantic coastwise trades only provided the stimulus for the SIU to obtain larger increases from the coastwise operators with whom it had agreements. The SIU increases ranged from $7.50 to $10 per month.[8] In February 1941, the NMU obtained a further "war emergency" increase of $7.50 per month from the offshore operators, and could now claim that "this marked the first time the NMU had assumed indisputable leadership in securing higher wages on both coasts."[9] Simultaneously, agreements for increases were reached by the SUP and the other unions on the West Coast.[10] Again in October 1941, almost simultaneous agreements were reached on both coasts. This time, the basic rate was increased by $10 per month and no change was made in the "war emergency" increases previously granted. Thus, the rate for an A.B. seaman on both coasts was now $100 per month, including a basic rate of $82.50 and "emergency" increases totaling $17.50.[11] The wage rates agreed upon at this time were to remain unchanged for the war's duration.

These changes in wage rates were as nothing compared with the constant adjustments in war risk bonuses. The feeling that the seamen were risking their lives while the ship operators were reaping great returns bred intense feeling regarding these bonuses. The instability and uncertainty resulting from the risks were heightened by the rapid shifts in the locale and nature of operations of the belligerents during the early part of the war. Competing union ambitions under such conditions could only add to the instability.

Upon the outbreak of war in Europe, the NMU sought to negotiate with the American Merchant Marine Institute on war risk bonuses, insurance, and increased manning scales. In the midst of negotiations, sitdown strikes occurred on several ships due to leave East Coast ports to repatriate Americans stranded abroad, with the crews refusing to sign on until definite agreement had been reached.[12] At this point, the Maritime Commission, while denying any intention of seeking to influence the private negotiations, announced a 25 percent war risk bonus on its own ships, together with provision for recompense in the event of loss of personal effects or internment.[13] These terms were far below the union demands, but the union, charging the commission with blocking real negotiations, held that it was compelled to accept similar terms from the private operators to avoid antagonizing public opinion under existing emergency conditions.[14] This resolution of the matter, however, was short-lived, for within a month the NMU was negotiating more favorable terms with individual companies, which included insurance against death and injury, as well as bonuses varying in amount on the basis of a rough estimate of the degree of risk involved.[15] In the spring of 1940, when Pacific areas became involved in war operations, West Coast unions were to negotiate bonuses based upon the Maritime Commission's precedent.[16]

As warfare became intensified on all fronts during the spring of 1941, the unions renewed their demands for improved bonuses and insurance provisions. Adjustments were frequent, with the operators contending that they were caught between competing union demands.[17] Periodically, ships' departures were delayed because the crews felt that they were being inadequately compensated for the dangers involved.[18] In August 1941, therefore, the Maritime Commission called a conference in the hope that a blanket agreement could be reached to stabilize war risk bonuses nationally. The Commission sought to obtain agreement on a plan of its own whereby bonuses would be based upon the index of hull insurance. The effort met with success only for licensed personnel; the situation remained uncontrolled for unlicensed personnel.[19]

The issue of war risk bonuses was brought to a head once again in September when the SIU went out on strike against East Coast ships due to leave for the war zones. The union was demanding increases in the bonuses on African and Far Eastern runs, the establishment of bonuses in West Indies and South American runs, and an increase in the amount of the $5,000 war risk insurance. Nine ships were immediately affected.[20] The Maritime Commission notified the parties that the lines would be seized by the government unless the matter was submitted to arbitration. When the parties failed to accede, the commission seized three Alcoa ships and manned them with crews obtained through the offices of the Shipping Commissioners.[21] Within one week after the outbreak of the strike, twenty-five ships were tied up. The strike was finally terminated twelve days after its start, when the case was certified to the National

Defense Mediation Board, and the Maritime Commission made its exit from the scene.[22] Acting with expedition, the National Defense Mediation Board recommended increases in the bonus rates. The recommendation increased the bonus from $60 to $80 for African and Far Eastern runs, that a bonus of $100 be established for the port of Suez, and that the other demands be denied.[23] These recommendations were accepted and served to bolster a precarious stability until American entry into the war.

THE UNITED STATES IN THE WAR

The entry of the United States into the war on December 7, 1941, required some change in the existing relationships between management and labor. In the merchant marine, more than in any other sphere of operations, it was immediately apparent that any possible economic strife attendant upon the workings of normal collective bargaining relations had to be avoided if government domination were to be avoided. If all disputes were settled amicably, thus ensuring stability in ship operations, any proposals that the merchant marine should be operated and manned by the Navy would be forestalled. The presence of strong maritime unions, aware of the role of government domination during and following the first World War, also acted as a brake upon any governmental proposals and policies for altering established patterns of labor relations in the merchant marine.

Within a week of the attack on Pearl Harbor, a conference of shipowners and maritime labor representatives was called under the auspices of the Maritime Commission and the Department of Labor. While national representatives of labor and management were still deadlocked over the terms of a more inclusive understanding on wartime labor relations, the maritime conference achieved prompt success. By December 19, 1941, a "Statement of Principles" had been developed by maritime labor and management in which they agreed that strikes and lockouts would be banned for the war's duration, and that collective bargaining rights, obligations, and procedures would be unimpaired.

Special provision was made with respect to the troublesome and temporary war risk bonus question. At that time varying bonuses were being paid by different operators for the same voyage, and insurance ranged from $2,000 to $5,000. The problems involved in negotiating bonuses, since the parties were inadequately informed regarding the risks involved in traversing specific areas, were acknowledged. The need for national uniformity in war bonuses, as well as in insurance, proportionate to the risks involved was expressed by the signatory parties. A Maritime War Emergency Board, consisting of three members to be named by the President — with one member to be selected from the

Department of Labor and a second from the Maritime Commission — was established to meet this need, and to decide all unsettled disputes which might arise between labor and management relating to the interpretation and application of a uniform system of war risk compensation. On December 19, the President appointed the following to the board: Frank P. Graham, President of the University of North Carolina; John R. Steelman of the Department of Labor; and Edward Macaulay of the Maritime Commission. By January 10, 1942, the board was issuing decisions which carried out the functions delegated to it by the unions and operators.[24]

The "Statement of Principles" proved to be only a partial answer to the problem of stabilizing wartime maritime labor relations. In February 1942, the War Shipping Administration was established with Admiral Emory S. Land as Administrator (he was already Chairman of the Maritime Commission). Since the WSA had complete authority to requisition, purchase, and operate American shipping, it was apparent that assurances solely by private operators regarding the continuance of customary collective bargaining processes were inadequate. Fears that the merchant marine would be operated by the Navy were allayed, however, when the WSA adopted the policy of having qualified ship operators act as the government's agents in operating their own requisitioned ships and, subsequently, the vast tonnage of government-constructed shipping.

Government requisition and ownership raised manifold problems regarding collective bargaining relationships. Would existing agreements between ship operators and unions be recognized by the government? In view of the Maritime Commission's policy of nonrecognition of collective bargaining representatives on its own ships, was the vast shipbuilding program of the government to constitute a threat to union security? Similarly, would the vast government training program required to man the new ships threaten the existence of the unions? These and other questions were of pressing concern to the unions.

The question of the recognition of existing collective bargaining arrangements was of immediate concern; the answers to the other questions could be developed, once understandings on fundamentals had been reached. Such understandings were reached between the WSA and the maritime unions in May 1942, but not until certain WSA proposals which the unions viewed as intended to supersede existing agreements had been altered. These proposals would have established a tripartite board within the WSA to determine wages, war risk bonuses, insurance, and working conditions, and to modify or retain existing contract provisions in order to establish national uniformity. It had also been proposed that the respective unions establish manpower pools which could be called upon to furnish men.[25] Union reaction had been instantaneous. The proposals ignored collective bargaining rights, the unions charged, and would wipe out the hiring halls.[26] The Maritime War Emergency Board supported the union position, pointing out to the WSA that any change in existing agreements without mutual consent among the signatories of the "Statement of Principles" would be a "violation of the mutual assurances and promises therein contained." [27]

The unions had been unified in pressing the War Shipping Administration to modify its proposals. But in the working out of specific terms of understanding, union rivalries and doctrinal differences again became manifest. Separate "Statements of Policy" were agreed upon between the WSA and the West Coast unions, the NMU, and other principal maritime unions. Under these, the WSA agreed to recognize the terms of existing collective bargaining agreements, as well as to respect customary arrangements for obtaining personnel, including the union hiring hall. The unions agreed to refrain from exercising the right to strike for the war's duration; and, in the interests of effective discipline, to eliminate crew mass meetings, to recognize the master's authority, and to settle all grievances in accordance with the terms of existing contracts. The West Coast unions agreed that "existing collective bargaining agreements be frozen for the duration of war," for, as explained by the SUP, "our main consideration was to put a period to the constant attempt on the part of the shipowners or other groups to move in on our agreements." [28] Terming the West Coast unions' agreement "treachery," the NMU obtained a "Statement of Policy" providing for the continuance and observance of existing agreements and permitting their change by mutual agreement between the WSA and the NMU.[29] Thus, the NMU left open an avenue for obtaining those West Coast conditions which remained unachieved on the East Coast.

By May 1942, the WSA and the unions had laid the groundwork for the good labor relations which made it possible for the merchant marine to be operated without any significant impediment during the war years.

THE UNIONS AND THE GOVERNMENT

"There was not one strike in the maritime industry during the war. With the exception of a few minor and isolated misunderstandings, there were no delays in the sailing of vessels as the result of a labor dispute . . ." reported the WSA in 1946.[30] It was more than the mere wartime necessity of getting troops and supplies abroad which contributed to this record. WSA policies aiming at maximum implementation of the intent of the "Statements of Policy" helped immeasurably. Nevertheless, there was constant union vigilance to ensure that these policies did not infringe upon contractual rights. Bureaucratic regulations, governmental policies at variance with established practices, rival unionism, and lack of uniformity in working conditions were constant irritants. Some of these problems were solved to the mutual satisfaction of all involved; others resulted in grudging adjustments on the part of the unions; and, finally, a number remained unresolved. At no time, however, was there any question regarding the devotion of the maritime unions and their members to the larger duty of aiding in winning the war.

Once the continued functioning of the union hiring halls had been guaranteed by the "Statements of Policy," the keystone for coöperation with the maritime unions had been set. The contemplated expansion of the merchant marine, and the necessity for recruiting a vast force of former seamen as well as new recruits to man these ships, threatened to deluge the existing union membership. Thus, between 1941 and 1945, expansion of the merchant marine had increased the number of available deepsea jobs from about 55,000 to about 200,000.[31] Simultaneously, through the efforts of the War Shipping Administration's Recruitment and Manning Organization and its Training Organization, the labor force was increased from about 75,000 to a peak of 250,000.[32] About 168,000 men were graduated from training schools during the war.

Despite this potential threat to union security, a working relationship was established between the WSA and the unions which was generally harmonious. This relationship was based, according to Marshall E. Dimock, Director of the RMO, on the clearly enunciated principle that "we recognized the central role of the union hiring halls; we were determined not to infringe upon the agreements between operators and unions; we wanted the hiring halls to continue to meet the principal manpower requirements of the merchant marine and were content to supplement their work." [33] To implement this policy, instructions were issued which required the agents of the WSA to obtain necessary personnel through their normal and customary channels. Thus, agents who had union agreements would call upon the union hiring halls for necessary personnel. The union in turn would call upon the RMO for men when sufficient union members were not available. Unorganized companies, however, could call upon the RMO directly for necessary personnel. Manpower reserves were maintained by the RMO at various ports to meet last-minute manning problems. The men in these pools were paid a daily wage and subsistence allowance until they were shipped.[34]

A second set of problems arose which required resolution of differences regarding union representation policies on government-owned and bareboat-chartered vessels, where the crew was in the government's employ, and seamen's rights on privately-owned or time-chartered vessels, where the crew was employed by the private operator. The issue of collective bargaining rights on government-owned ships had been a major object of contention between the unions and the Maritime Commission. It would have arisen again had the WSA chosen to take an intransigent stand regarding the bargaining rights of employees on government-owned ships. Here, again, union rights could have been undermined as the merchant marine expanded fourfold under the impetus of government-financed construction. With established ship operators operating their own and government-owned ships, seamen would have shifted from one to the other with resultant changes in bargaining rights. The new operators to whom ships were also being assigned would have been under no obligation to deal with any union.

Recognizing the explosive possibilities of such a situation, the WSA called upon the National Labor Relations Board to function in its customary manner in representation cases on government-owned or bareboat-chartered ships. Nevertheless, the WSA maintained the position that it did not thereby "recognize that the National Labor Relations Board has jurisdiction over employees of the War Shipping Administration and that this question shall be reserved for future determination and adjudication in the event it should ever become pertinent and material in any proceeding or case." The NLRB agreed to these terms. This agreement was adhered to scrupulously during the war years, the only serious difficulty developing in the case of the major oil companies "during the period when tanker operations were most acute." These companies had combined "to form a corporation to take a General Agency and, even in the face of a directive from the Administrator, refused to respect the commitments which the Administrator had made to the Board, and declined to permit representation questions to be determined." [35]

The varied nature of the employment relationships arising out of the varied charter and ownership arrangements in turn produced confusing differences in the rights of seamen regarding such matters as old-age pensions and compensation for illness or injury arising out of shipboard employment. On time-chartered vessels, where they were employees of the ship operators, seamen had rights to old-age pensions under the Social Security Act; wages, maintenance, and cure for illness or injury incurred in the service of the vessel; and to sue for injury or death under the Jones Act. On bareboat-chartered and government-owned ships, they were considered government employees with rights under the United States Employees' Compensation Act, but no rights under the Jones Act; no rights to wages, maintenance, and cure for illness or injury; with exemption from the Social Security Act; and possible Civil Service status. The uncertainty arising from this dual situation was eliminated by a statute passed in March 1943, which put all seamen on equal terms by giving them only the rights of seamen in private employment, and excluding them from the operation of statutes normally applicable to government employees.[36]

The responsibility for formulating labor policies which would ensure stability was assigned to the Maritime Labor Relations Organization of the WSA, established in June 1942 with Hubert Wyckoff as Director. This organization was under the supervision of the Deputy Administrator for Labor Relations, Manning, Training, and Recruitment, Captain Edward Macaulay. In seeking to apply the basic policies of the WSA and to maintain labor stability in the face of the constant pressures of the rival unions, the Maritime Labor Organization sought to attain two goals: first, to achieve nationwide uniformity in wages and working conditions; and, second, to maintain the relative position of the rival unions as it had existed prior to the war. Regarding the first matter, national uniformity in wages and working conditions for unlicensed seamen had been virtually complete before the war. Therefore the WSA program for complete uniformity was significant chiefly in the case of licensed officers. A National War Labor Board decision, however, by awarding several adjustments in a case involving the NMU and East Coast operators, was to bring East Coast working conditions up to West Coast levels.

The government was constantly subject to the pressures of the rival union organizations during the war years, particularly in the assignment of new ships. With each union seeking to protect and enhance its own strength, the WSA was frequently caught in the crossfire. In assigning new ships to operators, some consideration was evidently given to the matter of maintaining the relative strength of the rival unions at prewar levels, although efficiency of operation was presumably the primary criterion.[37] In December 1942, a dispute developed between the NMU and the SUP regarding the jurisdiction of ships built on the West Coast which were being operated from the East Coast with West Coast crews. The three agents involved (Grace, Luckenbach, and Moore-McCormack) operated on both coasts, and had agreements with the respective unions on both coasts. As the ships were turned over to them, the agents called on the West Coast unions for crews. The NMU charged that this invaded its East Coast jurisdiction and disturbed the relative prewar position of the unions on East and West Coast ships of the companies involved. The SUP claimed that it had always manned the West Coast ships of these companies.

Confronted with a situation threatening to get out of hand, Admiral Land intervened and called a meeting. Since the unions were unable to reach any agreement, and since no other basis existed for settling this jurisdictional dispute, Land decided the dispute under the authority delegated to him by the President. His directive provided that all ships of the companies involved returning to East and West Coast ports, respectively, were to be considered East and West Coast ships, respectively, and were to be manned by the NMU and the West Coast unions, respectively, no matter how they were manned currently. In the future, as far as practicable, ships constructed on the West Coast would be allocated for West Coast operation and manned by West Coast unions. Similarly, ships constructed on the East Coast would be manned by East Coast unions. The directive indicated that, as far as possible, consideration would be given to the relative status of the labor organizations which had existed prior to the war.[38] This decision was to serve as a pattern for subsequent WSA policy.

Relations between the WSA and the maritime unions were complicated further by the divergent attitudes of the leading unions regarding governmental policies and controls. The NMU, on the whole, maintained a policy of coöperating closely with the WSA and other governmental agencies, while pressing constantly for increased labor representation in matters pertaining both to wages and working conditions, as well as on the broader issues in the war shipping program, such as manpower utilization and ship operation.[39] While the NMU succeeded in obtaining action on some of its manpower proposals, it was unsuccessful in obtaining standing tripartite advisory committees which would afford labor a direct voice in the conduct of the war shipping program. The coöperation of the NMU extended also to its adoption of shipping rules more stringent than those subsequently adopted by the RMO, whose observance was to be a condition for continued draft deferment.[40] In addition, an upgrading school was voluntarily established by the union. But an undercurrent of suspicion of governmental activities persisted within the NMU. While it acknowledged the coöperation of the RMO, it expressed the fear that this organization could be utilized for the "eventual destruction of the maritime unions." [41] As the war proceeded and WSA officialdom rejected its proposals, the NMU expressed greater fear for the security of the union hiring halls, and made charges that "certain elements in WSA were in collusion with some of the ship operators who still hoped to break the Union." [42]

The position of Lundeberg's SIU-SUP differed sharply from that of the NMU. This organization, while coöperating fully in advancing the war effort, continued as formerly to oppose governmental regulations at every step, regarding them as efforts to hamstring the seamen and weaken their organizations. It attacked NMU proposals for the establishment of tripartite boards to determine wages and working conditions because it would inevitably lead to supersession of the union by such a "superboard." [43] The NMU shipping rules were attacked as "semi-

Fascistic." [44] Increased governmental controls were resented on the grounds that the seamen were contributing adequately to the war effort by continually sailing ships into the war zone.[45] Every action of the RMO was watched to ensure that the unions' jurisdiction was not being usurped. Vehemently objecting to the authority delegated by Selective Service to the RMO to certify active seamen for deferment, the SIU-SUP refused at first to sign RMO draft registration cards, comparing them to blacklists and "fink" books.[46] It finally receded from this position, voting to accept the cards on the grounds that the army was threatening seamen with draft induction. As a last gesture of opposition, the organization agreed that its members would furnish information to government officials, but that they would not sign the cards.[47] An RMO regulation for annual medical examinations was attacked as threatening the elimination of over-age seamen, with the result that the regulation was amended to exclude such a possibility.[48]

To WSA proposals for conferences to establish incentives to reduce turnover, Lundeberg replied that the WSA was "undermining the collective bargaining structure of the seamen's unions." [49] A conference of SIU-SUP officials in April 1945 summed up the views of the organization as follows: "It is the opinion of the delegates that the WSA had no business to stick their nose into labor relations . . . this was strictly a matter between the unions and the operators. . . ." [50] They adopted motions calling for the abolition of the RMO and the Labor Relations Organization of the WSA, as well as the elimination of all governmental boards dealing with labor relations.

Contributing to the SIU-SUP dislike for governmental intervention were the charges of discrimination brought against the Atlantic and Gulf District of the SIU by the Fair Employment Practices Committee. The union was accused of "checkerboarding" the crews on the ships covered by its agreements — that is, not mixing white and Negro seamen, at least in the same department. In requesting replacements from the RMO, the union would specify whether it desired whites or Negroes. When the RMO, in line with its policy of rotary shipping, dispatched Negroes where whites had been requested, or vice versa, the union would reject such individuals. To the charges of discrimination, the union countered that it practiced segregation, the only basis for harmonious operations; not discrimination. It charged that the New York Office of the RMO refused to send Negroes when requested to do so, sending them to ships with white crews when the union hiring hall was closed; and that the officials of that office were seeking to carry out "social-reformist theories." The union refused to participate in the hearings before the FEPC, except to file a statement charging the committee with bias. In September 1945, after the case had been under considera-

tion for two years, the FEPC issued a cease-and-desist order against
the SIU to abandon its policy of segregating crews. The decision, however, in its application to war work, was anticlimactic.[51]

All these differences between the maritime unions and the government agencies concerned with seamen's affairs had no effect on the even
flow of supplies and troops on ships manned by civilian seamen. The
contribution of the merchant seamen to the war effort received widespread public recognition during the war years. The casualty rate among
merchant seamen during the first part of 1943 was proportionately
greater than in all the armed services combined. During the course of
the year, 733 ships of over 1000 gross tons were sunk; and 5638 merchant
seamen and officers were dead and missing, 580 were prisoners of war.[52]
In recognition of their heroism and valor, Congress authorized the award
of special medals and decorations to merchant mariners. The special
nature of the war service of merchant mariners was further recognized
by Congress when it provided for reëmployment rights for seamen patterned after those for men inducted into the armed forces.[53] Legislation
was introduced into Congress intended to grant to seamen some of the
benefits granted to servicemen under the G.I. Bill of Rights. Although
such a measure was widely supported, opposition from the Armed
Forces prevented its passage.

The United Seamen's Service was established as a private organization
in 1942 by maritime industry and labor groups and social and public
organizations, with the assistance of the War Shipping Administration.
Its function was to provide seamen with services and facilities comparable to those available to servicemen through the USO and the Red
Cross. The facilities of the USS were used most extensively in medical
care, housing and recreation, personal service and overseas operation.
Medical care facilities included rest homes to cope with the effects of
convoy fatigue, and a chain of port medical offices in fifteen domestic
ports. Overseas operations included seventy units throughout the world.

Both Curran and Lundeberg were among the incorporators of the
USS. Lundeberg turned against the organization in February 1943,
charging that it was overstaffed, poorly and uneconomically administered, and provided little actual service to seamen. Although his charges
were answered, Lundeberg continued to oppose USS activities, and this
became the official SIU policy, although apparently most rank-and-file
members used the USS. This was also one facet of Lundeberg's emphasis
on self-reliance through the achievement of gains through collective bargaining, rather than acceptance of the fruits of philanthropy or charity.
The NMU continued to support the USS throughout the war, and
personal service offices were established in several NMU halls. With the
declining services available with limited postwar resources, however,

increasing opposition developed here too. And union opposition was matched by employer indifference in the postwar years.[54]

Merchant seamen received support in the halls of Congress against charges of excessive earnings and poor discipline. Average earnings for able seamen were shown to be in the neighborhood of $2600 during the period when highest war bonuses were in effect. The reports of serious discipline cases were shown to be applicable to an infinitesimal number of American seamen — one-half of 1 percent.[55]

LIMITATIONS UPON COLLECTIVE BARGAINING

The war years provided little opportunity for collective bargaining to extend its roots at the plant or company level, either in the maritime industry or in industry generally. Changes in wages and working conditions were the result, altogether too frequently, of decisions of the tripartite National War Labor Board; and labor peace was induced by wartime necessity. For the unions of unlicensed seamen, with governmental assurance of maintenance of the *status quo*, the war years were a period during which prewar gains were consolidated and efforts were made to obtain some improvements. However, between Pearl Harbor and the end of the war, basic wage rates remained unchanged for seamen; working conditions were altered only moderately — and then generally by War Labor Board decision, rather than by collective bargaining. Both the unions and the operators profited from the war — the former from the substantial increase in union membership and income; the latter, from expanded operations and the sale of old vessels. Wartime prosperity, however, did not conceal from the parties the necessity for looking toward the postwar era. For the unions, this meant conversion of the war risk bonus, which had been the major element increasing seamen's earnings, into the basic wage rate, and obtaining further improvements, particularly in hours of work. For the operators, the postwar outlook was one of renewed competition, with the necessity for maintaining operating costs at a minimum. Many operators were to take the position that wartime adjustments had been made by them as WSA agents, and not as the result of their willing agreement through collective bargaining. These positions were to be consistently maintained during the war years.

The adjustments in seamen's wage rates in 1940–41 had been substantial when viewed in relative terms; thus, the adjustment in the able seamen's rate had amounted to about 38 percent. However, the adjustments were hardly immoderate when viewed from the point of view of the absolute rate for a 56-hour work week — in this respect, the rate had increased from $72.50 to $100 per month. Of the increases, the operators had insisted that $17.50 be designated as wartime emergency increases, apparently with an eye to the uncertainty of shipping prospects when wartime prosperity ended. Since these pre-Pearl Harbor wage rate adjustments exceeded the amounts allowable under the wartime wage stabilization policy of the "Little Steel Formula," no further adjustments in basic wage rates were forthcoming for seamen until the end of the war.

The major source of increased income, however, was provided by war risk bonuses. A study undertaken jointly by the Bureau of Labor Statistics and the Maritime Commission showed that war risk bonuses accounted for approximately half the average gross income of unlicensed seamen during the year starting October 1, 1943. Thus, average gross earnings were $2596 for able seamen, $2648 for oilers, and $2335 for messmen; days worked averaged 286, 287, and 281, respectively; and war risk bonus earnings averaged $1230, $1291, and $1195 respectively. Basic wages generally accounted for about 35 percent of earnings, and overtime pay for about 15 percent.[56] So long as war risk bonuses continued, there was little pressure for changes in wages and working conditions.

The War Shipping Administration, while recognizing the processes of collective bargaining, instructed its general agents to obtain the approval of the administration before placing amendments and modifications of, or supplements to, their agreements into effect.[57] In this way, while not participating in collective bargaining, the WSA exercised control over its outcome in order to maintain and extend uniformity in wages and working conditions. This policy was justified on the grounds that lack of uniformity "was bad for morale and made it difficult to man vessels in the highly competitive wartime manpower situation in the industry."[58] When the National War Labor Board was given jurisdiction over the wage stabilization program in the fall of 1942, the War Shipping Administration immediately called upon the board to give special consideration to the wage stabilization problems of the maritime industry. In response to this request, the board established a tripartite War Shipping Panel to consider cases and wage stabilization problems relating to maritime labor. In tending to increase nationwide uniformity in deepsea wages and working conditions, the decisions of the panel and the board followed prewar trends and were consistent with the aims of the WSA.

War Labor Board decisions, however, played a relatively minor role in the affairs of unlicensed seamen during the war. Uniformity in wages, and substantial uniformity in working conditions for unlicensed personnel on deepsea vessels on both coasts already existed. The major differences were between the several overtime and penalty payment provisions of the NMU and West Coast agreements, since the West Coast provisions were more favorable. The NMU called upon the WSA and the NWLB to arrange a conference "for the purpose of establishing a national contract uniform in terms." [59] Failing in this, the union served notice of the reopening of its agreements in 1943 and demanded the more attractive overtime and penalty payment provisions of the West Coast agreements; as well as checkoff of union dues and a 44-hour week in port and at sea. The parties deadlocked, and the case went to the NWLB. The board, with industry members dissenting, granted the unions those provisions which were in line with West Coast agreements, but denied the reduced work week and the checkoff. The board also ordered elimination of the distinction between the basic wage rates and the emergency increases.[60] The agreements incorporating this NWLB order indicated that the companies were signing as "General Agents of the War Shipping Administration." [61]

Voluntary agreements and dispute cases involving virtually all the other unions of unlicensed personnel came before the board during the war. Changes involved primarily the elimination of existing inequities rather than establishment of new practices. Here again, as on matters of governmental policy generally, Lundeberg's SIU-SUP opposed further government intervention, even opposing the establishment of the special maritime panel.[62]

Pressure for changes in wages and working conditions was to increase as war risk bonuses were altered during the course of the war. The Maritime War Emergency Board had announced in an early decision that as changes occurred in war conditions, the board would modify, extend, or revoke the provisions of its decisions regarding bonuses, either on its own motion or after written petition and careful consideration of evidence presented by the parties affected.[63] According to the board, its actions were founded on the "basic theory that war risk bonus is payment for exposure to war hazard." [64] As the nature and degree of hazard changed, so would the bonus payment.

The terms of war risk insurance were combined in the Second Seamen's War Risk Policy — whose terms were prescribed in several of the board's decisions. Under this policy, seamen were insured for $5000, subject to an increase of $2500 in the event of total disability. Loss of or damage to personal effects and loss of wages during repatriation or detention were also covered by the policy.[65]

The board's first war risk bonus decision on January 10, 1942, during a period in which submarine attacks predominated, established bonuses ranging from 100 percent ($100 minimum) for voyages to European ports and across the Pacific, down to no bonus in the Gulf of Mexico, and increased the number of port bonus areas (ports subject to attack). By September 1, 1942, a voyage bonus of 100 percent was payable on substantially all voyages, except on the west coast of the Western Hemisphere. In March 1943, the board altered the basis of payment in view of the intensified surface and aerial action in localized areas of concentrated Allied shipping. Voyage bonuses were continued, but an area hazard bonus of $5 per day and port attack bonuses of $125 replaced the earlier port bonus. As robot and rocket bombs and suicide-bomber attacks were added to the earlier hazards, the board in April 1944 continued the 100 percent bonus ($100 monthly minimum) for vessels entering the marine approaches to combat areas, but reduced to 66⅔ percent ($80 monthly bonus) the voyage bonus for seamen on vessels entering other waters.[66] The area hazard bonus was extended, and a vessel attack bonus of $125 replaced the port attack bonus.

The board's decisions proved acceptable so long as the adjustments resulted in increased earnings. When the voyage bonus was decreased in 1944, however, the SIU-SUP charged the board with failing to adhere to the "Statement of Principles" because it had acted without calling upon the labor-management advisory board.[67] The signatories to the "Statement of Principles" were thereupon requested by the board to vote upon the question of continuing the board; a split vote supported its continuance.[68] The problem of war risk bonuses, however, remained unsettled; it was to become more acute as Allied victories continued, and was to reach a crisis with final Allied victory.

ELIMINATION OF THE WAR RISK BONUS

Victory at the end of the first World War brought the termination of war risk bonuses for unlicensed seamen, with no compensatory adjustments. At the end of the second World War, the maritime unions were alert to the imminent elimination of the primary source of the seamen's increased wartime earnings.

With the unconditional surrender of Germany, the Maritime War Emergency Board held extensive hearings regarding the action to be taken on Atlantic risk bonuses. The unions vehemently opposed any reduction. The board issued a new decision to be effective on July 15, 1945. Under this decision, the maximum bonus for Atlantic voyages was now fixed at 66⅔ percent ($80 monthly minimum) in the areas closest to Europe and Africa, and at 33⅓ percent ($40 monthly minimum) in the western reaches of the Atlantic. No change was made in the area and voyage bonuses on the Pacific and Indian oceans, nor in the vessel attack bonus.[69]

Faced with substantial reduction in the take-home pay, and with the likelihood that voyage bonuses would be eliminated completely in the near future, the unions launched an all-out campaign to obtain immediate wage adjustments. The NMU sought public support through advertisements in the newspapers of major cities, alleging that seamen's wage rates were substandard.[70] Although some Congressional support for postponing the bonus reduction was obtained pending a wage decision by the NWLB, the bonus reduction was put into effect.[71]

The NWLB had held during the war that war risk bonuses were not subject to wage stabilization principles, and did not come within its purview. However, the question of compensating for the reduction and elimination of the bonuses was now placed squarely before the board. In dispute cases involving the West Coast firemen, the marine cooks and stewards, and both East Coast unions, the unions demanded substantial adjustments to eliminate substandard wage rates, citing an hourly rate of 30¢ for ordinary seamen and 41¢ for able seamen; to offset loss of pay due to the bonus reduction; and to bring wages into line with shoreside wages so that seamen would not leave for more remunerative shoreside jobs. The operators opposed any increases on the grounds that the wages were not substandard, since seamen receive free subsistence and quarters; the bonuses had been intended solely for war risk; postwar foreign competition could not be met; and wage stabilization policy would not permit such adjustment.[72] They also proposed that operators be designated in the contract as general agents for the War Shipping Administration, rather than as employers, since they were operating on that basis.

The NWLB held public hearings during July 1945, at which the licensed officers also presented their views. In the meantime, the war was terminated in the Pacific, and the Maritime War Emergency Board announced that all bonuses would be terminated on October 1. In August an executive order was issued which relaxed wage stabilization policies somewhat. In the light of all these developments, the NWLB ordered a general increase of $45 per month, to be effective from the date of elimination of the voyage bonuses: October 1, 1945. This decision was arrived at, it was explained, after "weighing all the inequities in the case arising out of the issues of substandard wages, overtime, and the elimination of the bonus, and considering the fact that the wage increase will not be retroactive. . . ." To the operator demand regarding the manner of signing the contract, the board replied that "whatever the designation in the contract, the operators are the employers" and the question therefore had no significance.[73]

The operators had been completely unsuccessful in their efforts to separate the conditions of wartime operation from those of reconversion. The so-called emergency increases were now part of the wage structure, which had been further augmented by the largest single increase in the history of the merchant marine. While these actions had been largely government-sponsored, the unions had gained in finance and numbers during the war years. The reconversion period was to furnish opportunities for further substantial gains; but these gains were to be had only at the expense of substantial instability and a general inability to reëstablish collective bargaining on an effectively functioning basis. It was not long before events were to disprove the prophesy of the director of the WSA Maritime Labor Organization that the $45 increase made effective throughout the merchant marine "should ensure, for personnel purposes in this industry, 'effective transition to peacetime economy.'" [74]

CHAPTER 9

THE POSTWAR YEARS

THE MIXED OUTLOOK FOR THE MERCHANT MARINE

The merchant marine was slower to recover from the depression than American industry generally; on the other hand, it was affected more rapidly and intensely by the impact of the war in Europe, and by our entry into it. Therefore, there had been virtually no period of prewar "normalcy" for any burgeoning of the newly developed merchant marine policy and of the recognition of the unions. The war period served to strengthen the industry and the unions economically, and to make for greater cohesion among ship operators. The unions remained divided but there were developments toward greater unity, particularly on the West Coast.

The period since the end of the war, however, has been sufficiently protracted to provide an opportunity to observe the development of the merchant marine and of labor-management relations under private operation at least, if not under conditions of "normalcy." The general uncertainty in characterizing any set of conditions as normal for the American merchant marine is compounded in the postwar period by the role of the merchant marine in the continuing governmental aid program.

Opportunity and uncertainty have been the parallel prospects facing the shipping industry. On the one hand, there have been substantial opportunities. Ship operations had been very profitable during the war years, even after the WSA took over operations in 1942 and cut charter rates and even after taxes rose. The expansion in shipping and the conversion of old tonnage into cash through sale or payment of indemnity for loss at favorable rates resulted in substantial profits to shipping enterprise. It has been estimated that the net worth of dry cargo shipping companies more than doubled during the war, increasing from $273,000,000 in 1939 to over $587,000,000 at the end of 1944.[1] The favorable opportunities for American shipping immediately following the war enhanced this position. The Government made clear its intent to leave the ship operation field promptly, and restricted the operation of government-owned vessels to relief shipments of coal and grain and to supplying occupied areas; these ships were bareboat-chartered to private operators. Private ship operators, attracted by the favorable terms under the Ship Sales Act and the efficiency of operation of some of the war-built types, purchased ships which brought the American merchant marine to about one-third above its prewar size. Increased subsidy opportunities and appropriations also acted as an attraction. New legislation was enacted aiding the industry — particularly through the 50–50 cargo preference provision, which required that 50 percent of aid and surplus disposal cargoes financed through government funds be carried on American flag ships. Periodic crises, such as the Korean conflict, have expanded opportunities. An additional factor has been apparent in the most recent period; American shipping appears to be enjoying increased opportunities resulting from the expanded volume of world trade which has accompanied the restoration of the economies of the western European countries.

But the benefits have not been unalloyed, and the fluctuating opportunities for American ships and seamen are constant reminders of the clouding influences. The terms of the Ship Sales Act also made it possible for foreign countries to purchase ships; within a short period, the traditional maritime nations had restored their shipbuilding facilities, and were able to resume their prewar shipping superiority. The registry of ships under "flags of convenience" — the flags of countries such as Panama, Liberia, Honduras, and Costa Rica, which had little or no proprietary interest in the companies, and which exercised little control either over profits of the company, seaworthiness of the vessel, or wages and working conditions of the seamen — became an increasingly prominent factor in the competitive world maritime situation, creating disturbances not only in the high cost American merchant marine, but also in other better situated traditional maritime countries. The rises in subsidy costs and the increased applications for subsidies have made these the subject of not always friendly study by Congressional committees and the executive department disbursing agencies. Reduced appropriations for foreign aid programs, together with criticism of the 50–50 preference requirement have also added to the uncertainty. Throughout the period, the coastwise and intercoastal dry cargo trade has been unable to revive in the face of competition from rail and trucking.

The postwar dominance of American carrying capacity in the foreign trade has, therefore, been accompanied by substantial year-to-year fluctuations in the size of the active U. S. fleet. At the time of Japan's surrender, the War Shipping Administration had control of a fleet of about

4300 vessels with job opportunities for about 200,000 seamen. By July 1, 1948, the active fleet had dwindled to 1813 ships with jobs for 90,000 seamen. In the year preceding the Korean crisis, active ships numbered 1150, with jobs at about 62,000; during 1951 ships in operation increased to over 1400 with 85,000 jobs. Between 1951 and 1956, the number of active ships dropped to 1100, with jobs dropping to 59,000. The level of ship operations in the periods without defense emergencies has conformed substantially to the level recommended as the average justified on economic grounds and for minimum security needs by a presidential advisory committee in 1947. This was slightly above 1000 ships totaling between 11,000,000 and 12,000,000 deadweight tons, and requiring 65,000 licensed and unlicensed personnel. This level would equal the number of ships in operation in 1939; with the increased size and speed of the ships the former carrying capacity would be increased by one-third.[2]

The drop in active ships reflects the decline in the share of American trade carried on U. S. flag ships, as well as the drop from expanded wartime levels. In the immediate postwar year prior to the reconstruction of the European merchant marine, American ship operators mainly operating with chartered government-owned ships played a predominant part in the carriage of military supplies and aid to the devastated countries. In 1947 and 1948, American ship operators carried well over 60 percent of American foreign trade. With the revival of European merchant marines and the redevelopment of normal trade relationships attendant on economic recovery in the free world, the share of American trade carried by American ships has dropped to below 30 percent — a proportion largely dependent on the support provided American-flag ships through the 50–50 provision.

Shipboard employment has fluctuated with shipping opportunities. The range of variance in the postwar period from about 60,000 to about 100,000 has been less than that which occurred during the war when employment rose from 48,000 in 1942 to 160,000 in 1945. However, the sharp fluctuations within the narrower range have produced periodic dislocations — characterized generally by unemployment rather than by labor shortages. Only during the expanded demand for manpower during the Korean conflict were there substantial shortages. The general surplus of seamen available during most other periods is a basic factor in the labor-management relationships of the postwar period.

The mixed postwar prospects for the American merchant marine were further complicated by important uncertainties in the sphere of labor-management relations, particularly between 1945 and 1948. Prior to the war collective bargaining had barely been established when wartime ship operation and economic stabilization arrangements intervened to preclude any real opportunity for the conduct of activities generally associated with the process of collective bargaining. The ship operators had acted as the government's agents during the war; the unions had had little opportunity to demonstrate the influence of their growth and stability in the face of maritime stabilization regulations. Uncertainty over government withdrawal from both operations and stabilization persisted even after the war.

The difficulties in reëstablishing the basis for effective labor-management relations were manifest in shoreside situations which were less complex than those in the maritime industry, as the record of labor-management relations in 1946–8 demonstrates. To the general ingredients of instability, the maritime industry contributed its special character: the sharp drop in ship operations, the substantial decline from wartime wage earnings, the absence of effective labor-management relationships, and the presence of active rivalry between unions, reinforced by ideological differences. The enactment of the Taft-Hartley Act in 1947, and its ban on union preference in hiring, except under the provisions of a union shop arrangement in which new employees could enter the union within thirty days of entry on the job, enhanced the potential for instability. The maritime unions viewed the provisions of this act as a threat to the union preference hiring hall provision of their agreements.

That there was instability in maritime labor relations in the years immediately following the end of the war is hardly surprising, particularly when the shoreside record is considered. More significant is the fact that as a result of their experience the parties emerged with a desire for the establishment of stable relationships, particularly the West Coast operators. The desire may be attributed to the contrast between the 1946 and 1948 maritime strike situations. In 1946 the ship operators had been caught between the crossfires of rival unions and inconsistent governmental policies. In 1948, following the Taft-Hartley Act, the strike had been a private matter between the West Coast operators and the left-wing longshore and stewards' unions. In both cases, the unions had won. West Coast operators, like their East Coast colleagues, were now prepared to establish effective relationships, deëmphasizing their attack on the radical ideology presumed to be underlying the actions of these unions.

On the other hand, seafaring unions turned away from radical ideologies. Joseph Curran led a successful fight against the powerfully entrenched Communist groups in the National Maritime Union. Harry Lundeberg, long a bitter enemy of Harry Bridges, removed the West Coast stewards from control of the left-wing satellite National Union of Marine Cooks and Stewards. The primary concern of the seafaring unions was now to achieve economic gains for their memberships, and these gains have proved to be substantial.

The factors which produced substantial gains in wages and fringe benefits for American seamen in the postwar period were numerous and complex. The maritime unions now played an integral role in the American labor movement. They were aided in their militant efforts at achieving shoreside working conditions by the conditions favoring the economy at large and the foreign trade opportunities for the merchant marine. Improved earnings opportunities for seamen have offset the attraction of shoreside job opportunities and contributed to the maintenance of an adequate, and often more than adequate, labor reserve for manning the merchant marine. This reserve has assured that the union hiring hall could meet its responsibility in providing ship personnel. Governmental assistance through the foreign aid and cargo preference programs, and of partial aid through subsidies and other financial assistance has provided a favorable general climate. Additional factors accounting for union pressures for gains include: the uncertainty of the merchant marine's future and the desire to maximize conditions while favorable opportunities exist, in the hope of maintaining them in the future; the almost annual "round of increases" to shoreside workers, together with the mutual stimulation of wage adjustments and continued inflationary trends; and the intense competition among the maritime unions in which each competing group desires to take the credit for establishing the pattern for the industry. The early postwar efforts of the ship operators to resist adjustment of wages and working conditions, even at the risk of substantial strikes, has been replaced by bargaining positions conditioned by a combined concern with the maintenance of ship operation costs at minimum levels, as well as a concern with the immediate and short run opportunities available for American ships. An objective view of these policies of "expediency" as characterized by a spokesman for West Coast ship operators, suggests that American ship operators and seamen's unions function in collective bargaining as do the more assured parties in the more assured shoreside industries; it is only that the uncertainties are greater in the foreign competitive area.

Still serving as a deterrent to the developing stability in the industry is the continuing fractionalization of the union and management structure. The obstacles placed in the way of systematic bargaining and agreement by separate and rival organizations of seamen and longshoremen have been apparent, and have received much attention. The absence of operator unity, even within the same association, has not always received the same measure of attention.

THE POSTWAR STRUCTURE FOR COLLECTIVE BARGAINING

Both the companies and the unions emerged from the war in sound condition. The improved financial situation of the companies was matched with that of the unions resulting from the sharp gains in membership, and the absence of strikes under the maritime no-strike pledge. Unlike the development of closer relations among ship operators during the war, the union efforts at unity had lagged during the war years.

Wartime conditions produced greater cohesiveness among ship operators, all of whom were acting as agents of the War Shipping Administration. The National War Labor Board noted that such cohesion on the East Coast was "more pronounced." [3] On the West Coast, the Pacific American Shipowners' Association, already established as the offshore and intercoastal employers' instrument for collective bargaining, took over the function of negotiating for the operators of coastwise vessels organized in the Shipowners' Association of the Pacific Coast. A number of companies with contracts with the Seafarers' International Union, Atlantic and Gulf coasts, organized the Atlantic and Gulf Shipowners' Association in 1946 to negotiate uniform agreements with the SIU. Nationally, too, there were indications of closer relationships, when the National Federation of American Shipping was organized in 1944 by five major ship operating associations representing all American shipping, to keep "the nation's Merchant Marine from falling to pieces as it did after the war." The association did not deal with collective bargaining negotiations, although its research studies included labor reports.[4]

This cohesiveness weakened in the postwar years, even where the surface appearance was one of greater cohesion. Increased competition for cargoes and divergent positions on subsidies and other legislation resulted in the dissolution of the National Federation. The SIU employers' group was dissolved, and was replaced by an informal Atlantic and Gulf group. The East Coast operators continued to handle negotiations through separate dry cargo and tanker Committees for the Owners and Operators, Atlantic and Gulf coasts, which conduct negotiations with the NMU and unions of licensed officers, respectively. The committees include representatives of the American Merchant Marine Institute, and are serviced by its staff, but represent both Institute members and non-members. The president of the institute conducts negotiations on behalf of the committees; on the West Coast, negotiations are conducted by the staff of the Pacific Maritime Association. Representation accorded the different sectors of the industry, and subsidized and unsubsidized operations produces differences within the standing committees; differences in the forcefulness of bargaining positions between the dry cargo and tanker committees have also developed on occasion.

Even in the case of West Coast operator associations, where the extent of cohesiveness appears great, there is evidence of particularism. The "new look" in labor-management relations on the Pacific Coast, following the prolonged strike of longshoremen and marine cooks and stewards in 1948, was accompanied by a reorganization of the maritime employer organizations. The Pacific American Shipowners' Association, formerly dealing with ship unions, and the Waterfront Employers' Association, formerly dealing with longshore personnel, were combined into the Pacific Maritime Association. The staff of the association conducts negotiations on behalf of its members, and members are bound by majority vote on penalty of resignation. Despite the appearance of greater unity and centralization, however, major differences have arisen among the member companies over tactics in dealings with the rival seafaring and longshore unions, and on other association policies. Instability in interunion differences has been heightened by employer actions apparently intended to play one union off against another; employer differences have also resulted in the opposite effect, with unions playing off one employer against another. Resultant differences have apparently included discussion of the advisability of continuing to combine ship and longshore employers in a single association. The apparent greater centralization within the PMA has been reduced by the withdrawal of authorization to the association to bargain on their behalf by three of its members.[5]

The vast expansion in union membership during the war brought with it a windfall of union dues which vastly improved the financial status of the unions. The expansion in union membership between 1939 and 1946 was as follows: NMU, from 51,300 to 77,500;[6] SIU-SUP, from 15,000 to 62,000;[7] Marine Firemen, Oilers, and Watertenders, from 4,000 to 19,500;[8] Marine Cooks and Stewards, from 4,500 to 15,000.[9] The finances of the unions rose at a greater rate than the membership because of the prolonged peace in labor relations during the war. Characteristic of the trend for maritime unions was the change in the fortunes of the Pacific Marine Firemen's Union. Thus, in 1938, the union was in debt to the extent of $22,300; but by the end of 1941, it had a surplus of $60,000; and by the end of the war, it had a cash surplus of $871,000, with a strike fund of about $300,000, had modernized its hall in San Francisco, and had purchased a valuable lot in that city, as well as buildings to serve as union halls in San Pedro and Baltimore.[10]

There were several flaws in the unions' position, however. Division was paramount, the rivalries among the competing unions continued sharp and unabated. As the merchant marine sloughed off from its wartime peak, the unions could anticipate a sharp and early reduction in membership and income. Thus between January 1946 and November

1947, dues-paying members of the Marine Firemen's Union declined from 19,500 to 9000, including both regular members and permitmen.[11] In the case of the NMU, dues-paying members during the first six months of 1947 averaged 75,073, but dropped sharply to 60,000 in 1948 and again to 45,700 in 1949.[12] The drop in union membership failed to keep pace with the drop in vessels in active operation, however. Hence, although there were frequent shortages of men in some of the skilled ratings, in others and in the unskilled ratings, men were finding increased difficulty in obtaining jobs. In 1947, the NMU membership of 71,000 exceeded the 50,000 jobs available to its members by 50 percent — exceeding substantially the normal shore reserve of 10 to 20 percent.[13] These handicaps made it essential to recoup job losses, and resulted in the redoubling of efforts on the part of the maritime unions to obtain maximum gains so long as profitable carrying opportunities were available to the ships in operation.

The postwar period saw the renewal and intensification of desires to extend the organization of seamen. The Sailors Union of the Pacific had succeeded in winning several elections among the crews of West Coast tanker companies during the war years, and completed its organization among unlicensed crews in 1946 with a victory on the ships of the Standard Oil Company of California. The union's success in organizing all three departments on board these ships, in contradistinction to the three-union organizations among the three departments on board dry cargo ships, was a new departure which, as subsequent developments indicated, presaged closer action among the dry cargo ship personnel. From 1950 on, Lundeberg's Sailors' Union of the Pacific was locked in a battle which was fought in the courts and on the docks for control of the jobs still held by the expiring National Union of Marine Cooks and Stewards. A major aid in the fight was the creation of the Pacific District of the SIU, including the three autonomous unlicensed unions. The action of the licensed officers in negotiating together since 1955, and a single unit for the unlicensed seamen, along with the longshore negotiations, means that the Pacific Maritime Association now conducts three sets of negotiations, whereas formerly it conducted from six to ten.

On the East Coast, as Joseph Curran pointed out in his fight against the powerful Communist clique in the NMU, the left-wing officials in charge of the Lakes and Isthmian organizing drives had been preoccupied with ideological concerns rather than with organizing, and had dissipated the organizing funds. The successful fight to eliminate the Communists persisted for several years, and the National Maritime Union, with the Communists eliminated, was able to maintain its position as the largest single maritime union.[14]

The Atlantic and Gulf District of the Seafarers' International Union sought to enhance its jurisdiction by conducting organizing drives among unorganized seamen and those in independent unions. Its successes in the Isthmian and Cities Service drives were major additions to its contracted companies in situations, particularly the latter, where substantial company opposition was encountered.[15]

The licensed officers' unions, the Masters, Mates and Pilots, and the Marine Engineers' Beneficial Association, affiliated with the AFL and CIO respectively, continued to represent the great majority of licensed officers. The organization of a rival union to the MEBA in 1949, the Brotherhood of Marine Engineers, affiliated with the SIU, resulted in the loss of jobs with two companies to the BME. The licensed unions have continued to follow the patterns set by the militant unlicensed unions. Their drive for recognition of the hiring hall reflects the uncertainty over jobs for their members and the direct influence of practices in the unlicensed unions pressured for by former unlicensed seamen upgraded to licensed ratings during the war.

CHARACTERISTICS AND DEVELOPMENTS IN COLLECTIVE BARGAINING

Under wartime wage stabilization and virtual governmental control of the merchant marine, the maritime unions sought to obtain improvements through legislation. They aimed for wage increases, a reduction in the 56-hour week at sea and 44-hour week in port; unemployment insurance; and a seamen's bill of rights (modeled after that for G.I.'s).

The efforts to achieve some of these aims through legislation were only partially successful. The effort to extend the coverage of the Fair Labor Standards Act to seamen in order to obtain a 40-hour week at sea and in port failed. The CIO Maritime Committee had urged extension on the grounds that a 40-hour week was both practicable and necessary, claiming that the watch system could be changed from three watches to four per day, thereby providing employment for one-third more men.[16] Frank J. Taylor, testifying on behalf of the American Merchant Marine Institute, opposed any reduction in the work week on the grounds that existing shipboard accommodations were not adequate for the additional personnel which would be needed; competition would be impossible with foreign shipping or with domestic land transportation; and "utilization of free time becomes a real problem even today where a man is on watch only eight hours out of twenty-four. . . ." [17] Admiral Land's opposition to the proposal as War Shipping Administrator apparently impressed the Senate Committee. According to Land, Congress had originally exempted merchant seamen from the act because their "profession is unique and should not be classified with professions ashore" and he stated no change had occurred to warrant altering the exemption.[18] But what was not forthcoming through legislation was achieved in two stages — in 1946 and 1951–2 — through collective bargaining, when the government was in substantial control of the merchant marine.

The proposed seamen's bill of rights had been watered down until it came to substantially less than the G.I. bill of rights. The opposition of the armed services served as an effective deterrent to enactment. Only in the matter of achieving unemployment insurance, originally promised in 1939, were the seamen successful. In 1946, Congress passed a measure under which the states would administer a program of unemployment insurance for seamen, who were to be covered by the provisions of the state law in which the employer's headquarters or home office was located. These political activities for improvement of the seamen's status were transitory. The end of the war produced a natural shift to the collective bargaining sphere of action.

Reference has already been made to the climate of uncertainty which surrounds the American merchant marine. For ship operators, it is the uncertainty of the volume of cargo and passenger traffic; the renewed effective foreign competition, the mounting operating and overhead costs; the continued government aid in the form of subsidies and cargo preference; the role of the government during emergency periods and the tactical effects of rival union drives on negotiations. The uncertainties confronting the unions are equally great: uncertainty over the ability of the industry to provide an adequate number of jobs for the core group of union seamen; the possibility of diluting these opportunities further if unrestricted entry into the industry is permitted; the impact of the ban of the Taft-Hartley Act on the union preference arrangements in the industry; the possibility of encroachment on both territorial and work jurisdiction; and the necessity for maintaining a position of leadership in the frequent negotiations in the industry. This complex of factors has been aggravated by the presence of a complicated rival union situation. Its outward manifestation in collective bargaining relationships has been what the ship operators have referred to as "whipsawing." The operators have contended that they have been caught between rival unions in negotiating. To this, the union reply has been that the operators have not been loath to play off one union against another.

The complexities of the situation and its characteristics, however, should not becloud the general improvement which has marked labor-management relations in the maritime industry. On the East Coast, offshore labor-management relations have been generally good, both in the major segment of the industry centered about the NMU, particularly since the successful battle against the Communist clique, and in the SIU Atlantic and Gulf sector. The longshore situation on the East Coast, however, has been a continuing source of instability and prolonged work stoppages in recent years. On the West Coast, the "new look" in maritime labor relations following the 1948 longshore strike has resulted in improved relations both in longshore and offshore operations.

In dealing with the gains made by the seamen's unions since 1945, it is hardly sufficient to provide a mere recital of these: the process by which these were negotiated is essential to an understanding of the interaction of the rival union situation and the numerous uncertainties cited above. Both the summary of gains, and some brief accounts of leading negotiations are essential.

The seafaring unions have achieved their objective of "first class" status for their constituents in the postwar years. The full employment conditions on shore and the regular increases in wages and working conditions gained by shoreside workers have aided the militant seamen's unions in their efforts. In addition, the often intense differences among the maritime unions and the jealously guarded jurisdictions have made each seek to outdo the other group. Separate contract expiration dates have served as levers in this competitive process — with one group of contracts centered around the NMU contract expiring on June 15, and the SIU-SUP contracts expiring on September 30, although if one group obtained more favorable terms one year, these have usually been roughly approximated by the other bargaining groups within the same year.

The underlying urge toward national uniformity in wages and working conditions has maintained a close similarity in basic wages and working conditions. In recent years, however, the form of the wage system has differed, with the NMU maintaining the 40-hour at sea basic work week, and the SUP choosing to incorporate the increased earnings resulting from this provision into its basic rate. There have also been variations in the forms taken by numerous pension and health and welfare plans financed by employer contributions.

Since the $45 adjustment directed by the National War Labor Board in 1945 which occurred when war risk bonuses were being cut back, the NMU ablebodied seamen's rate increased by 130 percent, from $145 to $353 in 1956 on the East Coast. Earnings have increased even more with the liberalization of overtime payments, and with the reduction of the basic work week in two steps, although the actual work week for men on watch remains at 56 hours: from 56 to 48 hours on shipboard, from 48 to 40 in port in 1946, and from 48 to 40 on shipboard in 1951–2. However, with the necessity for continuing the 56-hour week, overtime costs, which averaged 8 percent of basic rates in 1939–41, are estimated to have increased to about 40 percent on all coasts. In 1955, on the West Coast, where average overtime earnings have generally been higher, the SUP agreed to incorporate into the base rates an average representative of overtime earnings for work on Saturdays and Sundays, and for work within the regular eight-hour workday. The A.B. rate, $453 in 1956, includes the allowance for such overtime earnings.

In addition to increases in wages, maritime agreements have followed shoreside trends in establishing welfare and pension plans and in ensuring vacations to all those maintaining continuous service through an industry-wide pooling of vacation allowances. Showing prompt reaction to shoreside developments, health and welfare plans were negotiated promptly in 1949–50 by the seamen's unions, and pension plans followed shortly. The NMU also followed on the footsteps of the United Automobile Workers in obtaining an "employment security plan" in 1955 in lieu of a wage increase.

Closer examination of the postwar developments reveals the extent to which expediency has characterized wage negotiations in this industry. The reductions in the work week occurred in 1946 and 1951–2 when there were direct governmental pressures for the maintenance of an adequately staffed merchant marine. Governmental intervention was particularly direct in the agreement on the first work week reduction in 1946. Expediency was maintained by the parties through the provision for reopenings at six-month intervals, with frequent negotiations or arbitration awards to "equalize" rates between both coasts or to provide increases to meet rises in the Consumer Price Index.

Maritime operators have acknowledged this expediency, but they insist that they have had to accept these increased costs because of the impact of forces beyond their control, including the fluctuation of merchant marine opportunities, whipsawing by strong rival unions and the prominent role of government in a number of increases.[19] They cite the results of the study of the industry undertaken for them which show that the postwar rate of increase in maritime base rates and earnings has far outstripped those of shoreside manufacturing workers; that the earnings level exceeds those of such shoreside industries as basic steel, autos, shipbuilding and others; and that operating costs far exceed those on foreign vessels.[20]

Although acknowledging that American maritime wages far exceed those of foreign seamen, the maritime unions contend that they are merely seeking to bring the seamen's conditions into line with the American standard of living. The unions contend that more appropriate is a comparison between the seamen's status in this country and abroad with their respective shoreside counterparts. On this basis, it is contended that American seamen fare substantially less favorably than do foreign seamen. They cite the A.B. seamen hourly base rate (in 1956, approximately $1.90 per hour) as evidence that it is in line with average manufacturing rates; on earnings, they emphasize the casual and intermittent character of seafaring job opportunities in contrast to shoreside employment and the necessary length of the shipboard work week. They have emphasized also the other side of the relationship; that governmental welfare and social security benefits are more important in foreign countries, that employer payments for these are made through established funds, and do not appear in the wage, and that comparisons with foreign rates are invalid because of currency devaluation.[21]

The combination of circumstances under which these gains were made varied widely during this period. Governmental activities and policies were prominent in various ways in several of the negotiations. Rival union efforts to develop effective alliances were also apparent in some of these, as were altered approaches to collective bargaining. A detailed history of the specific collective bargaining negotiations would only make for confusion in the plethora of negotiations in which the industry has been involved. Instead, brief summaries are presented of the key features in those bargaining situations particularly affected by the fragmentation of organization on both the labor and management sides.

The Reconversion Period (1946)

The first reduction in the basic work week was obtained in the protracted negotiations in 1946. These occurred at a time when 80 percent of ship operations were being conducted for the account of the War Shipping Administration and when substantial governmental intervention in numerous reconversion period strikes was taking place. The CIO maritime unions — including the International Longshoremen's and Warehousemen's Union and the National Maritime Union had organized the Committee for Maritime Unity, to which the AFL unions had replied with the formation of a Maritime Trades Department. The strategy of the former was to seek to obtain combined negotiations with both East and West Coast operators; this was partially obtained when, at the urging of Secretary of Labor Schwellenbach, the operators on both coasts agreed to joint negotiations with several qualifications.[22] The ship operators were ready to grant major concessions, but were unwilling to accede to any reduction of the basic work week at sea, holding that this was merely a disguised wage increase.

In the face of apparent stalemate, Granville Conway, War Shipping administrator and Philip Murray, president of the CIO intervened. Conway offered the seafaring unions a reduction in the work week at sea to 48 hours, along with the 40-hour week in port which the operators had offered, and wage ($17.50) and overtime increases. Murray placed pressure on Bridges to accept the terms of an earlier fact-finding board recommendation. The agreements concluded on Conway's terms were subject to the approval of the National Wage Stabilization Board, since they involved increased costs to the government; these were approved immediately by the board on the grounds of "the application of special standards to the unique situation in this industry," since the combined postwar adjustments in the maritime industry now were well in advance of those granted in industry generally.[23]

Subsequently, the SUP and the SIU, which had refused to participate in the joint negotiations, concluded their own agreements. These agreements followed the earlier, with one exception — the SUP agreement provided a $22.50 increase for the A.B. rate, while the SIU obtained a $27.50 increase. The West Coast Marine Firemen's Union, party to the first set of negotiations, was given "most favored nation" treatment, by the operators, and its firemen's rate was brought up to the SUP level.

The War Shipping Administration approved the agreements, but the Wage Stabilization Board disapproved the increases in excess of $17.50. To do otherwise, the board held, would make a sham of wage stabilization, and, in any event, its action did not preclude the ship operators from absorbing the small additional cost involved — about $1.00 per day per ship. There was sharp opposition in all quarters to the Board action — SUP, NMU and operators — and a strike was called by the AFL unions on September 5 with Lundeberg announcing that the strike was one to protect collective bargaining. The CIO unions on both coasts supported the strike with pledges that they would not cross AFL picket lines.[24] On a rehearing, the Wage Stabilization Board sustained its previous action.[25] On September 12, the strike was terminated when John R. Steelman, director of the Office of War Mobilization and Reconversion amended the wage regulations to permit the government to absorb the increases.[26] Immediately following the termination of the SIU-SUP strike, the NMU, the MCS, and the MFOWW struck since Steelman's order applied only to the increases for the AFL seamen. The AFL Maritime Trades Department, organized to counterbalance the Committee for Maritime Unity, now agreed to recognize the picket lines of the striking unions. An arbitration proceeding, as the result of the June 15 agreement, became the vehicle for equalizing the terms for both groups of unions. When the Pacific American Shipowners' Association protested the strike as a violation of the terms of the June 15 agreement, the Maritime Commission, which had only recently taken over government ship operations from the now defunct WSA, pressed the operators, and the strike was terminated on September 24.[27]

All these events were followed almost immediately by another and even more protracted set of work stoppages tying up the ships in October, when the contracts of the licensed officers were open. The stumbling block to agreements was the demand for union preference — the strike persisted on the East Coast until October 27, when agreement was reached on limited union preference, and until November 23 on the West Coast, where the operators successfully opposed the proposal.[28]

To add to the complexity of the situation, Bridges contended that his agreement was still open at the time of the licensed officers' strike, although the ILWU had obtained virtually all of its demands, including a June 15 expiration date, and went on strike. His reason for striking reverted to the long-standing jurisdictional dispute between the SUP and the longshoremen over the work of handling the cargo of the steam schooners. This demand may have been intended in part to retaliate for the SUP's manning of all departments of the several dry cargo vessels operated by the American Pacific Steamship Co., an action which had resulted in a jurisdictional dispute then preventing all shipments to and from Coos Bay, Oregon. The company had formerly been a tanker company, and had dealt with the SUP in all three departments. In taking over dry cargo operations, and extending its tanker agreements to these, a situation without precedent was created. When the *Mello Franco* had put in at Coos Bay at the end of June, the ILWU was joined by the MFW and the MCS in picketing the ship. The SUP retaliated by "freezing" the port and refusing to sail in or out. The SIU on the East Coast placed picket lines in several East Coast ports around ships manned by members of the Committee for Maritime Unity, and the ships were immobilized when the ILA refused to cross the picket lines. A fact-finding board was appointed by the secretary of labor; but resolution of the dispute was only obtained following arrangements for selling the ship to a foreign country.[29]

The Taft-Hartley Law (1948)

A substantially different climate surrounded negotiations following the enactment of the Taft-Hartley Act in June 1947. Government operations had largely ceased, and ship operations were almost completely under private control in line with the policies established by the Ship Sales Act of 1946. The provisions of the Taft-Hartley Act with greatest implications for the maritime industry were, first, the ban on discrimination against any prospective employee because of union or nonunion affiliation, and, second, the restriction on union security to a union shop contract — which appeared to prohibit the union preference arrangement in maritime agreements, under which ship operators obtained their personnel through union hiring halls. Particularly significant, too, seemed the provision of the act requiring all union officials to file non-Communist affidavits as a condition for enjoying the protective features of the act, since it operated to exclude all unions which refused or were unable to file these affidavits.

The first impact of the act upon the maritime industry was felt in the SUP negotiations in September 1947. The membership of the SUP had voted to direct their officers to file the non-Communist affidavits, but "with great reluctance," since "it is against our principles to tell any snoopers what our affiliations are." [30] When it came to the union preference issue, Lundeberg and Gregory Harrison, counsel of the Pacific American Shipowners' Association, met with Senator Taft who assured them that he would help out since the parties felt that a solution could be found.[31] A solution was finally worked out which provided that the employers "would prefer applicants who have previously been employed on vessels of one or more of the company signatories to this agreement. . . ." In its turn, the union agreed "that in furnishing deck personnel through the facilities of their employment office it will recognize such preferences. . . ." When ordinary seamen with prior experience are not available, "the union in dispatching seamen will prefer graduates of the Andrew Furuseth Training School" (the latter being the union-organized and operated school).[32] Although the employers insisted upon interpreting this clause to mean that they could hire either union or nonunion men as and where they choose, they continued to call upon the SUP hiring hall for men.[33]

The "Lundeberg formula" for settling the hiring hall issue came in for attack by the CIO unions as "a seriously weakened hiring hall clause." On the other hand, the SIU-SUP rebuffed Curran's efforts to obtain industry-wide unity in preparation for the 1948 negotiations, stating the "SUP and SIU want unity with *bona fide* American trade unionists. But we do not want unity with an organization which has followed the Communist Party line for years. . . ." [34] Curran, now in the throes of a battle to eliminate Communist influence, was placed in the position of having to meet with the left-wing maritime unions in the CIO. The conference called by the CIO unions in November 1947 to obtain unity was to consist of only four of the CIO unions — the NMU, the MCS, the ILWU, and the ACA. Even these unions were to disagree over the course of action to be taken in the event of a strike in June. A split occurred over Bridges' proposal for a merger between the ILWU and the NMU with the left-wing group in the NMU supporting the proposal and the Curran-led group opposing it.[35]

The negotiations for the 1948–9 contract were opened by notices from the employers on both coasts calling upon the CIO unions and the MFOWW to agree to changes in the agreements to conform to the requirements of the Taft-Hartley Act. Denying any intent to break the unions, the ship operators contended that any other course would leave the employers open to suit for damages. Charging that the employers were seeking to break them, the unions insisted that the *status quo* be maintained. The resultant stalemate over the hiring question virtually precluded negotiation on the remaining questions at issue.

Early during the negotiations, the Pacific American Shipowners' Association and the SUP agreed to extend until September 30, 1949, their contract which was not due to expire until September 30, 1948. In addition to continuance of the "Lundeberg formula" on industry seniority, their agreement provided for an increase in wage rates, bringing the able seamen's rate, for example, to $210; and put the SUP ahead of the CIO once again.[36] This time, apparently, there was to be no question as to which union initiated the pattern.

The West Coast employers offered the West Coast CIO and independent seafaring unions a clause similar to that of the "Lundeberg formula." In the case of the ILWU, however, the Waterfront Employers' Association proposed doing away with union preference, as well as eliminating the necessity for obtaining union approval before registering a man; and proposed replacing the union-selected hiring hall dispatcher with an impartially selected impartial dispatcher. East Coast employers, represented by the Committees for Companies and Agents, offered to replace the offending union preference clause with one providing for companies to "give due consideration to members of the Union who possess the required qualifications." The companies indicated that they would continue to call on the union hiring hall in most cases, but not exclusively.[37]

When it appeared that a strike would occur on June 15, President Truman appointed a Board of Inquiry in accordance with the provisions of the Taft-Hartley Act. The parties reiterated their positions before the board — the employers denied any intent to eliminate the hiring halls, the unions charged that the provisions of the Taft-Hartley Act failed to meet the peculiar short-term employment conditions of the maritime industry. Injunctions were issued by courts on the respective coasts, under the provisions of the Taft-Hartley Act, delaying the execution of any strike until September 2, presumably giving the parties further opportunity to negotiate.[38]

East Coast negotiations proceeded during July and August, a period which saw the overwhelming defeat of the left-wing groups in the NMU. Early in August, the operators agreed to maintenance of the *status quo* regarding union preference and the union hiring hall, subject to determination of the legality of these practices by a court of "competent jurisdiction." The prolonged delay in settling the controversy actually proved to be a blessing for the NMU.[39]

The dispute on the West Coast continued in a vastly different atmosphere. The parties would meet only at the specific request of the Federal Mediation and Conciliation Service. As expressed in a final report to the President during August, it was the view of the Board of Inquiry that the disputes involving the longshoremen and the Marine Cooks and Stewards "provide little basis for a conclusion other than despair." In no uncertain terms, the board reported that "if deterioration in so bad a situation is possible, the situation has deteriorated." The employers' charges of Communist domination leveled at the unions of longshoremen and marine cooks, and the unions' countercharge of union-busting, were characterized by the board as not "ephemeral charges made with tongue in cheek. . . . They are professed as firm convictions fully supported. They permeate the whole fabric of the parties' relations and gnaw at its every strand. They create a sense of despair and frustration which accompanies every attempt at negotiation." Negotiations were conducted in a humorless, unsympathetic, and intolerant atmosphere. "The institutional attitudes are blamed upon the leaders; and the leaders grate upon each other as persons beyond their responsibility as leaders." [40]

The Board of Inquiry reported the parties' inability to agree on any issue, and particularly on the hiring hall issue.[41] However, shortly before the expiration of the injunction period on September 2, the International Longshoremen's and Warehousemen's Union and the operators appeared to have reached agreement on applying the East Coast formula to the hiring hall problem — that is, maintaining the *status quo* pending determination by a court of "competent jurisdiction." Progress was also reported in negotiations with the other unions. On the eve of September 2, however, the negotiations became stymied over the wage question. At the final session, where negotiations collapsed, Harry Bridges reverted to his earlier stand, demanding continuance of the present hiring hall "with no strings attached." On September 2, the injunction against a strike was dissolved, and a strike was called by West Coast longshoremen and the seafaring employees, immobilizing all shipping other than tankers. The Waterfront Employers' Association and the Pacific American Shipowners' Association announced that "survival of the industry and the public welfare" required adoption of a policy of refusing to bargain with any union which had failed to file the non-Communist affidavits called for by the Taft-Hartley Act. Announcing that "certain Communist-dominated unions in Pacific shipping have made continuous operation impossible. Therefore, we have made our declaration of domestic independence — independence of Communist control of labor on shore and ship," the shipowners' associations sought to enlist wider support.

The ship operators maintained a steadfast position during the first two months of the strike, making the filing of non-Communist affidavits conditional for dealing with the unions. Maritime workers and the public were bombarded with releases calling attention to the "Communist Party Line leadership that does not want agreement between employers and employees." According to Frank Foisie, president of the Waterfront Employers' Association, the strike was "inevitable" and the issue was a fight for survival of "either shipping or Communism." The "fourteen years of appeasement" of these "Communist-controlled unions," he found, have "failed us as signally and disastrously in Pacific Coast shipping as it has our nation in its relations with the Soviet Union this same period of years." [42]

Representatives of CIO President Philip Murray were also active during October, seeking to end the strike. Their presence indicated that the CIO supported the strike, despite the anti-Communist stand of CIO leaders. The National Maritime Union, too, adopted a policy of complete support for West Coast strikers. Its policy was implemented by refusal to man any ships which might be reallocated from the West Coast to companies under contract with the NMU. [43]

One paradox which developed during the strike related to the handling of Army cargoes. Harry Bridges had indicated that the members of his union were willing to handle such cargoes under prestrike wages and working conditions. Informed of this offer by Secretary of the Army Kenneth C. Royall, the West Coast ship operators refused to handle such cargoes, contending that "it would not be in the best interests of the Army mission to resume the handling of its cargoes if it required again saddling the operation with the harassment and sabotage of Communist Party Line labor leadership." [44] Confronted with this refusal, the Army arranged with a contractor who was not a member of the Waterfront Employers' Association to handle Army cargoes. Longshoremen would be employed at prestrike wages and were to be obtained through the union hiring hall. Thus, for much of the strike period, members of the ILWU were handling Army cargoes, while private ship operators were refusing to deal with the "Communist-led unions."

A basis for the resumption of negotiations was provided in the so-called "Roth Formula" drafted by Almon Roth, president of the San Francisco Employers' Council. The terms of the "formula" were intended to avert future strikes, as well as provide an immediate basis for settlement. They provided that the CIO would participate with the ILWU in the negotiations and would underwrite the "faithful performance" of the contract by the ILWU. Every effort would be made to settle future disputes through collective bargaining. The CIO and the San Francisco Employers' Council would withhold assistance from their respective constituents unless they approved action involving a strike or lockout. With the union's acceptance of these terms, the employers dropped their demand for the filing of non-Communist affidavits. [45]

Negotiations were resumed on November 11 for the first time since the outbreak of the strike on September 2. Agreements were reached with all the striking unions by the first week in December. In the case of the longshoremen and the unlicensed personnel, the agreements provided for retention of existing hiring and hiring hall arrangements and substantial increases in wages and working conditions. Shipowners and union officials announced that the agreements were "based on complete good faith," and they joined in predicting that the contracts and "the new spirit can mean a new era for West Coast Shipping." [46]

The strike settlement left a major problem unsettled — that of Harry Lundeberg's Sailors' Union of the Pacific. The tying up of the dry cargo ships had deprived the members of the SUP of employment, although they were not on strike. When a settlement of the strike appeared in the offing, it was now Lundeberg's turn to charge that the SUP jurisdictional rights were being handed over to the ILWU by the ship operators, and he threatened to prevent ship sailings unless these jurisdictional rights were protected and increased wages were granted. Subsequently, when ship sailings were delayed even after assurances were forthcoming that no jurisdictional claims were involved in the strike settlements, it was apparent that Lundeberg was seeking adjustments in excess of those granted the striking unions. These tactics were successful, for by the end of December the SUP received wage increases equaling those granted to the other unions, plus a $7.50 per month "clothing allowance." [47]

The significance of the 1948 strike was twofold — first, it demonstrated the ability of left-wing controlled unions to obtain and maintain rank and file solidarity in the face of ideological attack by the operator group. Second, it gave support to the dissidents among the operator group who had seen no reason for the strike in the first place, and who were joined by major ship operators who now sought, not only immediate settlement, but a reorientation which would avoid similar expeditions into futility, and would aid in the growth of the industry. One outcome of this study was a decision to combine the two existing associations into the Pacific Maritime Association, which would deal with both seamen and longshoremen. A second was the decision on the principle of greater participation by ship operators in negotiations.[48] The record of the years since 1948 indicates that the "new look" in West Coast maritime labor relations has had lasting effect. Labor-management relations in the West Coast maritime industry appear to have lost the intransigent character of the period between 1934 and 1948, when operator attitudes reinforced the constant fear on the part of the unions that their status had not been accepted, and that the operators were seeking at least a partial return to the era of employer domination. The subsequent period has not been without its problems and instability;

but these have been the product of union rivalry rather than of ideological conflict between labor and management. The record, particularly in recent years, shows continuing improvement in both longshore and seafaring relations.[49]

Limited Mobilization (1951–1952)

The developments in the limited Korean crisis period were reminiscent in a measure of the interunion crossfire in 1946. Again, this was a period of substantial government operation, and of stabilization controls, but substantially more limited in scope and intensity than during the war. In this situation, it was the CIO unions who led off again with a brief strike in June 1951, which was terminated with agreement to establish the forty-hour week at sea in two steps by the end of the year, and a wage increase. The Wage Stabilization Board reduced the wage increase to conform to stabilization regulations and approved the reduction in the work week.[50] With the exception of the SUP, these adjustments were extended to the remainder of the industry.

In November, 1951, the SUP concluded agreement on terms which differed from the earlier pattern. It provided for wage increases averaging 13 percent as against the 6.2 percent and work week reduction approved by the board; and an innovation which distinguished between overtime and penalty pay — the overtime pay, at $2.35 (at time and one-half equivalent) was to be paid for "true" overtime — time worked outside regular working hours — after 8 hours per day and after 56 per week; penalty pay at $1.63 (a straight time equivalent) was to be paid for Sunday and holiday work and for hours worked between 48 and 56 hours per week at sea; and for certain extra duties performed during regular working hours. The board approved this increase.[51]

Matters stood thus only briefly. In February, 1952, the SUP advised the Pacific Maritime Association of its intention to reopen the contract. Failure to reach agreement on the union demand for the 40-hour week at sea and for a wage increase resulted in a 63-day strike which began on May 27. To the ship-operator charge that the SUP strike was directed at achieving gains in its rivalry with the ILWU both over the scope of work issue, and over the impending elections in the Marine Cooks and Stewards competition, Lundeberg replied that these issues had been injected by the Pacific Maritime Association. He charged, too, that the association was coddling Bridges and the ILWU, and that it was now directing its fire against the SUP.[52] The operator insistence on clarifying the jurisdiction of the scope of work between the SUP and the ILWU in handling ship's stores arose out of the charge that there had been numerous work stoppages over the work.[53] The strike was ended with agreement on the 40-hour week and a wage increase. The insistence of the association on clarity on the work issue resulted in a memorandum, but the basic issue persists.

Through arbitration proceedings, the other seafaring unions proceeded to obtain the restoration of parity which had been disturbed by the two agreements. The Marine Firemen's Union had led off in November at the time of the initial SUP agreement under its "most favored nation" arrangement.[54] Arbitration awards involving the CIO unions were handed down in November.[55] All the adjustments were subsequently made effective after the termination of the Korean crisis price-wage stabilization controls.

New Departures from Uniformity (1955)

Bargaining in the maritime industry in 1955 occurred at a time when a thorough congressional investigation of maritime labor relations was under way.[56] The committee had before it a bill which proposed to amend the Merchant Marine Act of 1936 by requiring that maximum limits as well as minimum be fixed on wages, working conditions, and manning for operating subsidy payments. Ship operators and unions, alike, were agreed in their opposition to the setting of maximum limits on operating subsidies. Maritime management opposed the subsidy maximum limitation as resulting in the undesirable control of wages by government in peacetime; as setting up a limited, unrealistic, and unfair area of wage control; and as resulting in violation of the parity principle in the payment of subsidies. The unions were opposed to the measure as an unwarranted restriction on collective bargaining, and as having insidious precedent-setting implications for shoreside labor-management relations.

Although legislative action was not forthcoming, the hearings undoubtedly had some influence on the collective bargaining which was then taking place. East Coast operators took a strong stand in opposition to any wage increases, and proposed to reduce operational costs by eliminating allegedly obsolete working provisions calling for penalty payments which were initiated prior to the institution of the 40-hour week. The National Maritime Union, taking its cue from the attainment of supplementary unemployment benefits in the auto industry, directed its demands to the establishment of such a plan for seamen. The substantial turnover in employment among seamen and the continui excess reserve available for ship jobs were viewed by Joseph Curran making such an arrangement particularly desirable to achieve stab' in employment for seamen. A brief strike occurred when the operators insisted upon clear understanding that seamen who quit jobs voluntarily would not be eligible for such payments. The dry and passenger operators were the first to conclude agreement tc tribute 25¢ per man per day for the establishment of an employment security fund whose benefit arrangements would be developed subsequently. The tanker operators held out for several days longer than did the dry cargo operators, possibly because of greater concern with the shoreside implications of another foothold for employer-financed supplements to unemployment compensation. The contribution to the pension and welfare plan was also increased by 25¢ per man per day — but there was no wage increase, and the union had not requested one.[57]

Harry Lundeberg, on the other hand, proposed the incorporation into the base rates of amounts representative of the average of overtime earnings for work on Saturdays and Sundays, and for work within the regularly scheduled eight-hour day. The new A.B. rate of $423 replaced the former rate of $302, and included the allowance for their overtime earnings and an additional increase of $25. "True" overtime would now be paid at time and a half for work after 56 hours per week and 8 hours per day. The restoration of the 56-hour basic work week at sea was justified by the SUP as eliminating much internal disagreement among union members whose earnings have differed on the various trade routes. The congressional proposal on maximum limits for operating subsidies was also cited.[58] The other members of the SIU-Pacific Coast District made varying choices in their negotiations. The Marine Cooks and Stewards followed the SUP pattern; the Marine Firemen's Union chose to continue the existing provisions for penalty payments after 40 hours at sea, and for extra duties performed during the regular eight-hour work period.[59]

In one major respect, however, there was conformity in all of the maritime agreements in 1955. They provided for three-year terms, with annual wage reopenings. The lengthened contract periods were hopefully viewed as auguries of greater stability.

THE HIRING OF SEAMEN AND THE TAFT-HARTLEY ACT

The key role occupied by the fight for job control makes it a measurable pulse of the state of labor-management relations in the maritime industry. The fears that the Taft-Hartley Act would destroy or at least disrupt the functioning of the union hiring halls have not materialized. The provisions of the act have, however, under the pressure of unfair labor charges against the union preference-hiring hall provisions in the contracts in 1947, resulted in contractual changes and in new concepts in the operation of the halls.

The joint responsibilities under which both unions and management are placed by the act's provisions for the avoidance of discrimination in employment on the basis of union or nonunion status, has resulted in closer relations between them in efforts to work out arrangements to meet the pressures for conformity with the act's provisions. The accommodations have sought to preserve the union hiring hall and to protect the job security of the union members who have normally followed the sea, while avoiding discrimination between union and nonunion members. In an industry marked by brief duration of employment relationships and substantial turnover, and therefore apparently unable to utilize the union shop provisions of the Taft-Hartley Act, a unique seniority concept has been developed to achieve job security which has received various adaptations by the respective unions. A notable feature has been the development in several instances of joint labor-management arrangements dealing with aspects of the union hiring hall referral system.

The altered position on the management side has been reflected by the maritime industry spokesmen who appeared in the hearings leading to enactment of the Taft-Hartley Act prior to the "new look" in labor-management relations on the West Coast, and also in the hearings subsequent to the enactment of the act. Almon Roth, president of the National Federation of American Shipping, appeared as a spokesman for the maritime industry before the congressional committees considering the revision of the National Labor Relations Act. He supported general propositions for revision of existing legislation similar to those developed by the National Association of Manufacturers, for example: subjecting unions to the same contractual responsibility as employers; eliminating all sympathetic strikes and secondary boycotts; outlawing the closed shop; outlawing strikes to gain recognition; excluding supervisors from the National Labor Relations Act; and opposing compulsory arbitration.[60] On proposals to outlaw industry-wide or multi-employer bargaining units, however, Roth dissented; his grounds were that established patterns of collective bargaining in the industry would be destroyed.[61] Roth charged that the union-controlled hiring halls were used to prevent the development of any ties of loyalty between shipowners and seamen. "We think we should have the right to employ and select our employees and use them continually under the same operation and develop their skills," argued Roth; "we do not get that under the hiring-hall system." [62]

In 1948–1949, the ship operators were confronted with the necessity of shifting their viewpoints on the union hiring hall. The company charges filed against the National Maritime Union by Great Lakes and East Coast companies, and rival union and individual charges on the West Coast resulted in a series of NLRB decisions holding that union-preference hiring hall arrangements in existence at that time were illegal, since they resulted in the operation of the hiring halls to discriminate against nonunion or probationary trip card men.[63] The West Coast operators had just endured a prolonged strike, out of which a new approach to bargaining had emerged. The realities involved in maintaining stable relationships with the unions and the demonstrated utility of the halls resulted in a changed attitude which both accepted the union hiring halls and was constructively critical of their operation. Improvements have been sought through bargaining, and the absence of the hiring hall as an issue in contract negotiations since 1948 reflects the constructive nature of labor-management relationships in the industry.

The altered position of the ship operators is reflected in testimony on union proposals for the legalization of the union hiring hall which have been pressed since 1949. In the 1950 hearings, the Pacific Maritime Association pointed out that the effect of the act was to permit employers to negotiate with the unions to obtain all their personnel through a lawfully operated hiring hall, but that it placed the onus on the operators to police the operation of the halls, or else to assume the penalty of assuming financial responsibility for the actions of the union. The former was considered as detrimental to stable relations, and the latter as unfair. It was proposed to make the union alone responsible for the legal operation of the hall, and to require the government to assume full responsibility for enforcement.[64] The American Merchant Marine Institute indicated that it was interested in resolving the problems which had arisen out of the NLRB decisions, through collective bargaining. Although not necessarily opposed to the union operation of the hiring hall, the operators were dissatisfied with the workings of the rotary system which "impairs the employer's right to select his employees and substitutes a mere right of rejection which can be exercised only where the man referred by the union is physically unfit, manifestly incompetent, or has been guilty of misconduct." This qualified position was taken at a time when East Coast operators were opposing the demands of the licensed officers for hiring hall arrangements.[65]

In the 1953 hearings on revision of the Taft-Hartley Act, the testimony of the operators on both coasts indicated their willingness to operate under the union-controlled hiring hall, and they referred to evidence of the operation of the halls in conformity with the law. There was divergence, however, on the details of their position. The AMMI opposed any exemption of the industry from the closed shop provisions of the act on the grounds that "this would continue all of the evils of the closed shop system."[66] The Pacific Maritime Association, however, proposed legislation which would permit the establishment of hiring halls with a limited list of registrants to whom the union shop provisions of the act could be made applicable.[67]

In taking a position at variance with the unions on the exemption of the hiring halls from the act, the employers made clear their acceptance of the legal operation of the halls and their willingness to accommodate to the legal decisions through collective bargaining. This has been reflected in the relative ease with which remedies were achieved in the face of NLRB actions on complaints of discrimination.

The unions also altered their positions in regard to the necessity for modifications in the hiring hall to accommodate to the changed situation produced by the Taft-Hartley Act. Although all would prefer to see the halls exempted from the act's provisions, they have negotiated changes in contract provisions, and in most instances in the operations of the hiring hall to preserve the hall, to enhance the bargaining relationship, and to strengthen the union. The evolution of the position on the hiring hall has been particularly evident in the case of the NMU. Here the internal dissension produced by the fight against the Communist clique, and subsequently by nonparty radicals, would have turned an administration position of accommodation to the Taft-Hartley Act into a weapon of attack against Curran. Even after the radicals were expelled, and NLRB and court actions indicated the necessity for some accommodation, a split developed within the union administration, with two officials urging a fight against the act. The Curran-led majority took the position that such a fight could only weaken the union, and that accommodation which the union itself could determine, with negotiation with the ship operators where appropriate, would protect against the weakening both of the hall and the union.

The first step in the development of accommodation to the act's ban on hiring arrangements which would discriminate between union and nonunion members was the development of what has come to be known as the "Lundeberg" formula. The terms of this arrangement were concluded by Lundeberg and the Pacific American Shipowners' Association in the fall of 1947.[68] This provided for the retention of the union hiring hall, but substituted for the union preference clause the provision for preference to those with prior employment on the vessels of the contract covered companies and preference to new entries from among the graduates of the Andrew Furuseth Training School, organized and operated by the SUP. With the work force fully organized in unions for more than a decade, the effect of this industry seniority clause was to protect the prior job rights of union members, although there was the possibility that expellees from the union might bring charges under the act. In practice, no change was necessary in the operation of the hiring hall; Lundeberg stated emphatically in the 1950 Congressional hearings on the hiring hall: "we operate identically the same way today as we did before the passage of the Taft-Hartley Act." [69]

Subsequently, the Supreme Court sustained the NLRB finding that the NMU Lakes hiring hall was illegal, and additional NLRB decisions outlawed other arrangements deriving from union preference-hiring hall clauses. As a result, the industry service seniority arrangement, tied to the vessels of the companies in the bargaining unit, was extended to most agreements in the remainder of the industry.[70]

The situation, however, has continued to be a changing one as the result of the great fluctuations in the employment of seamen during the Korean crisis. To accommodate the greatly expanded needs created by the military crisis, the seamen's unions issued permit cards to large numbers of new entries, permitting them to sail without lifting the restrictions on the numbers admitted as members. With the downturn in shipping employment in 1953, there was substantial unemployment among both union and nonunion seamen. In case of the NMU alone, there were 24,000 permit men in addition to the 40,000 members of the union in 1953,[71] with about 26,000 jobs under the union's jurisdiction. Under the pressure of a large number of cases filed with the NLRB charging discriminatory treatment in the union hiring halls, additional changes were made in the agreements covering East Coast seamen. A seniority group system was formulated intended to give prior protection to the core group of seamen, who in the vast majority were union members and considered to be permanently attached to the industry, while the system tried to avoid discrimination to nonunion seamen and to new entries. In 1953, the NMU agreement was modified to spell out the standards for seniority preference, and seamen sailing on company vessels prior to June 1948, and sailing continuously thereafter, were given first preference.[72] Continued charges of discrimination by more recent entries resulted in further change in 1954, with the establishment of a four-group system, with first preference going to those in the "regular employment pool" (Group 1) who had been employed or registered for employment on union-contracted vessels during the second half of 1953, the seniority preference base period.[73] The SIU-A and G agreements also were modified in 1955 to establish a "pooling of employment" system on SIU contracted vessels. A three-class seniority group system was established, with first preference going to those who had shipped regularly since before 1951, and up through 1954.[74]

West Coast agreements have also seen greater elaboration of the employment clauses. The SUP agreement has been altered — it now includes a provision to give preference to those with more than three years' seniority. The Marine Firemen's agreement sets service during the year beginning in October 1953 as the base seniority period, with seniority going to those who are employed for more than six months thereafter on the contracted companies' ships; the agreement provides that membership in the union is not to be a condition of employment. The Marine Cooks and Stewards' agreement, adopted following the prolonged NLRB proceedings described later, provided eligibility to those who were eligible to work on the companies' ships in October 1952, and worked for six months thereafter, and established a procedure for nonmembers to bid for jobs in the hiring hall.

A concomitant feature of the changes which have been incorporated into the agreements is the increased participation of the ship operators in the hiring arrangements, although the unions continue to run the hiring halls. The seniority arrangements themselves have been the subject of successful negotiations, and appear in the agreements. The agreements also establish joint arrangements for the handling of charges of discrimination in the actual functioning of the union hiring hall. Thus the NMU agreement establishes a procedure for the handling of individual complaints regarding improper classification through a permanent Appeals Board. The SIU-A and G agreements provide for a joint Seafarers' Appeals Board which establishes the shipping rules and regulations governing the hiring halls and decides on individual complaints regarding the administration of the employment clause. The detailed arrangements in the Pacific Coast Marine Cooks and Stewards' agreement provides for joint determination of additional classes of eligibility as the needs of the industry require; the unions' shipping rules are specifically concurred with by the contracting companies.

Another notable development of the period has been the pressure for and attainment of union hiring halls for licensed personnel. Their unions, as representatives of supervisory personnel, are excluded from coverage by the Taft-Hartley Act, thus permitting them to bargain for such arrangements. The Masters, Mates and Pilots and the Marine Engineers' Beneficial Associations had to contend with strong employer opposition to hiring halls. The issue was pressed militantly by the licensed officers' unions, confronted by fluctuations in job opportunities with many of their members "on the beach." The breakthrough came on the West Coast in 1949 and was followed by similar agreements for dry cargo ships following a strike on the East Coast in 1951, and an arbitration award covering East Coast tankers in 1952. The role of the licensed unions' hiring hall is more restricted than the unlicensed unions' halls, both by practice and contract provisions. Masters, chief engineers and first officers are excluded from the hall provision, and all licensed officers may be employed continuously by the company. With the widespread practice of continuous employment for licensed personnel, the hiring hall serves primarily to equalize opportunities for intermittent employment.

COUNTERPRESSURES FOR UNION RESTRUCTURING

The prewar efforts at maritime union unity had been of brief duration and of limited success during the period of common crisis. The Maritime

Federation of the Pacific had been moribund long before its official demise in 1940, and renewed efforts at unity did not materialize until the war's end. The counterpressures which had persisted from the prewar period were fused with a new combination of factors which established a new orientation, but failed to shift the balance toward greater unity.

In the prewar period, and in the immediate postwar period, the basic pressure toward temporary but partial unity was the concern that employer efforts would be directed toward a weakening of the position of the unions. This remained a pressing factor until the West Coast employers adopted the "new look" orientation after the 1948 strike. But even common fears in the embattled prewar period had seen the dominant role played by the efforts of the leading maritime union leaders to establish strong and effective loci of strength from which they could independently extend and strengthen the position of their unions. Lundeberg had refused to accept Bridges' efforts to use the Maritime Federation of the Pacific for this purpose; Curran was only able to continue with the Committee for Maritime Unity for a brief period. The admixture of power drives and ideological overtones, and the collaboration of left-wing cliques among the various maritime unions made it inevitable that there could be no coöperation with Bridges unless he was in the saddle. Curran's battle to eliminate the Communist-controlled clique, therefore, was bound up with his refusal to permit Bridges to control the affairs of the National Maritime Union.

The strong anti-Communist position of the SIU-SUP and the successful NMU drive against Communist influence eliminated the ideological basis for noncoöperation between these organizations. Economic gains were now the primary concern of both seafaring groups, and it was possible to meet together on matters of common concern which involved the preservation of all of the seamen's benefits. But these *ententes cordiales* were of brief duration, dissolving as new issues and divergent tactics materialized.

The competing loci of strength were extended and entrenched in the postwar period. On the West Coast, the Sailors' Union of the Pacific successfully enlarged its area of strength through the extension of the three-department SIU Pacific District, originally established to cover tanker operations, and subsumed a federation of the three-unlicensed West Coast unions. This broadened locus of strength permits rationalization of bargaining; it also permits a broader base from which to cope with any disputes which may arise with Bridges' ILWU over the scope of work. On the East Coast, the Atlantic and Gulf District under the leadership of Paul Hall, its secretary-treasurer since 1948, has successfully conducted organizing drives, notably on the ships of the Isthmian and Cities Service companies, and has played a prominent role in the support of the newly organized International Brotherhood of Longshoremen against the now independent International Longshoremen's Association. The tie between the autonomous Pacific District and the Atlantic and Gulf District through the Seafarers' International Union provides a basis for mutual aid on both coasts in organizing drives, strike action, and limited pooling of manpower. The scope provided by the SIU has been enhanced by the chartering of the Marine Firemen's Union in 1953; the Brotherhood of Marine Engineers in 1949 (rival to the Marine Engineers' Beneficial Association then affiliated with the CIO) and such other unions as the Inland Boatmen's Union, at one time a CIO affiliate, and several fishermen's and cannery workers' unions. A renewed effort has also been made with the AFL-CIO merger to energize the Maritime Trades Department, which was headed by Harry Lundeberg prior to his death, and is now headed by Paul Hall.

The other locus of strength among the seamen is the National Maritime Union, the largest single maritime union, with 55 percent of the unlicensed jobs in the American merchant marine (approximately 25,000 to the 19,000 of the combined SIU-SUP). The CIO Maritime Committee served as a coördinating group for legislative activity for the NMU, the American Radio Association, the Marine Engineers' Beneficial Association, and the Industrial Union of Marine and Shipbuilding Workers prior to the merger.[75]

The CIO unions organized the Committee for Maritime Unity in 1946 to present a united front in the event of a strike and to meet the growing strength of the SIU. The task of achieving unity among the CIO unions and others outside the Lundeberg fold was not an easy one. Within the National Maritime Union there had already occurred rumblings portending a split between a group led by Joseph Curran, president of the union, and the Communist-oriented elements led by Ferdinand Smith, secretary, and Howard McKenzie and Frederick Myers, vice-presidents.[76] In view of the similarity between the points of view of the NMU left-wingers and Harry Bridges, it could be anticipated that Curran would look at Bridges' renewed proposal for a single national maritime union with a critical eye.[77] The Marine Engineers' Beneficial Association, a CIO affiliate, and the independent Marine Firemen, Oilers, Watertenders, and Wipers' Union, led by Vincent J. Malone, could be expected to lean to more conservative views than those of the other maritime unions.

A preliminary meeting was held in Washington during February 1946, which was attended by the representatives of the six CIO maritime unions (the American Communications Association, Inland-boatmen's Union, International Longshoremen's and Warehousemen's Union, National Union of Marine Cooks and Stewards, Marine Engineers' Beneficial Association, and the National Maritime Union) and the independent

Marine Firemen's Union. The meeting unanimously adopted a "Program for One National Union for Maritime Workers." The preliminary terms provided for a national organization whose functions would be mainly to coördinate the strike actions of the constituent unions, which would continue to be autonomous. A major goal of this "national union" was to achieve one national uniform agreement. The organization was to establish national research and political action departments and to publish a newspaper for maritime workers. A convention was scheduled in San Francisco to establish this union formally in May. At the Washington session Curran expressed the hope that the AFL maritime unions would join the Committee for Maritime Unity, thus ensuring the success of the program.[78]

The prospects for successfully forming such a limited national union were diminished, however, when Vincent Malone, secretary of the Marine Firemen's Union, resigned from the Committee for Maritime Unity. Implying that his union had more to gain by remaining independent, he pointed out that there had been intimations that the marine firemen would receive jurisdiction over the 2000 engine room jobs on West Coast tankers if they affiliated with the AFL. Furthermore, citing the activities of the left-wing elements within his union, he pointed out that the proposed confederation would only lead to intensification of these activities.[79]

Thus, when the Committee for Maritime Unity reconvened in San Francisco in May, with a substantial tumult, the representatives from the MFOWW and the MEBA attended only as observers. Furthermore, although the convention subscribed to the program for a national union, its major concern was the more immediate one regarding the nature of joint action in the event of a strike if the prolonged negotiations begun in September did not result in satisfactory agreements.

The significant result of the convention was the decision to call a joint strike on June 15, subject to ratification by the individual unions. The program for joint action in the event of such a strike announced that "the maritime unions now join together in support of the wage increases and other improvements demanded by each of the participating unions." Troop and relief ships might be worked during the strike "if agreement is reached to operate such ships under fair and equitable conditions." The World Federation of Trade Unions was to be contacted at once to work out a plan to obtain support from foreign trade unions. "To the extent possible and practical" the unions were to conduct joint negotiations with the ship operators. Curran and Bridges were elected cochairmen of the committee to coördinate the activities of the unions in the event of a strike. It was apparent within a few weeks that this limited agreement was the product only of common uncertainty, and would disappear when more basic conflicts prevented any further obscuring of cleavages. During the 1946 negotiations, the CMU countered a threat of government operation of the merchant marine with a call to the World Federation of Trade Unions to refuse "to work ships manned by the Government and declared scab ships with the exception of troop and relief ships as we determine them." [80] This action, in complete disregard of the national CIO, resulted in Philip Murray's intervention in the negotiations, and was settled when the War Shipping Administration offered a reduction in the work week as well as a wage increase (pp. 231–232).

The 1946 achievements of the Committee for Maritime Unity had been important, and were not overshadowed by the subsequent adjustments won by the AFL unions. Besides reduction of the basic work week and increased base rates the committee succeeded in changing the previous contract expiration date from September 30 to June 15. This new date was more advantageous since it occurred at the season of highest shipping operations both on the ocean and on the Lakes, preventing the possibility of importation of strikebreakers from the Lakes and making strike action possible during the season when ship operators were most vulnerable; furthermore, this earlier date provided the CIO unions with the opportunity to set the pattern for the entire industry, since the SUP contract continued the September 30 date. By the end of 1946, the contracts of all the unions affiliated with the Committee for Maritime Unity provided for the June 15 expiration date, and greater unity appeared in the offing for 1947.

Immediately following the successful campaign waged in June 1946, however, the prospects for continued growth of the committee seemed uncertain. On the one hand, there were occasional *pronunciamentos* from the cochairmen, Bridges and Curran, between June and September to the effect that the committee would pursue its goal for unity in the maritime industry.[81] The vote in the affiliated unions, with the exception of the MFOWW, was overwhelmingly in favor of the establishment of a national union consisting of autonomous maritime unions.[82] On the other hand, the indications of disunity were numerous, even in victory. The Pacific Marine Firemen and the Marine Engineers' Beneficial Association did not adopt the committee's program for a national union. Malone, head of the MFOWW, severed his personal connection with the CMU following the Fly Award, charging the committee with being dominated by the Communist Party. Developments within the National Maritime Union were to be even more significant for the future. Furthermore, the effort of the left-wing clique to use the CMU to dominate the National Maritime Union, made participation a basic issue in Curran's fight to eliminate Communist influence. When he resigned at the end of 1946, the CMU collapsed.

In May 1947, common uncertainty in the face of shipowner adamancy and the anticipated enactment of the Taft-Hartley Act reunited the leaders of the CIO maritime unions through the mechanism of the loosely constituted CIO Maritime Committee, whose functions formerly had been merely to represent the constituent unions on legislative matters. At a five-day conference, an agreement was reached which included provision for joint action in the event of a lockout of West Coast unions for refusing to change their position regarding contract extension. To avoid the pitfalls of the previous year's actions, it was agreed that Philip Murray would be requested to give his advice and opinion, and the CIO would be requested to call on the WFTU for assistance, if necessary. A meeting of all maritime unions was scheduled for June 14.

That this meeting was born of common necessity rather than of mutual understanding was demonstrated by Curran's subsequent comments to the effect that the ILWU, with its thirty delegates, had dominated the conference to obtain support for its predetermined position to request extension of the existing contract alone. The actual extent of this coöperation, therefore, was reflected in Bridges' action in reaching agreement first with the Waterfront Employers' Association, extending the existing agreement for a year. Although conditional upon similar extensions by the four West Coast maritime unions still negotiating with the employers, this agreement had the effect of establishing the pattern for the others. On the East Coast, Curran, conducting the negotiations for the NMU, refused to yield in his demand for concessions on wages and working conditions. When the shipowners, in turn, refused to accede, a three-day strike was called which resulted in quick agreement upon a 5 percent increase, payment for work on holidays at sea, and additional vacation gains on tankers.[83]

The internal battle to eliminate left-wing influence from the NMU was conducted concurrently with these developments. Beginning with the 1947 national convention and continuing through 1950, Curran led a successful fight against the left-wing (see below).

The unity efforts of the CIO unions had their repercussions on the Seafarers' International Union. To counteract the longshoremen-seamen unity apparently achieved by the Committee for Maritime Unity, Lundeberg's organization looked for support from related shoreside unions. Consideration of a Maritime Trades Department within the American Federation of Labor had extended back to the first decade of the century, but had failed of success so long as the longshoremen were encroaching on the jurisdiction of the International Seamen's Union.[84]

The SIU had for some time been interested in the possibility of establishing a marine trades department within the AFL; this was attained when the 1945 convention of the AFL adopted a resolution to establish such a department.[85] In May 1946, a conference of AFL maritime unions requested a charter for such an organization. In August, the AFL executive council issued a charter to the Maritime Trades Department, which was to consist of the ILA, SIU, Masters, Mates and Pilots' Association, Brotherhood of Firemen and Oilers, and the Commercial Telegraphers' Union, with the Teamsters promising their coöperation. The department was to protect the unions from raids by the CIO unions. It was to function primarily through local port councils; assurances were given that no union would seek to dominate the others. The purposes of the department were announced as solely economic; it "shall at no time adopt or advance any political program or ideology." The primary purpose of the organization was to "assure a coördinated offensive against the number one enemy of labor, the Communists. . . ." [86]

The elimination of the ideological obstacle to coöperation by the competing seafaring union centers resulted in occasional mutual efforts as issues arose which were common threats to their security. On two such occasions since 1950, the seafaring unions have adopted common programs, only to have the coöperative effort disintegrate. The common programs have included among their leading purposes the protection of the hiring hall, assurance of continued aid to the merchant marine through the 50–50 cargo preference arrangements, restrictions on transfer of American ships to foreign flags, and elimination of the Military Sea Transportation Service as a competitor of private commercial shipping operations.

In March 1950, the seafaring unions, with the exception of the National Union of Marine Cooks and Stewards, met to develop joint support to amend the Taft-Hartley Act to legalize the hiring hall. At that time, the operation of the NMU hall on the Lakes had been found to violate the Taft-Hartley Act. The SUP was then confronted with court actions arising out of the expulsion of a dissident group in the Seattle branch, and the other unions were confronted by suits of individuals alleging discrimination in the operation of the halls.

Out of this two-day conference came an agreement to act to preserve the hiring hall. The agreement cited the actions of expelled Communists and Trotskyites in seeking to undermine the unions through attacks on the hiring halls. The unions agreed "not to use the antilabor provisions of the Taft-Hartley Act against each other, and each union agrees that it will give no aid and comfort to any group of individuals of any union using the Taft-Hartley Act in litigation against a union. Such cases will be regarded as internal matters of the union involved." [87] The conference also demanded the functions of the Coast Guard in supervising and disciplining seamen be returned to the Department of Commerce along with the

Bureau of Marine Inspection and Navigation; the Coast Guard was charged with arbitrary action in revoking licenses, and with excessive issuance of seamen's certificates in an industry substantially overmanned already. On the transfer of American owned ships to foreign flags, and transfers from maritime countries with high standards to the "flags of convenience" of countries with low standards, the conference pointed to the failure of governmental action, and referred to the need for "collective action" of the maritime unions and the labor movement generally.[88]

Shortly thereafter, the government called upon the maritime industry — management and unions — to collaborate in adopting a joint policy to meet the Korean emergency. In July, the maritime unions, both affiliated and independent and the ship operators, agreed to a Statement of Maritime Policy which provided for coöperation with the government in a screening program to keep security risks off the waterfront and the ships, on assurance that the program would not be directed against union activity and that tripartite port review boards and a tripartite national review board would be established. The statement also called on the government to utilize fully "the available pools of trained manpower comprised of thousands of seamen, licensed and unlicensed, longshoremen and the trained organizations of private steamship and stevedoring companies. . . ."[89] Concern was expressed for the implementation of the program when a tripartite national appeals board was not established immediately, but subsequently the Coast Guard screening program with its local and national tripartite review boards met with union approval.[90]

In anticipation of an expanded operation of government-owned vessels, a conference of maritime labor representatives was held in January 1951. The "Statement of Policy" for the operation of these vessels submitted by the unions called for labor representation in top policy-making positions in the maritime agencies, deferment for skilled seamen, private operation of the ships and civilian status for the seamen, full utilization of the manpower and facilities available in the union hiring halls, avoidance of any repetition of discriminatory regulations which were issued by the RMO during the war, and restriction of the Military Sea Transportation Service to the operation of troopships.

A joint meeting of representatives of shipping management and of the labor unions was held shortly after, to obtain agreement on the policy. The operators submitted their comments and, except for comments on the training procedures, there was substantial agreement. Unanimous agreement could not be obtained however. Lundeberg charged the operators with seeking to break the agreement, by establishing "the old fink" training programs and schools for seamen. The SIU subsequently withdrew its support from the program accepted by the unions in January, and approved by the Maritime Administration, charging that it had been disregarded in the subsequent formulation of regulations, which left the shipowners in control of merchant marine policies.[91]

It was not until 1953 that another effort was made at joint action. In the fall of 1953, Lundeberg called on Curran and the other seafaring union leaders to meet to consider the unemployment problems arising out of the cutback of the merchant marine following the end of the Korean crisis, threats to the 50–50 program and the marine hospital service, and foreign flag transfers. The invitation was accepted, and a meeting was held in January 1954 in Washington at which the Conference of American Maritime Unions was organized, including thirteen unions of ship personnel. Harry Lundeberg and Joseph Curran were named spokesmen for the unions. The program called for government aid to coastal and intercoastal shipping, restriction on transfer to foreign flags, restriction on the issuance of seamen's papers unless jobs are specifically available, legalization of the hiring halls, 100 percent cargo preference, continued services of the marine hospitals, endorsed the Coast Guard screening program and called for its tightening, and restriction of the Military Sea Transportation Service.[92]

An interesting development of the conference was the action of the East and West Coast ship operators in requesting joint meetings to discuss common problems relating to the merchant marine. Between January and April, weekly joint meetings of representatives of both management and labor on both coasts were held. The discussions included labor matters considered vital to both parties, including joint action to protect the hiring hall, uniform expiration dates, and penalty work payments. But the general understanding apparently reached on these matters did not receive specific implementation. Furthermore, there were differences between ship operators and the unions on the cargo preference provisions and flag transfer (the unions wanted 100 percent preference and were opposed to permitting transfer).[93] The joint effort so hopefully begun was soon to lapse.[94]

The CAMU continued to act on legislative matters for more than a year. In March 1955, Lundeberg withdrew from the conference. The impetus for this action was the attacks on his proposal to place American bulk carriers in a competitive position with foreign tramp ship operators in the Pacific, by offering to reduce manning scales and incorporate penalty payments in base rates by restoring the 56-hour basic work week, and increasing base rates to include the penalty amounts formerly earned for Saturday and Sunday work. The proposal included complete manning by licensed and unlicensed personnel affiliated with the SIU. The proposal was attacked as a "sellout" of conditions achieved by the seamen's unions, and an invasion of the jurisdiction of the licensed unions.[95] Lundeberg replied in kind, charging Curran with weakening the hiring hall without prior consultation with the other unions and attacking Curran's participation in the Labor-Management Maritime Committee with six subsidized companies.[96]

Any hope that the seafaring unions might achieve some rapport prior to the AFL-CIO merger convention in December 1955 proved to be in vain. The merger convention itself was presented with conflicting positions on the question of subsidies — with the NMU supporting subsidies as currently administered, and the Maritime Trades Department supporting an investigation of the current operation of subsidies. Curran indicated his refusal to join the Maritime Trades Department on the grounds that it had reconstituted itself in advance of the merger without any CIO unions in attendance. The NMU would be prepared to affiliate only if the department were reconvened to provide all the maritime unions with an opportunity to participate in its organization.[97]

THE EMPHASIS ON "PORK CHOPS"

The rebirth of seamen's organizations on both coasts in 1934–1937 had been associated with a radical militancy that had been fertilized in part by the "Wobblies" and the Communists. The waterfront, with its background of employer domination and casual employment ties, provided radicals with an opportunity to associate themselves with the loyalties engendered by militant union activity. The seamen, inherently individualists skeptical of the conservative traditions of shoreside society, were not unwilling to permit the radicals to play a prominent part in the affairs of their unions so long as ideological considerations were secondary or at least parallel with the economic goals of the unions. When these interests clashed, "pork chop" unionism achieved precedence, but not without substantial battles.

In the prewar period, the issue of Communist influence had been drawn in the Maritime Federation of the Pacific, when Lundeberg had made clear his antagonism against the efforts of the left-wing to dominate the other members of the federation. The result was a bitter hostility toward Communist infiltration which permeated the constituent unions of the Seafarers' International Union. Bred in a revolutionary syndicalist environment, Lundeberg came instead to concentrate on purely economic goals and to enhance the strength of his organization.

It was not long after the end of the war before Joseph Curran found that he, too, had to make the break if the union was to attain its economic goals. The efforts of Bridges and the left-wing within the NMU to use the Committee for Maritime Unity as a device to dominate the affairs and strategy of all the affiliated unions kindled the smoldering anti-Communist flame. This was to result immediately in the disruption of the

CMU, and ultimately, in the elimination of Communist influence from the leadership of the NMU. The ten-year honeymoon period for the NMU terminated when the activities of the left-wing clique demonstrated with crystal clarity that economic goals would be sacrificed to the current stratagems of the Communist Party.

There had been persistent indications of a split between a "right-wing" group led by Joseph Curran, president, Jack Lawrenson, vice-president, and M. Hedley Stone, treasurer; and a left-wing group under the leadership of Ferdinand Smith, secretary, and Howard Mackenzie, vice-president. The left-wingers sought to attribute the 1946 successes to Harry Bridges, charging Curran with having been unwilling to take an adamant stand in negotiations. Curran had replied vehemently to these charges, pointing out that the gains had been achieved only through collective action. He had charged, further, that the left-wing-dominated organizing department had been used for campaigning purposes instead of organizing the ships of the Isthmian Steamship Co., with the resultant loss of these ships to the SIU. Curran's view of the nature of Communist activity in the union at this juncture (July 1946) was expressed in these terms: "I do not believe it is the policy of the Communist Party, but I have to be shown, to take over control of the Union. As a matter of fact, I believe it to be their principle that they want only the right of any member of their party to join the Union, run for office, and get on the floor, and speak their piece as they see fit. We agree with that, and we had to fight for that policy." However, he charged, individual Communists were attempting to obtain control and to discredit "anyone who will stand in their way, including the President of the Union." [98] In Curran's opinion, the feasibility for continuing the CMU still existed. By December 1946, however, he was to change his view.

On December 27, 1946, the *Pilot* appeared with a front page caption wishing "A Happy New Year" to the members of the NMU. The inside pages of the newspaper carried several articles by the various officials of the union which pointed toward a year of cleavage and disunity. Immediate cause of the controversy was Curran's resignation from the CMU with the support of Lawrenson and Stone. In support of his action, he charged that four small West Coast seafaring unions, including some 25,000 members, together with the ILWU, a shoreside organization, were attempting to control the policies of the 75,000-member National Maritime Union. [99] He charged that the CMU had been used by the West Coast unions, under Bridges' leadership, to enforce mistaken tactics and to slander AFL and independent seamen's unions. The NMU, he announced, "cannot at this date become a B-class union to be used to heighten the prestige of a few individual leaders and be used by them to promote hatreds and disunity among the seamen as a whole under the guise of false unity. . . ." He appealed for a joint organization of the seamen's unions of all affiliations — CIO, AFL, and independent — "for the purpose of getting the best possible wages, hours, and conditions for all seamen. . . ." As further evidence of the motives of the West Coast unions, he pointed out that in the negotiations over the wage reviews then pending, the ILWU and the MCS had already decided upon arbitration, before the NMU had even met with the operators.

The left-wing leaders in the NMU replied with a counterblast. In individual statements, they charged the Curran action as leading to "confusion and disunity," and cited the past lack of success of efforts to achieve unity with the AFL unions. Most vehement of the replies came from Joseph Stack, a vice-president, who charged that "the actions and manner in which the President of our Union resigned as Co-Chairman on the Committee for Maritime Unity and his statement for the press and *Pilot,* amount to treason against the membership of the NMU. . . ." Curran was accused of having convinced the members of the NMU Negotiating Committee, including Stack, "to use his approach" and to give up the demand for the work week reduction in the June 1946 negotiations. By contrast, according to Stack, there had been the militancy of the CMU, "particularly on insistence of Harry Bridges . . . which revived the fight for the 40-hour week. . . ." [100]

The clash between the Curran-led and left-wing groups within the NMU was now in the open and fairly clearly defined. The left-wing leaders, ignoring the interests and position of the East Coast seamen, were apparently bent upon imposing Harry Bridges' control over the NMU. Furthermore, political considerations, such as attacks on American foreign policy, reflecting the line of the Communist Party, were becoming overwhelming concerns of the left-wing leaders to the exclusion of the economic goals of the seamen. Curran's group had split increasingly from the left wing as economic goals were minimized and political considerations extraneous to and in conflict with the seamen's welfare came to predominate. Although prior to the war the Communists had been regarded as allies strengthening the union, now Smith, MacKenzie, and Stack were charged by Curran with being Communists who ignored the union's interests.[101] Seeking to supplant the Bridges' alliance, the Curran wing became increasingly seamen-minded and sought to attain an alliance of all the seafaring unions. In this they were to be unsuccessful. But in their battle to eliminate Communist control from the affairs of the NMU, they succeeded fully.

The anti-Communist group gained an initial success in its attack upon the CMU. Although the left-wing dominated executive council of the NMU voted against Curran's resignation, it opposed any referendum on the issue until after a CMU meeting scheduled for March 15.[102] This meeting was never to occur. The committee was dissolved early in February. In announcing the dissolution, the CMU categorically stated that: "The reasons advanced by Curran to justify his resignation were carefully reviewed by the CMU Executive Committee and were found to have no substantial foundation in fact. . . ." The decision to dissolve the CMU was attributed "to the regrettable fact that Curran's resignation has rendered the CMU ineffective for all practical purposes." [103] On his part, Curran viewed the dissolution as a "great victory for the rank and file" of the NMU.

The problem of unity in the face of anticipated adamancy on the part of the ship operators reasserted itself as June 15 approached, the contract expiration date for the CIO maritime unions and MFOWW. Shadowing the negotiations was the imminent passage of the Taft-Hartley Act with its restrictive provisions. The operators proposed to extend the agreements until September 30, the date on which the AFL agreements would expire. Curran, for the NMU, and Malone, for the MFOWW, presented counterdemands for wage increases and improvements in working conditions. Bridges and Hugh Bryson, president of the Marine Cooks and Stewards, restricted their demands to extension of the existing agreement for another year, explaining that the disunity caused by the "stab in the back" to the CMU had made the presentation of new contract demands impractical.[104]

The success of the NMU strike in 1947, with resultant wage increases, permitted Curran to contrast his own success with Bridges' failure in achieving gains for the seamen. He also pointed out that Bridges' action in meeting with William Z. Foster and other Communist Party leaders during the NMU strike had served to embarrass NMU efforts.[105] The way was now open to fight the battle to eliminate the Communist leadership from the NMU at the Sixth Biennial Convention scheduled for September 1947.

The issue of eliminating Communist domination was the keynote of the 24-day convention. By parliamentary maneuvers, the left-wing minority made every effort to prevent passage of Curran's constitutional recommendations to give the rank and file greater control over actions of the leadership between conventions, and to restrict offices and membership to bonafide seamen. Throughout the convention, Curran fought the "Communist-dominated disruptive forces," citing their record of malfeasance in the Isthmian organizing drive, their encouragement of job action in the settlement of beefs, their actions in ignoring the interests of the NMU, their tactics in filling vacant offices between conventions from among their supporters, and their efforts to stir up racial differences among the members in their efforts to "rule or ruin." The left-wing groups appealed for unity in the face of the threat to the unions from "pro-

Fascist forces." They directed their fire against the "monopoly-dictated foreign policy of the Truman-Republican coalition," and called for support of a third party.[106] The rank-and-file group led by Curran, however, prevented any beclouding of the issues. On the main proposals, the Curran group was victorious. It remained for the election and referendum on the constitutional amendments adopted at the convention which was to be conducted in 1948 to indicate the extent of victory.

The results, which were made known in July 1948, disclosed that the left-wing faction had been swept completely from office. Curran received approximately 30,000 votes to his opponent's 10,000; other Curran supporters won by two to one margins.[107] Commenting on the victory, Curran announced: "We are going to get rid of all who are not working for the membership. We are going to put this union back on a real trade union basis with a militant program intended to serve the members." The left-wing officials were subsequently tried on charges of seeking to "create chaos" and to seize control of the union, and were expelled.[108]

The efforts to eliminate the Communist clique continued, centering around constitutional revisions to bar "Communists, Nazis and Fascists" from admission into the union, and to expel those already in the union. An insurgent movement developed among nonparty communists, led by Jack Lawrenson, a vice-president who charged that Curran was ignoring the wishes of the rank and file. The battle, aptly described as one between the administration's desire for stable unionism and the insurgent desire for "permanent revolution," was fought in the 1949 convention, in which Curran succeeded in carrying his proposal to bar Communists from admission to membership, but lost on the revision to expel Communists.[109] The battle was marked by temporary seizure of the NMU headquarters building by 400 insurgent partisans. The administration reëstablished stability gradually. In the election which followed in 1950, Curran received a majority of 5 to 1 (23,409 to 4,532 for his opponent), John MacDougal defeated Lawrenson by a vote of 13,301 to 8,353.[110] A referendum subsequently supported a constitutional amendment to exclude Communists, Nazis and Fascists from membership.[111] The victory of "pork chop" unionism was complete.

Lundeberg's SUP was also involved in battles to deal with radical groups whose activities infringed on the union's security. The battles involved an internal insurgent movement with ideological coloration in the port of Seattle, and a competitive action with Bridges' ILWU to wear the mantle of the National Union of Marine Cooks and Stewards.

The Seattle situation developed out of the SIU drive to replace the Communist-dominated Canadian Seamen's Union on Canadian shipping.[112] The insurgents, led by John Mahoney, challenged the action of the SUP in supporting the SIU affiliate. This challenge was also bound up with opposition to the SUP policy of expanding jurisdiction on the West Coast. The insurgents were charged with being "Trotzkyites," their cause being actively taken up by Trotzkyite groups. The union action in expelling the participants in the insurgent movement was subsequently the subject of much litigation.[113]

The most protracted action, one persisting from 1948 until 1955, involved the successful SUP drive which eliminated Communist influence from West Coast seafaring operations through the National Union of Marine Cooks and Stewards. The NUMCS had played a satellite role to Bridges' ILWU. Both unions were expelled from the CIO in 1950 on the grounds that their policies "have been, in the past, and are today, directed toward the achievement of the purposes of the Communist Party rather than the objectives set forth in the constitution of the CIO."

The drive to eliminate the left-wing union began with SUP support of a rival union among anti-Communist dissidents in Seattle during the 1948 strike. A group of these were subsequently expelled from the union, and were denied the opportunity to obtain employment through the NUMCS hiring hall. Their action in filing unfair labor practice charges against the union and the companies was subsequently to produce an NLRB decision which effectively weakened the union's position.

During 1950–1951, the National Maritime Union made efforts to take up the jurisdiction of the expelled union. The result was to produce renewed activity by the SUP, which offered the stewards a charter, with autonomy in the SIU, if reorganization would eliminate Communist influence.[114] The NMU petition for an election was dismissed in May 1951 when it failed to marshal sufficient sign-up cards. Thereafter, a petition was filed by the newly formed unit of the SIU, the Marine Cooks and Stewards, AFL. During much of this period, there were outbreaks of violence as ships preparing to sail were picketed by men expelled from the NUMCS for anti-Communist activity.

The action of the NLRB in the case involving those expelled for their activity in Seattle during the 1948 strike sealed the fate of the union. The NLRB found that the union had used the hiring hall to discriminate against the expellees, and that the companies shared responsibility for this discrimination. The board ordered the companies to cease and desist from recognizing the union, thereby terminating the contractual relationship. The expellees were ordered to be given priority in hiring, with back pay for the period involved.[115]

The board's action left a hiatus in the hiring arrangements. This was filled when a court order established a central registration office to be used by members of both unions. The offices were established by the Pacific Maritime Association in June 1952 and were run under the supervision of a court appointed referee. A central registration list was maintained on which any man who had sailed on a PMA ship since December 1946 was entitled to be placed.

During 1952–1953, the NUMCS continued on the downgrade — its president, Hugh Bryson, was indicted on charges of perjury in filing Taft-Hartley non-Communist affidavits. Bridges took up the cudgels for the NUMCS, establishing a stewards' department in the ILWU. When the NLRB refused the ILWU a place on the ballot in the 1954 elections on the grounds that it had filed too late, the ILWU and the NUMCS urged the men to vote neither — and the vote showed 1285 for neither and 743 for the MCS-AFL.[116]

The affiliation of the Marine Firemen's Union with the SIU now permitted the SUP to alter its tactics. It now requested that the Pacific Coast District of the SIU — consisting of the three unlicensed unions — be treated as a single unit.[117] The board granted the petition. In the ensuing election in April 1955, the SIU-Pacific District was the winner with 3931 votes to 1064 for the ILWU, and 327 "neither" votes. For the Pacific Maritime Association, which supported the SUP petition, the single unit offered the possibility of a rationalization of bargaining relationships. For the SUP-SIU, it meant the elimination of a channel for Communist intervention in the seagoing area; in the continuing battle to circumscribe the power sphere of the ILWU, a new and potentially effective weapon had been won.[118]

AN ANALYTICAL COMMENTARY

THE IMPULSE TO ORGANIZATION

The basic impulse to union organization in the maritime industry has proceeded from three interrelated factors: first, the effort to protect and circumscribe the seamen's vocation; second, to protect the seamen in the sale of their labor in the face of constant uncertainty over job opportunities; and, third, to ensure to seamen some measure of the great gains in standards of living achieved by shoreside workers — to achieve the status of "first class" citizens. These have been the basic economic and social determinants of all of the seamen's unions.

The efforts of the maritime unions have been directed toward the protection, determination and enforcement of craft requirements. With the increased specialization and job dilution which accompanied the shift from sail to steam, the seamen's unions adopted a policy directed toward ensuring that governmental regulations supported the skill requirements set forth in the union constitutions as requirements for membership and promotion. The Seamen's Acts of 1915 and 1936 defined the skill requirements for some of the basic crafts and set requirements for manning and upgrading. This was not unlike the craft requirements which the building trades unions were able to obtain through local statutes to protect the skills of the trade. But this was only a partial approach to the problem of delimiting and protecting the seamen's status.

The second factor, that of ensuring the seamen with some protection in the sale of their labor, resulted in the adoption of several different approaches. The unions were originally too weak to gain collective bargaining status and to achieve union preference in hiring through the hiring hall, a virtual closed shop again comparable to the arrangements in the building trades. The substantial fluctuations in cargo and passenger carrying opportunities for the American merchant marine, together with the use of seamen of all lands on American ships, made it doubly difficult for union seamen to obtain employment in the face of the early opposition of the ship operators to the unions. Skill restrictions, language restrictions, citizenship restrictions, were all directed toward protection of the status of the American seamen. The legislative program sought to achieve what collective bargaining could not attain. The unions would organize and rationalize the market of skills made requisite under the Federal statutes. Unless employers turned to the union for the necessary skills, their ships would sail without adhering to statutory requirements. Union seamen could then request government officials to inspect the ship to determine whether legal requirements were being met. Furthermore, to ensure that these skills could not be met by the recruitment of foreign seamen, the unions successfully pressed for language and citizenship requirements to preclude the employment of more than a small percentage of foreign seamen.

The third factor, achievement of the status of first-class citizenship, underlay all the organizing efforts of the seamen. To meet the view that they were an irresponsible lot, who were incapable of looking out for their own interests and required special treatment as wards in admiralty and charity cases, the seamen sought to escape from their subjugated state. They achieved this by establishing land-based organizations with full-time officials who could look after their interests while they were at sea. The striving for status included elimination of some of the archaic statutes restricting the seamen: imprisonment and fine for desertion and excessive logging for shipboard violations of discipline. They also required the achievement of status that comes with association with one's fellows in organizations of their own making. The early experience with employer domination of the labor market reinforced the bond between the seamen and their unions.

These drives to organization were thwarted during the first three decades of the century by the counterorganization of employer associations whenever union organization appeared to be effective. Only in the coastwise steam schooner trade on the West Coast did effective and lasting organization and collective bargaining develop prior to the first World War, and this was the product of a combination of factors — the schooner trade was largely an industrial carrier type of operation subsidiary to lumber operations, hence ship labor costs were a relatively minor element in total costs under favorable market conditions; the labor force on the steam schooners was a relatively homogeneous one, coming largely from northern Europe; and the job duties required of this labor force were especially arduous because the performance of longshore work as well as seamen's duties was required in isolated and small ports with inadequate shoreside manpower.

The East Coast, with its ample shoreside forces, and its constant stream of immigrants did not offer special opportunities for organization. Nor did the offshore operations on the Pacific Coast. Countered by effective employer opposition whenever efforts were made to improve the condition of the seamen, the early federation of seamens' unions, the International Seamen's Union, was unable to adopt a policy which might have made organization effective. It could not overcome the craft particularism which was reflected in separate unions for the three departments on both coasts; it was unable to overcome the particularism attendant on the different conditions of the East and West coasts; and its inability to overcome the prejudices toward Negroes, Orientals, and seamen of other nationalities precluded the all-embracing organization without which insecurity continued to threaten all.

The failure of the ISU was magnified by the complete success of employer domination of the labor market during the twenties. For the employers operating expensive units of capital equipment, requiring quick turnaround and ready manning, the organization of the labor market had now become a *sine qua non* for effective ship operation, as well as to meet the union challenge. That the unilateral control of the market was used to drive labor costs down was almost inevitable in the sharp competitive situation which has always confronted American ship operations. But this only served to add to the explosive potentialities of a situation made volatile by the more generalized attack on the labor movement. When the American labor movement was to assert itself, the maritime unions were in the forefront of the most militant unions.

The establishment of effective union organization in the maritime industry in the thirties was basically the result of the new balance in the relations between labor and management in American industry established under New Deal labor legislation. The maritime unions were able to grow and to develop as the labor movement generally took on new life. They were also supported by the renewed interest of the Federal Government in the establishment of a modern merchant marine; the provision of operating subsidies was tied directly to labor costs, to equalize labor costs on American subsidized ships with those of competitive foreign operations.

Divergent tactics produced effective organizations on both coasts. On the West Coast, new organizations in reality came to fill the shells of the old. The strength of the maritime unions in the achievement of organization to meet effective employer organizations lay in the federation of waterfront unions. The continuance of craft organizations among the seamen's unions, which would otherwise have been a source of weakness, was made possible through the Maritime Federation of the Pacific, which was the product only of mutual insecurity in the face of continued employer opposition. The development of ideological differences between Bridges and Lundeberg, coupled with personality differences among the union leaders, and the mutual willingness of ship operators and union officials to play off one against the other, resulted in an early sundering of the weak federation of crafts. But by this time, the war was upon the country; and it was not long after the war that there was a realization among West Coast operators that their views and dealings with the unions had lagged behind the developments in union organization and in transportation both on land and sea, and the requirements of their own industry for profitable survival.

On the East Coast, a militant rank-and-file movement developed against the old-line union leadership; out of it developed a new organization. Deriving its origins from a background of employer domination, corrupt and inept leadership, discrimination and local corruption, there was substantial opportunity for inroads by radical groups including Communists, Wobblies, and Trotskyites. The new organization was different from the West Coast organization in that it combined members of all departments in a single union, which adopted a policy of aggressive nondiscrimination. The rank-and-file group had enlisted the aid of the West Coast unions in its early battles; the continuing strength of Curran's NMU was in its combination of all departments, its uniform agreements with the leading American lines, and its willingness to accept all as eligible to membership — regardless of race, creed, or nationality.

The postwar organizations of the maritime unions on both the East and West coasts have shown parallel trends. The NMU and the SIU had already organized all the respective departments into respective single unions prior to the war. During the war and since, the SUP has conducted a drive to increase the area of its job jurisdiction, as well as to establish affiliation with the other craft unions, a trend which has resulted in joint action, and could possibly result in eventual unity. A single organization already exists on West Coast tankers, where the SUP has organized all three departments. On dry cargo ships, the separate craft unions still exist on a departmental basis, but they are now part of the Pacific District of the SIU, with joint bargaining an accomplished fact.

It may appear paradoxical that the seamen's unions have failed to achieve a national union when the conditions under which shoreside national unions have been established appear to be particularly operative in the maritime context. In the case of the shoreside craft unions, it has been said that "mobility of labor alone, apart from extension of product markets, might have been sufficient to induce the formation of national union." [1] There is no greater mobility than that of the seaman; his contacts with the seamen of both coöperating and rival unions in the various ports of call, both at home and abroad, appear to be unlimited. Yet, a single national union, or even federation of unions, has failed to materialize.

The explanation resides in a number of factors inherent in the organizations of the industry and of the unions. At present, the focuses of union organization are coastwise in character, with rival organizations on the Atlantic and Gulf (the National Maritime Union and the Seafarers' International Union, Atlantic and Gulf District) and the SIU-Pacific Coast consisting of the Sailors Union of the Pacific, the Marine Firemen's Union, and the Marine Cooks and Stewards. Unlike the emergence of the national craft union as a centralizing force to cope with the limitations of the local union as the center of organization, the seamen's unions have been centrally organized from their inception. The port organizations play a minor role in the seamen's unions — they are wayside stations to ensure adequate replacements for ships, and for the handling of "beefs." While meetings are held in the ports, the actions taken at such meetings have only local significance. Policy matters which are subject to approval by the membership and elections of officers, including port patrolmen, are determined on the coastwide basis. The administration of the port is subject to the direction of the executive council. Strike actions, whether coastwide or local, may only be taken on approval by the council. In the case of the licensed officers' unions, which are organized as national unions, the local unions do, however, exercise substantial authority.

The centralization of authority within the unlicensed unions has had the effect of producing several concentrations of strength around centralized organizations which are comparable to national unions in the scope of their jurisdiction and extent of their authority.[2] This is, perhaps, the last remaining obstacle to the achievement of some form of national unity — the merger of the AFL-CIO has eliminated the divisive effects of separate affiliations; the East and West Coast structural differences are gradually disappearing; the ideological bases for differences have been eliminated.

These changes have also had their effect on the divergent practices in regard to nondiscrimination. The successful elimination of the Communists from the NMU was in part the result of Curran's success in demonstrating that the nondiscrimination policies followed by the union under his leadership had no connection with the ideological ties with which the Communists sought to associate it. The persistence of rank-and-file loyalty to the Communist-oriented leadership of the NUMCS was in large part the product of the ready acceptance by the union of Negro and Oriental members; the left-wing leadership sought to use charges against the exclusionary policies of the SUP in the fight to retain jurisdiction of the stewards.[3] The success of the Pacific District of the SIU in gaining the stewards jurisdiction is thus not merely an increase in strength for the SIU unions, it has resulted in the affiliation of the SUP and the Marine Firemen with the mixed membership of the Marine

Cooks and Stewards. The Atlantic and Gulf District of the SIU, the subject of wartime charges of discriminatory practices which the Fair Employment Practices Committee was unable to resolve, has also made substantial strides. This was the result of an agreement made with the New York State Commission Against Discrimination in 1951 to end discrimination, both in "checkerboarding" steward department complements and in restricting "colored" members to the stewards' department.[4]

The organizing forces have made for increasing similarities among the seamen's unions, despite the differences in their origins and backgrounds. The differences are not insubstantial — they have resulted in differences in tactics — but concentration on nonideological economic gains, and the creation and preservation of job opportunities for the seamen is now the prime aim of all of the seamen's unions.

Seamen's organizations stimulated employer organization. At first, the employer organizations were ephemeral, lasting only as long as necessary to meet the threat of union organization, but subsequently persisting as union organization persisted. This was particularly true on the West Coast, where the open-shop drive at the turn of the century was particularly prominent in San Francisco. But divergence of economic interests produced splits among employer groups — and the coastwise steam schooner operators accepted the unions and maintained collective bargaining relations for most of the period from 1900 to 1921. The offshore operators successfully maintained the open shop for most of the period, making limited concessions during the first World War. Here, too, organization was the accompaniment of the limited recognition of the unions. But with the end of the first World War, the organization became the backbone of an anti-union drive which culminated in complete employer domination with the offices of the Pacific American Steamship Association serving as the means for control of the labor force.

On the East Coast, the weakness of the seamen's unions and the greater diversity in operations and ports resulted in a loose organization of companies which functioned together only at the threat of union gains in strength and in demands. Effective and lasting organizations developed during the first World War partly because of the desire to operate in unified fashion in meeting the unions, but also to facilitate dealings with the Federal Government which was the wartime operator of the merchant marine, with the companies acting as its agents. The East Coast association also participated in the anti-union action in 1921; here, however, the fragmentation of the labor force, rather than its marshalling as on the West Coast, became the means for employer control.

The development of collective bargaining since the thirties has been accompanied by strong employer associations on both coasts. The American Merchant Marine Institute, heir to the earlier East Coast association, has had to make relatively few organizational changes in establishing rapport with the unions. The greater predominance of subsidized operators, the absence of a tradition of association control of the labor force, the absence of alliances between the maritime industry and shoreside industry to fight union organization, the tradition of loose affiliation to accommodate the large number of companies with varied operations — all account for the greater ease with which the accommodation was made to collective bargaining on the East Coast. The historical coöperation of West Coast maritime employers with land-based drives against union organization, and the direct exercise of employer control of the labor force during the twenties help explain the intensity of the obstacles to the more facile accommodation to the necessities of collective bargaining on the West Coast. This was only achieved as the result of the apparently useless strike, particularly from the employer's point of view, in 1948. The result was a major reorganization in the employer organization to reëstablish a new and workable collective bargaining relationship with the West Coast seamen and longshoremen.

The structural aspects of this new organization, the Pacific Maritime Association, in which collective bargaining is carried on directly by the staff of the association in dealing with both longshore and seamen's unions, differs from that of the American Merchant Marine Institute, whose orientation is solely shipside. In conjecturing on the likelihood of national unity among the seafaring unions, a further step is the possibility of national bargaining. The necessity for union restructuring to meet the requirements of this development would also require structural accommodations within the employer associations.

THE SETTING FOR COLLECTIVE BARGAINING

The structural organization of collective bargaining in the maritime industry has developed out of the nature of the employment relationship. Since to a major extent employment in the industry continues to be based upon the single round-trip basis and ship operators share in a common labor pool which is available when ships have to be sailed; it is unnecessary for seamen to be kept on a payroll on a permanent basis — thus labor costs can be reduced to a minimum between trips. Under such conditions, uniformity in wages and working conditions becomes a major concern of both ship operators and maritime unions, although the reasons and the timing of these concerns may not always coincide.

Thus, if ever a single maritime union, or a federation of maritime unions under a single aegis, exists representing all the seamen, its goal will be uniformity in wages and working conditions as insurance against reductions, particularly when shipping opportunities fall off. The past effect of rival unionism has demonstrated, however, that although the tendency toward nationwide uniformity may be apparent, the goal will constantly be receding as the various unions get side-tracked into jockeying for lead position, frequently with tacit or overt assistance from among the ship operators.

Uniform wages and working conditions, at least on a coastwise basis, are considered desirable goals by ship operators as well as unions. This is particularly true during periods of prosperity, when ship operators might have to outbid one another to obtain necessary personnel in a labor market restricted by the attraction of shoreside employment. The need for uniformity is felt less during periods of recession and depression when the hard core of the maritime labor force is augmented by many former seamen and shoreside unemployed. In the absence of union organization, the tendency during such periods has been for individual ship operators to reduce labor costs to minimum levels. Under the conditions of union organization prevailing in recent years, the unions have continued to make substantial gains even in the face of declining job opportunities and the presence of substantial unemployed reserves.

The logic of economic conditions as well as union pressures has, therefore, acted to produce coördinated employer action. As a result, collective bargaining in the maritime industry has tended constantly toward negotiations on an industry-wide basis, at least within a geographic area. Both employers and unions have organized on a coast-wide basis, with negotiations and agreements covering their respective jurisdictions. This is the basis for the consistent opposition by the maritime management associations to legislative proposals to strike at "industry-wide bargaining," by narrowing the scope of bargaining units to individual employers. The shipping industry's position in support of continuance of coastwide bargaining was set forth by Almon Roth in the hearings on the revision of the Wagner Act in 1947, and this has continued to be the position of the industry. Roth stated at that time that the established patterns of collective bargaining in the maritime industry would be destroyed by outlawing multi-employer bargaining. "Each company would need to deal with an independent union that dealt with it alone," he pointed out, and "full compliance with the law would lead to variations in wage rates and working conditions." This would permit unions to play off one employer against another.[5]

The model for bargaining in the maritime industry is that of a multi-employer association, dealing with a union representing a group of employees of the member companies. This model substantially simplifies the complex character of the structure for bargaining, and requires elaboration of the structural and frictional limitations on the generalized model.

There are major differences in the structure for bargaining on the two coasts. The first arises out of differences in union structure. On the East Coast, there are separate and rival union organizations of unlicensed personnel necessitating separate multi-employer arrangements. In the case of the NMU, a standing committee of members of the American Merchant Marine Institute conducts negotiations; in the case of the SIU, its contracted companies, some of whom are members of the Institute, meet together as an informal group for the purpose of conducting negotiations. Separate committees have conducted negotiations with the licensed officers and the radio operators for some time. On the West Coast, it is only since 1955 with the establishment of the Pacific District of the SIU that the Pacific Maritime Association has conducted a single negotiation with the three unlicensed unions; prior to that, separate negotiations were conducted with the individual unions. Similarly, negotiations have been combined for licensed personnel in recent years; whereas formerly separate negotiations were conducted.

A second difference arises out of the structural and administrative distinctions between the Pacific Maritime Association and the American Merchant Marine Institute. The primary purpose of the Pacific Maritime Association is to deal with both the seafaring and longshore labor relations of the West Coast maritime industry. The association is authorized to negotiate contracts for both segments of the industry, subject to the approval of the majority vote of the membership. The membership includes American-flag shipping companies with 11 of 21 directors of the association (2 for passenger lines, 3 intercoastal, 1 coastwise, 1 Alaska, 4 offshore); and the shoreside groups comprising foreign lines (2 directors), stevedores (2), terminal operators (2), and area members (1 each for port areas of Southern California, of Oregon and Columbia River, and of Washington). The shipping companies maintain a separate identity in the negotiation of agreements with the seafaring unions, and a majority of their votes is required to implement an agreement by the PMA. Once approved, the contract is signed in the name of the association and is binding on all of the members.[6] Resignation is required of any member who does not accept the majority-approved contract. Majority vote also determines the action to be taken by the association in the case of violations of the contract by the union; a two-thirds vote is necessary on a decision to suspend or terminate a contract with a union for such violation. The PMA constitution provides for financial aid to a member affected by a union breach of contract. The staff members of the association conduct the negotiations, although since the 1949 re-organization, ship operators participate to a greater extent than formerly.[7] The association staff is also directly responsible for the handling of disputes and grievances which arise under the contracts; the association designates the employer members of the joint port committees to handle grievances.

The contrast with the American Merchant Marine Institute is substantial. The membership of the Institute is restricted to American-flag ship operators, numbering approximately 70; it is not concerned with longshore operations. It is concerned with a wide range of matters, including various governmental subjects, many matters relating to technical industry problems, relations with the public; labor relations are only one aspect of its interests. Furthermore, the Institute itself does not conduct negotiations — these are conducted by standing committees which negotiate separately with the unions representing licensed officers, radio operators, and unlicensed personnel. Nonmembers of the Institute, as well as members, are represented on the committees whose membership is divided among representatives of the Institute and of the subsidized and unsubsidized offshore lines, and the (unsubsidized) inter-coastal lines, tramp and industrial carrier operations. The individual companies which are represented by the committees are not bound by its negotiations; the standard agreement resulting from the negotiations is signed by the individual companies. The coördinating role of the Institute in labor relations is performed through the conduct of negotiations by its president, and through the designation by the Institute of the employer members of the permanent Joint Disputes Board to handle grievances which individual companies cannot resolve with the union.

A further difference between the model of multi-employer bargaining and the realities of the bargaining situation results from the preceding differences. The model would presuppose joint action by employers, particularly where they are bound by such specific terms as laid down for the Pacific Maritime Association. In practice, this has not been the case. The evidence since the combination of the longshore and shipping associations in 1949 has been of splits among the shipping companies over the tactics to be followed in dealing with the unions. In the 1948 strike there was some opposition within the employer group to strike action against the ILWU; the split was wide open when major companies joined in opposing continuance of the strike. In 1952, two offshore companies with substantial passenger operations were willing to settle with the SUP rather than risk a strike. They subsequently withdrew their authorizations from the PMA to conduct negotiations on their behalf. The differences which have arisen have been accompanied by charges that the association membership is too all-inclusive to permit adequate treatment of particular offshore company needs; that there are companies which favor either the SUP or the ILWU, thus adding to the volatility of an already delicate situation; and that the association has failed to meet forthrightly the conflicting demands in the rivalry between the SUP and the ILWU over their respective work jurisdictions.[8] The East Coast situation is simplified by the absence of any necessity for a single association to deal with rival unions, and this may account in part for the absence of overt frictions among the companies coöperating in bargaining. The greater informality in the relationships among the operators may also serve as an escape mechanism for the frictions which undoubtedly arise among such a diverse group of ship operators.[9] East Coast longshore negotiations, a continuing source of difficulties in recent years, are handled by employer associations organized on a port basis.

There are further variations in the pattern of multi-employer bargaining in the maritime industry. The National Maritime Union is the collective bargaining agent for unlicensed personnel on board tanker vessels operated by about twenty companies from East Coast ports. While these companies have no formal organization for collective bargaining purposes, eight to ten of them generally collaborate through an informal committee in conducting negotiations with the union. Generally following the pattern established by the dry cargo companies, on some occasions they have set the pattern to avoid strikes. Here, again, the standard tanker agreement is signed by the individual companies. On the West Coast, the SUP negotiates separate agreements with each of the tanker operators.[10]

The apparent simplicity of the model of multi-employer bargaining in the maritime industry, therefore, must be modified to take account of a substantial maze of factors. These include separate multi-employer negotiations with rival unlicensed unions and with licensed unions (and a wholly independent organization by ports for dealing with longshoremen) on the East Coast, separate negotiations with actively rival longshore and seafaring, and with licensed unions on the West Coast. Added to these are the internal disagreements which have arisen in the employer associations, particularly on the West Coast, and the apparent inability of the associations on both coasts to do little more than keep one another informed of developments and views. The maze has been made even more complex by the effect of varying contract expiration dates in formalizing the play of rival union forces. Yet despite the organizational maze, a substantial degree of uniformity in wages and working conditions has been maintained in the industry, and stability in labor-management relations has been increasingly apparent in the postwar period.

Both the spirit in which labor-management relations in the industry have been conducted, and the strike record bear out the fact of improvement — although it can hardly be said that ideal relationships have been established. The achievement of this increased stability in the face of the divisive effects of union rivalry, aided and abetted on occasion by a divided employer situation, and by continued uncertainty for the industry, represents no mean achievement.

The Pacific Coast situation has shown particular improvement. The reorganization of the separate longshore and shipping employer associations into the Pacific Maritime Association, to accommodate to the "new look" labor relations policy of achieving stability, has been accompanied by an acceptance of bargaining with the ILWU.[11] This acceptance, and the comparative stability in the longshore situation since 1948, has served to focus on the jurisdictional issues which continued between the SUP and the ILWU, over their respective scope of work and over the stewards work area in the vacuum created by the demise of the NUMCS. The scope of work issue has been complicated by the action of the association in acknowledging the overlapping claims of both unions, which has served to add fuel to the flames of conflict on occasion. There have been numerous stoppages in the period as a result of these, but their effects have been generally localized.[12] The formation of a three-union collaborating unit for unlicensed personnel in 1955 through the Pacific Coast District of the SIU to negotiate with the association should ease the negotiating burdens on the association. It has meant that the three-seafaring West Coast unlicensed unions now have the same contract expiration date — September 30, as does their East Coast affiliate.[13] The agreements with the licensed unions also provide a common date, that of June 15, which is also the NMU contract date.

The stability in labor-management relations is reflected in the reports of the Pacific Maritime Association, and in the strike record. The Pacific Maritime Association has commented on the reduction of jurisdictional disputes "to a minimum."[14] The strike record shows a spectacular drop in the incidence and intensity of work stoppages since 1948 (see Table 2).

The record of offshore labor-management relations on the East Coast also reflects general stability. The continuing substantial strike activity in East Coast maritime labor relations reflects the continued instability in longshore labor-management relations attendant on disclosure of racketeer domination, rank-and-file unrest, government intervention, expulsion from the AFL, limited extent of internal elimination of corrupt influence, and employer opposition to coastwide bargaining. The seamen have been affected by the longshoremen's numerous stoppages, and the unions have taken different sides, but the instability has not been of their making.[15]

Table 2

Maritime strikes — West Coast ports 1946–1956[1]

Year	Number	Workers involved	Man days lost during year
1946	27	84,000	1,550,000
1947	17	8,370	57,300
1948	22	29,700	1,620,000
1949	9	1,040	25,900
1950	7	370	6,760
1951	17	19,100	134,000
1952	14	25,800	412,000
1953	11	11,500	14,600
1954	8	510	4,180
1955	9	14,200	33,600
1956	5	3,330	37,700

[1] Includes strikes of both seamen and longshoremen.
Source: U. S. Department of Labor, Bureau of Labor Statistics.

The evidences of the increased stability in the offshore segment of the industry is shown in the brief association of ship operators and unions in 1954 in a joint effort to arrive at agreement on legislative matters pertaining to the broad interests of the industry and on approaches to achieving further stability in labor-management relations. The latter included joint support of the union hiring hall, and determination of a uniform contract termination date. The failure of this brief essay into the area of mutual solution of their problems to provide immediate solutions does not detract from the significance of the effort itself. A further evidence of the feasibility of joint labor-management coöperation in matters of broad concern to the industry is the Labor Management Maritime Committee, which consists of six subsidized operators and the National Maritime Union, and which has been concerned with fostering the interests of the merchant marine.[16] This was an outgrowth of meetings in which Philip Murray, president of the CIO participated with Curran and representatives of the companies in seeking to enhance the position of the American-flag merchant marine. The committee has considered shipboard safety problems and prepared materials on foreign flag labor costs. The Atlantic and Gulf District, SIU and its contracted operators have developed an industrywide safety program directed at preventing costly accidents.[17]

There is still room for improvement in labor-management relations in the industry, as evidenced by the operator's associations endorsement in 1955, of the establishment of a special maritime labor board to deal with disputes in the industry. That this endorsement included divergences in East and West Coast positions, and that there was substantially less than unanimity among East Coast operators, does not minimize the dissatisfaction out of which these positions developed. These included the inability to attain a single contract expiration date and the attendant continuance of the whipsawing potential; the numerous scope of work stoppages on the West Coast, and the absence of an adequate machinery to cope with these problems.

Since the inception of collective bargaining, maritime trade agreements have always provided for machinery to handle grievances. This is particularly necessary in an industry where disputes relate to such pressing matters as overtime payments, crew quarters, and manning. Such a matter as dissatisfaction with quarters does not permit of prolonged negotiation. Job action on the part of crew members, or direct action to secure improvements through refusal to sign articles, is a ready substitute for the less direct outlet of the grievance machinery. In the past, the ship operators' emphasis on the use of the grievance machinery and on recourse to arbitration where necessary has been viewed by seamen as a device to postpone the settlement of grievances in the hope that the union demands will be thwarted. Furthermore, the tradition of direct action to rectify grievances is so strong in the industry, that it has been worth a union official's position to take a strong stand in favor of strict adherence to the grievance machinery. Even with the stress placed by the maritime unions on the need for responsible behavior on the part of their members, job action has not been eliminated as a possible recourse in particular situations.

The use or disuse of the grievance machinery does not necessarily furnish a true index to the state of the collective bargaining process in the industry. The use of less formal procedures than those set down in the contract may be evidence of a flexible approach on the part of the parties, in the interest of obtaining prompt and fair settlements. Employer insistence on rigid adherence to contract provisions may produce an opposite reaction, a resort to job action on the part of crews. All the language in the contracts relating to the settlements of disputes becomes meaningless in the absence of the assurance on both sides that the collective bargaining process has been accepted in good faith.

Contract provisions relating to the adjustment of grievances differ among the various unions. In practice, however, the procedures for handling disputes up to the arbitration level are basically similar. Preliminary efforts at settling disputes on board ship are the duties of the respective ship delegates for the various departments on board West Coast ships: the departmental delegates and ship's delegate on SIU ships, and the departmental delegates and ship's committee on NMU vessels. These crew spokesmen attempt to settle disputes with department heads or with the master, if necessary. If they fail, they turn over a written record of the grievance to the union patrolmen when the ship arrives in port. The patrolmen and the port agents examine the grievances for their validity under the provisions of the agreement. If these are deemed valid, efforts are made to settle the disputes with the master, the department head, or other company official located in the port. If the deadlock persists, the issue is referred to the national officials of the union who then take the matter up with the appropriate official at the company headquarters.

Each West Coast agreement provides for a port committee at San Francisco consisting of three representatives of the PMA and three of the respective union. The duties of the port committee are to investigate and adjudicate all grievances and disputes between the parties. The San Francisco port committee has veto power over actions by committees at San Pedro, Seattle, and Portland involving basic interpretations of the agreement; all issues unsettled in the outports are referred to San Francisco. The agreements provide for arbitration of any disputes which the San Francisco port committee is unable to resolve. The MFOWW and MCS agreements provide for standing referees, while the SUP agreement provides for an *ad hoc* referee. The MFOWW and the MCS permitted the grievances to go to arbitration in practice, but the SUP has consistently opposed arbitration.

The degree of control exercised by the Pacific American Shipowners' Association through the San Francisco port committee is lacking on the East Coast. The standard NMU dry cargo agreement supplements the grievance machinery for the union and the individual signatory company with a Permanent Disputes Board consisting of three each appointed by the union and the American Merchant Marine Institute. In the event that the company and union representatives fail to settle the dispute, it is referred to the Permanent Disputes Board, which is to transmit its decision to all of the companies for uniform application.

The scope of work and uniform contract date problems are broad and basic problems; their breadth extends beyond the established grievances procedures. The manner in which the grievance machinery has been by-passed on numerous occasions only adds to the difficulties encountered in dealing with the basic issues. The operators on both coasts have apparently preferred to permit flexibility in the handling of grievances rather than adherence to the machinery in the contract, in the interest of avoiding any issue which would force a showdown. To the extent that this serves to add to stability, it is commendable; but proper use of the grievance machinery by both sides can provide major assistance in the achievement of a climate that will aid in the solution of the broader problems through the efforts of the parties themselves.

If any single theme pervades the union claim to loyalty on the part of seamen, it is the key role of the union hiring hall in eliminating the discriminatory employment practices of the pre-union job control era. The role of rotary shipping through the hiring hall, with the measure of employment opportunity which it provides, despite the casual nature of shipping employment, is an integral part of this theme. The unions have grudgingly yielded to the requirements of the Taft-Hartley Act that the union hiring hall must be operated in nondiscriminatory fashion providing equal employment opportunities to union and nonunion members alike. The concessions to the act's requirements have constantly sought to protect the prior right of those who have continued to follow the sea as the source of their vocation, the vast majority of these being union members. The facility in making adjustments with the ship operators in the operations and administration of employment practices to meet the act's requirements has not eliminated the union concern that additional legal pressures for change may be forthcoming; and the unions have continued to press for exemption of the union hiring hall from the provisions of the act.

The unions constantly urge as a reminder the condition of the seamen before the union-controlled hiring hall was achieved, implying that through its achievement all other improvements were attained. The discriminatory employment practices antedating the renewal of collective bargaining in the thirties are still vivid for many who still follow the sea. Accounts of crimping abuses are hardly apochryphal. There are rankling memories of the favoritism and kickbacks associated with pierhead hiring (or shipping off the dock), as well as with the longshoremen's shape-up. Employment offices maintained by individual companies during the twenties and early thirties, as well as the multi-employer Marine Service Bureau on the Pacific Coast, while more orderly and efficient than the other hiring methods, were also used in discriminatory fashion, particularly against union members. It took hiring through the union hiring hall, argue the seamen, to do away with discrimination and all the companion evils of casual employment.

The maritime job market continues to be characterized by three factors which give the nature of the union security relationship and the role of the hiring hall a persistently vital role in the security of the union and its members, even with the acceptance of collective bargaining and the hiring hall by the operators. These factors are, first, the persistence of the casual nature of the employment relationship; second, the frequent excess of members and nonmembers beyond the reserves necessary to meet the requirements of turnover; and, third, the necessity for maintaining an employment pool to permit prompt crewing of ships in this modern era of fast ship turnaround.

The casual nature of the maritime employment relationship persists. The traditional terms of maritime employment — employment of seamen on a single round trip basis — have continued to the present. Experience with the present-day industry-wide vacation plans indicates that the majority of seamen continue to be employed on a discontinuous (or broken time) basis by more than one employer. Thus, during 1956, 70 percent of the seamen who qualified for vacation benefits on dry cargo vessels and 80 percent on tankers received the vacation benefits available for those with discontinuous service records under one plan. The remainder received the larger benefits available to those with continuous service with one employer during the course of a year.[18] There is, of course, no legal bar to continuity in employment nor is there any contractual bar. In fact, West Coast dry cargo agreements specifically provide that union members in good standing may remain continuously in employ on the same vessels, provided that this is acceptable to both the employers and the members in question. The standard NMU agreement goes even further, permitting unlicensed personnel to remain continuously in a company's employ, subject to the restriction that transfer from one of the company's ships to another ship depends upon the individual's length of continuous service with the company in a particular rating. However, operators generally have not chosen to exercise their prerogative to achieve greater continuity of employment.

The excess of necessary reserves to meet turnover requirements, the second feature of the maritime labor market, is closely intertwined with the first feature. With a substantial number of unemployed seamen available, and the regular termination of employment upon the end of a voyage, the unions contend that the competition for job opportunities could be utterly disruptive in the absence of some regularizing arrangement, such as the preference given to union members (those regularly following the sea) and the union hiring hall. The unions have pointed to the vast number of men who acquired appropriate government-issued seamen's papers during the recent World War and the Korean crisis who could conceivably deluge the regular maritime work force. Job opportunities during the postwar years have fluctuated greatly, both because of substantial increases and declines in shipping facilities to meet the wartime emergencies, and the fluctuations attendant upon the shifts in carrying opportunities for the merchant marine. One instance of adjustment may serve to indicate the problem. In 1952, there was a sharp drop in employment opportunities as vessels were being returned to the government when foreign aid programs were curtailed and foreign trade dropped. At that time, the Pacific Maritime Association reported that the total available labor pool on the West Coast amounted to 24,700 at a time when available jobs were dropping rapidly from 18,500 in February, leveling off to 10,700 in October. Under normal conditions, a reserve of 25 percent is needed to accommodate for turnover; under the circumstances cited, more than one of two seamen were "on the beach." [19]

In most shoreside industries, turnover is relatively small in the short run, and workers are further protected by seniority rights in layoff and recall. Hence, employer control of hiring has little effect on the security of the union, and the Taft-Hartley Act union shop provision under which workers may be required to become members of the union thirty days after hiring is feasible by the stable nature of the employment. Seamen who are terminated at the end of a voyage, or whose ship is laid up permanently, have no seniority rights. Furthermore, a union security clause may have little meaning in a situation where a round trip may take less than thirty days.

The seafaring unions' approach to job security for their members before the enactment of the Taft-Hartley Act was through the combination of contractual union preference, hiring hall arrangements, and the limitation on the admission of new members to the union. At that time, the agreements in the maritime industry provided, in general, that employers would give preference in employment to union members. Although the union preference provision appears on its face to be less stringent than a closed or union shop provision, in conjunction with the union hiring hall, its effect is the same as that of the closed shop. The union provisions differed in detail, but they were all intended to provide the union membership with preference in employment. This preference was consistently enforced in all cases on the Atlantic and Pacific coasts through union hiring halls, whether or not referred to specifically. All the maritime unions maintained limits on the number of new entries into the union. To ensure adequate resources, permits or trip cards were issued to qualified seamen. Limited numbers of trip card men were admitted to probationary membership when the regular membership roles were declining or when the employment prospects over an extended period appeared bright. In all instances, regular union members received preference in employment opportunities over trip card men, whatever their registration dates in the hiring hall.

This combination of arrangements — union preference-union hiring hall, with resultant preference to union members in hiring and promotions — was found to be in contravention of the Taft-Hartley Act.

The accommodation made by the unions, and the operators, as described earlier, has been to develop a concept of unit-wide seniority, based on the prior employment of the seamen on the vessels of the companies covered by a particular bargaining unit. This concept has been further developed by setting a base period service date, with those seamen (whether union or nonunion) who served during that period treated as part of a regular employment pool, and receiving priority in employment opportunities. Additional classes for those with lesser service, or less continuous service, and for those who are entering the industry are also provided. The increased participation of management through the establishment of joint boards to hear complaints regarding the appropriateness of the classification accorded an individual, and in the joint determination of the shipping rules under which the hiring halls function, has also been described. Obviously, the unions are concerned with the preservation of the role of the hiring hall in maintaining job security for their members who continue to follow the sea; the intent of the revisions in arrangements is to meet the nondiscriminatory requirements of the Taft-Hartley Act with a minimum of dislocation. Although nonmembers are now shipped, every effort is made to ensure that these are limited to the relatively few eligible for the highest priority classes. The unions are continuing to maintain controls over the numbers who are admitted to regular membership.[20]

The third feature of the maritime labor market, the necessity for the maintenance of an adequate manpower reserve to meet the rapid turnaround needs of the modern merchant marine, helps explain the values which operators have acknowledged for the central hiring hall. Stringent government regulations regarding the qualifications and certification of crew members require that an adequate labor pool be available constantly from which ship operators may promptly draw necessary replacements. Without the union hiring halls, ship operators would either have to maintain individual labor pools, or they would have to combine to maintain a single labor reserve. In either case, the expense would have to be borne by the companies for a function now performed by the seamen, themselves, through their unions. That the expense can be not insubstantial is demonstrated by the experience of the Pacific Maritime Association in operating the court-directed central registration office for the recruitment of West Coast stewards — the cost of operations for the three-year period was reported as totaling $350,000.[21]

Supported by the union membership, the administration of the union hiring halls is controlled by the democratic process within the unions. Each union has its own set of shipping rules to govern the employment process. While these rules differ in detail, they are all intended to assure each union member a fair and equal opportunity in obtaining employment. In all cases, the rules are subject to membership approval. Instances in which the shipping rules have been violated, with individuals obtaining positions through favoritism, are apparently rare. Penalties for violations of the shipping rules are severe.

The shipping rules of all the unions provide for the rotary system of hiring in order to equalize work opportunities among the membership. Under this system, when members are discharged from a ship, they report to the union hiring hall where they are given shipping cards indicating the date and hour of registration. All jobs are posted on bulletin boards in the hiring halls prior to the regularly scheduled time when the dispatcher will attempt to fill them. When jobs are announced by the dispatcher, interested men with the appropriate experience submit their cards. The dispatcher sorts the cards and gives the job to the individual with the earliest shipping card, that is, the man longest on the beach. If there is any question regarding this individual's qualifications, under the rules the dispatcher is empowered to ask for discharge papers to establish the applicant's eligibility.

The expiration date of a shipping card depends upon a number of factors. To ensure that work opportunities are shared only by those who want work, the card is effective only within specific time limits. These vary with the extent of employment opportunities — when shipping is brisk and jobs are plentiful, the time limit may be 30 to 45 days; when shipping is slow and jobs are scarce, the time limit may be 90 days or more. Any man who does not ship within the time limit loses his shipping date and must reregister. Seamen are usually given the right to consider and reject assignment for two or three jobs, after which they lose their shipping dates. Several unions make regular attendance at union meetings a requirement for keeping registration dates.

While the operator calls upon the union for necessary personnel, all the agreements permit him to reject men who he considers to be unfit, unsuitable, or unsatisfactory. The West Coast agreements require the employer to furnish a written statement regarding his reasons for rejecting any man sent by the union. These agreements, as well as the SIU agreements, also provide that such employer action may be taken up through the grievance machinery. The NMU agreement provides that the union will be given verbal information at its request regarding a company's reason for rejecting any employee furnished by the union. Several of the agreements require the unlicensed personnel to submit to physical examinations required by the operators as a condition of employment. The unions have the right to request review of the decisions of the company doctors, and the matter may go to arbitration by outside doctors.

A number of additional reservations apply to the union hiring hall as the sole source of unlicensed personnel. The agreements generally exclude certain supervisory, highly skilled or key ratings from the personnel mandatorily furnished operators by the union. Thus, the Marine Firemen's Union agreement permits the companies to assist in selecting electricians, icemen, and plumbers at the union hall, or to obtain men from other sources if no union members are considered qualified. Chief stewards are among the classifications in the NMU agreement which may be obtained from within or without the union. The hiring exceptions made to allow individual employees to remain in continuous employment with a single employer have been indicated above.

The union hiring hall has since the mid-thirties become an established feature of employment in the maritime industry and has been extended to the licensed personnel. Although there are operator complaints regarding the limitations on selecting competent personnel through rotary shipping, the employer's right to select capable personnel has not been completely usurped, for the agreements specifically protect this right. Nor is continuous employment prohibited, for the agreements protect this practice, too. Rather, the hiring halls have provided an assured source of qualified labor to the maritime industry at a minimum cost. They have contributed much to restoring to seamen the dignity and self-respect which were lacking under other systems of employment. It is no wonder, therefore, that the maritime unions have made every effort to circumscribe the effects of the Taft-Hartley Act on the hiring halls. The economic imperatives to which the industry alludes in protesting economic concessions to the seamen are the very ones which appear to the seamen to require that some control be exercised over the size of the labor force available to ship operators.

TRENDS IN WAGES AND WORKING CONDITIONS

A revolution has occurred in the economic status of American seamen since the end of the war. This is paradoxical in a sense, in that it has occurred during a period marked generally by declining and limited job opportunities for seamen. This is explained, however, by the continuing opportunities for the segment of the merchant marine remaining in operation, under the stimulus of aid cargoes, subsidies, and the world-wide increase in the volume of trade, despite the sharp increase in shipping competition. The maritime unions have sought to counter the limited job opportunities available to their members, by ensuring as high an earnings level as possible during periods of employment. The pressures of rival unionism have also acted to push up the level of labor costs.

Ship operators have differed in their explanations of the reasons for the rise. Some unsubsidized operators have charged that operating subsidies have eliminated subsidized management's incentive to restrain rising wage costs, and, in turn, have raised labor costs for the entire industry, subsidized and unsubsidized sectors alike.[22] Other maritime operators have acknowledged that expediency has been the major determinant of their reaction to union demands and that they have had to accept these increased costs because of the impact of forces beyond their control; including the fluctuation of merchant marine opportunities, whipsawing by strong rival unions, and the prominent role of government in a number of increases.[23] They cite the results of the study of the industry undertaken for them which show that the postwar rate of increase in maritime base rates and earnings has far outstripped those of shoreside manufacturing workers; that the earnings level exceeds those of such shoreside industries as basic steel, autos, shipbuilding and others; and that operating costs far exceed those on foreign vessels.[24]

Although acknowledging that American maritime wages far exceed those of foreign seamen, the maritime unions contend that they are merely seeking to bring the seamen's conditions into line with the American standard of living. The unions contend that more appropriate is a comparison between the seamen's status in this country and abroad with their respective shoreside counterparts — on this basis, it is contended that American seamen fare substantially less favorably than do foreign seamen. They cite the A.B. seamen hourly base rate (approximately $1.90 per hour in 1956) as evidence that it is in line with average manufacturing rates; on earnings, they emphasize the casual and intermittent character of seafaring job opportunities in contrast to shoreside employment and the necessary length of the shipboard work week. They have emphasized also the other side of the relationship: that welfare and social security benefits are more important in foreign countries, and that employer payments for these are made through established funds, and do not appear in the wage; and that foreign currencies have been devaluated.[25]

The revolution in the wages and working conditions in the status of the seamen has seen the development of a basic wage structure whose level is in line with general shoreside industry wage levels, and of substantially increased earnings levels. The effect of shoreside wage and related movements has been particularly apparent in the prompt and successful efforts of the maritime unions to obtain the new fringe benefit features which have developed in shoreside labor-management relations. The attainment of pensions, health and welfare plans, and, in the case of the National Maritime Union, of a supplementary unemployment benefit plan have all been prominent features in maritime collective bargaining. Jointly administered plans for industry-wide pooling of employer contributions for these purposes, and for the provision of vacation benefits, have made these benefits feasible in an industry marked by casual employment relationships.

The rival union situation has had both centrifugal and contripetal tendencies on wage relationships. Division has occurred as each union has sought to lead or to establish a separate pattern. The necessity of keeping up with the rival union has resulted in pressures to obtain identity in levels or in the amounts of increase. Wage rates were fairly identical on both coasts up to 1955, but earnings levels were higher on the West Coast. The licensed unions, which customarily follow the patterns established by the unlicensed unions, have maintained parity on both coasts. Although the cost increases for contributions for fringe benefits have generally been equal, the forms the benefits have taken have varied among the unions. The centrifugal forces were most apparent in 1955 when the NMU improvements took the form of the establishment of the Employment Stabilization Plan and increased welfare benefits; the SUP altered its wage system to incorporate penalty overtime payments into the base rate, along with additional wage increases; and the Atlantic and Gulf SIU received wage increases and increased welfare benefits.

Apparently there have been occasions when a gain made by one union, but not sought by another, has required downward adjustment to avoid overpricing its labor force, with the possibility that the shipment of the products would be transferred to companies dealing with a rival union.[26] Numerous wage reviews have been submitted to arbitration by the maritime unions, with the exception of the SUP and the SIU, and the arbitrators have frequently acted to restore parity in basic wage levels among the unions. Similarly, government action during periods of wage stabilization controls has been based on the maintenance of parity.

Wages and Earnings

The wage structure on board American ships is relatively simple. The number of classifications are small, the job duties are well established by custom and contractual description, and the internal relationships have been roughly maintained for many years. The rates for such key classifications as ablebodied seamen and firemen-watertenders are uniform on all vessels. The tanker wage structure is comparable to that of dry cargo ships, and customarily follows the patterns of the dry cargo industry. The wage structures on passenger vessels, with their provision for numerous specialized service ratings is more complex. Manning scales and wage structures also make provision for additional ratings to meet additional duties required on various types of ships. In the case of vessels with greater power tonnage, the wage scales of licensed officers are graduated upward to meet increased responsibilities and experience requirements and differentials are also provided for the unlicensed classifications which require greater experience and responsibility.

The wage structure is based on monthly payments. On the East Coast, there is uniform practice of overtime payment for all time worked beyond 40 hours at sea; and since the 56-hour week has continued, all men on watch automatically receive penalty payment for weekend work. On the West Coast, the SUP negotiated a change in its wage structure in 1955, by which penalty payments for weekend and other work were incorporated into the base rates, with "true overtime" to be paid for work beyond 8 hours per day and 56 per week. The result was an ablebodied seamen's rate of $453 per month. For the purpose of treating base rate movements independently of earnings, the East Coast scale is more appropriate under the circumstances. Changes in the basic rate structure are shown in Table 3 for class "B" (C-2 and C-3) freighters on the Atlantic and Gulf Coast between 1939 and 1956.

Unlicensed personnel received greater relative increases during the period — the amounts of increase amounting to three to four times their original base rates, while the rates of licensed officers rose 2 to 2.5 times. The absolute increases to licensed personnel have exceeded those of the unlicensed personnel; the latter, starting from substantially lower base rates, have however received greater percentage increases. The effect of the varied increases has been to reduce the percentage spread between the A.B. rate and the captain's rate by one-half. The lower licensed ratings have received somewhat greater increases than the top ratings, reducing the spread between these to some extent. Among the unlicensed personnel, the deck and engine department received the largest relative increase, while the stewards' department received lesser relative increases. However, the relative spreads within the respective groups of licensed and unlicensed groups have not been altered appreciably.

The base rate structure is only one contributory part of the total earnings of the seamen. In the war and postwar period, overtime earnings became a major element. Overtime payments during the period of employer job control were meager and intermittent. One element in the resumption of collective bargaining in the thirties was provision for overtime pay for extra work performed, accompanied initially by the employer option to pay cash or grant compensatory time off. The option was eliminated in the West Coast contracts following the 1936–7 strike, and overtime pay has been important since that time.

It has been estimated that payments for overtime and penalty work between 1939 and 1941 for A.B. seamen averaged approximately 8 percent

Table 3

Typical manning scales and basic wage rates for U. S. Flag Class B[1]
freighters, 1939–1956, Atlantic and Gulf Coast

Deck department	1939			1956			% of Increase 1956 over 1939
	Man-ning	Monthly rate	% of A.B. rate	Man-ning	Monthly rate	% of A.B. rate	
Master................	1	$335	465	1	$1093	364	226
Chief Officer...........	1	190	264	1	670	201	252
2nd Officer............	1	175	243	1	591	177	237
3rd Officer............	1	162	225	1	545	164	236
4th Officer............	0	—	—	1	500	150	—
Purser................	0	—	—	1	547	164	—
Radio Officer...........	1	132	183	1	536	161	306
Bo's'n................	1	85	118	1	445	134	423
Carpenter............	1	85	118	1	408	123	380
Maintenance Men......	0	—	—	2	375	113	—
Able-Bodied Seamen....	6	72.50	100	6	333	100	362
Ordinary Seamen.......	3	55.00	77	3	258	77	370
Engine Department							
Chief Engineer........	1	310	430	1	993	299	220
First Asst. Engineer.....	1	205	285	1	670	201	226
Second Asst. Engineer...	1	175	243	1	591	177	237
Third Asst. Engineer....	1	160	222	1	545	164	240
Fourth Asst. Engineer...	0	—	—	1	500	150	—
Licensed Jr. Engineer...	0	—	—	1	466	140	—
Chief Electrician.......	0	—	—	1	529	159	—
Second Electrician......	0	—	—	1	493	148	—
Deck Engineer........	1	117.50	162	—	—	—	—
Oilers................	3	82.50	114	3	333	100	306
Firemen, Watertender...	3	82.50	114	3	333	100	306
Wipers...............	2	60.00	83	3	312	94	420
Stewards Department							
Chief Steward..........	1	125.00	173	1	435	131	248
Chief Cook............	1	110	153	1	393	118	254
Cook and Baker........	1	90	125	1	383	115	—
Second Cook..........	0	—	—	1	345	104	283
Messman or Utility Man	6	60	83	6	256	77	321
	38			47			

[1] In the negotiation of agreements, ships are designated by power tonnage. Class "B" includes C-2 and C-3 power tonnage classes.

Source: Based on data obtained from Maritime Administration, U. S. Department of Commerce. According to information furnished by the Maritime Administration, this manning scale falls within the range of "typical manning scales."

of their base rates. Wartime exigencies resulted in the increase of overtime pay to about 48 percent of base rates; these were reduced to 27
percent on the East Coast and 35 percent on the West Coast in the period
immediately following the war's termination. Overtime costs were automatically increased by the two-step reduction in the work week at sea
from 56 hours to 48 in 1946 (an 8 percent increase) and to 40 in 1951–2
(a 9 percent increase). This was automatic overtime pay, since watch-
standing requirements at sea remained unchanged; with the numbers in
the crew unchanged, the actual work week remained at 56 hours. Thus,
automatic overtime increases together with additional premium pay work
items resulted in overtime costs averaging 41 percent on East Coast ships
and over 52.6 percent on West Coast ships.[27]

The total monthly earnings of an A.B. seaman on the East Coast, as
recently estimated by the American Merchant Marine Institute, amount
to about $530. This amounts to hourly earnings of approximately $2.06,
on the basis of an average of 60 hours actually worked per week.[28]
Studies of average duration of regular employment during the course of
a year showed nine to ten months average duration during the war, and
eight months in the immediate postwar period — both periods of ready
employment opportunities.[29] The sixfold increase in the monthly earnings
of the A.B. seamen has occurred during a period when average hourly
earnings of manufacturing workers increased threefold, and consumer
prices doubled.

The substantial increase in operating costs resulting from overtime
penalty payments has made these a constant subject of discussion in labor-
management relations, and of governmental studies. These payments
arise out of the many provisions of the contracts which provide payments
for work outside the customary hours of work, for work outside regular
duties performed during regular hours of work, and for the performance
of dirty or hazardous work. The unions have argued that a primary
purpose of penalty pay provisions is to discourage ship's officers from assigning unjust and unreasonable tasks to seamen. They have argued that
the ship operators, by proper planning, can avoid penalty payment of overtime for controllable items. They have argued also that the monthly earnings are not substantial when consideration is given to the long hours
worked by the seamen, and to the restricted duration of employment during
the year. The CIO Maritime Committee submitted an extensive statistical
exhibit to the House Committee on Merchant Marine and Fisheries in
1955 demonstrating that the wages of American seamen bore no better
relationship to shoreside industrial wages than those of foreign seamen
to their respective domestic industry wage levels. It stressed also that
foreign seamen receive substantial social security benefits which do not
appear in their pay envelopes.[30]

The ship operators have argued the necessity of reducing penalty payments as one important avenue to the reduction of costs. Proposals have been made to eliminate double overtime for what are claimed to be routine duties for work performed on Saturdays, Sundays and holidays, to reëvaluate duties now considered additional, and to add these to the regular duties of the jobs. The Pacific Maritime Association has adopted a policy of obtaining cost information from its members and analyzing the components of overtime and penalty pay costs; explicit data showing the variations by type of payment, department, trade route and vessel have been published in a series of reports.[31]

The combination of shipowner and Congressional pressures resulted in a major change in the West Coast wage structure in 1955. Harry Lundeberg's SUP negotiated a wage agreement which incorporated amounts equivalent to the payments for noncontrollable penalty payments — amounts paid for work within the spread of the eight-hour workday and penalty time paid for standing watches on Saturday, Sunday and holidays — into the monthly base rate. This is accompanied by a "true" overtime rate, which is close to time and a half, which is to be paid for work outside the regular 8-hour day and 56-hour week at sea; the overtime rate in the other seafaring agreements, which continue to be based on the 40-hour week, is approximately a straight time rate. Although controllable operations requiring penalty payments were left open to employer control, appreciable effects on penalty payments were not apparent several months after the new structure was developed.[32]

Fringe Benefits

The prompt reaction of the maritime unions to shoreside trends in fringe benefit arrangements has brought substantial improvement in the status of seamen and of their families. It has also meant that the industry has had to assume increased costs to conform to the American pattern of private arrangements to provide benefits which are either not provided or only partially provided through government. In the case of the maritime industry, this has added to the cost handicaps in meeting the competition of ships of nations which provide substantial social welfare benefits through comprehensive governmental plans.[33]

The government provided benefits received by American seamen which, while substantially less than those provided seamen of other countries, are not unimportant; traditionally, they are entitled while employed to free hospitalization and medical care through the Public Health Service. Seamen, like industrial workers generally, are covered by both the unemployment compensation and old age and survivors' insurance provisions of the Social Security Act. American seamen are not covered by a Federal workmen's compensation statute as are longshoremen, a matter of conscious choice by union officials and apparent preference for the maintenance of the provisions of the Jones Act of 1920, making ship-owners liable for damages for certain injuries suffered by seamen while employed, and permitting seamen to file suits in the courts.

The provision of vacation, welfare, pension, and supplementary unem-ployment benefits in the maritime industry has resulted from the "in-dustry-wide" pooling of employer contributions to respective funds for the separate purposes. The effect of these joint labor-management trust fund arrangements covering the union-contract employer group has been to provide additional frequent contacts for labor and management to meet in regard to the regular and continuing problems which require solu-tion in the day-to-day administration of the plans. The mutual interest in solving problems, rather than in resolving positions based on divergent interest, has tended to strengthen bargaining relationships.

It was only the industry-wide pooling of employer contributions which made vacations effective for seamen on dry cargo ships, although vacation provisions had been in effect in prior contracts providing for vacations for continuous service with one company; the discontinuous service of most seamen, however, precluded any widespread vacation practice. The in-dustry-wide arrangement is based on the pooling of service during the year with the contracted employers; a seaman with service during the year may receive up to fourteen days' vacation a year, and a seaman with continuous service with one company receives an additional seven or fourteen days, depending on the contract. Similar provisions are effective for both licensed and unlicensed personnel, and for dry cargo and tanker operations. Seamen who work continuously with one company are re-quired to take their vacations, thus providing relief both from the ship's regimen and an opportunity for relief work for others.

The welfare and pension arrangements negotiated since the SUP-SIU drive for these provisions began in 1949 have been extended to all of the unions and personnel in the industry. There are numerous variations in the financing of the plans — some are based upon benefits, others are based upon lump-sum employer contributions; and there are variations in their administration, and benefits. Separate pension and vacation plans are currently operative for the three unlicensed West Coast unions, but arrangements are under way to combine these, to permit the pooling of service and funds. The Marine Engineers' Beneficial Association has an integrated plan covering both coasts. The pension plans generally provide for retirement pensions which range from $65 to $100 per month at age 65, to supplement Social Security benefits, and for disability retirement. The fifteen welfare plans now in operation in the industry show a wide range of benefits. All provide benefits to dependents of employees, as well as to employees; fewer provide hospital and medical care benefits to the dependents of pensioners, as well as to pensioners. Employees generally receive life insurance and hospitalization benefits. SIU welfare funds are being used for the construction of clinics to provide diagnostic examinations of seamen as a means of preventing illness. Most of the plans provide for hospitalization and maternity benefits for members' dependents. Provision for pensioners and their dependents are more sparse — some plans provide death benefits for pensioners, and limited amounts of hospital and medical care for pensioners and their dependents.

The NMU employment security plan, which was adopted in 1955 and effected in 1956, is unique in the industry. The intent of the plan is to provide for benefits during periods of unemployment when seamen are inadequately covered by state unemployment benefits. Benefits are paid when the seaman is unemployed under the following circumstances: layoff from ship (up to 3 weeks); reshipment after disability (to 5 weeks); disability preventing reshipments (13 weeks); to care for a disabled spouse (5 weeks); legal proceedings (5 weeks); reship after vacation time (4 weeks). The full $30 per week benefit is paid when the seaman is not entitled to state unemployment compensation payments; $15 is paid during any week he is eligible for such payments.[34]

Manning, Quarters, and Duties

The provisions of the trade agreements reflect the unique characteristics of maritime employment in various respects. Provisions with regard to manning and quarters conform to certain Federal regulations which set minimum requirements, but also fill in some of the gaps left by such regulations. The complete description of customary duties and the work for which penalty payments are to be made arises in a measure out of the completeness of the captain's control of discipline at sea.

Manning requirements have long been a major cause of contention between the maritime unions and the ship operators. Since the first decade of the century, the minimum crew requirements in the deck and engine departments for each vessel have been fixed by Federal steamboat inspectors. Manning scales have been spelled out in the agreements only in those areas which are not covered by government regulations. Until recently, therefore, bargaining was limited to the stewards' department, which is not covered by Federal regulation. The absence of such regulations apparently furnished a stimulus for setting up specific manning scales in the stewards' department to insure adequate provision for meals. Current agreements provide specifically for collective bargaining on manning scales in the stewards' department. During the past decade, the Pacific Marine Firemen's Union agreement has also specified a manning scale for refrigerator engineers on refrigerator ships.

More recently, however, collective bargaining has achieved changes in manning through negotiation. Thus, in 1948, the SIU obtained a contract provision that manning scales in the deck and engine departments would not be altered "unless such changes are mutually agreed to by both the Union and the Company." The NMU contract provides for the referral of questions with regard to manning in the deck and engine departments to a joint industry committee with authority to make final and binding decisions. Unlike the effort at uniformity which this industry-wide approach permits, manning matters on the West Coast are handled entirely by the individual companies without recourse to the facilities of the Pacific Maritime Association.

The changes in manning which have occurred on one class of vessels — the typical freighter — are reflected in Table 2. Between 1939 and 1950, the manning scale on these ships was increased from 38 to 47, with changes as well as additions in jobs. These were the concomitant of increased duties and increased personnel requirements resulting from altered ship facilities, such as electrically powered booms, and additional booms and hatches; increased and more complicated payroll record keeping requirements; and, in particular, the reduced work week for day men and for the stewards.

The opportunity for the unions to assert some influence on manning has also presented itself, as new types of ships have been put into operation. Management has strongly resisted union demands in this area, and the evidence indicates that the results of such negotiations have been tied to fairly clearcut connection between requisite duties and the personnel complement. There is no evidence of any featherbedding in manning arrangements.

The hope held out for reduced unit costs in ship operations as the result of the operation of ships of substantially greater carrying capacity would of course have its effect on manning. The awesome 100,000-ton supertankers, which can carry six times the load of the ordinary tanker, require less than twice the crew of the latter. The less spectacularly enlarged bulk carriers and intermediate supertankers also require reduced labor complement per ton carried. The process of "jumboizing" ships may achieve reduced unit operating costs, but the employment problems for seamen may be intensified.

For quarters, as for manning scales, the area of bargaining is restricted to matters outside the provisions of the pertinent Federal statutes and regulations. The Seamen's Act of 1915 fixes minimum space requirements for each seaman at 120 cubic feet and 16 square feet of floor space; and requires quarters to be "securely constructed, properly lighted, drained, heated, and ventilated, properly protected from weather and sea, and, as far as practicable, properly shut off and protected from the effluvium of cargo or bilge water." The act also requires that crew quarters should not be used for stores or cargo; that hospital compartments should be provided; and that washing places and washing outfits should be provided. The act of 1936 requires monthly inspection of crew quarters by inspectors of the Bureau of Marine Inspection and Navigation to "satisfy themselves that such quarters are of the size required by law or regulations issued thereunder, are properly ventilated and in a clean and sanitary condition, and are equipped with the proper plumbing and mechanical appliances required by law or regulations issued thereunder, and that such plumbing and mechanical appliances are in good working order and condition." Violation of these requirements makes the master or ship's officer who is willfully responsible for the violation liable to a fine not in excess of $500, and can result in withdrawal of a ship's certificate of inspection.

The unions have generally been unsuccessful in obtaining a voice in the matter of the arrangement and construction of crew quarters through collective bargaining. However, in designing merchant ships for government account, the Maritime Administration has generally sought to provide a maximum of two berths per room, and privately designed ships generally follow suit. American ship construction standards are considered the highest in the world.[35] The provisions of the trade agreements are restricted to matters relating to the equipment, comfort, and cleanliness in the quarters assigned to the crew. All the agreements contain some provision assuring proper equipment for the use of the crew, such as washing machines, blankets, mattresses and pillows, dishes of crockery, clean towels and bed linen, and soap and matches. Specifically required also are proper ventilation for crew quarters, full length lockers, washrooms with hot and cold water, and messrooms separate from sleeping quarters. The NMU agreement establishes a joint industry quarters committee to deal with questions which may arise over quarters.

A characteristic feature of maritime trade agreements is the detailed listing of the working rules for the unlicensed crew members in the respective departments. All the agreements state that the individual crew members will be required to perform the regular and customary duties of the rating for which they have been signed on. In addition, many of the specific duties which are considered regular and customary are spelled out in the provisions of the contracts. The provision of penalty payments for exceptional duties, and for hazardous or obnoxious cargo — carried or duties involved, has already been described.

A further indication of the growing scope of collective bargaining is reflected in the recent negotiations on the East Coast to restrict the master's statutory authority to fine seamen for infraction of the lawful commands at sea or willful neglect of duty. The unions' view that this authority, part of the maritime code, is archaic, received support in the report of the Maritime Labor Board in 1940; legislative action was not forthcoming, however.[36] In the campaign to restrict fines for logging, Joseph Curran charged that the latitude given the master to determine the extent of the penalty was a throwback to the era of indentured servitude; and following negotiations on this matter in 1955–1956, the NMU and the SIU reached agreement with their respective contract groups, to restrict the master in penalizing a seaman for missing a watch to the actual amount he would have earned during that time. The understandings were concluded on the basis that these would not impede the lawful exercise of the captain's authority on shipboard.

The impact of union organization and the great changes flowing therefrom have resulted in substantial changes in the complexion of the maritime labor force, which are apparent from the limited data available.

The citizenship restrictions have had their impact, and the increased requirements for specialist ratings have also had their effect. Alien seamen filled over 50 percent of the jobs on American-flag ships prior to the first World War, and 40 to 50 percent during the twenties; these have been displaced by the citizenship requirements and the entry of American citizens into the merchant marine. The modern work force includes a group of older men who turned to the sea for want of other opportunities, and have been associated with most of the history of union organization. Increasingly, young men have entered the industry attracted by the challenge of the increasingly complicated technology of the ship, and the opportunity to obtain specialist ratings. In addition, the merchant marine continues to serve as a bridge for newcomers to the continental United States — now it is American citizens from Puerto Rico, rather than foreign immigrants, who play a prominent part in the maritime labor force.[37]

Improved earnings and the reduction in the time of round trip voyages have eliminated basic factors which made for the relative isolation of the seamen in the past. The effect is reflected in the sharp increase in the number of married seamen during the past twenty years. One study showed 8 percent of seamen as married in 1934–1935; another showed an increase from 28 to 50 percent in the number listing wives as next of kin between 1940 and 1951. The majority showed the next of kin to be living in the port area. The incidence of marriage among seamen is presently estimated at well above 50 percent.[38]

The number of men remaining in the industry with long years of shipboard service are further indications of the increased stability in the work force. In one union, over one-third of the union members have had thirteen or more years of service as seamen; this is probably typical of the membership of all of the unions.

The continued casual nature of the employment relationship in the industry notwithstanding, there is evidence of increased continuity of service with individual companies. In dry cargo operations, where an employment has been considered as particularly casual, about 30 percent of those receiving vacation benefits under the NMU plan in 1956 received the larger benefits based on continuous employment with a single company.

Although these are limited data, they suggest that at least the core of a stable labor force is in the making in the American merchant marine. Its stability includes participation in the normal relationships which shoreside workers enjoy. The threat to this stability, however, is the uncertainty of job opportunities during periods of sharp fluctuation in the shipping opportunities for American flag vessels.

CONCLUSIONS AND PROSPECTS

The numerous and complicated facets of the successful efforts to organize seamen require a concluding evaluation of developments to date and a focussing on remaining problems. The answers to the following questions may provide a measure of the insight necessary in evaluating "where we have been" and "where we are going."

(1) What have been the aims of the seamen's organizations, and have they been achieved?

(2) What has been the impact of organization on the industry?

(3) In the problems which remain, what should be the role of the government?

(1) *What have been the aims of the seamen's organizations, and have they been achieved?*

The primary goal of the seamen's organizations has been to develop stable and effective trade unions which would assure adequate representation of the seamen's interests. Only limited organization existed among the seamen's organizations until the mid-thirties. With the renascence of the trade union movement in the thirties, the strength of the seamen's unions on the West Coast was recouped, and effective organization developed on the East Coast. Through strong organization, these unions were initially able to withstand threats to hard-won concessions, and more recently have gone on to make great gains that have brought their wages and working conditions into line with both shoreside levels and trends. The strength of the organizations has been demonstrated through the periods when the weakening effects of factional strife could have threatened survival. The stability and strength of the seamen's organizations has stemmed from the effective leadership of the late Harry Lundeberg and Joseph Curran, the democratic organization of the unions, and the general growth of the trade union movement. The seamen's organizations and their leaders on both coasts have participated fully in the activities of the trade union movement as a whole, and occupy respected positions in the labor movement.

The goal of job control, so central to the purpose of trade unionism in the maritime industry, has been achieved to a degree unacceptable to old sailing ship men of the ilk of Andrew Furuseth. The latter sought a job control which was based merely on recognition of the craft, as typified by the able seamen's requirements in the Seamen's Act of 1915. Opposing any equalization of work opportunities through rotary hiring, they argued that masters should be free to select union members on the basis of ability. The ISU failed, however, to achieve job control through statutory requirement alone, since modern vessels required skills different from those required on the old sailing ships. Besides, only some degree of equalization of work opportunities could assure a stable maritime labor force, as well as a stable union membership. The role of the union hiring hall, with rotary hiring, is now an accepted institution in maritime labor relations.

The ability of maritime labor and management to achieve constructive adjustments to the Taft-Hartley requirements of nondiscrimination on account of union or nonunion membership reflects the progress that has been made in the collective bargaining relationship. These adjustments have been made through negotiations during the past decade without the hostility which marked the issue in the early prewar days of the developing relationship; the accommodations have been treated as problems of joint responsibility and not of differences over principles. This does not mean that there are no problems. The unions would prefer to have the hiring halls exempted from the provisions of the Taft-Hartley Act. The ship operators complain of the inadequacies of the rotary shipping system in ensuring that only qualified and responsible seamen are referred to openings. But these are not issues which are raised as periodic salvos in a hostile climate; they are among the constructive contentions for improving the status of the industry and of its labor force.

Another major goal of the seamen's organizations — the achievement of "first class citizenship" for the seamen has been achieved in recent years to an extent which Andrew Furuseth could never have foreseen. He set the pattern for effective political action by the seamen's leaders in obtaining a favorable governmental climate for improvement of the seamen's status; but the gains achieved under the leadership of Curran and Lundeberg have been the result of economic action primarily. The gains made by the seamen during the past ten years have constituted a minor economic revolution. The seamen's wages and working conditions now compare favorably with those of the average American industrial worker, but the continued uncertainties over job opportunities and full time annual employment may still be disadvantages.

Political activity for economic ends, however, is necessarily a major concern of the seamen's unions. The ever present concern of the Congress and the executive agencies with the state of the merchant marine and of the role of labor-management relationships as one integral part of the industry's conditions naturally produce a political orientation on the part of both labor and management. The political interest of the unions has been oriented toward legislative actions which would protect and enhance the state of the American flag merchant marine, and to avoid governmental action which would restrict the scope of private collective bargaining relationships in the industry, or would encroach upon the purely civilian status of the merchant marine and its personnel. The American seafaring unions are among the staunchest supporters of a modern, well-equipped, and well-manned American flag merchant marine. There may be differences with the ship operators over some of the details of the program for achieving such a merchant marine, but on basic aims, and on most of the important elements of the program, there is substantial agreement.

One major goal of the seamen's organizations has not been achieved — the welding of all seamen's unions into a single national union. This is true despite the elimination of two former major obstacles to unity — the intensification of the rivalry among the seamen's unions by the AFL-CIO split, and the presence of Communist influence in some of the unions. But although these influences may be eliminated, there are still the continuing factors of competing concentrations of strength, differing economic interests by virtue of the differing composition of the operator contract groups with which the unions deal, and the inability of the ship operators themselves to achieve unity.

The failure to achieve unity has been bound up with the often intense union rivalries which have had their impact in the "whipsawing" of operators to obtain somewhat greater gains than those achieved by their rivals. The rivalry, it should be noted, is not restricted to the seamen's unions — on the West Coast, particularly, ideological differences, jurisdictional feuds over the respective scope of work of seamen and longshoremen, and the constant battle to extend jurisdiction over common areas between the seamen's and longshoremen's unions has produced much more intensive rivalry. On balance economically, the "whipsaw" in maritime labor-management relations has had negative value. The economic gains it has produced have been minor on most occasions; most of the gains achieved by the unions have been achieved in the initial bargaining, under the favorable carrying conditions and the attractions of shoreside work. On the negative side, which outbalances the gains, the whipsaw has caused loss of earnings because of work stoppages; has required the expenditure of substantial time and energy in negotiations and arbitration proceedings on the part of labor and management which cannot be matched in shoreside negotiations; and has made for a continuing general uncertainty in labor-management relationships, despite the vast progress which has been made.

The rival union situation has restricted union leaders in sitting down with management to discuss possible approaches to meeting the problems of the industry, for fear of recrimination from rivals; and specific actions which do not follow the mainstream can be cause for substantial attack both from without and within the organization. The use of grievance machineries and of arbitration, difficult under the best of circumstances in an industry marked by casual employment and quick turnaround, is further restricted by the destructively critical effect of rival unionism on efforts to establish labor-management coöperation. That efforts in the direction of increasing coöperation have occurred despite the likelihood of attack is evidence of the character of the leadership of the seamen's union; but the uncertainty prevails, and more basic joint approaches to the problems of the industry could be made if union rivalry were eliminated.

(2) *What has been the impact of organization on the industry?*

A recent Congressional report (The Bonner Committee) on the state of labor-management relations in the maritime industry appropriately described the broader milieu in which these relations were operating in the following terms:

Time and again it has been said that the American merchant marine is a sick industry. This has been denied by some. The facts are, however, that we have six or seven hundred less ships in our active fleet than military authorities estimate to be necessary for national defense purposes; the domestic and intercoastal trades have all but vanished from the seas; the tramp fleet, which is being sustained almost entirely by the 50–50 law and Government-aid cargoes, is doomed to obsolescence and eventual liquidation; the United States has dropped far down among the nations of the world in the number of ships being built; and the maritime unions have thousands of men on the beach. These are hardly the characteristics of a strong merchant marine.[1]

Within this context, it is apparent that labor-management relations and labor costs are but isolated elements among a host of factors which affect the status of the merchant marine. The complexity of the labor-management relationships is not self-impelled — it arises from a multitude of factors including the economics of the industry, the diversity of company organization, operations and trade routes, divergent structural arrangements for collective bargaining in management associations, and the presence of internal differences in position; the impact of government through subsidies, the operations of the Military Sea Transportation Service, and mediation and other efforts to forestall work stoppages and to improve waterfront conditions; the continuing excess of the labor pool over shipping requirements, except in periods of crisis; the impact of the Labor-Management Relations Act on the hiring hall; and the plethora of union organizations, with rival concentrations of strength. These factors do not include the impact of shoreside changes in wages and working conditions on maritime labor relations.

The influences operating on the maritime industry and on labor-management relations in the industry are therefore many and varied. Their influence on labor-management relations is probably much greater than the reverse; but union organization has undoubtedly left its mark on the industry's position.

The gains achieved by union organization in wages, hours, and fringe benefits have brought the seamen to the status of their American shoreside counterparts. The resultant increased labor costs have only added to the comparative disadvantages under which American ship operators have always labored — even under the aegis of employer domination of hiring. The cost impact has been intensified by the requirement that all American flag ships carry 75 percent of American citizens in their crews; subsidized ships, whose unfavorable labor cost differentials are equalized through subsidy payments, must have American citizens among at least 90 percent of their crews.

The efforts of tramp operators to discuss concessions with the unions on labor costs have been clouded by the presence of rival unions. In the absence of a united seamen's union movement, it is not possible to assay the willingness of the unions to grant concessions to maintain job opportunities. This does not mean that such concessions are necessarily desirable — they must be evaluated realistically against the actual effects of minor labor cost concessions on the actual continuance of the operation, as well as on pressures from other ship operators, and possibly even from the government, to extend such concessions.

The manpower impact of the unions on the industry and on the nation's needs has been of great importance to efficient operation. The unions and their hiring halls have ensured a continuing and regular supply of qualified citizen seamen to man American-flag ships. During wartime emergencies, these formed the core for the operation of the merchant marine, while additional personnel were being trained to meet the expanded requirements of a government-operated naval auxiliary. Operator criticism of the hiring hall relates to particular features of the rotary system and to training of new entries; on the basic matter of the values of the hiring hall, and of its continuance under union auspices, there is no disagreement.

The pressure of strong union organizations has provided a powerful fillip to the groups who have supported an American-flag merchant marine and government aid for this purpose. Operating subsidies, of course, are directly related to the status of American seamen in relation to foreign seamen. But union assistance to the merchant marine has been even more direct through the support given to cargo preference legislation, restriction on MSTS operations, and assurance of civilian operation, even during periods of government operation and control of the merchant marine.

The problem of lack of unity on the labor side has its counterpart on the industry side. The differences among ship operators are reflected not only in collective bargaining dealings, they are also apparent in the numerous organizations which represent the various segments of the industry on matters of governmental policy.

Employer organization appears to have been impelled by two factors — labor organization and governmental concern with the merchant marine. The ability of the unions to achieve unity would undoubtedly act as a stimulus to closer action on a national scale by the ship operators on a national basis — in the event of such a development, the successful British experience with the joint National Maritime Board may prove instructive.[2] In the meantime, both shipowners and unions must strive for greater unity to ensure the stability needed by an industry whose future is extremely insecure.

There are indications that ship operators have failed to adjust their personnel management practices to meet both the changed conditions in the merchant marine and the trends in shoreside management. Seamen continue to be treated as casual workers whose demands can be met by the enforcement of discipline during the voyage. Dissatisfied men can be replaced at the end of a voyage, and the cause of grievances need not be adjusted. The effect of collective bargaining in making itself a permanent and natural element in the relations between shipowners and seamen should be reënforced through the companies' adoption of personnel practices designed for constructive preventive measures. Such action, with union coöperation, would avoid much of the instability fostered by rival unionism.

(3) *In the problems which remain, what should be the role of government?*

In an industry which is so closely identified with governmental aids and governmental defense, trade, and aid policies, it is perhaps inevitable that there should be a predisposition to resort to specialized governmental agencies in the solution of labor problems. This was true in 1937, when the Maritime Labor Board was established, and it was true again in 1955. In both cases, there was operator support and union opposition; in 1955, however, the operator position was substantially less than unified.[3] The establishment of a board with merely mediatory authority in 1937 did not appreciably affect the course of maritime labor relations; and it was seriously questioned whether the presence of the board did not serve to confuse and complicate the functions which are normally exercised by the generalized Federal Mediation and Conciliation Service. The more recent proposals would have established a mediatory board with strike-delaying authority. Yet the experience with the national emergency strike provisions of the Taft-Hartley Act, and particularly in the maritime industry, has demonstrated that such authority to delay has not precluded prolonged strikes on the expiration of the "cooling off" period.

The unanimous position of the operators, along with the unions, in opposition to any limitation on the substantive aspects of bargaining would indicate that it was not proposed to give the board more than mere mediatory authority. There was complete unanimity in opposition to a bill to amend the Merchant Marine Act of 1936 by requiring that maximum limits, as well as minimum, be fixed on wages, working conditions, and manning scales for operating subsidy payments. The position of maritime management was based on opposition to peacetime limits on wages, the limited and unfair restriction of wages in one industry, with the rest of the economy free of such control, and the violation of the principle of parity in subsidy payments. The unions opposed all the measures as unwarranted restrictions on collective bargaining and as having pernicious precedent-making possibilities for shoreside labor-management relations.[4]

The aforementioned Bonner Committee report showed admirable perspicacity in its evaluation of the problems confronting the maritime industry. In viewing the current deficiencies, of the merchant marine, the committee report concluded that these are "the result of a combination of factors and that neither labor costs nor labor relations are the sole causes." In reaching the conclusion that it was for the parties themselves to solve their problems, with general assistance from the government in the provision of information and the conduct of conferences, the committee report emphasized that "this is not to minimize the importance of the problems in the maritime labor field, but rather to caution against any hope that an easy solution to the difficulties of the industry can be found in any one area."[5] The recommendations of the committee called for efforts among the labor unions to adjust their differences, for efforts within management to achieve unity and establish company administrative arrangements for effective handling of labor management relations, and called on the government to arrange conferences to obtain agreement on such major problems as uniform expiration dates and an umpire system for major disputes, and to reëxamine governmental policies bearing on the merchant marine.

This approach would continue the private nature of collective bargaining in the industry, through which substantial advances have been made in recent years. Any governmental machinery which does not evolve out of joint negotiations and out of the joint determination of the parties to be bound by such machinery would be likely to recreate the climate of hostility in labor-management relations which has disappeared from the industry. Even jointly determined machinery may prove to be inadequate in the face of substantially altered circumstances, as has perhaps been true in the railroad industry.

Ample opportunities exist for further development of *bonafide* collective bargaining in the maritime industry, and thus for stable maritime labor relations. Strong and democratic unions have developed; responsible leadership exists both among labor and management. The federal government is underwriting the costs of the American standard of living for a substantial portion of the American merchant marine. This is the cost of maintaining an additional arm of security in an imperfect world. So long as the threat of war exists, assistance to the privately-operated merchant marine is necessary — carefully audited to ensure that the public interest is being protected. But just as necessary to the public interest as merchant vessels, it must be remembered, are the seafaring workers represented by their responsible trade unions.

NOTES

NOTES

The Economic Setting

1. Direct railroad control of these operations, together with high rates and discriminatory rate practices, made these inefficient and costly operations; J. G. B. Hutchins, *The American Maritime Industries and Public Policy, 1789–1914* (Cambridge, 1941).

2. Senate Committee on Interstate Commerce and Shipping, *Final Report on Merchant Marine Study and Investigation* (1950), pp. 84–86; see also Daniel Marx, Jr., *International Shipping Cartels* (Princeton, 1953).

3. These estimates are based on data in the following: Senate Committee on Interstate and Foreign Commerce, *Merchant Marine Studies and Investigations* (1952), pp. 341–343; House Committee on Merchant Marine and Fisheries, *Study of the Operations of the Military Sea Transportation Service* (1954), p. 611; Carl E. McDowell and Helen M. Gibbs, *Ocean Transportation* (1954), p. 217.

Chapter 1

The Seamen in 1900

1. Commissioner of Navigation, *Annual Report* (1894), p. 30.

2. *American Federationist* (1900), p. 94.

3. Commissioner of Navigation, *Annual Reports* (various years).

4. W. Macarthur, "The American Seamen under the Law," *The Forum* (February 1899), pp. 726–728.

5. House Committee on Merchant Marine and Fisheries, Hearings on H. R. 383, *To Prohibit Shanghaiing and Peonage in the United States* (February 1906).

6. *Coast Seamen's Journal,* June 22, 1892 and April 5, 1893.

7. Commissioner of Navigation, *Annual Report* (1886), p. 191.

8. *Merchant Marine Commission Hearings* (1905), pp. 13 and 1570.

9. Commissioner of Bureau of Labor Statistics, State of California, *Investigation into the Condition of Men Working on the Waterfront and on Board of Pacific Coast Vessels* (1887), p. 4.

10. *Ibid.*, p. 3.

11. Commissioner of Navigation, *Annual Report* (1903), p. 49.

12. Commissioner of Navigation, *Annual Report* (1895), p. 28.

13. *Ibid.*, Reports of 1885, p. 271 and 1890, p. 7.

14. In Harden V. Gorden (2 Mason 541, 555) cited in Commissioner of Navigation, *Annual Report* (1893), p. 15.

15. Robertson *v.* Baldwin — the *Arago* Case — cited in *Coast Seamen's Journal,* March 24, 1897.

16. Organization on the Great Lakes antedated that on the coasts. A. E. Albrecht, *International Seamen's Union of America* (1923), p. 74.

17. James Fall, *British Merchant Seamen in San Francisco, 1892–1898* (1899), p. 74.

18. *Coast Seamen's Journal,* January 25, 1893; October 18, 1893 and January 8, 1896.

19. Samuel Gompers, *Seventy Years of Life and Labor,* I (New York, 1943), 347.

20. *Coast Seamen's Journal,* January 20, 1892.

21. *Ibid.,* January 3, 1900.

22. *Ibid.,* August 31, 1892.

23. *Ibid.,* March 9, 16 and 23, 1892.

24. Testimony of Vernon C. Brown, president of Maritime Exchange of New York, before Committee on Merchant Marine and Fisheries on February 18, 1896, cited in *Coast Seamen's Journal,* October 21, 1896.

25. *Congressional Record,* 54th Congress 2nd Session (1897), pp. 548–550.

26. *Coast Seamen's Journal,* February 10, 1897.

27. *Congressional Record,* 55th Congress 3rd Session (December 12, 1898), p. 129.

Chapter 2

Beginnings of Collective Bargaining, 1900–1916

1. Senate Committee on Commerce, 62nd Congress, 3rd Session, Hearings on H. R. 23673, *Involuntary Servitude Imposed upon Seamen,* pp. 666, 670, 672 and 852.

2. Paul Taylor, *Sailors' Union of the Pacific* (New York, 1922), p. 2.

3. *Coast Seamen's Journal,* August 14, 1901.

4. *San Francisco Chronicle,* July 30, 1901.

5. *Ibid.,* August 9, 1901.

6. *Coast Seamen's Journal,* November 6, 1901.

7. California Bureau of Labor Statistics, *11th Biennial Report* (1904), p. 66.

8. The latter claim was questioned, however, since it was reported that these shipowners had been paying dividends of 30 to 35 percent. *San Francisco Call,* August 5, 1906.

9. *San Francisco Chronicle,* June 7, 1906.

10. *Ibid.,* June 15, 1906.

11. *Ibid.,* June 15, 1906.

12. *Coast Seamen's Journal,* July 11, 1906.

13. *San Francisco Chronicle,* June 22, 1906 and July 14, 1906.

14. *San Francisco Call,* September 1, 1906.

15. *Pacific Marine Review* (January 1907).

16. Merchant Marine Commission, *Report and Hearings* (1905), p. 1341.

17. Committee on Merchant Marine and Fisheries, Hearings on H. R. 11372 et al. (1912), p. 418.

18. *Coast Seamen's Journal,* July 18, 1906.

19. I.S.U. *Proceedings of 12th Convention* (1907), p. 25.

20. *Coast Seamen's Journal,* June 24, 1908.

21. I.S.U. *Proceedings of 16th Convention* (1911), p. 139.

22. I.S.U. *Proceedings of 20th Convention* (1916), p. 126.

23. Andrew Furuseth, *American Sea Power and Seamen's Act* (1917), p. 9.

24. I.S.U. *Proceedings of 14th Convention* (1909), p. 10.

25. *Coast Seamen's Journal,* July 13, 1910.

26. I.S.U. *Proceedings of 15th Convention* (1910), pp. 35–37.

27. *Marine Journal,* October 16 and November 11, 1902.

28. *Coast Seamen's Journal,* June 17, 1903; February 17, 1904 and May 25, 1904.

29. *New York Times,* June 11, 1904. A strike was called in 1904, for example, but it proved unsuccessful after strikebreakers were brought in from southern ports.

30. *New York Times,* June 18, 1911.

31. *Marine Journal,* July 1, 1911.

32. *Coast Seamen's Journal,* September 13, 1911.

33. *The Longshoremen* (July 1912).

34. *New York Call,* July 29, 1912.

35. Senate Committee on Commerce, 62nd Congress 3rd Session, Hearings on H. R. 23673, *Involuntary Servitude,* p. 418.

36. *New York Call,* July 29, 1912 and *New York Times,* July 4, 1912.

37. *New York Times,* July 12, 1912 and July 21, 1912.

38. *New York Call,* July 27, 1912.

39. *Coast Seamen's Journal,* October 1, 1913.

40. *I.W.W. Proceedings of 8th Convention,* pp. 5 and 6; Paul F. Brissenden, *History of the I.W.W.* (New York, 1920).

41. Albrecht, *International Seamen's Union,* p. 116.

42. Greater success was achieved in establishing uniform practices relating to initiation fees and membership dues. The emphasis upon obtaining organization among all seamen, and in removing all obstacles to such organization gave the impetus to a concerted attempt to establish such uniformity. A subject of early concern was the variation among fees collected by the respective unions. Dues ranged from 50¢ to 75¢ per month; and initiation fees were generally $5, but those of the Pacific Coast Marine Firemen's Union were $50. In 1908, a policy was adopted restricting financial assistance for organizing purposes to those unions whose initiation fees did not exceed $10. By 1919, substantial uniformity was reported — dues were $1; and initiation fees were generally $5 or $10, with $15 being charged by the Pacific Marine Firemen's Union. *I.S.U. Proceedings of 7th Annual Convention* (1902), p. 72; *ibid., Proceedings of 22nd Annual Convention* (1919), p. 18.

43. *I.S.U. Proceedings of 16th Annual Convention* (1911), pp. 204, 208.

44. House Committee on Merchant Marine and Fisheries, *Hearings on the Seamen's Bill* (January 1912), pp. 182–184, 198.

45. *I.S.U. Proceedings of 12th Convention* (1907), p. 71; *14th Convention,* p. 48.

46. Furuseth, *Second Message to Seamen* (1919), p. 7.

47. *Coast Seamen's Journal,* August 6, 1902.

48. Text of agreement in Furuseth Papers in possession of Paul Scharrenberg.

49. *A.F.L. Proceedings of 22nd Annual Convention* (1902), p. 189.

50. *A.F.L. Proceedings of 25th Annual Convention* (1905), pp. 218–219.

51. *A.F.L. Proceedings of 28th Annual Convention* (1908), p. 256.

52. *A.F.L. Proceedings of 33rd Annual Convention* (1913), p. 340.

53. *I.L.A. Proceedings of 22nd Convention* (1913), p. 103.

Chapter 3

Andrew Furuseth and the Seamen's Act

1. Wilson letter to William B. Wilson, September 13, 1918 (Wilson papers).

2. S. Perlman and P. Taft, *History of Labor in the United States, 1896–1932* (1934), pp. 161–162.

3. Andrew Furuseth, *Equity Power and Its Abuse* (1917), p. 10.

4. *Marine Journal,* October 16, 1909; October 15, 1913.

5. Albrecht, *International Seamen's Union,* p. 71.

6. *Solidarity,* May 10, 1913.

7. Letter from Walter Macarthur to Ira Cross, March 13, 1935 (Macarthur Papers in the Bancroft Library, University of California).

8. Alvin S. Johnson, "Andrew Furuseth," *The New Republic,* November 11, 1916, p. 41.

9. Thus, under American law, the line operating the *Titanic* was able to limit its entire liability for the effects of the disaster to about $5,000, the value of the lifeboats which were rescued. *Encyclopedia of the Social Sciences* (New York, 1933), article on "Maritime Law," 10:128.

10. Andrew Furuseth, "The Decay of Seamanship," in the *I.S.U. Proceedings of 18th Convention* (1914), p. 80.

11. Andrew Furuseth, *American Sea Power and the Seamen's Act* (1917), p. 1.

12. House Committee on Merchant Marine and Fisheries, 61st Congress 1st Session, Hearings on H. R. 11193, *American Seamen,* 1:13 (1910).

13. Senate Committee on Commerce, 62nd Congress 3rd Session, Hearings on

H. R. 23673, *Involuntary Servitude Imposed Upon Seamen* (1912–13), pp. 542–543.

14. Andrew Furuseth, "The Decay of Seamanship," in the *I.S.U. Proceedings of the 18th Convention* (June 1914), p. 80.

15. Merchant Marine Commission, *Report and Hearings* (1905), p. 13.

16. House Committee on Merchant Marine and Fisheries, Hearings on S. 529, *Shipping Bill* of the Merchant Marine Commission (1906), pp. 110–111.

17. *Coast Seamen's Journal*, April 15, 1908.

18. *Coast Seamen's Journal*, August 5, September 2 and 9, 1908.

19. *Ibid.*, September 22 and December 15, 1909.

20. *Ibid.*, September 28, 1910.

21. House Committee on Merchant Marine and Fisheries, 61st Congress 1st Session, Hearings on H. R. 11193, *American Seamen*, 2:2 (1910).

22. *Congressional Record*, October 18, 1913, p. 5697.

23. *Pacific Marine Review* (February 1914).

24. Senate Committee on Commerce, 62nd Congress 3rd Session, Hearings on H. R. 23673, *Involuntary Servitude Imposed Upon Seamen.*

25. House Committee on Merchant Marine and Fisheries, Hearings on 11193, *American Seamen* (1910), p. 7.

26. House Committee on Merchant Marine and Fisheries, Hearings on S. 136, *The Seamen's Bill* (1914), p. 408.

27. *Shipping Illustrated*, July 27, 1912.

28. Letter from John Bassett Moore to Woodrow Wilson, October 16, 1913 (Wilson Papers).

29. Evidence of this altered situation was furnished by President Wilson's appointment of Furuseth as a member of the American delegation to the International Conference on Safety at Sea at London, in 1913. Furuseth interpreted the appointment as representing the President's desire that "the great body of seamen, the men before the mast . . . be represented at the conference in order that the hopes, aspirations and experience of the seamen may be heard there." However, Furuseth found little support for his views among the government and shipowner representatives attending the conference. He resigned from the American delegation when it appeared that provisions might be adopted which he deemed inadequate for safety at sea. He acknowledged that he might "in his ignorance have violated some of the rules or proprieties governing such a mission, but I had to follow my conscience. . . ." Secretary of Commerce Redfield charged Furuseth with having "failed to grasp the obligation of courtesy to you [the President] and through you to the people of the United States . . . that he rather regarded the matter as an opportunity to forward certain individual views and that when these views failed to receive full approval in some respects, he abandoned the general task for which he was appointed. . . ." Furuseth letters to Woodrow Wilson, October 29, 1913 and January 12, 1914 and Redfield letter to Wilson, February 2, 1914 (Wilson Papers).

30. *Congressional Record*, 63rd Congress 1st Session, October 21, 1913, pp. 5073, 5777.

31. *Congressional Record*, 63rd Congress 2nd Session, February 27, 1915, pp. 4807, 4819.

32. Letter from Woodrow Wilson to Furuseth, March 2, 1915 (Wilson Papers).

33. Letter from Wilson to Newton D. Baker, March 5, 1915 (Wilson Papers).

34. Letter from Furuseth to Wilson, March 6, 1915 (Wilson Papers). Senator LaFollette advised the seamen, upon passage of the act, that "The Fourth of March 1915 is your emancipation day. The Act approved by President Wilson makes America sacred soil and the Thirteenth Amendment finally becomes a covenant of refuge of the seamen of the world." To Andrew Furuseth, he paid tribute for "intelligent, courageous, and unswerving devotion to your cause for 21 years." LaFollette letter to *Sailors' Union of the Pacific*, March 6, 1915, in the *Coast Seamen's Journal*, March 10, 1915.

35. The qualifications set for able seamen on the seas were: age nineteen years or older, and three years of service on deck at sea or on the Great Lakes. On the Great

Lakes, the experience requirement was only eighteen-months' service. A further exception was made for school-ship graduates, who could obtain A.B. certificates upon examination as to competency after twelve months' service; however, school-ship graduates might comprise only 25 percent of the total A.B. complement required by the act. Public Law No. 302, 63rd Congress.

36. *New York Times*, October 21, 23, 27, and 28, 1915.

37. *Literary Digest*, December 4, 1915, p. 1270.

38. Proceedings of the American Academy of Political Science, New York, *The American Merchant Marine* (October 1915), pp. 68, 133, 119.

39. *New York Times*, July 9, 1915.

40. One ship which he kept in operation even after the passage of the Seamen's Act in November 1915, and even after he had received an offer of one million dollars for it, brought him a profit of $250,000 (the original cost of the ship) in a single voyage to the Orient. Moreover, on completion of the trip the ship was sold to Japanese shipping interests at a price in excess of one million dollars. House Committee on Merchant Marine and Fisheries, Hearings on H. R. 10500, *Creating a Shipping Board, a Naval Auxiliary, and a Merchant Marine* (February 1916), p. 244.

41. Article in Fairplay, cited in *Pacific Marine Review* (July 1915).

42. *Visalia Daily Times*, December 6, 1915.

43. *Pacific Marine Review* (October 1916).

44. *Marine Journal*, October 16, 1915.

45. *New York Times*, June 12, 1915.

46. *Ibid.*, July 25, 1915.

47. *Boston Herald*, July 3, 1915.

48. *Marine Journal*, April 1 and 15, 1916.

49. Proceedings of the Academy of Political Science, *The American Merchant Marine*, p. 15.

50. Statements by Gerard Henderson, editor of *Harvard Law Review; ibid.*, p. 76.

51. *Congressional Record*, 64th Congress 1st Session, p. 1197; Proceedings of the Academy of Political Science, *The American Merchant Marine*, pp. 15, 54.

52. *Ibid.*

53. Gerard Henderson, "Seamen's Law on Safety at Sea," *New Republic*, October 16, 1915, p. 280 and "Seamen's Law and World Wages," *New Republic*, October 9, 1915.

54. Letter from William C. Redfield to Samuel Gompers, March 7, 1916 (Wilson Papers).

55. House Committee on Merchant Marine and Fisheries, 64th Congress 1st Session, Hearings on H. R. 10026, *Amendment of the Seamen's Act of 1916*, pp. 128–129.

56. G. P. Sturgis, "Futility of the Seamen's Act," *The Industrial Economist* (April 1916), p. 28.

57. Andrew Furuseth, *The Seamen's Act* (1917), p. 25.

58. Letter from Woodrow Wilson to Samuel Gompers, February 29, 1916 (Wilson Papers).

59. Letter from Robert P. Bass to Woodrow Wilson, November 30, 1918 (Wilson Papers).

60. *Ibid.*

61. *Coast Seamen's Journal*, October 18, 1916; Andrew Furuseth, *American Sea Power and the Seamen's Act* (1917), p. 21.

62. House Committee on Merchant Marine and Fisheries, Hearings, *The Establishment of an American Merchant Marine* (1920), p. 275.

63. Robert W. Bruère and H. Blankenhorn, "For an American Merchant Marine," *New Republic*, August 27, 1919.

64. *Marine Journal*, November 23, 1918.

65. *I.S.U. Proceedings of 23rd Annual Convention* (1920), pp. 130–140.

66. *Pacific Marine Review* (August 1919).

67. Commissioner of Navigation, *Annual Report* (1921), p. 22; *Annual Reports*

(1916–1923). While the data upon which these statistics are based are not exhaustive, they are useful in indicating the trend in employment.

68. Senate Committee on Commerce and House Committee on Merchant Marine and Fisheries, Joint Hearings on S. 3217 and H. R. 10644, *Amending Merchant Marine Act of 1920* (1922), p. 285.

69. Dillon *v.* Stratheam, 256 Fed. 631.

70. Letter from Andrew Furuseth to Woodrow Wilson, November 16, 1918 (Wilson Papers).

71. Reply from Woodrow Wilson to Andrew Furuseth, November 18, 1918 (Wilson Papers).

72. *I.S.U. Proceedings of 23rd Annual Convention* (1920), pp. 57–61. Furuseth contended that "a super legislature" would be established which would "assume jurisdiction over the daily life of the working people throughout the world."

73. *Monthly Labor Review* (November 1920).

74. In the case of the Lake Carriers' Association, "minor changes" requested were elimination of the three-watch provision for firemen, especially for short trips; and inclusion of the right to ship certificated lifeboatmen where A.B.'s were not available. First Merchant Marine Conference (1928), pp. 15, 24.

Chapter 4

The First World War and After

1. Commissioner of Navigation, *Annual Report* (1916), p. 11.

2. *I.S.U. Proceedings of 19th Annual Convention* (1915), pp. 20–22, 43.

3. *New York Times,* April 16 and 18, 1916.

4. *I.S.U. Proceedings of 19th Annual Convention* (1915), p. 27.

5. United States Shipping Board, *Second Annual Report* (1918), p. 8.

6. United States Shipping Board, *Minutes,* January 27, 1917, January 9, 1918 and September 19, 1918.

7. R. P. Bass, *Supplementary Report to the Shipping Board,* December 31, 1918, pp. 2, 6 (S.B. Archives).

8. R. P. Bass, Letter to R. B. Stevens, December 26, 1918 (S. B. Archives).

9. *Coast Seamen's Journal,* April 25, 1917.

10. On a ship which formerly had 8 on deck, there would now be 6 able seamen, 2 ordinary seamen, and 2 boys. *Coast Seamen's Journal,* January 9, 1918.

11. The subsequent investigation disclosed that, while possession of the discharge book was virtually compulsory for employment during normal times, the vicissitudes of wartime labor shortages had resulted in some relaxation of this requirement, although men who had such books still received preference in employment. The practice of using the books as a blacklisting device against men advocating union organization appeared to have been discontinued during the war, but it was reported that its past history had created a continuing spirit of hostility which might impede the stability of essential operations during the war. In addition, the book continued to serve as a means of rating the men, and a bad mark made it extremely difficult for a man to obtain further employment.

The Shipping Board announced in November 1917 that the continuous discharge book should be abolished and replaced by individual certificates of service which should contain no rating of an individual's services. Since the Lake shipping season was almost ended for that year, it remained until the following season to determine how the Lake Carriers' Association would carry out the provisions of the order. With the opening of the 1918 season, it was soon apparent that the situation on the Lakes had hardly improved. The Shipping Board was advised that, while the continuous discharge book had been eliminated, a "certificate of membership" had been substituted which contained a pocket in which all discharge certificates had to be kept. The seamen regarded this as a mere subterfuge and as an actual continuance of the earlier system.

The association refused to attend the Marine Conference held in April 1918 on the grounds that attendance at a conference jointly with union representatives would constitute admission that the unions represented the Lakes seamen, a fact which the association denied. (A separate conference was held with the association.) The association's refusal to join with the unions in developing a system of recruitment and training, and refusal to sign the "Call to the Sea" increased the bad feeling. The unions again scheduled a strike to take place by July 29, 1918. During June and July, the board was to suggest, and then to direct, that the discharge certificate not be in book form and that it be the sole property of the seamen who were not to be required to deposit or display it at the time of employment. Within two days of the strike deadline, the Shipping Board announced the establishment of a Lakes training station and ordered the association to follow the example of the Atlantic operators in coöperating in the training of seamen. The association was also ordered to sign the "Call to the Sea," as modified to prohibit hiring through the association's assembly halls. The strike was called off. The "Call to the Sea" was finally signed by all the officers of the Association by October 1918. Paul F. Brissenden, *Employment System of the Lake Carriers Association* (Washington, D. C., 1916); *U. S. Shipping Board Report*, Marine and Dock Labor (1919), p. 25.

12. Both opposed operation by the Navy Department. Generally, the trade publications of the ship operators also opposed manning by Navy crews, although there were some attacks on the men furnished by the unions. Cf., *Marine Journal*, December 22, 1917; January 19, 1918. However, compare also with the view éxpressed in issue of June 8, 1918, favoring use of enlisted naval men.

13. Transcripts of Hearing, *Marine Conference*, April 29, 1918.

14. *U. S. Shipping Board*, Marine and Dock Labor (1919), pp. 184–186 for text of awards.

15. *Ibid.*, p. 40; George E. Barnett, "Trade Unionism and the Standardization of Wages During the War," *Journal of Political Economy* (October 1919), p. 680.

16. Memorandum from R. P. Bass to Board, November 2, 1918 (S.B. Archives).

17. P. M. Zeis, *American Shipping Policy* (Princeton, 1937), pp. 112–113.

18. *Pacific Marine Review* (January and August 1919); also *Marine Journal* (July 1919).

19. Letter from R. P. Bass to R. B. Stevens, June 12, 1919 (S.B. Archives).

20. U. S. Shipping Board, *Second Annual Report* (1918), pp. 79–82.

21. House Committee on Merchant Marine and Fisheries, 66th Congress 1st Session, *Inquiry into the Operations of the United States Shipping Board* (1919), p. 87.

22. Memorandum from R. P. Bass to Shipping Board, October 28, 1918 (S.B. Archives).

23. This resulted primarily from the loose organization within the Shipping Board, which permitted the Division of Operations to duplicate the functions of the Sea Service Bureau and of the Marine and Dock Industrial Relations Division. Until the Armistice, the Division of Operations maintained its own offices to recruit experienced men for ships operated directly by the board, and called upon the Sea Service Bureau only for inexperienced men. The staff of the Operating Division had been drawn from among the shipowning groups. The Director of the Division, J. H. Rosseter, was an officer of one of the few open shop ship companies on the West Coast. It was discovered during the summer of 1918 that the Division of Operations was manning Shipping Board ships on the Lakes completely through the offices of the Lake Carriers' Association. A near crisis developed, and the division agreed informally to call on the unions first, thereafter. Furuseth also charged that the Atlantic Agreement was being violated. To obtain conformance with the provisions of the agreement, the board issued instructions in July 1918 directing that preference in employment of deck crew members on Shipping Board vessels operating from Atlantic and Gulf ports be given to union members where they were available. These instructions were regarded as substantially conforming with the Atlantic Agreement. House Committee on Merchant Marine and Fisheries, *USSB Inquiry* (1919), pp. 65, 110.

24. J. H. Rosseter, Director of Operations for the Shipping Board appeared on behalf of the West Coast operators in opposition to Furuseth. U. S. Shipping Board, *Minutes of Proceedings,* October 29, 1918, pp. 38, 50–51 (S.B. Archives).

25. Thus R. P. Bass advised Henry Howard, director of the Recruiting Service, in answer to a query on the matter of furnishing marine labor in the event of a strike, against rendering such assistance for "in its practical application, I am afraid that this method of dealing with the situation would enable the operators to make use of your service systematically to break all strikes. . . ." Letter of January 3, 1919 (S.B. Archives).

26. H. B. Ehrmann, *Memorandum to U. S. Shipping Board,* June 24, 1919 (S.B. Archives).

27. U. S. Shipping Board, *Proceedings of the Joint Shipping Industrial Conference,* June 4–5, 1919, Washington, D. C.; *New York Herald Tribune,* July 3, 1919.

28. U. S. Shipping Board, *Minutes of Proceedings,* June 4, 1919 (S.B. Archives).

29. Letter from R. P. Bass to R. B. Stevens, June 12, 1919 (S.B. Archives).

30. *I.S.U. Proceedings of 23rd Annual Convention* (1920), pp. 28, 288–289.

31. Testimony of E. H. Duff, counsel, American Steamship Owners' Association, before House Committee on Merchant Marine and Fisheries, 66th Congress 1st Session, *To Promote Welfare of American Seamen* (1919), pp. 39–40.

32. Alvin Johnson, "Is Revolution Possible?", *New Republic,* November 26, 1919, p. 368.

33. R. W. Bruere and H. Blankenhorn, "For an American-Manned Merchant Marine," *New Republic,* August 27, 1919, p. 118.

34. *New York Times,* July 14, 15, 16, 17, 19, 21, 22, 1919.

35. Telegrams from R. B. Stevens to Henry Howard, July 10 and 11, 1919 (S.B. Archives).

36. *New York Times,* July 23, 1919.

37. H. B. Ehrmann, Report for Week Ending July 26, 1919 (S.B. Archives).

38. U. S. Shipping Board, *Minutes of Proceedings,* August 8, 1919 (S.B. Archives).

39. *Pacific Marine Review* (July 1920) and P. Taylor, *Sailors' Union of the Pacific* (New York, 1923).

40. Among the most emphatic supporters of these efforts were companies who boasted: "We can and do employ Chinese whenever we can get away with it with the unions. . . ." House Committee on Merchant Marine and Fisheries, Hearings, *Establishment of an American Merchant Marine* (1920), p. 489.

41. *Marine Journal,* September 18, 1920.

42. *Marine Journal,* May 20, 1920; June 12, 1920; August 21, 1920.

43. U. S. Shipping Board, *Fifth Annual Report* (1921), p. 13.

44. The first formal evidence of the board's nonparticipation policy was the announcement that the board would withdraw from the tripartite National Adjustment Commission for longshore labor on October 1, 1920. The Shipping Board's subsequent role in the longshore negotiations demonstrated the bent in labor matters which the board was developing. The board's director of the Marine and Dock Industrial Relations Division, Darragh DeLancey, with Admiral Benson's support, formulated a plan of coöperation with shipping interests in preparation for negotiations. Memorandum from DeLancey to Benson, July 9, 1920 (S.B. Archives); Letter from DeLancey to S. C. Meade, July 13, 1920 (S.B. Archives); Letter from De-Lancey to Department of Justice, July 15, 1920 (S.B. Archives; Memorandum from DeLancey to Benson, August 13, 1920 (S.B. Archives); Memorandum from Benson to DeLancey, September 2, 1920 (S.B. Archives).

45. Telegrams from Benson to E. E. O'Donnell, June 9, 1920 (S.B. Archives).

46. U. S. Shipping Board Press Release, July 27, 1920.

47. Memorandum from DeLancey to Benson, September 9, 1920 (S.B. Archives).

48. Circular Letter, November 1920 (S.B. Archives).

49. *I.S.U. Proceedings of 25th Annual Convention* (1922), pp. 32–33.

50. *Monthly Labor Review* (1921), pp. 430–431.

51. *Marine Journal,* February 19, 1921.

52. A split within the longshoremen's union developed, and a company union, the Longshoremen's Association of San Francisco, was established with the aid of the shipowners. This union, the so-called blue book union, was the only union with which the Waterfront Employers' Association was to deal until 1933. Cross, pp. 251, 255; *Coast Seamen's Journal*, June 7 and 21, 1916 and September 24, 1919.

53. *I.S.U. Proceedings of 24th Annual Convention* (1921), p. 134.

54. *Coast Seamen's Journal*, June 2 and 16, 1920.

55. *I.S.U. Proceedings of 24th Annual Convention* (1921), pp. 116–118.

56. *Ibid.*, p. 35.

57. *Marine Journal*, January 15, 1921.

58. American Steamship Owners' Association, *Minutes of Committee on Wages and Working Conditions Aboard Ship*, February 7, 1921 (AMMI files).

59. A Shipping Board staff member reported the association's revised position, as told him confidentially by E. E. O'Donnell, chairman of the Association's Committee on Wages and Working Conditions: "After conference with the Shipping Board on reasonable reductions they will submit it to unions for agreement with 30-day revocation clause. If unions decline, break would then follow. O'Donnell suggests Pacific coast matter be handled in orderly manner and that shipowners should show willingness to discuss their problems with unions meantime S.B. maintaining neutral position. O'Donnell thinks, however, that demand for 10 percent decrease not enough. Should be 25 percent allowing room for bargaining. That this procedure would better serve both coasts and satisfy public." The steps subsequently followed both by the Shipping Board and the American Steamship Owners' Association were very similar to, if not identical with, this strategy. Telegram from J. C. Jenkins to DeLancey, March 9, 1921 (S.B. Archives); Telegram from J. C. Jenkins to De-Lancey, March 9, 1921 (S.B. Archives).

60. *New York Times*, April 6 and 14, 1921; *Journal of Commerce*, April 9, 1921.

61. *Journal of Commerce*, April 26, 1921; *New York Times*, April 28, 1921; *Benson Statement*, April 27, 1921 (S.B. Archives).

62. *Pacific Marine Review* (June 1921).

63. Furuseth asked him whether preference in employment would be given first to American citizens and next to those who had declared their intentions of becoming citizens. To this, Benson replied that preference would be given to Americans and only to properly qualified declarants. Even this inadequate guarantee was opposed by the spokesmen for the private ship operators who opposed any hard and fast requirements, although they stated that they favored employment of American personnel on American ships. Secondly, Furuseth asked whether the 15 percent reduction applied to the base rate only, or to total earnings. To this, an unequivocal reply was given that it applied to base rates alone. (This reduction, then, together with the proposed elimination of overtime would reduce take-home pay by as much as 40 percent.) To Furuseth's inquiry regarding the continuation of three watches at sea on deck, Admiral Benson replied that this could be considered only after the wage reduction was accepted. On the fourth question, regarding continuance of permission for union delegates to visit ships, Benson stated that the demand "indicated a lack of confidence and a desire for interference, and that he did not see why leaders of unions should be permitted on board ships to interfere directly with the men employed there." *Pacific Marine Review* (June 1921); *Journal of Commerce*, April 30, 1921; U. S. Shipping Board, *Report of Industrial Relations Division*, Weekly Report of April 30, 1921 (S.B. Archives).

64. U. S. Shipping Board Press Release, April 29, 1921 (S.B. Archives).

65. *New York Times*, May 3, 5 and 13, 1921; *New York Call*, May 3, 1921; U. S. Shipping Board, *Report on Marine and Dock Industrial Relations Division* (1922), pp. 16, 29–32.

66. *American Marine Engineer* (July 1921), p. 25.

67. *New York Times*, June 15 and 17, 1921; *New York Call*, June 18 and 22, 1921.

68. *San Francisco Chronicle*, May 17; June 15, 30; July 9 and 21, 1921.

69. *Pacific Marine Review* (August 1921); *San Francisco Chronicle,* July 31, 1921.
70. *Congressional Record,* 67th Congress 1st Session, July 25, 1921.
71. A. Furuseth, "Mastery of the Sea," *New Republic,* July 20, 1921, p. 209.

Chapter 5

The Collapse of Unionism, 1921–1933

1. U. S. Shipping Board, *Ninth Annual Report* (1925), pp. 6, 190–191; National Industrial Conference Board, *The Merchant Marine Problem* (1929), p. 38.
2. "Report of American Shipowners Conference" in *Pacific Marine Review* (June 1925).
3. U. S. Shipping Board, *Thirteenth Annual Report* (1929), p. 6.
4. General Report of the Postmaster-General to the President, January 1, 1935, in Committee on Merchant Marine and Fisheries, 74th Congress 1st Session, Hearings on H. R. 7521, *To Develop an American Merchant Marine* (1935), pp. 1098, 1101–1103.
5. *Pacific Marine Review* (August 1921; October 1921; January 1922).
6. Nevertheless, additional efforts were apparently necessary to reduce turnover, for the operators of lumber schooners offered bonuses after six-months' continuous service with one company. *Pacific Marine Review* (January 1925).
7. W. S. Hopkins, "Employment Exchanges for Seamen," *American Economic Review* (June 1935), pp. 251, 254.
8. Senate Committee on Commerce, 69th Congress 1st Session, Hearings on S. 1079, *Continuous Discharge Book for American Seamen* (1926), pp. 32, 149.
9. American Steamship Owners' Association, *Minutes of Committee on Seagoing Personnel,* November 2 and 17, 1922; January 5, March 30, 1923; December 16, 1924; March 24, 1925 (AMMI records).
10. *Marine Journal,* July 23 and August 13, 1921.
11. U. S. Shipping Board, *Minutes of Proceedings,* June 28, 1921 (S.B. Archives); Letter from Furuseth to Lasker, October 8, 1921 (S.B. Archives).
12. U. S. Shipping Board, *Report on Marine and Dock Industrial Relations* (1922), p. 33.
13. W. S. Hopkins, "Employment Exchanges for Seamen," p. 255. IWW and the ISU attacked the company employment offices. The *Marine Worker,* journal of the Marine Transport Workers' Industrial Union, IWW, described the "Sea Service Bureau, Lake Carriers' Assembly Room, Company Employment Office, Fink Hall — whatever they are called" as "slave markets, where seamen are sold." However, the care of the slave was characterized as better than that of the "free and equal" seaman who "is left to starve or depend on uncertain 'charity' " if he is "left stranded on the beach" when shipping is slow. The physical appearance of the hall was described vividly as "dirty, bare . . . crowded with standing men — benches take up too much room, and the boss likes to see his hall packed to capacity with willing slaves, so the men must stand — a counter, a desk, and some blackboards — such is the usual appearance of a seaman's slave market. The crowd seems apathetic and resigned. . . . The telephone rings. The crowd becomes expectant. The agent gets up from his desk. The crowd begins to surge around the counter. The agent comes forward and announces what jobs are open. There is a rush and a scramble round the counter, each man trying to get his paper into the hands of the agent or to attract his attention. . . ." *Marine Worker,* April 1, 1924.
14. On reconsideration of the case, a district court decision found that the association was no longer acting in restraint of trade, and the Supreme Court denied further review of the case. *Monthly Labor Review* (January 1927), pp. 132–134; (December 1928), pp. 127–130.
15. U. S. Shipping Board, *Wages and Working Conditions Aboard Ship* (1921) (S.B. Archives); Shipowners' Association of the Pacific Coast, *Wage Scales and Conditions of Employment* (1921).

16. *Pacific Marine Review* (February 1922).

17. American Steamship Owners' Association, *Minutes of Committee on Wages and Working Conditions Aboard Ship,* September 28, 1921 (AMMI records); U. S. Shipping Board, *Report on Marine and Dock Industrial Relations* (1922), p. 17.

18. *Marine Journal,* January 7, 1922; *Joint Hearings to Amend Merchant Marine Act of 1920* (1922), p. 436.

19. *Marine Journal,* February 4, 1922; Shipowners' Association of Pacific Coast, *Wage Scales and Conditions of Employment* (1922).

20. U. S. Shipping Board, *Report on Marine and Dock Industrial Relations* (1922), pp. 22–23, 26–27, 58.

21. *Joint Hearings to Amend Merchant Marine Act of 1920* (1922), p. 436.

22. U. S. Shipping Board, *Report on Marine and Dock Industrial Relations* (1922), p. 3.

23. American Steamship Owners' Association, *Annual Report* (1924), pp. 25–26; American Steamship Owners' Association, *Minutes of Proceedings of Committee on Seagoing Personnel,* April 2, 1923; Department of Commerce, *Merchant Marine Statistics* (1924), pp. 59–60.

24. Letter from Secretary of Labor Davis, May 4, 1923 (S.B. Archives).

25. *Seamen's Journal,* June 1, 1923.

26. *I.S.U. Proceedings 31st Convention* (1929), p. 174; American Steamship Owners' Association, *Minutes of Proceedings of Committee on Seagoing Personnel,* January 21, 1927 (AMMI files).

27. U. S. Shipping Board, *First Merchant Marine Conference* (1928), p. 55; *I.S.U. Proceedings of 30th Convention* (1927), p. 18.

28. U. S. Shipping Board, *Annual Reports* (1923–1929); Commissioner of Navigation, *Annual Reports* (1923–1929).

29. *Congressional Record* 74th Congress 2nd Session, June 19, 1936, p. 10068; Senate Committee on Commerce, 71st Congress 2nd Session, Hearings on S. 306 and S. 314, *To Amend Certain Laws Relating to Seamen* (1930), p. 129; House Committee on Merchant Marine and Fisheries, 70th Congress 1st Session, *The Merchant Marine* (1928).

30. U. S. Shipping Board, *Third National Conference on the Merchant Marine* (1930), pp. 66, 76–77, 82.

31. H. S. Perry, "The United States Shipping Industry," *Annals of the American Academy of Political and Social Science* (September 1937), p. 93.

32. U. S. Department of Commerce, *Statistical Abstract of the United States* (1946), p. 542; R. H. Overstreet, *History of the Proposed Code of Fair Competition for the Shipping Industry* (1936), Exhibit 63-I (NRA Archives).

33. U. S. Shipping Board, *Report on Marine and Dock Industrial Relations* (1932), p. 42; memorandum from C. W. Sanders to T. V. O'Connor, October 26, 1932 (S.B. Archives).

34. U. S. Maritime Commission, *Economic Survey of the American Merchant Marine* (1937), pp. 44, 53; *New York Times,* March 10, 1935.

35. *New York Times,* September 30, 1934.

36. U. S. Office of Federal Coördinator of Transportation, *Hours, Wages, and Working Conditions in Domestic Water Transportation* (1936), pp. 52, 296.

37. H. C. Metcalf, *A Sound Employer-Employee Relations Program for the Shipping Industry* (1937), pp. 60–62.

38. *Seamen's Journal,* July 20, 1921; G. P. West, "Andrew Furuseth and the Radicals," *The Survey,* November 5, 1921, p. 208. The agreement also provided that seamen would work with union and nonunion longshoremen alike; this was merely a statement of the policy usually followed by both seamen and longshoremen. P. S. Taylor, *Sailors' Union of the Pacific* (1923), p. 143.

39. Furuseth's intolerant treatment of the dissident elements in the SUP was the subject of a gentle reprimand from Lincoln Steffens. "You should deal very patiently with the young and sincerely revolutionary group in the Seamen's Union," Steffens suggested; "You were handicapped the other night by your impatience, Andy. You

were too indignant to make your case count. I understood your impatience, I felt how you felt and I suffered so much I could hardly stand it. It has been a tragedy to me to see younger men trying things I have tried and found futile, but I have learned, too, that the way I learned is the way they are going to learn; by trying and failing, and so gaining a little wisdom, which they in turn will see youth ignore, despise and disregard. It's the way of the world." Steffens possessed a resiliency in conduct of which Furuseth was incapable. Letter from Lincoln Steffens to A. Furuseth, September 12, 1921 (Furuseth papers). *The Seaman* was published in Washington from October 1921 through January 1922. *San Francisco Chronicle,* November 22, 1921; letter from Furuseth to Axtell, December 29, 1921 (in possession of S. B. Axtell).

40. Letter from Furuseth to Axtell, December 29, 1921 (in possession of S. B. Axtell).

41. Letter from Secretary Davis to President Harding, May 4, 1923 (S.B. Archives).

42. *Seamen's Journal,* February 15, 1922.

43. Leo Wolman, *Ebb and Flow of Trade Unions* (1936), pp. 186–187.

44. *I.S.U. Proceedings of 25th Annual Convention* (1922), pp. 167, 179; *I.S.U. Proceedings of 29th Annual Convention* (1926), p. 38.

45. Furuseth left the American Civil Liberties Union because he refused to participate in any activities in defense of the Wobblies. He warned the seamen against consorting with the IWW on the grounds that: "America gave you freedom, and if you listen and agree to proposals that the American people have stamped as criminal, you become allied with those who advocate it and must take the consequences." For those seamen and longshoremen who were jailed under the criminal syndicalism laws of California, he could only say "They have made their own bed, and while we are sorry for anybody who is in prison, they must lie in it as they have made it." These views contrasted sharply with those which furnished the impetus for the enactment of the Seamen's Bill. *Seamen's Journal,* November 23, 1921, November 1, 1923; P. Taylor, *sup,* pp. 145–146; Letter from Andrew Furuseth to Roger Baldwin, December 26, 1922 (Furuseth papers).

46. *Seamen's Journal,* December 14, 1921; Transcript of interview between ISU Officials and Admiral L. C. Palmer, Emergency Fleet Corporation, January 25, 1924 (S.B. Archives); *Pacific Marine Review* (September 1924).

47. Senate Committee on Immigration, 69th Congress 1st Session, *Hearings on S. 3574* (1926), p. 40; House Committee on Immigration and Naturalization, 69th Congress 2nd Session, *Hearings on S. 3574* (1927), pp. 9, 13; *Congressional Record,* 73rd Congress 2nd Session, March 5, 1934, pp. 3736–3741.

48. Senate Committee on Commerce, 71st Congress 2nd Session, Hearings on S. 306 and S. 314, *To Amend Certain Laws Relating to American Seamen* (1930). It was also proposed to have seamen on foreign ships enjoy the full benefits of the Seamen's Act while in American ports.

49. *The Marine Worker,* March 15, 1922; March 15, 1923; April 1, 1924.

50. *Marine Worker,* April 1, 1924; Marine Transport Workers' Industrial Union, *Exposed* (1923), p. 4.

51. John S. Gambs, *The Decline of the I.W.W.* (1932), pp. 70–71.

52. George P. West, "Andrew Furuseth Stands Pat," *The Survey,* October 15, 1923; *New York Times,* April 24, 25, 26, 28, 1923.

53. *Marine Worker,* July 29, 1923, October 1, 1923; David J. Saposs, *Left-Wing Unionism* (1926), p. 157.

54. *Marine Worker,* April 1, 1925; October 1, 1925; May 1, 1926.

55. Marine Workers' Industrial Union, *4 Fighting Years* (1933); *Marine Workers' Voice* (November 1932, April 1933).

56. *Marine Workers' Voice* (April 1934); MWIU, *4 Fighting Years.*

Chapter 6
Resurgence and Disorganization, 1933–1937

1. The ISU proposals also included: wage increases, three watches for deck and engine crews, limitation of working hours in the stewards department, in port — an 8-hour day, half day on Saturday, no work on Sundays and holidays, and payment for any overtime work, prohibition of the substitution of workaways for crew members, prohibition of company hiring halls, and right of union representatives to visit ships.

2. American Steamship Owners' Association, *Minutes of Committee on Seagoing Personnel*, October 1, December 18, 1933 (AMMI records).

3. R. H. Overstreet, *History of the Proposed Code of Fair Competition for the Shipping Industry* (1936) Appendix, Exhibit 1 (NRA Archives). Both the ISU and the MWIU opposed the failure to grant recognition. Roy Hudson, appearing on behalf of the MWIU claiming to represent 12,000 longshoremen and seamen, presented similar objections.

4. Overstreet, *History of Proposed Code*, Appendix, Exhibit 2.

5. *Ibid.*, Exhibit 14.

6. U. S. National Longshoremen's Board, *Mediation Proceedings, op. cit.*, p. 92. In other Pacific ports, the employment of longshoremen was controlled by employer hiring halls.

7. Herman Phleger, *Testimony in Behalf of Waterfront Employers — Pacific Coast Longshoremen's Strike of 1934*, September 25, 1934, p. 11; National Longshoremen's Board, *Mediation Proceedings*, pp. 87 and 92.

8. At the mediation hearings before the National Longshoremen's Board in July, the MWIU presented a list of "approximately 800 names of men of various organizations, as showing us to represent them on any hearings. . . ."

9. P. S. Taylor and N. L. Gold, "San Francisco and the General Strike," *Survey Graphic* (September 1934), p. 406.

10. P. Eliel, *Waterfront and General Strikes* (San Francisco, 1934), p. 101.

11. T. G. Plant, *Statement on Pacific Coast Longshoremen's Strike of 1934 to National Longshoremen's Board* (1934), pp. 27–29. "No question of union recognition or collective bargaining is involved. The companies are ready and willing to deal collectively with the representatives of their employees . . ." reported one spokesman, "but the first and essential step is for the unions to show their credentials. The steamship companies will coöperate in the elections necessary to establish the facts of representation. . . ."

12. *New York Times*, July 15, 1934.

13. Letter from Robert F. Hand, vice-president, Standard Shipping Co. to American Steamship Owners' Association, June 14, 1934 (AMMI records).

14. *New York Times*, June 17, July 1, 1934; Eliel, *Waterfront and General Strikes*, p. 76.

15. Los Angeles Port was being kept open at cost of $100,000 a week for special policemen, watchmen, higher wages and "other items incident to meeting the strikers' challenge." *New York Times*, July 17, 1934.

16. The first NLRB was established on June 29, 1934, to replace the moribund National Labor Board. The National Longshoremen's Board and the National Steel Labor Relations Board were established on June 26 and June 28, respectively. *Monthly Labor Review* (August 1934), pp. 316–317.

17. *New York Times*, July 1, 1934.

18. *Ibid.*, July 4, 1934; Taylor and Gold, *Survey Graphic* (1934), p. 407.

19. *New York Times*, July 5, 1934.

20. Taylor and Gold, *Survey Graphic* (1934), p. 407.

21. *New York Times*, July 7, 1934.

22. National Longshoremen's Board, *Report*, pp. 11–12, 89; Eliel, *Waterfront and General Strikes*, pp. 134 and 139.

23. Taylor and Gold, *Survey Graphic* (1934), p. 411. This disinterested view is that "in 1934 the presence of Communists on the scene, and such influence as they exerted on men and tactics was seized upon to defeat aggressive, but essentially orthodox unions and unionists."

24. *New York Times*, July 18, 1934.

25. National Longshoremen's Board, *Report*, pp. 17, 18–19, 22–23.

26. *Ibid.*, Appendix. The American-Hawaiian Steamship Co., as well as the tanker operating petroleum companies, however, insisted upon elections to determine the appropriate representatives of the seamen. The ISU unions were victorious in all cases, with the exception of the Standard Oil Company of California where neither the ISU nor the independent unions managed to attain a majority. The Masters, Mates and Pilots' Association was certified among the licensed deck officers in all cases except Standard Oil of California and Swayne and Hoyt. The results were similar among the engineers where the Marine Engineers' Beneficial Association was generally certified.

27. The award for the steam schooners, which had traditionally maintained higher wages and better working conditions than other West Coast operations, set rates of $70 for able seamen, and $95 for stewards; 70¢ per hour for overtime, to be paid for work in excess of 8 hours at sea or in port and for all work in port on Sundays and holidays; and a premium of 25¢ per hour for handling certain unpleasant cargoes.

28. National Longshoremen's Board, *Report*, p. 36.

29. *West Coast Sailors*, April 22, 1938.

30. Letter from Robert F. Hand.

31. Letter from Seafarers' Council to R. J. Baker, June 14, 1934 (AMMI records).

32. Letter from Ross J. Baker, president, American Steamship Owners' Association to Ben Golden, executive secretary, New York Regional Labor Board, July 24, 1934 (AMMI records). Only the tanker operating members of the association indicated their willingness to meet with the unions; and they reached agreement with the unions on wage increases during August. *New York Times*, August 15, 1934.

33. The MWIU claimed that it had succeeded in establishing union control of employment through a union hiring hall in Baltimore for a period of three months. MWIU, *Centralized Shipping Bureau* (New York, 1934).

34. *New York Times*, September 21, 25, 1934.

35. American Steamship Owners' Association, Minutes of Meeting with Mr. Garrison, October 1, 1934 (AMMI records); *Marine Workers' Voice*, November 1934. The shipping industry was not directly under the jurisdiction of the board since no code had been established.

36. *New York Times*, October 8, 11, 12, 15, 1934; *Marine Workers' Voice*, November 1934.

37. *Monthly Labor Review* (January 1936), p. 11.

38. *Seamen's Journal*, January 1, 1935.

39. *Ibid.*, December 1, 1934.

40. *Monthly Labor Review* (August 1935), pp. 380–382.

41. Cf. Robert J. Lampman, *The Rise and Fall of the Maritime Federation of the Pacific, 1935–41*, Pacific Coast Economic Association, Proceedings of 25th Annual Conference, 1950. Lampman stresses the role of the federation as an "instrument of regional revolt" against the old-line leadership.

42. *Voice of the Federation*, June 21, 1935; January 30, 1936; March 17, 1938.

43. Benjamin Stolberg, *The Story of the C.I.O.* (1938), p. 190; *United States News*, September 20, 1946, p. 81; *Voice of the Federation*, October 31, 1935.

44. The charges against Lundeberg and the SUP which resulted in expulsion from the ISU included admission to membership of individuals belonging to organizations hostile to the ISU (i.e. the IWW) and strikes in violation of the 1934 agreements. *Seamen's Journal*, April 1936, pp. 134–136.

45. *Voice of the Federation*, January 30, 1936; August 13, 1936.

46. R. A. Liebes, "Longshore Labor Relations on the Pacific Coast," *1934–42* (1942), p. 196 (unpublished Ph.D. thesis, University of California).

47. *Voice of the Federation*, January 30 and July 23, 1936; November 27, 1935; June 14, 1941.

48. Maritime Federation of the Pacific, *Fourth Annual Convention* (1938), p. 128.

49. *New York Times*, May 31, 1935.

50. *Ibid.*, August 4 and 11, 1935; *Voice of the Federation*, August 10 and 23, 1935. During September the shipowners finally broke the boycott by calling in gang after gang of longshoremen for a period of two weeks, and discharging the members of each gang as they refused to handle the "hot cargo," finally forcing the matter to arbitration over the issue of alleged violation of contract. The boycott, which had been in effect for three months, was lifted when the arbitrator decided that the longshoremen were violating their agreement. *New York Times*, September 29 and 30, 1935; *Voice of the Federation*, October 10, 1935.

51. The seamen were preparing to demand wage increases, payment for all over-time work in cash only, and longshoremen's conditions for longshoremen's work (6-hour day in port and a 65¢ hourly rate instead of and 8-hour day in port and a rate of about 39¢ an hour). *Voice of the Federation*, August 23, October 17, November 27 and 21, 1935; January 5 and February 7, 1936; American Steamship Owners' Association, *Bulletin*, September 6, 1935.

52. *Voice of the Federation*, January 9 and February 6, 1936.

53. *Voice of the Federation*, June 4 and 11, 1936. The IUMSWA was permitted to retain its membership in the San Pedro District Council of the Maritime Federation of the Pacific.

54. *Voice of the Federation*, April 16, 1936; *New York Times*, April 16 and 22, 1936.

55. *I.S.U. Pilot*, March 13, 1935.

56. Temporary achievement of control by the rank and file in the port of Philadelphia and establishment of a union hiring hall ended when investigating ISU leaders found that "the Communists were in control of the port" and enlisted the aid of the police to clear the union hall of "all Communists and nonunion men"; *I.S.U. Pilot*, April 19, 1935; Atlantic and Gulf District, I.S.U. Report of Subcommittee (AMMI records).

57. *New York Times*, September 1, 1935.

58. Court Action was brought against officials of Marine Firemen's Oilers' and Watertenders' Union for alleged unlawful amendment of the constitution and resulted in a decision sustaining the officials on the grounds that they had acted under emergency conditions brought on by the "unlawful conduct and resulting breach of conduct of the plaintiffs themselves." *New York Times*, August 22, 1935; May 19, 1936. Appeal by a number of members of the three East Coast unions resulted in the establishment of a "Citizens' Committee to Investigate Conditions in Eastern and Gulf Districts of the International Seamen's Union," consisting of Walter Gellhorn, Sterling D. Spero, and Samuel P. Puner. One meeting was held, attended by about 380 members of the three unions, at which charges were brought against the officers. Letter from Walter Gellhorn to writer, December 9, 1947.

59. *I.S.U. Pilot*, November 29, December 20, 1935.

60. American Steamship Owners' Association, *Report of Seagoing Personnel Committee*, March 10, 1936 (AMMI records).

61. *New York Times*, March 3, 5, 6, 15, 20, 1936. The Department of Commerce subsequently retracted its charge that such a strike in a safe port constituted mutiny. *New York Times*, July 25, 1936.

62. *Seamen's Journal*, April 1, 1936.

63. *I.S.U. Pilot*, March 20 and April 3, 1936; *New York Times*, March 23, 24; May 2, 13, 16, 26, 30, 1936; *Seamen's Journal*, June 1, 1936. The International Juridical Association submitted a "Report on the Status and Working Conditions in

the American Merchant Marine" to Secretary of Commerce Roper on July 24, 1936. Among the members of the committee were: Bruce Bliven, Paul F. Brissenden, Walter F. Gellhorn, Amos Pinchot, George Soule, Dorothy Van Doren, Herbert T. Wechsler, and William McFee.

64. *New York Times,* August 20 and 22, 1936.

65. American Steamship Owners' Association, *Bulletin,* September 11, 1936; *New York Times,* October 1 and 2, 1936.

66. *New York Times,* November 1, 1936.

67. *Pacific Marine Review* (October 1936).

68. The companies proposed to hire longshoremen and seamen directly, wherever the unions failed to furnish suitable men, or where there were no union men available. The unions, on the other hand, were demanding continuance of hiring through the union hall, but were willing to concede to an employer's right to reject men if he furnished written reasons for so doing. They denied the likelihood that a situation would arise where the unions would be unable to furnish men, in view of the surplus of experienced personnel in ratio to available jobs. *Voice of the Federation,* September 24, 1936.

69. R. Bookhout, "Why We Struck," *Atlantic Monthly* (August 1937), p. 248.

70. Pending the outcome of the commission's investigation, the parties were informed, they "not only are requested, but they are also expected, to continue operating under agreements now in force. They are reminded that the first obligation of each of them in this emergency is to the public." *New York Times,* October 14, 1936.

71. *Voice of the Federation,* October 15, 27, 1936; *New Republic,* November 18, 1936, p. 61.

72. The six seagoing unions representing the licensed and unlicensed personnel bolted the inquiry, "refusing to be a party to the shipowners' evident attempt to convert the Maritime Commission into an arbitration board." While they were willing to coöperate with any fact-finding investigation conducted by the commission, the unions stated that they "clearly cannot recognize the Commission's authority either to determine any of the issues in dispute or deprive their membership of their legal rights for collective bargaining to determine wages, hours, and other conditions of labor. . . ." The commission finally withdrew from the situation, later acknowledging publicly that it had no authority to intervene in strike situations. *New York Times,* October 31, 1936; November 3, 1936; January 4, 1937; *Voice of the Federation,* November 5, 1936.

73. "Their strategy," announced a press report, "will be to fold their arms until business losses in coast cities, plus privation to thousands of wage-earners either on strike or laid off because of the strike, produce a public opinion favorable to strike-breaking." *New York Times,* November 1, 1936.

74. *Voice of the Federation,* December 24, 1936; *New York Times,* December 24, 25, 1936.

75. *Voice of the Federation,* November 26, 1936.

76. *New York Times,* October 29, 31; November 1, 2, 7, 23; December 1, 1936.

77. Letter from R. J. Baker, president of American Steamship Owners' Association to F. A. Bailey, November 23, 1936 (AMMI records).

78. *Ibid.*

79. *New York Times,* December 18, 1936; January 17, 1937.

80. *Voice of the Federation,* December 24, 1936.

81. National Maritime Union, Proceedings of Second National Convention (1939), pp. 477–478.

82. However, there was much dissatisfaction in the affected locals of the MMP and MEBA, and one local of the MMP refused to ratify this action of the national officials. *New York Times,* January 15 and 17, 1937.

83. *Ibid.,* January 25, 1937.

Chapter 7

Reorganization and Uncertain Stability, 1937–1941

1. Maritime Labor Board, *Report, 1940*, p. 252:

Strike year	Number of workers involved	Number of man-days lost
1936	49,215	1,361,021
1937	14,841	732,153
1938	8,471	54,551
1939	8,619	112,336

2. American Steamship Owners' Association, *Bulletin*, January 29 and February 12, 1937; *New York Times*, February 2, 3 and 19, 1937.

3. Senate Committee on Commerce and Committee on Education and Labor. 75th Congress 3rd Session, *Joint Hearings on S. 3078* (February 1938), pp. 866–868; *New York Times*, April 18, 22 and 30; May 6; July 20 and 23, 1937.

4. Statement by Vincent J. Malone of the Marine Firemen's Union, *Voice of the Federation*, July 29, 1937.

5. MMU, *Proceedings First Convention* (1937), p. 282; NMU *Constitution* (1937), Art. 19.

6. NMU, *Proceedings of First Convention* (1937), p. 86.

7. *Rank and File N.M.U. Pilot*, March 1 and April 22, 1938; *New York Times*, August 31 and October 11, 1938; *National Maritime Union, Labor Spies in the N.M.U.* (1946), p. 37.

8. *The Pilot*, June 2 and 16, 1939; NMU, *Labor Spies in the N.M.U.* (1946); NMU, *Proceedings of Second National Convention* (1939), pp. 55, 80, 383; *New York Times*, July 4, 1939.

9. NMU, *Proceedings of Second National Convention* (1939), pp. 162–164, 192, 225, 395, 407–408. The spirit of greater circumspection extended even to such a basic tenet of the union as equal opportunities for all its members, and for Negroes in particular. The convention reported that achievement of equality had been prevented by the crews as well as by ship operators. The leadership and membership agreed there was no immediate solution for this problem, and referred it to the National Council for the handling of particular situations.

10. *New York Times*, June 4, August 5 and 29, October 3 and December 8, 1937; *A.F.L. Seamen's Journal*, January 12, 1938.

11. *A.F.L. Seamen's Journal*, September 3, 1938; *Seafarers' Log*, August 18, 1939; *West Coast Sailors*, October 28, 1938.

12. *West Coast Sailors*, May 25, 1937; *Voice of the Federation*, April 22, 1937.

13. *I.S.U. Pilot*, February 23, 1937; *Voice of the Federation*, March 18, 25; June 17, 1937; *West Coast Sailors*, June 11, July 23, 1937; *The Pilot*, July 2, 1937.

14. *New York Times*, July 18, 1937; *Voice of the Federation*, July 15, 1937.

15. *West Coast Sailors*, July 30, 1937; *New York Times*, July 18, 1937; National Maritime Union, *Proceedings of Second National Convention* (1939), p. 154.

16. *Voice of the Federation*, October 14, 21, 1937; *West Coast Sailors*, October 15, 1937.

17. *Voice of the Federation*, January 13, 1938; *West Coast Sailors*, April 15, 1938.

18. *West Coast Sailors*, April 15, 1938. The NMU subsequently withdrew its claims to jurisdiction over the Shepard Line. *Voice of the Federation*, September 29, 1938. The SUP charged that an NLRB certification of the NMU on the ships of the Shepard Line was invalid since the SUP had a written agreement with the company at the time and had not been notified of the election. One of the company's ships was declared "hot" and it was met by an SUP picket line in San Francisco during April 1938. Bridges refused to recognize the picket line as legitimate and authorized the longshoremen to crash it and work the ship. SUP picket

lines against the company's ships in East Coast ports, however, were recognized by Ryan's ILA; but the NMU established counter picket lines. On the West Coast, Lundeberg received support from such AFL groups as the longshoremen in Seattle-Tacoma, who were thereupon locked out, the teamsters, the San Francisco Labor Council, and the Masters, Mates, and Pilots' Association.

19. *West Coast Sailors,* June 3, 17 and 24, August 28, 1938; American Federation of Labor, *Proceedings of 59th Convention* (1939), pp. 48, 395.

20. The unions included the National Maritime Union, Marine Cooks and Stewards of the Pacific, Marine Engineers' Beneficial Association, Federated Council of Fishermen, International Longshoremen's and Warehousemen's Union, Inland Boatmen's Union, and the American Communication Association.

21. *West Coast Sailors,* February 4 and 11, 1938; *Voice of the Federation,* April 29, 1937; Maritime Federation of the Pacific, *Proceedings of 4th Annual Convention* (1938), p. 108. Just as he had supported the NMU in the dispute involving the Shepard Line, Bridges was also to support the Ship Scalers and Painters in a jurisdictional dispute with the Sailors' Union during October 1940. *New York Times,* October 20, 1940.

22. *The Pilot,* March 28, 1941; *West Coast Sailors,* November 11, 1944. The NMU was successful in obtaining certification only in the case of the Union Oil Co.

23. U. S. Department of Labor, Handbook of Labor Statistics, 1:339 (1941).

24. Maritime Federation of the Pacific, *Proceedings 8th Annual Convention* (1941), p. 45.

25. American Steamship Owners' Association, *Bulletin,* June 18, 1937.

26. *I.S.U. Pilot,* May 11, 1937.

27. *New York Times,* October 15, 1937.

28. During most of the elections, the AFL failed to have any representative present despite adequate notice, "thus putting the government agency in the embarrassing position of conducting the election with only the rival organization present." Analysis based upon testimony of Elinore M. Herrick before the Senate Committee on Commerce and Committee on Education and Labor, 75th Congress 3rd Session, *Hearings on S. 3078* (1938), pp. 866–884; Maritime Labor Board *Report* (1940), p. 128; *New York Times,* reports during June 13, 15, 19, 22 and 25, July 7, 18, 22, 27, 29 and 30, August 17, 19, 20, 21 and 22, September 1, 8, 11, 12, 23 and 30, December 1937 and January 29, February 3 and 5 and March 17, 1938.

29. American Steamship Owners' Association, *Bulletin,* June 18, 1937; November 19, 1937; Testimony of Mrs. Herrick, *Hearings on S. 3078* p. 884.

30. *New York Times,* February 18, March 8, June 27, 1938.

31. AMMI *Bulletin,* November 4, 1938; *The Pilot,* September 2, 1938.

32. *New York Times,* May 18, 1939; *The Pilot,* June 16, 1939.

33. AMMI statement to Maritime Labor Board, October 16, 1939 (Maritime Labor Board Archives).

34. J. Curran, *The N.M.U. Forges Ahead* (1939), p. 30.

35. Maritime Federation of the Pacific, *Proceedings of Fifth Annual Convention* (1939), pp. 28–29; the proposal was rejected by a vote of 1256 to 984. *The Pilot,* September 19, 1941.

36. Maritime Federation of the Pacific, *Proceedings of Fifth Annual Convention* (1939), p. 21; *Voice of the Federation,* May 31, 1941.

37. *Pacific Marine Review* (April 1937).

38. *Ibid.,* June 1937.

39. *Ibid.,* March 1938. Roth was later appointed to direct the San Francisco Employers' Council, which was organized in December 1938 to "secure collective action by employers and groups of employers to the end that stable, peaceful, and harmonious relations between employers and employees will be prompted and established. . . ." Council's Articles of Incorporation, as quoted in Maritime Labor Board, *Report* (1940), p. 91.

40. Maritime Labor Board, *Report* (1940), pp. 182–185, 194, 250.

41. *New York Times,* September 3, 9, 16, 1938.

42. *Ibid.*, October 2 and 9, 1939; *Voice of the Federation*, October 5, 1939. In the negotiations with the Shipowners' Association of the Pacific Coast, operators of coastwise steam schooners, a deadlock developed between marine firemen and the ship operators. After a two-week strike, an agreement was reached without the firemen's obtaining their basic demand: overtime for Saturday work. *New York Times*, November 12 and 18, 1939; *Voice of the Federation*, November 9 and 23, 1937.

43. The Bureau of Navigation and Steamboat Inspection, charging that about one third of the certificates in the possession of seamen were counterfeit, recommended that these be replaced by continuous discharge books and that all seamen be examined thoroughly before being issued their A.B. certificates. An "Interdepartmental Committee on Shipping Policy" in 1935 included among its labor recommendations the provision for a Federal Maritime Authority to handle "the review and settlement of all maritime labor problems," along with broader responsibilities for improving the condition of the American merchant marine; determination of minimum wages for unlicensed personnel by the Federal Maritime Authority (such a minimum not to stand in the way of better wages and working conditions which might be determined through collective bargaining); study by the authority of maritime conditions; and a continuous discharge book. ISU and shipowner proposals were the sources of these combined recommendations. In House Committee on Merchant Marine and Fisheries, 74th Congress 1st Session, Hearings on H. R. 7105, *Merchant Marine Policy*, pp. 1115–1116.

44. Only under such a system, claimed Furuseth, is skill and good reputation recognized; "no private shipping office, whether kept by owners, unions, or individuals, has ever been able to keep itself honest and clean. . . ." Similarly he opposed schools for merchant seamen as failing to provide the training and experience which could only be obtained at sea. House Committee on Merchant Marine and Fisheries, 74th Congress 1st Session, Hearings on H. R. 7521, *Merchant Marine Policy* (1935), pp. 505, 540.

45. The Pacific American Steamship Association expressed its stand in terms similar to those which had received such a favorable press in the agitation over the Seamen's Act in 1915: "the Trans-Pacific passenger business will be handed over to Japanese and Canadian systems, because you cannot drive young American boys by legislation to become flunkeys." House CMMF, 74th Congress 1st Session, Hearings on H. R. 6039 *et al*, *Seamen's Legislation* (1935), p. 15; Senate Committee on Commerce, 74th Congress 1st Session, Hearings on S. 2582, *Merchant Marine Act* (1935), p. 186; *Congressional Record*, 74th Congress 2nd Session, June 18, 1936, p. 9916.

46. Statements by Senator Royal S. Copeland and Representative Schuyler P. Bland; *Congressional Record*, June 18, 1936, p. 9886; June 20, 1936, pp. 10569–10571.

47. Statement by Senator Hugo N. Black, *Ibid.*, June 19, 1936, p. 10068.

48. The Merchant Marine Act of 1936, Public Law No. 835, 74th Congress was approved by the President on June 29, 1936. The Seamen's Act, Public Law 808, 74th Congress, was approved by the President on June 25, 1936.

49. This labor aspect of the maritime legislation had hardly been debated in Congress prior to passage. There had been a last minute effort to pass a shipowner-sponsored amendment to exempt the stewards' department from the citizenship requirement, but it had failed. And for the first time, a serious attack had been made upon the continuous-discharge book provision; Representative Vito Marcantonio charged that its real purpose was "to establish an effective system of blacklisting of seamen who have exercised their rights as Americans by having gone out on strike for decent living conditions." The move was unsuccessful. *Congressional Record*, 74th Congress 2nd Session, June 19, 1936, p. 10068; June 20, 1936, p. 10572.

50. All outstanding able seamen and lifeboatmen certificates had to be surrendered within six months; new certificates of service were to be issued to able seamen and lifeboatmen who were found to be qualified through examinations by local boards

of inspectors. For the first time, unlicensed members of the engine department with a rating above that of wiper and coal passer were required to hold certificates of service and were required to pass examinations testing their competence to obtain such certificates. All other unlicensed seamen were to be issued certificates of service without examination, upon taking an oath to carry out all the duties required by law and to carry out the lawful orders of their superior officers on shipboard. All certificates of service were now made subject to suspension or revocation on the basis already applicable to the licenses of ship officers. Sec. 1, Public Law No. 808, 74th Cong. Unlicensed seamen were to be covered by sec. 4450 of the Revised Statutes which provided for investigation and hearing by local boards of inspectors when seamen are charged with incompetency, negligence, misconduct, or breach of discipline threatening the safety of a vessel or its passengers. If found guilty of such charges, the seaman could have his certificates revoked or suspended.

51. *Voice of the Federation,* October 15, 1936.

52. Senate Committee on Commerce, 75th Congress 1st Session, *Presentation of Demands of "Striking Rank and File" Seamen Relative to Continuous Discharge Book* (1937), p. 4.

53. Following the termination of the 1936–1937 strike early in February, there was continued unrest in the maritime industry. When the local inspectors of the Bureau of Marine Inspection and Navigation sought to carry out the provisions of the law relating to the "fink" books, both the West Coast seamen and the eastern militants refused to accept the continuous discharge books, and a number of ships were tied up by job actions. The East Coast rank-and-file seamen were forced to recede from this position, however, because there were enough ISU men willing to accept the books who could be used to replace them. A partial victory was won by the unions when court orders were issued on both coasts restraining shipping commissioners from refusing to attend the signing on of seamen who did not accept continuous discharge books. *I.S.U. Pilot,* February 9, 1937, February 23, 1937; *New York Times,* February 13, 14 and March 5, 1937.

54. House Committee on Merchant Marine and Fisheries, Hearings on H. J. Res. 121 and 143, *Continuous Discharge Books for Seamen,* 75th Congress 1st Session (1937), pp. 321–324, 368; Public Law No. 25, 75th Congress 1st Session. The act made it a misdemeanor on the part of any person, company, or corporation to require any seaman to carry the continuous discharge book as a condition for continuation of or for obtaining employment.

55. As described by Representative Bland, these proposals were clearly preliminary and exploratory in order "to secure a frank expression of opinion as to measures that will protect the public and, at the same time, do justice to all interests involved." Hearings were held on these proposals during May 1937. S. 1710 and H. R. 5193, 75th Congress 1st Session. However, these measures differed from their model in requiring that the representatives of the respective parties "shall be native-born or fully naturalized citizens of the United States." House Committee on Merchant Marine and Fisheries, 75th Congress 1st Session, *Hearings on H. R. 5193* (1937).

56. House Committee on Merchant Marine and Fisheries, 75th Congress 1st Session, *Hearings on H. R. 5193* (1937), pp. 23, 104, 107, 126, 132, 173.

57. Senate Committee on Commerce, 75th Congress 1st Session, Report No. 184, Part 4, *"Morro Castle" and "Mohawk" Investigations* (1937), pp. 3–5. Committee included Admiral H. G. Hamlet of the Coast Guard as chairman; Howard C. Cullman, Port Authority of New York; and P. F. King of Sailors' Haven, Boston, as public members; Paul Scharrenberg, D. E. Grange, and John Bley of the ISU as seamen's representatives.

The labor members of the committee indicated their general agreement with the report, but took exception to the views regarding the hiring hall and the Maritime Federation of the Pacific. On the former, they stated that the matter was adequately covered by the West Coast agreements; on the latter, they pointed out that seafaring personnel had participated in maritime federations for many years.

Howard S. Cullman, vice-chairman of the New York Port Authority and a public member of the committee, called attention to the fact that the report of the Personnel Advisory Committee left much to be desired. He objected strenuously to the report as viewing the "maritime personnel situation . . . from the ivory tower of the committee room" without "the vitalizing evidence of first-hand testimony, of direct contact with the issues and people involved." He questioned the impartiality of a committee which had included only ISU representatives, and he leveled the charge of superficiality against the report on the grounds that "without delving into its cause, the Committee laments the sad state of discipline in our merchant marine," pp. 28–31.

58. *Algic* Defense Committee, *Story of the Algic Case* (1937), pp. 4–5, 7. The committee reported that no individual performing "necessary" work had attended the crew's meeting which voted to refuse to perform the work. Only those performing routine day work attended; *New York Times,* September 11, 1937.

59. *New York Times,* September 13, 1937; December 19, 1937. The counts on which the men were convicted carried maximum sentences of five years' imprisonment or $1000 fine or both. However, nine men were sentenced to two months in jail and five men were fined $50. *New York Times,* December 21, 1937.

60. *Washington Post,* November 6 and 7, 1937; December 19, 1937 and January 16, 1938; Frederick Myers and Ferdinand C. Smith were listed as graduates of the Communist Party's marine school at Camp Nitgadaiget, New York. Somewhat less spectacular and widespread publicity was accorded the views of those who considered the charges against the maritime unions as being limited in grasp and prejudicial in intent. Captain Felix Riesenberg, who had served as an advisor to the Maritime Commission on labor matters several months earlier expressed this view as follows: "If you don't mind sleeping in a narrow bunk on a dirty mattress crawling into a dark hole deep in the afterpeak of a ship, over the screw, where the fumes from showers and toilets permeate the humid air; and if lack of ventilation or light has no terrors for you and you like to take your meals in a smelly messroom just off a hot galley, sitting at a narrow bench covered with soiled oilcloth and facing a blank wall not too clean, with a slovenly messboy shoving a plate of greasy stew over your shoulder — if these things please you and you are thankful for them and obedient, you are a 100 percent American seaman, a credit to the flag and to the United States. On the other hand, if you kick about such things, and if you take part in 'inciting to riot,' join in sit down strikes, and in that way interfere with the earnings of a cargo steamer, you are a Communist. . . ." Felix Riesenberg, " 'Communists' at Sea," *The Nation,* October 23, 1937, pp. 432–433.

61. House Committee on Merchant Marine and Fisheries, 75th Congress, 2nd Session; *Hearings on H. R. 8532* (1938), pp. 764–765.

62. Senate Committee on Commerce and Committee on Education and Labor, 75th Congress 2nd Session, *Joint Hearings on S. 3078* (1937–8), pp. 10–13, 968–983.

63. *Congressional Record,* 75th Congress 3d Session, Appendix, January 31, 1938, pp. 398–399; May 10, 1938, p. 6534; June 11, 1938, p. 8913.

64. Public No. 705, 75th Congress. The new labor provisions were added in June 1938 as Title X to the Merchant Marine Act of 1936. This measure stated that it was "the policy of the United States to eliminate the causes of certain substantial obstructions to the free flow of waterborne commerce and to mitigate and eliminate these obstructions when they have occurred by encouraging the practice and procedure of collective bargaining" and the prompt settlement of all disputes. The measure was clearly temporary and exploratory in intent, and was to expire in June 1941. To the Maritime Labor Board, with jurisdiction over longshoremen and seamen, was given the responsibility for encouraging employers and employees to enter into agreements and to settle all disputes amicably. The parties could call upon the board for assistance in settling disputes, or the board could proffer its own services as mediator. However, no penalty was prescribed for refusal by any or all parties to accept the board as a mediator. Furthermore, jurisdiction over questions of representation and unfair labor practices in the maritime industry was specifically reserved

to the NLRB. To the Maritime Labor Board was also assigned the task of submitting to the President and to Congress by March 1, 1940, a comprehensive plan for a permanent Federal policy for stabilizing maritime labor relations.

65. *AMMI Bulletin*, November 18, 1938.

66. *New York Times*, November 2 and 3, 1939, and May 7, 1940. Included among the charges were the following: While only 7 percent of the membership were Communists, 85 to 90 percent of the union's office personnel in New York were Communists; the Communist Party controlled elections in New York through a small bloc; the great majority of the unions officers were Communists or fellow travelers.

67. William McFee, "Sea Going Soviet," *Saturday Evening Post*, September 12, 1940; Charles Y. Harrison, "Stalin's American Merchant Marine," *American Mercury* (October 19, 1940); "Hitler's Plan to Seize the American Merchant Marine," *Cosmopolitan* (1941). Thus, where a "Maritime Commission representative" was quoted to the effect that "the use of a little emery dust could cripple the vessel and leave her helpless on the seas," the commentator failed to point out that there was not the slightest hint of sabotage among the charges against the unions. Again, federal agents were reported to be at work on the Atlantic Coast "following clues concerning a possible link between NMU officials and Gestapo (secret service) headquarters in Berlin." Harrison, *American Mercury* (Oct. 1940), pp. 138–139; upon a request by the NMU to be permitted to answer any evidence prepared by the FBI, President Roosevelt replied that the FBI had not undertaken such an investigation. NMU, *Proceedings of Third National Convention* (1941), p. 142.

68. Chamber of Commerce of U. S., *Committee Report on American Shipping Needs* (1940), p. 7. The Committee included officials of Matson, United Fruit, and Grace Lines.

69. The bill introduced by Representative Dirksen of Illinois also provided for continuous discharge books, control by the captain of the distribution of printed matter, and compulsory mediation for thirty days. House Committee on Merchant Marine and Fisheries, 77th Congress 1st Session, Hearings on H. R. 2662, *Merchant Seamen* (1941), pp. 37, 101, 142–146, 399, 404, 416–424. The bill provided that the government hiring halls operate with the advice of labor advisory boards regarding "the right and claims . . . of the various labor organizations."

70. Joseph Zisman, *Workmen's Compensation and the Protection of Seamen*, U. S. Bureau of Labor Statistics Bulletin No. 869 (1946), p. 57; *West Coast Sailors*, July 30, 1940. The Jones Act "gave the seaman the election between common-law and maritime rights. . . . Moreover, it made applicable in cases of personal injuries to seamen, the rights and remedies applicable in cases of personal injuries to railway employees — i.e., the removal or restriction of the employers' defenses." Zisman, *Workmen's Compensation*, pp. 29–30.

71. Testimony of Francis Walker, AMMI, before House Committee on Merchant Marine and Fisheries, 77th Congress 1st Session, Hearings on H. R. 5446, *Unemployment Insurance for Maritime Industry* (1941), p. 42; Gregory Harrison, PASA, before House Committee on Merchant Marine and Fisheries, 78th Congress 1st Session, *Unemployment Insurance for Merchant Seamen* (1943), pp. 48–60.

72. *Associated Oil Co. et al., and Sailors' Union of the Pacific*, 5 NLRB 893 (Cases R-477 to 481).

73. *Cities Service Oil Co. et al., and NMU*, 25 NLRB 12 (Case C-1270–72) in 6 *LRRM* 467–470. The Second Circuit Court of Appeals sustained the board's decision, but modified it to provide that the passes could be issued with a forfeiture provision if they were used as a means of collecting dues or soliciting new members. In 8 *LRRM* 540.

74. *Waterman Steamship Corporation and N.M.U.*, 7 NLRB 257 (C-375); *Peninsular and Occidental Steamship Co. and N.M.U.*, 5 NLRB 959 (Case No C-342). However, discharge of a union crew and replacement by members of a rival union was held not to be discriminatory where the employer customarily discharged the crew at the end of a voyage if the ship was to remain in drydock undergoing repairs for an extensive period, and recruited a new crew when repairs were completed.

The Supreme Court sustained the board's view of the effect of shipping articles on the employment relationship. *Calmar S.S. Corp. and N.M.U.,* 18 NLRB 1 (Case No. C-417-26 and C-428) in 5 *LRRM* 372-3.

75. Southern Steamship Co., 10 LRR *Manual,* pp. 544-553.

76. The members of the board were Robert W. Bruère, chairman, former head of the Cotton Textile National Industrial Relations Board and Labor Department conciliator; Louis Bloch, economist and labor specialist; and Claude E. Seehorn, former vice-president of the Brotherhood of Locomotive Firemen and Engineers.

77. Maritime Labor Board, *Supplemental Report* (1942), p. 18. The report states that the 25 "strike" situations involved a cumulative total of 8500 seamen, and the 15 "other disputes" involved 23,600 seamen, but it fails to furnish a breakdown of the numbers involved in the individual strikes. It may be noted, however, that the board was active in the 1939 East Coast tanker strike, which alone involved 4000. Maritime Labor Board, *Report* (1940), p. 39.

78. National Resources Planning Board, *Transportation and National Policy* (1942), p. 497. Maritime Labor Board, *Minutes,* September 20, 1939 (National Archives).

79. Lundeberg was reported as having refused to permit the board to mediate the dispute between the SUP and the steam schooner operators. Maritime Labor Board, *Minutes,* December 25, 1939, December 3, 1940 (National Archives). A Chamber of Commerce-sponsored report regarding "American Shipping Needs" in 1940 was reflecting the views of the generality of shipowners when it said that the board's record was "not impressive," and cited the Conciliation Service's performance as having been "energetically conducted and with a substantial degree of success." Chamber of Commerce of the United States (1940), pp. 11-12.

80. *Congressional Record,* April 21, 1941. In the hearings on extension, F. P. Foisie, on behalf of Pacific American Shipowners' Association and Shipowners' Association of Pacific Coast in Senate Committee on Commerce Hearings on H. R. 4107 (1941), pp. 53-54, stated that "it is commonly understood and believed that the Pacific Coast member [Bloch] owes his appointment to the influence of Messrs. John L. Lewis and Harry Bridges."

81. The bureau stemmed from two agencies which had for many years held jurisdiction over seamen as part of their more general responsibility for inspecting merchant ships. Within the bureau were the shipping commissioners (Sea Service Bureau) who, under the Shipping Commissioners' Act of 1872, supervised the shipment and discharge of seamen, arbitrated minor disputes, and maintained employment registers for seamen and shipowners who wished to make use of their services. The bureau's local steamboat inspectors had been responsible for the issuance of certificates of service to able seamen under the Seamen's Act of 1915. The bureau was abolished in 1946, and its functions relating to ship personnel were transferred to the Coast Guard. Reorganization Plan No. 3 of 1946, *United States Statutes at Large,* 79th Congress, 2nd Session.

82. Maritime Commission, *Annual Report* (1937), p. 93. Little stress was placed upon the thesis, appearing in the Commission's *Economic Survey of the American Merchant Marine* released shortly thereafter, to the effect that: "The shipowners themselves are in no small measure responsible for the present unfortunate situation. . . ." U. S. Maritime Commission, *Economic Survey of the Merchant Marine* (1937), p. 46.

83. A majority of the important maritime countries of the world had already ratified a 1920 draft convention of the ILO which had provided an indemnity of two months' wages to seamen on vessels lost or foundered. House Committee on Merchant Marine and Fisheries, 76th Congress 1st Session, Hearings on H. R. 4051, *Hiring of Seamen* (1939), p. 139.

84. New vessels designed by the commission were to provide for adequate messrooms; recreation rooms; facilities for berthing three or four men together on freighters, and not more than ten together on passenger ships; improved heating and venti-

lating systems; covering decks and crew quarters with moisture-proof material; and quarters behind the collision bulkhead, as a safety measure. U. S. Maritime Commission, *Annual Report for Period Ending October 31, 1937* (1938), p. 7; *ibid., Economic Survey of the Merchant Marine* (1937).

85. House Committee on Merchant Marine and Fisheries, 76th Congress 1st Session, Hearings on H. R. 4051, to amend section 301 of Merchant Marine Act of 1936, *Hiring of Seamen* (1939), p. 5.

86. Maritime Labor Board, *Report*, pp. 42–43. Admiral Land refused to join the Maritime Labor Board in requesting the President for an opinion by the Attorney General on the question, giving as grounds: "we do not think that under existing contracts, there is any doubt as to the status of these employees that would justify our seeking confirmation of our opinion that they are employees of the government." Letter from Land to Bruère, June 1, 1939 (Maritime Labor Board Archives).

87. *N.M.U. Pilot*, April 8, 1938; *West Coast Sailors*, April 22 and July 15, 1938.

88. *Maritime Commission* Press Release, July 11, 1939; *West Coast Sailors*, July 13, 1939.

89. *West Coast Sailors*, July 13, 1939; Maritime Labor Board, "Hiring of Seamen," p. 22 (unpublished study).

90. U. S. Maritime Commission, General Order No. 25, *Establishing the U. S. Maritime Service*, July 14, 1938.

91. American Merchant Marine Conference, *Proceedings* (1939), p. 45; *West Coast Sailors*, August 5, 1938; November 24 and December 1, 1939.

92. NMU, *Proceedings of Second Convention*, 1939, pp. 156–157; *The Pilot*, November 17, February 7, 1941.

Chapter 8

American Seamen in the Second World War

1. Clair Wilcox, "The Merchant Marine," *Fortune* (November 1944), p. 111.

2. American Merchant Marine Institute *Bulletin*, December 5, 1941.

3. *New York Times*, January 17 and 28, 1940; Joseph Curran, *The N.M.U. Forges Ahead* (1940), p. 8; Maritime Federation of the Pacific, *Sixth Annual Convention* (1940), p. 185.

4. *New York Times*, November 11, 1939; Maritime Labor Board, *Supplementary Report* (1942), p. 4.

5. *New York Times*, November 14 and 17, 1939.

6. Letter from R. S. Field to R. Bruere, November 16, 1939 (Maritime Labor Board Archives). The letter went on to state that: "Outside of the feature of legal compulsion to issue such papers, I am of the personal opinion . . . that it is unhealthy to permit any field of labor to close its doors to all comers merely to secure better economic conditions for those already in the field, bearing in mind the essentiality of providing for the future by having a continuous flow of youth into this particular field. . . ."

7. *New York Times*, May 1, 1940.

8. *The Pilot*, July 12, 1940; *Seafarers' Log*, July 20, 1940. Like developments occurred again in 1941; *The Pilot*, March 21, 1941; *Seafarers' Log*, March 25, 1941.

9. National Maritime Union, *Third National Convention* (1941), p. 116. An "emergency" overtime increase of 10¢ was also granted.

10. *West Coast Sailors*, February 11, 1941.

11. The NMU also succeeded in obtaining changes in the hiring and hours provisions for the stewards' department which brought these further into line with West Coast conditions. *The Pilot*, October 31, 1941.

12. *New York Times*, September 17, 1939. Sixty-one members of the crew of the *American Trader* were charged with "refusing to obey the lawful orders of the master." The charges were dropped after the NMU and the American Merchant

Marine Institute reached agreement on war risk bonuses. *New York Times,* September 19 and 21, 1939.

13. *New York Times,* September 21, 1939.

14. *The Pilot,* September 22, 1939.

15. *Ibid.,* November 3, 1939.

16. *West Coast Sailors,* May 3, 1940.

17. *The Pilot,* May 30, 1941.

18. *New York Times,* May 16, July 3, August 10, 1941.

19. *Ibid.,* July 23, 1941; *Business Week,* September 27, 1941.

20. *Seafarers' Log,* September 15, 1941.

21. *New York Times,* September 18, 19 and 20, 1941.

22. *Ibid.,* September 25, 1941.

23. *Ibid.,* October 5, 1941. The board also recommended that future disputes be decided by a Presidential Board consisting of three impartial members.

24. *Ibid.,* January 5 and 12, 1941; House Committee on Merchant Marine and Fisheries, 80th Congress 1st Session, Hearings on H. R. 476, *Seamen's Bill of Rights* (1947), pp. 379–389. The War Shipping Administration subsequently subscribed to the "Statements of Principles."

25. *West Coast Sailors,* May 15, 1942.

26. *Ibid.,* April 10, 1942; *The Pilot,* May 1, 1942.

27. *West Coast Sailors,* May 1, 1942.

28. *Ibid.,* May 22, 1942.

29. *The Pilot,* May 15, 1942.

30. War Shipping Administration, *The Merchant Marine at War* (1946), p. 64.

31. Herman M. Sturm, "Merchant Seamen During the Reconversion," *Social Security Bulletin,* February 1947, p. 20.

32. *The U. S. Merchant Marine at War,* p. 55. Between January 1937 and August 1941, about 366,000 men had obtained certificates or licenses in American civilian shipping, of whom some 250,000 were regarded as potential recruits. M. Dimock and A. Wubnig, "Maritime Industry during World War II," *Yearbook of American Labor,* 1:311 (1945).

33. Marshall E. Dimock, *The Executive in Action* (1945), p. 59.

34. WSA, *General Order* 17, July 25, 1942, as amended July 27, 1943; *The U. S. Merchant Marine at War,* p. 56.

35. Letters from E. S. Land to the NLRB, October 20, 1942 and from H. A. Millis to E. S. Land, October 26, 1942, in WSA, *Consolidated Bulletin C. Merchant Seamen* (1945, Appendix 1); Assistant Deputy Administrator for Maritime Labor Relations, WSA, *Summary Report, July 10, 1942 to November 2, 1945,* p. 34 (Mimeo).

36. Public Law 17, 78th Congress. No legislative action was taken on the question of extending NLRB jurisdiction to seamen in government employ. The Committee on Merchant Marine and Fisheries was satisfied that the agreement between the WSA and the NLRB "would appear to assure seamen the substantial benefits of the National Labor Relations Act without infringing upon the well-established principles that the United States as an employer is not subject to the National Labor Relations Act." House Committee on Merchant Marine and Fisheries, 77th Congress 2nd Session, H. R. 7424, *Merchant Marine Omnibus Bill,* Hearings and Report, 2572, September 1942, p. 17.

37. *Summary Report June 10, 1942 to November 2, 1945,* pp. 13, 19; *The Pilot,* December 18, 1942; *West Coast Sailors,* December 4 and 11, 1942.

38. *West Coast Sailors,* January 1, 1943.

39. *New York Times,* April 10, 1943; NMU, *Proceedings of Fifth National Convention* (1945), p. 101.

40. *The Pilot,* January 16, 1942.

41. NMU, *Fourth National Convention* (1943), p. 89.

42. NMU, *Fifth National Convention* (1945), p. 100.

43. *West Coast Sailors,* January 2, 1942.

44. *Ibid.,* May 1, 1942.

45. *Seafarers' Log,* October 29, 1942.

46. *Ibid.,* April 16, 1943.

47. *Ibid.,* July 16, 1943.

48. *West Coast Sailors,* December 10, 1943 and January 7, 1944.

49. *Ibid.,* vol. 7, no. 4.

50. *Ibid.,* April 13, 1945.

51. *17 Labor Relations Reference Manual 2621;* House Special Committee to Investigate Executive Agencies, 78th Congress (1944), pp. 1996, 1999, and 2021; *New York Times,* October 11, 1944; September 8, 1945; *Congressional Record,* 78th Congress 2nd Session, pp. 5027–5028.

52. *The U. S. Merchant Marine at War,* pp. 6–7.

53. *Public Law 87,* 78th Congress.

54. This summary of the USS is based on the full account which appears in Elmo P. Hohman, *Seamen Ashore* (New Haven, 1952).

55. *Congressional Record,* March 23, 1943 and June 20, 1946.

56. These are rough estimates. There were also minor earnings from port work and explosives and penalty cargo bonuses. Committee on Merchant Marine and Fisheries, 80th Congress 1st Session, Hearings on H. R. 476, *Seamen's Bill of Rights* (1947), p. 394.

57. WSA, *Consolidated Bulletin C.,* p. 27.

58. *Summary Report,* June 10, 1942 to November 2, 1945, p. 19.

59. National Maritime Union, *Fourth National Convention* (1943), p. 371. The action of the board in establishing nation-wide uniform wage scale and working conditions for licensed officers was cited.

60. NWLB Press Releases, July 4, 1944 and July 30, 1944 (B 1619 and B 1619A).

61. Cf. agreement between various general agents for the War Shipping Administrator and the NMU, July 15, 1944.

62. *West Coast Sailors,* January 1, 1943 and April 14, 1944.

63. Committee on Merchant Marine and Fisheries, 80th Congress 1st Session, Hearings on H. R. 476, *Seamen's Bill of Rights* (1947), p. 382.

64. *Ibid.,* p. 381.

65. *Ibid.,* p. 388.

66. This was with the exception of waters adjacent to the West Coast of the Western Hemisphere, where a bonus of 25 percent ($30 monthly minimum was in effect. This was increased later, on the West Coast unions' petitions, to 33⅓ percent ($40 monthly minimum). *Ibid.,* p. 384.

67. *West Coast Sailors,* March 31, 1944.

68. Voting for the continuance of the board were the Pacific Marine Firemen, the East Coast MEBA, the operators, and the WSA. Supporting its termination were the SIU, SUP, MMP, West Coast MEBA, and the Independent Tankermen's Association. *West Coast Sailors,* June 9, 1944.

69. Hearings on H. R. 476, *Seamen's Bill of Rights,* p. 383.

70. NMU, *Fifth National Convention* (1945), p. 29.

71. *Congressional Record,* 79th Congress 1st Session, Appendix, p. 3174.

72. *26 War Labor Reports 509.*

73. *Ibid.,* p. 511.

74. *Summary Report,* June 10, 1942 to November 2, 1945, p. 37.

Chapter 9

The Postwar Years

1. Postwar Planning Commission, Postwar Outlook for American Shipping (1946), p. 10; Clair Wilcox, "The Merchant Marine," *Fortune* (November 1944), p. 111.

2. President's Advisory Committee on the Merchant Marine, *Report* (1947), pp. 52–54.

3. National War Labor Board, *Termination Report,* 1:958 (1948).

4. *The Log* (March 1944), p. 70.

5. Wages and working conditions have remained uniform. House Committee on Merchant Marine and Fisheries, Hearings on Labor-Management Problems of the American Merchant Marine (1955), pp. 288–291.

6. NMU, *Second National Convention* (1939), p. 225; NMU, *President's Report to Sixth National Convention* (1947), p. 86. The latter refers to "average dues paying members" during the two years ending March 31, 1947, and apparently includes members on the Great Lakes and on the Mississippi River.

7. Maritime Labor Board, *Report* (1940), p. 85; *Seafarer's Log,* February 8, 1946. The data do not indicate whether inactive members were included. Fishermen and cannery workers are apparently included in the totals.

8. Maritime Labor Board, *Report* (1940), p. 84; *Marine Firemen's Reporter,* January 21, 1946. These data refer to active book members and permitmen only. By August 1, 1946, the number of active members had declined to 16,713.

9. Maritime Labor Board, *Report* (1940), p. 85; National Union of Marine Cooks and Stewards, *First Constitutional Convention* (1945), p. 32.

10. *Marine Firemen's Reporter,* September 18, 1945.

11. *Ibid.,* January 21, 1946 and November 3, 1947.

12. NMU, *Proceedings of Seventh National Convention* (1949), pp. 86, 138–139; *The Pilot,* December 10, 1948.

13. *Idem.* The claimed membership of the NMU and the SIU-SUP alone equaled the number of actually employed unlicensed and licensed personnel, plus a 40 percent shore reserve. "While a part of this obvious inconsistency may be discounted as due to overenthusiasm of the union front offices, there are more basic reasons involved. Employment opportunities in the maritime field have fallen so rapidly that many who still carry papers and, for all we know, who may still pay union dues, are no longer a part of the true merchant pool." National Federation of American Shipping, *Research Report 47-3, Maritime Labor Agreements* (1947). A portion of the discrepancy can be explained by inclusion of members employed on the Lakes and the Mississippi, and as fishermen and cannery workers.

14. On the Isthmian campaign alone, $250,000 was spent. National Maritime Union, *Proceedings of Seventh National Convention* (1949), p. 129.

15. The SIU organizing campaign began in 1946; the first agreement was concluded in 1950. Paul Hall reported that, in the Cities Service situation, the NMU "in the interests of legitimate trade unionism, and to assist the SIU in smashing company unionism, had withdrawn all interest in the case. . . ." Committee on Labor and Public Welfare, Hearings on Labor-Management Relations in the East Coast Oil Tanker Industry (1950), p. 14. The Senate subcommittee report found that "the antiunion efforts of the Cities Service Corp. followed three types of strategy, namely: (1) Delaying tactics made possible by the provisions of the Labor-Management Relations Act of 1947; (2) An extensive system of labor espionage, accompanied by discriminatory hiring and firing, and other unlawful acts; and (3) The organization and support of a company-dominated union, Citco Tankermen's Association, which was set up to compete for members with SIU." Committee on Labor and Public Welfare, *Report on Labor-Management Relations in the East Coast Oil Tanker Industry* (1951), p. 3.

16. Subcommittee of Senate Committee on Education and Labor, 79th Cong. 1st Sess., Hearings S 1349, *Amendment of Fair Labor Standards Act* (1945), p. 1289.

17. *Ibid.,* pp. 877–878. The Lake Carriers' Association presented similar arguments, pp. 988–990.

18. *Ibid.,* p. 863. The report of the subcommittee stated that: "The exemption from overtime pay provisions was retained, in accordance with the recommendations of the War Shipping Administrator, but the Committee was impressed with the urgent need to find methods of reducing, or compensating for, the unduly long hours

worked at sea and on inland waterways." Subcommittee of Senate Committee on Education and Labor, 79th Cong. 2nd Sess., Report No. 1012 on S 1349 (1946), p. 10.

19. House Committee on Merchant Marine and Fisheries, Hearings on Proposed Amendments to 1936 Merchant Marine Act (1953), pp. 302–337; Senate Committee on Interstate and Foreign Commerce, Hearings on Merchant Marine Studies (1953), pp. 1159–1165.

20. Industrial Relations Counselors, Inc., New York, N. Y., *Industrial Relations in the Ocean Shipping Industry* (March 1953).

21. See, for example, Statement of CIO Maritime Committee, Merchant Marine Policies, Practices and Problems of Labor Management and Government, presented by Joseph Curran, 1955. Also testimony of Harry Lundeberg, House Committee on Merchant Marine and Fisheries, Hearings on Labor-Management Problems of the American Merchant Marine (1955).

22. The associations were the American Merchant Marine Institute, Pacific American Shipowners' Association and the Waterfront Employers' Association. The qualifications were that the union Committee of 15 was to be accepted as a "negotiating committee" rather than as a "unity Committee"; and it was agreed that the demands of each of the seven unions, although taken up at joint sessions, would be considered separately. *New York Times*, May 29, 30 and 31, 1946.

23. The unique circumstances considered by the Board were: First, the necessity that the crew remain aboard vessels around the clock while at sea, working seven days every week; and, secondly, that wartime wage adjustments had been on the basis of a special bonus arrangement peculiar to this industry. National Wage Stabilization Board, *Release No. 61*, June 15, 1946.

24. *The Pilot*, September 6, 1946.

25. NWSB, *Press Release 90a*, September 11, 1946.

26. *New York Times*, September 13, 1946.

27. The Commission directed the operators that "we want our ships to move, stop quibbling and go to work." *New York Times*, September 21 and 22, 1946.

28. *New York Times*, October 27, 1946; Pacific American Shipowners' Association, *Story of a Strike* (1946); *The Marine Fireman*, November 21, 1946.

29. Three-Man Commission, *Report of Facts Leading to the Tie-Up of the S.S. Mello Franco at Coos Bay, Oregon* (1946).

30. *West Coast Sailors*, September 5, 1947.

31. *Ibid.*, September 19, 1947.

32. *Ibid.*, October 7, 1947.

33. Presidential Board of Inquiry, *Minutes of West Coast Hearings* (June 1948), pp. 244–246.

34. *West Coast Sailors*, November 14, 1947.

35. *New York Times*, December 6, 1947.

36. *Pacific Coast Maritime Report*, April 20, 1948; *West Coast Sailors*, April 16, 1948.

37. Presidential Board of Inquiry, *Minutes of East Coast Hearings*, June 7, 1948, p. 99; *New York Times*, July 14, 1948. The East Coast tanker operators, however, extended their agreement with the NMU until 1950, including the union preference clause, and providing for an increase of $5 per month.

38. *New York Times*, June 20 and 24, 1948.

39. The NLRB found that the current operation of the hiring hall violated the Taft-Hartley Act, *New York Times*, August 19 and 21, 1948. During August the SIU had obtained an agreement upon increases of $25 per month to boatswains and $12.50 for all other ratings. The NMU was now able to obtain wage increases which would equalize NMU and SIU rates. The *New York Times* viewed the negotiations leading to this settlement as involving "fumbling and stalling all along the way, with the operators largely responsible," since an earlier settlement could have been achieved with substantially less concessions.

40. Board of Inquiry, *Final Report to the President on Labor Disputes in the Maritime Industry* (August 13, 1948), pp. 25–26.

41. The board reported that the employers "appear also to be dissatisfied with the current hiring practices apart from the question of law." *Ibid.*, p. 29.

42. *New York Times*, October 15, 1948. Only in the case of the independent Marine Firemen's Union, whose officials had filed the non-Communist affidavits, were the shipowners willing to offer a separate peace. However, when Vincent Malone, president of that union, made a counterproposal that operating representatives of the companies negotiate with rank-and-file representatives of all the striking unions, his proposal was rejected. A Bridges' proposal to withdraw from negotiations, leaving their conduct to a rank-and-file committee, was also rejected. *New York Times*, September 27, 29; October 19 and 20, 1948.

43. *The Pilot*, September 10, 1948.

44. The operators did offer to make arrangements with the Army "to supply gear, equipment and administrative personnel to handle its cargoes" if the Army requested. *New York Times*, September 12, 1948.

45. *West Coast Sailors*, November 12, 1948; *New York Times*, November 8, 1948.

46. *New York Times*, November 26, 1948.

47. *West Coast Sailors*, November 12, 1948.

48. To implement these intentions, shipowners, stevedoring contractors and ILWU representatives met in a two-day session in 1949 to explore "areas of mutual interest" to increase maritime work opportunities on the West Coast. *New York Times*, January 25, March 8, 1949; *The Dispatcher*, March 18, 1949. Clark Kerr and Lloyd Fisher, "Conflict on the Waterfront," *Atlantic Monthly* (September 1949).

49. Cf. Federal Mediation and Conciliation Service, *9th Annual Report* (1956), pp. 21–25; Betty V. H. Schneider and A. Siegel, *Industrial Relations in the Pacific Coast Longshore Industry* (Berkeley, 1956), pp. 77–86; Pacific Maritime Association, *Annual Reports*.

50. The board majority noted the virtual straight time rate of overtime pay, as contrasted with the general industry practice of a 40-hour week with time and a half for overtime. Wage Stabilization Board, *Release WSB-111* (September 19, 1951).

51. The basis for the board's action could only have been that the total effect of the increases would produce earnings consistent with those under the 40-hour week of the other maritime. However, in the earlier case, the board had stated it was acting on the "basis of wage and salary rates and not upon take home pay."

52. Seafarers' International Union, *Sixth Biennial Convention* (1953), pp. 78, 80, 81, 83. The view that concessions were deliberately given to the SUP prior to 1948 is suggested in W. Gorter and G. Hildebrand, *The Pacific Coast Maritime Industry*, 2 vols. (1952–1954).

53. Paul St. Sure, president of the PMA stated that: "As many as fifty work stoppages were recorded in the Bay area in April and May before the strike began," because the sailors demanded that the shipowners follow the letter of the contract requiring the PMA to take work from other unions that had been doing it for years. *New York Times*, July 18, 1952. The scope of work issue between the sailors and longshoremen on the West Coast persisted through the entire period. For discussion of the C-Trader dispute of 1950 see Seafarers' International Union, *Proceedings of Fifth Biennial Convention* (1951), pp. 88–89; the SUP position on the role of sailor's work in the 1952 strike is described in Senate Interstate and Foreign Commerce Committee, *Hearings on Merchant Marine Studies* (1953), pp. 1120–1128; the Pacificus dispute of 1954–1955 is described in House Committee on Merchant Marine and Fisheries, *Hearings on Labor-Management Problems*, 1955, pp. 43–48.

54. *Marine Firemen*, July 8, 1952.

55. By Aaron Horvitz, *New York Times*, November 14, 1952.

56. House Committee on Merchant Marine and Fisheries, *Hearings on Labor-Management Relations Problems of the American Merchant Marine* (1955).

57. *The Pilot,* June 23, 1955; *New York Times,* June 17, 18 and 22, 1955.

58. *West Coast Sailors,* September 16, 1955.

59. *West Coast Sailors,* November 25, 1955.

60. House Committee on Education and Labor, 80th Cong. 1st Sess., Hearings on *Amendment to the National Labor Relations Act* (1947), pp. 543–573.

61. *Ibid.,* p. 575. "Each company would need to deal with an independent union that dealt with it alone," he pointed out, and "full compliance with the law would lead to variations in wage rates and working conditions."

62. Senate Committee on Labor and Public Welfare, 80th Cong. 1st Sess., Hearings on S. 55 and S. J. Res. 22, *Labor Relations Program* (1947), pp. 606–607. Roth summed up his testimony as follows: "We believe the most stabilizing influence that can be brought to bear on industrial relations are a few unsuccessful strikes coupled with legislation to guarantee contract compliance and union responsibility, and to eliminate recognition and jurisdictional strikes, secondary boycotts and the sympathetic work stoppages." House Committee on Education and Labor, Hearings on *Amendment to the National Labor Relations Act,* p. 576.

63. National Maritime Union, 78 NLRB 971; National Maritime Union, 92 NLRB 1365; ARA, 92 NLRB 1344; Pacific Maritime Association, 89 NLRB 894.

64. Senate Committee on Labor and Public Welfare, Hearings on Hiring Halls in the Maritime Industry (1950), pp. 46–48.

65. *Ibid.,* p. 569.

66. Senate Committee on Labor and Public Welfare, Hearings on Taft-Hartley Act Revisions (1953), pp. 2573–2574.

67. *Ibid.,* p. 3147.

68. This followed discussions with Senator Robert Taft, co-author of the Taft-Hartley Act, *New York Times,* September 21, 1947.

69. Senate Committee on Labor and Public Welfare, Hearings on the Hiring Hall (1950), p. 169. Senator Taft commented on the decision in the Lakes NMU case as follows: "As far as this clause (the SUP clause) I do not believe this clause would ever be held illegal, but this opinion suggests that operations under it may in some way be held to be illegal." *Ibid.*

70. The SIU-A and G agreements, however, did not contain the industry seniority arrangement; they stated "It is specifically understood and agreed that membership in the union shall not be a condition of employment. . . ."

71. House Committee on Education and Labor, Hearings on Labor Relations Act (1953), p. 1466.

72. Second preference went to those who had sailed on company ships after June 1948, and last to those who had sailed on any American-flag vessel since that date.

73. This action was accompanied by a decision of the union administration to open membership to those meeting the union requirements. To charges that this would "flood" the union, Curran subsequently reported that between 1954 and early 1956 "fewer than 500 books" were issued; and that 3500 applications were pending. NMU *Pilot,* March 29, 1956.

74. In the case of ratings above the entry ratings, since before 1952, and up through 1954.

75. The Marine Engineers' Beneficial Association has recently disaffiliated over tactical differences with the NMU on dealing with the newly-organized American Coal Shipping Co. It has also concluded a no-raiding pact with the rival Brotherhood of Marine Engineers, *New York Times,* December 4, 1952.

76. *The Pilot,* November 23, 1945. There had been differences between the Curran group and the left-wing group on several administrative and constitutional proposals at the 1945 convention, NMU, *Fifth National Convention* (1945), pp. 35, 329. Curran has charged that Bridges proposed to extend the wartime no-strike policy into the postwar period, and that acceptance of this proposal would have undermined the militancy of the seamen's unions and threatened their existence. NMU, Sixth National Convention, 1947, pp. 292–293.

77. *New York Times,* January 14, 1946.

78. *Ibid.,* February 7, 1946; *The Pilot,* February 8, 1946.

79. *The Marine Fireman,* March 18, 1946.

80. *New York Times,* June 3, 1946.

81. *The Pilot,* June 15 and September 27, 1946.

82. *Ibid.,* August 24, 1946; *The Marine Fireman,* February 15, 1947.

83. *The Pilot,* June 20, 1947. The Marine Cooks and Stewards had held out in negotiations and struck on June 16, charging an employer lockout. This tactic enabled one left-wing-dominated union on the West Coast to lay claim to having showed militancy, and to having won increases for themselves, albeit first won by the NMU. *Voice of the Marine Cooks and Stewards,* June 26, 1947.

84. *The Pilot,* May 10, 1946; *New York Times,* May 7, 8, 9 and 12, 1946.

85. During the strike involving the International Longshoremen's Association in October 1945, the SIU-SUP supported Ryan to prevent the "NMU, MFOWW and MCS and other non-maritime communists" from prolonging the longshoremen's strike. *Seafarer's Log,* October 19, 1945. The CIO and independent unions sought to help the groups within the ILA who opposed Ryan, but denied any intention of raiding the ILA. *New York Times,* October 16, 1945.

86. Joseph Ryan of the ILA was its president. SIU, *Proceedings of First Convention* (1942); p. 140; *Seafarer's Log,* May 24, August 23, 1946; *New York Times,* July 29 and August 17, 1946.

87. NMU *Pilot,* March 23, 1950; Seafarers' International Union of North America, *Proceedings of Fifth Biennial Convention* (1951).

88. *West Coast Sailors,* March 24, 1950; NMU *Pilot,* March 23, 1950. On flag transfers, the Senate Committee on Interstate and Foreign Commerce, Merchant Marine Study and Investigation, 1950, made the distinction between investment of American capital in foreign industry and in a steamship line "operating out of Panama" — in that "a steamship operation domiciled in a nation whose reliance on foreign trade and shipping plays a minor role, does not generally constitute the type of investment which lends itself toward any significant contribution to the dollar position of such nonmaritime nations." The report also stated: "Reduced to its simplest terms, the testimony revealed that such transfers are for the purpose of avoiding the higher cost of American seagoing labor, the high safety standards required by American law, the higher rate of taxation on certain phases of steamship operations exacted by the American Treasury, and to avoid the 50 percent duty on any repairs performed in foreign shipyards. . . ." pp. 65–6.

The maritime unions have opposed the trade-out and build program of the Maritime Administration, which requires the building of new ships in American yards as a condition for immediate transfer. It is held that the terms of transfer require such ships to be "available" to the U. S. in the event of an emergency. The unions point to the immediate loss of jobs, and to the competitive disadvantage created for American flag ships. NMU *Pilot,* November 8, 1956.

The unions of the traditional maritime countries, including the American seafaring unions, have sought to meet the problem of the Liberian and Panamanian fleets through an organizing drive by the International Transportworkers' Federation. *West Coast Sailors,* September 28, 1956.

89. NMU *Pilot,* August 24, 1950.

90. In the early stages, the SIU charged that "the Coast Guard is more interested in getting rid of militant union men than of the Commies." Seafarers' International Union of North America, *Proceedings of Fifth Biennial Convention* (1951), p. 33. See *Seafarer's Log,* January 1, 1952, for later participation. Court decisions in 1955 and 1956 required the accused seaman to be confronted by his accuser. The Coast Guard held that this had caused a breakdown of the program. The screening program went over some 300,000 seamen, longshoremen and other waterfront workers between 1950 and 1957, and resulted in barring 1800. *Seafarer's Log,* March 15, 1957.

91. *West Coast Sailors,* April 20, 1951; Federal Maritime Board, *Annual Report* (1951), p. 52.

92. *New York Times,* January 20, 1954. The Military Sea Transportation Service was organized in 1949 to combine all the military sea transport service. Both the unions and ship operators have charged it with encroaching on commercial operations. In 1955, the MSTS was operating 287 vessels, with 11,000 civilian marine employees covered by civil service. The Defense Department has opposed attempts to make MSTS "in the status of an auxiliary to the private shipping industry." *Journal of Commerce,* March 16, 1956.

93. *Journal of Commerce,* January 28, 1954; *The Pilot,* April 15 and May 27, 1954.

94. The Labor-Management Maritime Committee, established in 1950 by the CIO unions and six subsidized operators, continued.

95. *New York Times,* March 22, 1955. Lundeberg indicated that the union would take up the slack between what the operators could pay and what the seamen normally earned. *New York Times,* March 21, 1955.

96. Seafarers' International Union of North America, *Proceedings of 7th Biennial Convention* (1955), p. 42.

97. *The Pilot,* March 15, 1956.

98. *The Pilot,* July 5, 1946.

99. He estimated the NMU membership at 90,000. *The Pilot,* December 27, 1947.

100. *Idem.* This argument was intended to justify the action of the left-wing members of the committee in recommending acceptance of the operators' offer of $12.50 per month increase, which was subsequently rejected by the membership.

101. *New York Times,* January 5, 1947.

102. *The Pilot,* January 14, 1947.

103. *Ibid.,* February 4, 1947; *Voice of Marine Cooks and Stewards,* February 20, 1947.

104. *Voice of the Marine Cooks and Stewards,* June 26, 1947.

105. *The Pilot,* July 11, 1947.

106. NMU, *Proceedings of the Sixth Constitutional Convention* (1947), pp. 468, 481 and 492.

107. *The Pilot,* July 30, 1948.

108. *The Pilot,* September 3, 1948.

109. The required two-thirds vote could not be obtained; the vote was 404 for the amendment, with 216 opposed.

110. A full account of the insurgent movement is provided in Philip Taft, *The Structure and Government of Trade Unions* (Cambridge, 1954), pp. 202–205.

111. NMU *Pilot,* January 11, 1951, the vote was 10,394 for and 1613 opposed.

112. See J. A. Sullivan, *Red Sails on Great Lakes* (1955), for description of Communist infiltration into the Canadian Seamen's Union by former president.

113. Seafarers' International Union, *Proceedings of Fifth Biennial Convention* (1951), pp. 86–87; *Sixth Biennial Convention* (1953), p. 73; Philip Taft, *Structure and Government,* pp. 209–212; Donald H. Wollett and Robert J. Lampman, "The Law of Union Factionalism — The Case of the Sailors," *Stanford Law Review* (February 1952), pp. 177–214.

114. *West Coast Sailors,* February 16, 1951.

115. 90 NLRB 1099.

116. *Seafarer's Log,* February 5, 1954.

117. The ILWU and the NUMCS moved to dismiss the SIU petition on the basis of alleged discriminatory membership policies against Negroes by the MFW and the SUP. The board's opinion states: "Even assuming such discrimination has existed in the past as alleged in the offer of proof, the board has no express authority to pass on eligibility requirements for membership in a labor organization." It indicated that it would police its certification to ensure representation of all employees in the unit. 110 NLRB No. 254.

118. Accounts of the demise of the NUMCS appear in June C. Record, "The

Rise and Fall of a Maritime Union," *Industrial and Labor Relations Review* (October 1956), pp. 81–92; Seafarers' International Union of North America, *Proceedings of 7th Biennial Convention* (1955), pp. 20–23; Senate Committee on Labor and Public Welfare, *The Marine Cooks and Stewards' Union* (1953). The NUMCS view appears in Senate Committee on Interstate and Foreign Commerce, *Merchant Marine Studies* (1953), pp. 1044–1056.

Chapter 10

An Analytical Commentary

1. Lloyd Ulman, *Rise of the National Trade Union* (1955), p. 67.

2. The Atlantic and Gulf, and the Pacific Districts of the SIU are comembers of the SIU and coöperate on matters of common interest, but they are autonomous in regard to the affairs within their respective jurisdictions.

3. Jane C. Record, "The Rise and Fall of a Maritime Union," *Industrial and Labor Relations Review* (October 1956).

4. New York State Commission Against Discrimination (1951), *Report of Progress*, pp. 61, 87.

5. House Committee on Education and Labor, *Hearings on Amendments to the National Labor Relations Act* (1947), p. 575; see also, testimony of J. Paul St. Sure, Senate Committee on Labor and Public Welfare, *Hearings on Taft-Hartley Act Revisions* (1953), pp. 1331–1332, and Walter E. Mahoney, *ibid.*, p. 2574.

6. A majority of the votes of all the members, both shipping companies and shoreside, is necessary to implement the longshore agreements. The votes of the members are determined by the amount of cargo handled, and in addition in the case of the shipping companies, the average number of seafaring employees. See Pacific Maritime Association, *Agreement of Consolidation and By-laws* (1949).

7. However, the more recent indications of splits among the operators suggest that this has not functioned as was anticipated. Cf. Betty V. H. Schneider and Abraham Siegal, *Industrial Relations in the Pacific Coast Longshore Industry* (1956), p. 86.

8. Testimony of J. Paul St. Sure, House Committee on Merchant Marine and Fisheries, *Hearings on Labor Management Problems of the American Merchant Marine* (1955), pp. 39–71; George Killion, *ibid.*, pp. 284–330; Thomas E. Cuffe, *ibid.*, pp. 330–362.

9. One indication of divergence of views among East Coast operators is reflected in the testimony of Francis Greene that there was a wide variation of opinion within the members of the institute on the merits and desirability of a bill to establish a special maritime labor board to stabilize labor relations in the industry. *Ibid.*, p. 814.

10. Several tanker operators on the East Coast negotiate with independent unions whose jurisdiction is restricted to a particular company. These companies include Standard Oil of New Jersey, Socony-Vacuum, Tidewater Oil, and Atlantic Refining Companies.

11. Harry Lundeberg charged that this new policy resulted in "appeasing" of the left-wing-controlled ILWU, *Proceedings of Fifth Biennial Convention* (1951), pp. 87–88.

12. The coastwide SUP strike of 1952 included economic issues, as well as the question of scope of work. See Schneider and Siegal, *Pacific Coast Longshore Industry*, pp. 77–87 for description of relations under the "new look."

13. Formerly, only the SUP contract expired on September 30; the contract termination date of the others was June 15, as was that of the NMU.

14. Pacific Maritime Association, *Annual Report* (1956), p. 3.

15. The postwar strike record in the maritime industry on the East Coast follows. The statistics almost wholly reflect longshore strikes except for the year 1956, which includes both seamen and longshoremen:

Maritime Strikes, Atlantic and Gulf Ports 1946–1956[1]

Year	Number	Workers involved	Man days lost
1946	31	230,000	3,270,000
1947	12	8,360	42,000
1948	13	47,900	605,000
1949	19	6,410	24,700
1950	11	⌠2,670	32,900
1951	23	34,600	325,000
1952	19	12,500	59,200
1953	37	68,900	243,000
1954	28	73,200	665,000
1955	25	39,200	156,000
1956	21	53,800	257,000

U.S. Department of Labor, Bureau of Labor Statistics. See, Charles P. Larrowe, *Shape-Up and Hiring Hall* (1955), for background of labor-management relations and hiring practices in longshoring.

16. National Maritime Union, *Proceedings of Tenth National Convention* (1955), pp. 79–80.

17. *Seafarer's Log*, November 9, 1956.

18. Data provided by office of NMU Vacation Plan Administrator.

19. Pacific Maritime Association, *Analysis of Strikes and Work Stoppages in the Maritime Industry* (1952), p. 11.

20. National Maritime Union, *Proceedings of Tenth National Convention* (1955), pp. 353–354; *The Stewards News*, March 22, 1957; *Seafarer's Log*, September 14, 1956.

21. Pacific Maritime Association, *Annual Report* (1955), p. 7. The report stated that "the new MCS-AFL agreement provides for union-operated hiring halls, resulting in a considerable saving to member companies."

22. House Committee on Merchant Marine and Fisheries, *Hearings on Proposed Amendments to the 1936 Merchant Marine Act* (1953), pp. 26–35.

23. House Committee on Merchant Marine and Fisheries, *Hearings on Proposed Amendments to 1936 Merchant Marine Act* (1953), pp. 302–337; Senate Committee on Interstate and Foreign Commerce, *Hearings on Merchant Marine Studies* (1953), pp. 1159–1165.

24. Industrial Relations Counselors, Inc., New York, N. Y., *Industrial Relations in the Ocean Shipping Industry* (March 1953).

25. See, for example, *Statement of CIO Maritime Committee, Merchant Marine Policies, Practices and Problems of Labor Management and Government,* presented by Joseph Curran (1955). Also testimony of Harry Lundeberg, House Committee on Merchant Marine and Fisheries, *Hearings on Labor-Management Problems of the American Merchant Marine* (1955).

26. In 1948 the Seafarers' International Union agreed to the discontinuance of a provision whereby its members received a penalty payment of 10 percent on ships carrying coal and coke. Since NMU agreements had not contained this provision, the carriage of these products had been shifted to ships manned by NMU members, with resultant loss of employment to SIU members. The moral of this development, according to the SIU, was that "as a trade union primarily interested in the economic protection of its membership, we can no longer ignore the harm inherent in a lack of uniformity throughout the industry. Although we may have contractual assurance of unmatched conditions and wages, the possibility of 'bargain rates,' made possible by other unions less aggressive than we, is always a danger." *Seafarer's Log*, August 20, 1948.

27. Maritime Administration, *Seafaring Overtime on Privately-Operated United States Flag Ships* (1954); see also *CIO Maritime Committee, Merchant Marine Poli-*

cies, Practices and Problems of Labor Management and Government (1955), pp. 33–35.

28. Monthly earnings figure from American Merchant Marine Institute, Statement on S. 1267, 1957; Hours estimate based on Industrial Relations Counselors, *Industrial Relations in the Ocean Shipping Industry* (1953), pp. 74–75.

29. Studies reported in ILO Preparatory Technical Maritime Conference, *Report on Wages, Hours and Manning* (1945), p. 64; and Bureau of Labor Statistics, *Employment Outlook in the Merchant Marine* (1951), p. 7. For a substantial group which worked irregularly, the average duration of employment was 3.5 months.

30. *CIO Maritime Committee,* pp. 29–47.

31. See several Pacific Maritime Association Reports on Seamen's Earnings and Vessel Labor Costs.

32. Pacific Maritime Association, *Seamen's Earnings and Vessel Labor Costs* (August 15, 1956). The only changes were in the watch payments for the unlicensed deck and stewards' departments, and these resulted from the adoption of the new pattern.

33. Robert Straus, "Medical Care for Seamen," *The Origin of Public Medical Services in the United States* (New Haven, 1950), p. 142.

34. The plan requires no waiting period; eligibility requirements consist of at least 200 days aboard NMU-contract vessels. NMU *Pilot,* January 31, 1957.

35. U. S. Department of Commerce, *Labor-Management Relationships in the Maritime Industry and the Subsidization of Seamen's Wages* (1955), p. 20.

36. National Maritime Union, *Proceedings of Tenth National Convention* (1955), pp. 59–62. *New York Times,* July 11, 1956.

37. A recent estimate shows 15,000 citizens of Puerto Rican origin in the maritime labor force. *New York Times,* May 31, 1957.

38. James C. Healey, *Foc's'le and Glory Hole* (1936), p. 68; American Merchant Marine Conference, *Proceedings* (1952), p. 198.

Conclusions and Prospects

1. House Committee on Merchant Marine and Fisheries, 84th Congress, 2nd Session, *Report on Labor-Management Problems of the American Merchant Marine* (1956), pp. 1–2.

2. L. H. Powell, Industrial Relations in the British Shipping Industry, *International Labor Review* (June 1952).

3. The proposals for a specialized agency took the form of "staff" proposals. One provided for the adaptation of the national emergency strike provisions (a 90-day injunction period) of the Labor-Management Relations Act to the industry, with an industry board to mediate disputes. An alternative proposal also established such a board with authority to "request" the parties to delay work stoppages for 45 days; failure to comply with the request would be treated as an unfair labor practice under the Labor-Management Relations Act.

West Coast dry cargo ship operators were particularly favorable to the staff proposals, and expressed the hope that they would aid in dealing with strikes over major issues or jurisdiction in which the operators were caught between competing unions. The spokesman for the American Merchant Marine Institute was more circumspect in supporting the proposals. He supported these "in principle" and pointed out that there were no jurisdictional disputes on the East Coast. The spokesman for the American Merchant Marine Institute did indicate, however, that its constituents were not unanimous in their position; furthermore, representatives of tanker operators, of the Lake Carriers' Association, and a number of individual operators expressed their opposition to specialized legislation in this field. House Hearings, *Merchant Marine Labor Problems* (1955), pp. 797, 802, 810, 814.

4. Joseph P. Goldberg, Maritime Subsidies and Maritime Labor Relations, *Proceedings of the Eighth Annual Meeting of the Industrial Relations Research Association* (1955), pp. 328–345.

5. *Report on Labor Management Problems,* p. 27.

BIBLIOGRAPHY

GENERAL LITERATURE

GOVERNMENT SOURCES

LABOR SOURCES

INDUSTRY SOURCES

MANUSCRIPT MATERIALS

NEWSPAPERS

GENERAL LITERATURE

Books and Pamphlets

Abbot, Willis J., *The Story of Our Merchant Marine*, New York, 1919

Academy of Political Science in the City of New York, *Proceedings, The American Mercantile Marine*, October 1915; *American Foreign Trade Relations*, February 1921

Albrecht, Arthur E., *International Seamen's Union of America* (Bureau of Labor Statistics Bulletin No. 342), 1923

American Merchant Marine Conference, *Annual Proceedings*, 1935–44

Anderson, Robert E., *The Merchant Marine and World Frontiers*, New York, 1945

Axtell, Silas B., *Merchant Seamen's Law*, New York, 1943

Brissenden, Paul F., *History of the I. W. W.: A Study of American Syndicalism*, New York, 1920

Bryan, Leslie A., *Principles of Water Transportation*, New York, 1939

Camp, William M., *San Francisco: Port of Gold*, New York, 1947

Cornell, Felix M. and A. C. Hoffman, *American Merchant Seamen's Manual*, New York, 1946

Crockett, Peter C., "Trans-Pacific Shipping Since 1914" (unpublished Ph.D. thesis in the University of California), 1922

Cross, Ira B., *A History of the Labor Movement in California*, Berkeley, 1935

Dalzell, G. W., *The Flight from the Flag*, Chapel Hill, 1940

Dimock, Marshall E., *The Executive in Action*, New York, 1945

Dimock, Marshall E., and A. Wubnig, *The Maritime Industry during World War II*. In Yearbook of American Labor, V. I, *War Labor Policies*, 1945

Eliel, Paul, *The Waterfront and General Strikes*, San Francisco, 1934

Encyclopedia of the Social Sciences, New York, 1933, articles on Maritime Law; Marine Insurance; Seamen; Shipping; Merchant Marine

Fainsod, Merle and L. Gordon, *Government and the American Economy*, New York, 1941

Fall, James, *British Merchant Seamen in San Francisco, 1892–8*, London, 1899

Foster, William Z., *From Bryan to Stalin*, New York, 1937

Francis, Robert C., "A History of Labor on the San Francisco Waterfront" (unpublished Ph.D. thesis in the University of California), 1934

Franklin, Charles L., *The Negro Labor Unionist of New York*, New York, 1936

Frankfurter, Felix and N. Greene, *The Labor Injunction*, New York, 1930

Furuseth, Andrew, *A Symposium on Andrew Furuseth*, New Bedford, Massachusetts, 1948

Gambs, John S., *The Decline of the I. W. W.*, New York, 1932

Goldberg, Joseph P., *Maritime Subsidies and Maritime Labor Relations*, in *Proceedings* of Industrial Relations Research Association, 1955

Gompers, Samuel, *Seventy Years of Life and Labor*, New York, 1943

Gorter, Wytze, *American Shipping Policy*, New York, 1956

Gorter, Wytze and George Hildebrand, *The Pacific Coast Maritime Shipping Industry, 1930–1948*, 2 vols., Berkeley, 1952–4

Gregory, Charles O., *Labor and the Law*, New York, 1946

Hale, E. K., "Personnel Management in Shipping," New York University, 1942 (unpublished M.B.A. thesis in Library of Congress)

Harvard University, Graduate School of Business Administration, *The Use and Disposition of Ships and Shipyards at the End of World War II*, Washington, 1945

Healey, James C., *Foc's'le and Glory Hole*, New York, 1936

Hohman, Elmo P., *History of American Merchant Seamen*, Hamden, Connecticut, 1956

Hohman, Elmo P., *Seamen Ashore*, New Haven, 1952

Hurley, Edward N., *The Bridge to France*, Philadelphia, 1927

Hurley, Edward N., *The New Merchant Marine*, New York, 1920

Hutchins, J. G. B., *The American Maritime Industries and Public Policy, 1789–1914*, Cambridge, 1941

Industrial Relations Counsellors, Inc., *Industrial Relations in the Ocean Shipping Industry*, New York, 1953

International Juridical Association, *Report on the Status and Working Conditions of Seamen in the American Merchant Marine*, New York, 1936

Johnson, Emory R. and collaborators, *History of Foreign and Domestic Commerce of the United States*, New York, 1915

Johnson, E. R., G. G. Huebner, and A. K. Henry, *Transportation by Water*, New York, 1935

Johnson, J. Augustus, *The American Sailor, an Address, 1899*, New York, 1899

Kaltenborn, H. S., *Governmental Adjustment in Labor Disputes*, Chicago, 1943

King, Jerome, *et al.*, *We Accuse*, New York, 1940

Lampman, Robert J., "Collective Bargaining of West Coast Sailors, 1885–1947" (unpublished Ph.D. dissertation in University of Wisconsin), 1950

Lang, Frederick J., *Maritime*, New York, 1943

Larrowe, Charles F., *Shape-Up and Hiring Hall*, Berkeley, 1955

Library of Congress, *Andrew Furuseth, A Bibliographical List*, 1942

Liebes, R. A., "Longshore Labor Relations on the Pacific Coast, 1934–42," 1942 (unpublished Ph.D. thesis in University of California)

McDowell, Carl E. and Helen M. Gibbs, *Ocean Transportation*, New York, 1954

Marvin, Winthrop L., *The American Merchant Marine*, New York, 1902

Marx, Daniel, Jr., *International Shipping Cartels*, Princeton, 1953

Marx, Daniel, Jr., "The United States Maritime Commission," 1936–40, 1946 (unpublished Ph.D. thesis in University of California)

Metcalf, Henry C., *A Sound Employer-Employee Relations Policy for the American Shipping Industry* (Bureau of Personnel Administration), 1937

Millikan, Max F., The Ocean Shipping Industry, in Adams, Walter, ed., *The Structure of American Industry*, 1950

National Conferences on Merchant Marine, *Annual Reports*, 1928–33, Washington

National Industrial Conference Board, *The American Merchant Marine Problem*, New York, 1929

Nevins, Allan, *Sail On*, New York, 1946

Northrup, Herbert R., *Organized Labor and the Negro*, New York, 1944

Palmer, Dwight L., "Pacific Coast Maritime Labor," 1935 (unpublished Ph.D. thesis in Stanford University Library)

Perlman, Selig and P. Taft, *History of Labor in U. S., 1896–1932*, New York, 1935

Robinson, R. M., "Maritime Labor in San Francisco, 1933–1937," 1937 (unpublished M. A. thesis in University of California)

Saposs, David J., *Left-Wing Unionism*, New York, 1926

Schneider, Betty V. H. and Abraham Siegel, *Industrial Relations in The Pacific Coast Longshore Industry*, Berkeley, 1956

Slichter, Sumner H., *Union Policies and Industrial Management*, Washington, 1941

Smith, D. H. and P. V. Betters, *The United States Shipping Board*, Washington, 1931

Ssu-Tu, Hsin, *The Merchant Marine Policy of the U. S.*, Philadelphia, 1935

Standard, William L., *Merchant Seamen*, New York, 1947

Standard, William L., *Merchant Seamen and the Law*, New York, 1945

Stanford University Division of Industrial Relations, Industrial Relations Paper #1, *Employee Relations in Ocean Shipping*, 1948 (mimeographed)

Stolberg, Benjamin, *The Story of the C. I. O.*, New York, 1938

Straus, Robert, *Medical Care for Seamen*, New Haven, 1950

Sullivan, John A., *Red Sails on the Great Lakes*, Toronto, 1955

Taft, Philip, *The Structure and Government of Trade Unions*, Cambridge, 1954

Taylor, Paul S., *Sailors Union of the Pacific*, New York, 1923

Thor, Howard A., "A History of the Marine Engineers' Beneficial Association" (unpublished M. A. thesis in University of California), 1954

TNEC, *Economic Power and Political Pressure*, Monograph No. 26, Washington, 1941

Twentieth Century Fund, *How Collective Bargaining Works*, New York, 1942

Twentieth Century Fund, *Labor and the Government*, New York, 1935

Walsh, J. Raymond, *C. I. O.*, New York, 1937

Willoughby, William F., *Government Organization in War Time and After*, New York, 1919

Witte, Edwin E., *The Government in Labor Disputes*, New York, 1932

Wolman, Leo, *Ebb and Flow of Trade Unionism*, New York, 1936

Zeis, Paul M., *American Shipping Policy*, Princeton, 1938

Zisman, Joseph, *Workmen's Compensation and the Protection of Seamen* (U. S. Bureau of Labor Statistics Bulletin No. 869), Washington, 1946

Periodicals

American Marine Engineer, 1921

Annals of the American Academy of Political and Social Science, "Transportation: War and Post War," November 1943

Barnett, George E., "American Trade Unions and the Standardization of Wages during the War," *Journal of Political Economy*, October 1919

Bates, Henry A. and D. L. Helm, "Wage Structure in Deep-Sea Shipping," *Monthly Labor Review*, July 1937

Bendiner, M. R., "Is It Safe to Go to Sea?", *The Nation*, April 29, 1936

Bloch, Louis, "The Seamen's Right to Strike," *American Labor Legislation Review*, June 1942

Bookhout, Russell, "Why We Struck," *Atlantic Monthly*, August 1937

Bruère, Robert W. and H. Blankenhorn, "For An American Manned Merchant Marine," *New Republic*, August 27, 1919

Business Week (items in various issues)

Cheyney, Alice S., "International Labor Conventions," *Monthly Labor Review*, April 1934

Cross, Ira B., "Sailors of the '49's," *Coast Seamen's Journal*, June 19, 1907; "First Seamen's Unions," *Coast Seamen's Journal*, July 8, 1908

Dabney, T. L., "Organized Labor's Attitude Toward Negro Workers," *The Southern Workman*, August 1928

Darcy, Sam, "The Great West Coast Strike," *The Communist,* July 1934; "The San Francisco Bay Area," *The Communist,* October 1934

Drury, Horace B., "The Labor Policy of the Shipping Board," *Journal of Political Economy,* January 1921

Eaves, Lucille, "Where San Francisco Was Sorest Struck," *Charities and the Commons,* May 5, 1906

Eliel, P. A., "Peace in West Coast Shipping Industry," *Annals of American Academy of Political and Social Science,* November 1942

Farnam, Henry W., "The Seamen's Act of 1915," *American Labor Legislation Review,* March 1916

Forsyth, Ralph K., "The Wage Scale Agreements of the Maritime Unions," *Annals of the American Academy of Political and Social Science,* September 1910

Fortune, "The American Merchant Marine," September 1937

Furuseth, Andrew, "The Campaign Against the Seamen's Act," *The Survey,* July 31, 1915

Furuseth, Andrew, "Mastery of the Sea," *New Republic,* July 20, 1921

Furuseth, Andrew, "Sea Service," *American Federationist,* February 1918

Goldberg, Joseph P., Collective Bargaining in Maritime Shipping Industry, *Monthly Labor Review,* September 1950

Goodrich, Carter, "Maritime Labor Treaties of 1936," *Monthly Labor Review,* February 1937

Harrison, Charles Y., "Stalin's American Merchant Marine," *American Mercury,* October 1940

Henderson, Gerard, "Seamen's Law and World Wages," *New Republic,* October 9, 1915; "Seamen's Law on Safety at Sea," *New Republic,* October 16, 1915

Hohman, Elmo P., "The Important Place of Seamen in Our National Economy," *American Labor Legislation Review,* June 1941

Hopkins, William S., "Employment Exchanges for Seamen," *American Economic Review,* June 1935

Hutchins, J. G. B., "The Declining American Maritime Industries: An Unsolved Problem," *Journal of Economic History,* Supplement VI, 1946

Jones, F., "Composition of the Labor Force of the Merchant Marine," *Monthly Labor Review,* April 1937

Keay, Frances A., "The Sailor in Port: Philadelphia," *Charities and the Commons,* 1907

Kennedy, Philip B., "The Seamen's Act," *Annals of American Academy of Political and Social Science,* January 1916

Kerr, Clark and Lloyd Fisher, "Conflict on the Waterfront," *Atlantic Monthly,* September 1949

Kleiler, Frank M., "Maritime Labor Grows Up," *Survey Graphic,* January 1939

Kossoris, Max D. and J. Zisman, "Workmen's Compensation for Seamen," *Monthly Labor Review,* June 1946

Literary Digest, "The Full Crew Seamen's Law," March 20, 1915

Macarthur, Walter, "The American Seamen Under the Law," *The Forum,* February 1899

Macarthur, Walter, "Efficiency of Ships' Crews," *Charities and the Commons,* May 19, 1906

Monthly Labor Review, "Maritime Strikes of 1936–7," April 1937

Monthly Labor Review, "Maritime Labor Force in the United States," September 1942

Powell, L. H., "Industrial Relations in the British Shipping Industry," *International Labor Review,* June 1952

Record, Jane C., "The Rise and Fall of a Maritime Union," *Industrial and Labor Relations Review,* October 1956

Riesenberg, Felix, "Communists at Sea," *The Nation,* October 23, 1937

Rice, William G., Jr. and W. E. Chalmers, "Improvement of Labor Conditions on Ships by International Action," *Monthly Labor Review,* May 1936

Rothschild, V. H., 2nd, "The Legal Implications of a Strike by Seamen," *Yale Law Journal,* May 1936

Silver, Jonas, "War-Risk Bonuses for Seafaring Personnel," *Monthly Labor Review,* January 1944

Sturgis, George P., "Futility of the Seamen's Act," *The Industrial Economist,* April 1916

Sturm, Herman M., "Merchant Seamen During the Reconversion," *Social Security Bulletin,* February 1947

Taylor, Paul S., "Eight Years of the Seamen's Act," *American Labor Legislation Review,* March 1925

Taylor, Paul S. and Gold, N., "San Francisco and the General Strike," *Survey Graphic,* September 1934

West, George P., "Andrew Furuseth and the Radicals," *The Survey,* November 5, 1921

West, George P., "Andrew Furuseth Stands Pat," *The Survey,* October 15, 1943

Wilcox, Clair, "Merchant Marine," *Fortune,* November and December 1944

Williams, James H., "The Sailor and the Law," *The Independent,* November 15, 1900

Williams, James H., "The Autobiography of a Labor Leader," *The Independent,* November 6, 1902; "How We Live to Make Her Go," *The Independent,* January 7, 1902

GOVERNMENT SOURCES

Reports of Federal Agencies

Advisory Committee on the Merchant Marine, *Report,* 1947

Bureau of the Census, *Transportation by Water,* 1906, 1916, 1926

Commerce Department, *Merchant Marine Statistics,* 1924–1941; Maritime Commission Annual Reports; Federal Maritime Board and Maritime Administration, Annual Reports; Maritime Commission (Postwar Planning Committee), *The Postwar Outlook for American Shipping,* 1946; *A Review of Maritime Subsidy Policy,* 1954; *A Review of Labor-Management Re-*

lationships in the Maritime Industry and the Subsidization of Seamen Wages, 1955; *Seafaring Overtime on Privately Operated United States Flag Merchant Ships*, 1954

Federal Coördinator of Transportation, *Hours, Wages and Working Conditions in Domestic Water Transportation*, 1936

Industrial Commission, *Report*, 1900–1 (vols. IV & IX on Transportation)

Labor, Secretary of, *Annual Reports*, 1917–22

Maritime Labor Board, *Report to the President and Congress*, 1940; *Supplemental Report to the President and Congress*, 1942

Maritime War Emergency Board, History of (by Francis B. Goertner), 1950

National Labor Relations Board, *Written Trade Agreements in Collective Bargaining*, 1940

National Longshoremen's Board, *Mediation Proceedings*, July 9–11, 1934; *Hearings of Protests by Steamship Companies and Seamen on Rules of Eligibility to Vote in Election*, December 1934; *Report to the Secretary of Labor*, February 1935, with appendixes

National Resources Planning Board, *Transportation and National Policy*, 1942

National War Labor Board, *The Termination Report: Industrial Disputes and Wage Stabilization in Wartime*, 1948

Navigation, Commissioner of, *Annual Reports*, 1884–1932

Pacific Coast Longshore Fact-finding Board, *Report and Recommendations*, 1946

Presidential Board of Inquiry, *Reports on Labor Disputes in the Maritime Industry*, 1948

Shipping Board, *Annual Reports*, 1916–1931; *Reports on Marine and Dock Industrial Relations*, 1922–1931; *Proceedings of the Joint Shipping Industrial Conference*, 1919; *Report of the Marine and Dock Industrial Relations Division; Work, Wages, and Industrial Relations During the Period of the War*, 1919; *Report to Merchant Marine Planning Committee of United States Shipping Board on the Handicaps Against American Ships Engaged in Foreign Trade* (by Haag, A. H.), Washington, 1927

Social Security Board, *The Maritime Industry and Unemployment Compensation* (by Constance A. Kiehel), 1939

War Shipping Administration, *Comparative Analysis of Union Agreements of General Agents of the War Shipping Administration, Covering Unlicensed Personnel on Dry Cargo Vessels*, 1944 (mimeographed), 1945; *Merchant Seamen* (Consolidated Bulletin C — mimeographed), 1945; *The United States Merchant Marine at War*, 1946

National Archives

Maritime Labor Board Archives

National Recovery Administration Archives, *Hearings on Proposed Code*, 1933–4; miscellaneous correspondence; R. H. Overstreet, "History of the Proposed Code of Fair Competition for the Shipping Industry" (4 vols.), 1936 (unpublished)

United States Shipping Board; Archives of Marine and Dock Industrial Relations Division; Minutes of Proceedings of U.S.S.B.; Papers of W. S. Benson; A. D. Lasker

Congressional Publications

Congressional Record, 1890–1956

House Committee on Education & Labor, *Hearings on Amendments to the National Labor Relations Act,* 80th Cong., 1st Sess., 1947; Hearings on H. R. 5008, Hiring Practices, Maritime Industry, 81st Cong., 1st Sess., 1949

House Committee on Immigration and Naturalization, *Deportation of Alien Seamen,* 69th Cong., 1st Sess., 1926

House Committee on Immigration and Naturalization, Hearings on S3574, *Deportation of Deserting Alien Seamen,* 69th Cong., 2d Sess., 1927; Report No. 1924 to accompany H. R. 12173, *Deportation of Alien Seamen,* 72nd Cong., 2d Sess., 1933; Hearings on S.202, *Deportation of Alien Seamen,* 71st Cong., 3d. Sess., 1931; Report No. 2922 on S.202, *Deportation of Alien Seamen,* 71st Cong., 3d Sess., 1931

House Committee on Merchant Marine and Fisheries, Hearings on *Bills Regulating Allotment of Seamen's Wages,* 54th Cong., Sess., 1896; Hearings on *Bills Relating to Rights & Duties of Seamen,* 54th Cong., Sess., 1896; House Report No. 1660 on H. R. 2663, *To Amend the Laws Relating to Navigation,* 54th Cong., 1st Sess., 1896; House Report No. 1868 on H. R. 6399, *Laws Relating to American Seamen,* 54th Cong., 1st Sess., 1896; Hearings on H. R. 12351 and 18682, *Better Security of Lives of Passengers and Crews,* 60th Cong., 2d Sess., 1910; Hearings on H. R. 11193, *American Seamen,* 61st Cong., 1st Sess., 1910; Hearings on H. R. 23673, *The Seamen's Bill,* 62nd Cong., 2d Sess., 1911–12; Report No. 645 on H. R. 23673, *The Seamen's Bill,* 62nd Cong., 2d Sess., 1912; Hearings on H. R. 11372 et al., 62nd Cong., 2d Sess., 1912; Hearings on S. 136, *The Seamen's Bill,* 63rd Cong., 2d Sess., 1913–1914; Report No. 852 to accompany S. 136, *Welfare of American Seamen,* 63rd Cong., 2d Sess., 1914; Report No. 1439, *Conference Report on Seamen's Bill,* S. 136, 63rd Cong., 3d Sess., 1915; Hearings on H. R. 10026, *Amendment of the Seamen's Act,* 64th Cong., 1st Sess., 1916; Hearings on H. R. 10500, *Creating A Shipping Board, A Naval Auxiliary, and a Merchant Marine,* 64th Cong., 1st Sess., 1916; Hearings on H. R. 8069, *Welfare of American Seamen,* 66th Cong., 1st Sess., 1919; *Inquiry into Operations of the United States Shipping Board,* 66th Cong., 1st Sess., 1919; Hearings on the *Merchant Marine,* 70th Cong., 1st Sess., 1928; Hearings on H. R. 6789, *Payment of Seamen's Wages,* 71st Cong., 2d Sess., 1930; Hearings on *Safety of Life and Property at Sea,* Part 3; Hearings on H. R. 6039, 6040, 6041, 74th Cong., 1st Sess., 1935; Hearings on H. R. 7521, *To Develop an American Merchant Marine,* 74th Cong., 1st Sess., 1935; Report No. 1322 on H. R. 8597, *Seamen's Legislation,* 74th Cong., 1st Sess., 1935; Conference Report No. 3041 on H. R. 8597, Amend Sec. 13

of *Act To Promote Safety at Sea*, 74th Cong., 2d Sess., 1936; Hearings on H. J. Res. 121 and H. J. Res. 143, *Continuous Discharge Books for Seamen*, 75th Cong., 1st Sess., 1937; Hearings on H. R. 5193, *Maritime Labor Bill*, 75th Cong., 1st Sess., 1937; Hearings on 7017, *Right of Appeal from Suspension of Licenses and Certificates of Service*, 75th Cong., 1st Sess., 1937; Hearings on S. 2084, *et al.*, *School Ship Graduates*, 75th Cong., 1st Sess., 1937; Report No. 784 on S. 2084, *Graduates of Approved School Ships*, 75th Cong., 1st Sess., 1937; Hearings on H. R. 8532, *Amending Merchant Marine Act of 1936*, 75th Cong., 2d Sess., 1937–8; Conference Report to Accompany H. R. 10315, *Amendments to the Merchant Marine Act of 1936*, 75th Cong., 2d Sess., 1938; Hearings on H. R. 6745 *et al.*, *Eight Hour Day for Seamen*, 75th Cong., 3d Sess., 1938; Hearings on H. R. 4051, *Hiring of Seamen*, 76th Cong., 1st Sess., 1939; Hearings on H. J. Res. 194, *Conditions Pertaining to Lascar Seamen*, 76th Cong., 1st Sess., 1939; Hearings on H. R. 9918, *Citizenship Requirements for Manning of Vessels*, 76th Cong., 3d Sess., 1940; Hearings on 9982, *Shipment and Discharge of Seamen*, 76th Cong., 3d Sess., 1942; Report No. 2892 on H. R. 9982, *Shipment and Discharge of Seamen*, 76th Cong., 3d Sess., 1940; Report No. 2918 on H. R. 9918, 76th Cong., 3d Sess., 1940; Hearings on H. R. 2662, *Hiring Halls Under the Control of Shipping Commissioners*, 77th Cong., 1st Sess., 1941; Hearings on H. R. 4107, *Maritime Labor Board*, 77th Cong., 1st Sess., 1941; Report No. 354, *Two Year Extension of the Maritime Labor Board*, 77th Cong., 1st Sess., 1941; Hearings on H. R. 5446, *Unemployment Insurance for the Maritime Industry*, 77th Cong., 1st Sess., 1941; Hearing Pursuant to H. R. 281, *Authorizing Investigation of National Defense Program. Repatriation of American Seamen*, 77th Cong., 2d Sess., 1942; Hearings on H. R. 6503 and S. J. Res. 130, *Extension of Various Emergency Laws*, 77th Cong., 2nd Sess., 1942; Hearings on H. R. 7424, *Merchant Marine Omnibus Bill*, 77th Cong., 2d Sess., 1942; Hearings on H. R. 1361 *et al.*, *Rights and Benefits to American Seamen*, 78th Cong., 1st Sess., 1943; Hearings Prints Nos. 1 and 3, *Unemployment Insurance for Merchant Seamen*, 78th Cong., 1st Sess., 1943; Reports Nos. 1232 and 1313 on H. R. 4163, *Relating to Benefits to Merchant Seamen*, 78th Cong., 2d Sess., 1944; Report No. 1017 on H. J. Res. 245, *Authorizing Employment of Aliens upon American Ships*, 78th Cong., 2d Sess., 1947; Report No. 1215 on H. R. 3259, *Clarification of Certain Services Performed by Seamen*, 78th Cong., 2d Sess., 1944; Hearings on H. R. 2346 *et al.*, *Benefits to Merchant Seamen*, 79th Cong., 1st Sess., 1945; Hearings on H. R. 476, *Seamen's Bill of Rights*, 80th Cong., 1st Sess., 1947; Hearings on *Proposed Amendments to the 1936 Merchant Marine Act*, 83rd Cong., 1st Sess., 1953; *Study of Operations of Military Sea Transportation Service*, Hearings and Report, 83rd Cong., 1954; *Study of the Operations of the Maritime Administration and the Federal Maritime Board*, 84th Cong., 1955; *Hearings and Report on Labor-Management Problems of the American Merchant Marine*, 84th Cong., 1955–6; Special Committee on Un-American Activities, *Investigation of Un-American Propaganda Activities in U. S.*, 75th Cong., 3d Sess., 76, 77, 1939–42.

Senate Committee on Commerce (to 1944) and Interstate and Foreign Commerce, Report No. 1657 on S. 95, *Laws Relating to American Seamen*, 55th Cong., 2d Sess., 1898; Report No. 2755, *Report of the Merchant Marine Commission* and Hearings, 58th Cong., 3d Sess., 1905; Report No. 10 on S. 529, *Development of the American Merchant Marine and American Commerce*, 59th Cong., 1st Sess., 1905; Document No. 701, *Better Security of Life at Sea; Commission on Revision of Laws Relating to Safety of Life at Sea*, 60th Cong., 2d Sess., 1909; Report No. 482 on S. 5757, *Desertion of Seamen from U. S. Vessels*, 62nd Cong., 2d Sess., 1912; Hearings on H. R. 23673, *Involuntary Servitude Imposed Upon Seamen*, 62nd Cong., 3d Sess., 1912–13; Document No. 211, *Joint Letter from Secretary of Commerce and Secretary of Labor on Senate Bill 4, Involuntary Servitude Imposed Upon Seamen*, 63rd Cong., 1st Sess., 1913; Hearings on S. 136, *The Seamen's Bill*, 63rd Cong., 1914; Hearings on H. R. 15455, *Creating a Shipping Board, and etc.*, 64th Cong., 1st Sess., 1916; Hearings Relative to the *Establishment of a Merchant Marine*, 66th Cong., 1st Sess., 1919–20; Joint Hearings (Senate Committee on Commerce and the House Committee on Merchant Marine and Fisheries) on 3217 and H. R. 10644, *To Amend Merchant Marine Act of 1920*, 67th Cong., 1st Sess., 1922; Hearings on S. 1079, *Continuous Discharge Book for American Seamen*, 69th Cong., 1st Sess., 1926; Report No. 833 on S. 2945, *Payment of Seamen on Foreign Vessels*, 70th Cong., 1st Sess., 1928; Hearings on S. 306, and S. 314, *To Amend Certain Laws Relating to Seamen*, 71st Cong., 2d Sess., 1930; Hearings on S. 2582, *Merchant Marine Act*, 74th Cong., 1st Sess., 1935; Report No. 1461 on S. 2003, *Welfare of American Seamen*, 74th Cong., 1st Sess., 1935; Hearings on S. 3500 *et al.*, *Merchant Marine Act*, 74th Cong., 2d Sess., 1936; Report No. 1721 on S. 3500, *Merchant Marine Act*, 74th Cong., 2d Sess., 1936; Report No. 184, Part 4, *"Morro Castle" and "Mohawk" Investigation*, 75th Cong., 1st Sess., 1937; Hearing, *Presentation of Demands of Striking "Rank and File" Seamen Relative to Continuous Discharge Book*, 75th Cong., 1st Sess., 1937; Report to Accompany H. R. 5487, Report No. 200, 75th Cong., 1st Sess., 1937

Committee on Education and Labor, Hearings on S. 3078, *Amending Merchant Marine Act of 1936*, 75th Cong., 2d Sess., 1937–8; Report on S. 3078, *Amending Merchant Marine Act of 1936*, Report No. 1618, 75th Cong., 3d Sess., 1938; Report No. 2166 on H. R. 9982, *Shipment and Discharge of Seamen*, 76th Cong., 3d Sess., 1940; Hearings on H. R. 4107, *Maritime Labor Board*, 77th Cong., 1st Sess., 1941; Report No. 1140 on H. R. 4163, *Relating to Benefits to Merchant Seamen*, 78th Cong., 2d Sess., 1944

Committee on Interstate and Foreign Commerce, Merchant Marine Study and Investigation, Senate Res. 50, 81st Cong., 1950; Merchant Marine Studies, S. Res. 173, 83rd Cong., 1953–4

Committee on Immigration, Hearings on S. 3574, *Deportation of Certain Alien Seamen*, 69th Cong., 1st Sess., 1926; Report No. 1037 on S. 717, *Deportation of Alien Seamen*, 70th Cong., 1st Sess., 1928; Hearings on S. 202, *Deportation of Certain Alien Seamen*, 71st Cong., 2d Sess., 1930; Hearings on S. 7, *Deportation of Certain Alien Seamen*, 72nd Cong., 1st Sess., 1932; Report No. 677 on S. 7, *Deportation of Certain Aliens*, 72nd Cong., 1st Sess., 1932; Hearings on S. 868, *Deportation of Alien Seamen*, 73rd Cong., 2d Sess., 1934; Hearings on S. 379, *Deportation of Certain Alien Seamen*, 74th Cong., 1st Sess., 1935

Committee on Education and Labor, *Violation of Free Speech and Labor*, Hearings Parts 60 and 61, 1940; Report No. 46, Part 3, *Industrial Espionage*, 75th Cong., 2d Sess., 1937; Report on *Employers' Associations and Collective Bargaining in California*, Parts 1–9, 77th Cong., 1942; Subcommittee on Education and Labor, Hearings on S. 1349, *Amendment of Fair Labor Standards Act*, 79th Cong., 1st Sess., 1945; Committee on Education and Labor, Report No. 1012, *Amendments to Fair Labor Standards Act of 1938*, 79th Cong., 2d Sess., 1946

Committee on Labor and Public Welfare, Hearings on S. 55 and S. J. Res. 22, *Labor Relations Program*, 80th Cong., 1st Sess., 1947; Hearings on S. 249, *Labor Relations*, 81st Cong., 1st Sess., 1949; *Hiring Halls in Maritime Industry*, Hearings on S. 2196 and Report 1827, 81st Cong., 1950; *To Legalize Hiring Halls in Maritime Industry*, Hearings on S. 1044, 82nd Cong., 1951; *Labor Management Relations in the East Coast Oil Tanker Industry*, Hearings and Report S. Res. 140, 81st Cong., 1950–1; *Communist Domination of Certain Unions*, 82nd Cong., 1951; *The Marine Cooks and Stewards Union*, Staff Report, 82nd Cong., 1953; Taft-Hartley Act Revisions, Hearings, 83rd Cong., 1953

Joint Committee on Labor Management Relations, *Report on Labor-Management Relations in West Coast Maritime Industry*, 80th Cong., 2d Sess., 1948

Special Committee to Investigate Air and Ocean Mail Contracts, *Preliminary Report*, 74th Cong., 1st Sess., 1935

Special Committee to Investigate Conditions in the American Merchant Marine, *Hearings*, 76th Cong., 1st Sess., 1939

Special Committee to Investigate Executive Agencies, *Hearings*, 78th Cong., 1st and 2d Sess., 1944

State Publications

California Bureau of Labor Statistics, *Annual Reports; Investigation into the Conditions of Men Working on the Waterfront and on Board of Pacific Coast Vessels*, 1887

New York State Commission Against Discrimination, *Report of Progress*, 1951

Compilations of Laws and Decisions

Department of Commerce, *Navigation Laws of the United States* (by Frederick Artz), Washington, 1940

Lewis, Elmer A. (Compiler), *Seamen's Act as Amended and other Laws Relating to Seamen*, Washington, 1942

National Affairs, Bureau of, *Labor Arbitration Reports*, Washington, 1946–7; *Labor Relations Reference Manual*, Washington, 1936–1945; *War Labor Reports*, Washington, 1942–1945

LABOR SOURCES

American Federation of Labor

Proceedings of Annual Conventions

Andrew Furuseth

American Sea Power and the Seamen's Act, 1917

The Decay of Seamanship in Europe and America, Senate Doc. 216, 63rd Cong., 1st Sess., 1913

Equity Power and Its Abuse, 1927

International Conference on Safety of Life at Sea, 1929

Labor and Freedom (Address before Illinois Constitutional Convention) in Bulletin No. 3, Illinois State Federation of Labor, 1930

"Lest We Forget," American Federationist, May 1935, Supplement

The Seamen's Act, Document No. 694, 64th Cong., 2d Sess., 1917

Second Message to Seamen, Chicago, 1919

Watch and Watch at Sea, Senate Document No. 693, 64th Cong., 2d Sess., 1917

(With V. Olander) *Welfare of American Seamen, A Memorial*, Senate Document 452, 63rd Cong., 2d Sess., 1914

Congress of Industrial Organizations

Proceedings of Annual Conventions

CIO Maritime Committee

After the War — What?, 1944

The CIO Maritime Committee Postwar Program, 1944

The Maritime Commission vs. the Seamen

Who's Guilty?, 1940

East Coast Unions (before 1937)

Atlantic Coast Seamen's Union, *Constitution and By-Laws*, 1891; *Yearbook*, 1900

Eastern and Gulf Sailors' Association, *Constitution and By-Laws*, 1917

Marine Cooks and Stewards' Association of Atlantic and Gulf, *Constitution and By-Laws*, 1907, 1916

Marine Firemen, Oilers and Watertenders' Union of the Atlantic and Gulf, *Constitution and By-Laws*, 1902, 1913

Industrial Workers of the World

Solidarity, 1910–13
Industrial Worker, 1910–13
California Defense Bulletin, 1918–19
Industrial Unionist, New York, 1920–21
The One Big Union Monthly, 1919–21
(Marine Transport Workers' Industrial Union, No. 50), The Marine Worker,
 1922–26; Exposed, 1922

International Longshoremen's Association

The Longshoreman, 1912–13

International Longshoremen's and Warehousemen's Union

The Dispatcher

The International Seamen's Union

The American Seaman, 1910
Proceedings of Annual Conventions, 2d through 33d, 1892–1936
The Seaman, October 1921–January 1922
Seamen's Journal, 1892–1937
ISU Pilot, 1935–1937

Marine Workers' Industrial Union

Sparks, N., The Struggle of the Marine Workers, New York, 1930
The Marine Workers Voice, 1932–35
Four Fighting Years, New York, 1933
Centralized Shipping Bureau, New York, 1934
Dunne, William F., The Great San Francisco Strike, New York, 1934

Maritime Federation of the Pacific

Constitution and Rules of Order, 1940
The National Seaman, Proposed Constitution for One National Industrial Union
 of All Seamen, December, 1937
Proceedings of Annual Conventions, 1935–1941
Voice of the Federation, 1935–41
Yearbook, 1940

National Maritime Union

Constitution
Algic Defense Committee, Story of the Algic Case, 1937 (Pamphlet)
Curran, Joseph, The NMU Forges Ahead, 1940; Merchant Marine Policies,
 Practices, and Problems of Labor, Management and Government, 1955
Labor Spies in the NMU, New York, 1939
Pilot, 1937–1956
Proceedings of Biennial Conventions, First through Ninth, 1937–1955

Rank and File Pilot, March–June 1938
Standard, William L., *The Coming Ship Subsidy Scandal*, 1939
This is the NMU, A Picture History of the National Maritime Union, C. I. O.,
    1953
Two Years, New York, 1939

Pacific Coast Marine Cooks and Stewards

Constitution and By-Laws, 1906, 1938, 1945
Proceedings of Biennial Conventions, 1945, 1947
Twelve Thousand Marine Cooks and Stewards, 1944
Voice of Marine Cooks and Stewards, 1944–1949 (names)
Stewards News, 1951–1956 (M.C.S., Pacific District, S.I.U.)

Pacific Coast Marine Firemen

Constitution and By-Laws
Marine Firemen's Reporter, 1945–6
The Marine Fireman, 1946–1956
The Story of the Marine Firemen's Union, 1945

Sailors' Union of the Pacific

Constitution and By-Laws
Lundeberg, Harry, *Facts About the Seamen's Trade Union Movement*, U.S.A.,
    1956
West Coast Sailors, 1937–1956

Seafarers' International Union

AFL Seamen's Journal, 1938
Atlantic and Gulf District, *Seafarers' Log*, 1939–1956, *SIU at War*, 1944
Constitution, 1944
Proceedings of Biennial Conventions, 1942, 1945, 1947

INDUSTRY SOURCES

American Bureau of Shipping, *The American Merchant Marine*, 1933
American Merchant Marine Institute, *Employment Facts Concerning an AB
    Seaman in the American Merchant Marine*, 1948 (mimeographed) *Bulle-
    tin*, 1938–47
American Steamship Owners' Association, *Amended Articles of Association*,
    New York, 1920; *Annual Report*, 1923–4; *Bulletin*, 1935–8; *Labor Files*,
    1921–1956 (AMMI) files
American Syren and Shipping
Chamber of Commerce of U. S., *Merchant Marine Conference*, 1925; *Refer-
    endum No. 12 on the Report of the Special Committee on the Seamen's
    Act*, 1916
Coast Committee for the Shipowners, *A.B.C.'s of the Maritime Strike*, Decem-
    ber 1936

Committee on American Shipping Needs, *Report,* 1940
Committee on Merchant Marine, *Report,* 1917
The Log
Marine Journal
Marine Progress
National Federation of American Shipping, Research Report 47–3, *Maritime Labor Agreements,* 1947
Pacific American Shipowners' Association, *Hot Cargo,* October 1935; *Amended Articles of Incorporation and Amended By-Laws,* 1944; *Story of a Strike,* 1947; Educational Pamphlet Series, 1947–8
Pacific Coast Maritime Report, 1947–8
Pacific Maritime Association, *Agreement of Consolidation and By-Laws,* 1949; *Analysis of Strikes in the West Coast Maritime Industry,* Reports for 1951, 1952, 1953–4, 1956; *Annual Reports,* 1953–1956; *Fringe Benefits under the Pacific Coast Maritime Contracts,* 1956; *Seamen's Earnings Under Pacific Coast Contracts,* Reports for 1953, 1954, 1955
Pacific Marine Review, 1904–1947
Phleger, Herman, *Oral Argument Before the Pacific Longshoremen's Board,* 1934
Plant, T. G., *Statement to National Longshoremen's Board,* July 1934
San Francisco Chamber of Commerce, *Law and Order in San Francisco,* 1916
Shipping Illustrated

MANUSCRIPT MATERIALS
Private Collections

American Merchant Marine Institute, Labor Files
Letters from Andrew Furuseth to Silas Blake Axtell, 1917–21 (in possession of S. B. Axtell)
Papers of Andrew Furuseth and ISU, in possession of Paul Scharrenberg
Papers of Ira Cross, Bancroft Library, University of California
Papers of Walter Macarthur, Bancroft Library, University of California

Library of Congress

Woodrow Wilson Papers
E. C. Plummer Papers

NEWSPAPERS

New York Times
Journal of Commerce
San Francisco Chronicle
New York Herald
San Francisco Call
New York Call
Washington Post

INDEX